Popular Politics and Resistance Movements in South Africa

Popular Politics and Resistance Movements in South Africa

Edited by William Beinart and Marcelle C Dawson

WITS UNIVERSITY PRESS

Published in South Africa by:

Wits University Press
1 Jan Smuts Avenue
Johannesburg
2001
http://witspress.wits.ac.za

ISBN 978-1-86814-518-8

Cover photograph: Africa Media Online – Graeme Williams – Protest
March

Cover design by Hybridesign
Book design and layout by Sheaf Publishing
Printed and bound by Creda Communications

Contents

Contents

Contributors

William **Beinart** is professor of Race Relations at the University of Oxford. In recent years he has been involved in establishing the African Studies Centre and the School of Interdisciplinary Area Studies at Oxford and is currently president of the African Studies Association of the UK. He is author of *Twentieth-century South Africa* (2001); *Rise of Conservation in South Africa* (2003); with Lotte Hughes, *Environment and Empire* (2007); and with Luvuyo Wotshela, *Prickly Pear: The Social History of a Plant in South Africa* (forthcoming). He is currently researching and supervising on environmental history and popular politics in Southern Africa.

Julian Brown completed a DPhil thesis on 'Public protest and violence in South Africa, 1948–1976' at the University of Oxford. He is currently engaged as a post-doctoral research fellow in the NRF Programme in Historical Research, 'Local Histories and Present Realities', at the University of the Witwatersrand. His research focuses on the development of political and factional identity in the northern Free State.

Tracy Carson began her doctoral studies at Oxford University in 2004 on a British Marshall Scholarship. Upon completion of her DPhil in 2008 she was awarded a US Fulbright Scholarship to continue her research in Cape Town, South Africa. She is currently completing a two-year internship with the US federal government as a Presidential Management Fellow and her first book, *Tomorrow It Could Be You: Strikes and Boycotts in South Africa, 1978–1982*, will be published in 2010.

Marcelle C. Dawson works as a senior researcher attached to the South African Research Chair in Social Change at the University of Johannesburg. She obtained a DPhil in Politics from the University of Oxford in 2008. She is a member of the editorial collective of the *South African Review of Sociology*, the official journal of the South African Sociological Association. Her work has been published in *Race, Ethnicity and Education, Journal of Higher Education in Africa, Citizenship Studies* and *Globalisation and New Identities: A View from the Middle* (Jacana Media, 2006). Dawson researches and supervises topics related to social movements, popular protest, service delivery and democracy. Her current projects include the policing of protest in post-apartheid South Africa and 'southern theorising' of social movements.

Tim Gibbs is based at St Antony's College, Oxford, where he is completing his doctoral thesis on nationalism and Transkei's elite during the apartheid period. He took his undergraduate degree at Cambridge University and completed a master's in Development Studies at the University of KwaZulu-Natal, writing a dissertation on the textiles trade unions in Lesotho. His work has been published in the *Journal of Southern African Studies.*

Rebecca Hodes is deputy director of the AIDS and Society Research Unit at the University of Cape Town. She completed her DPhil at the University of Oxford in 2009. Extracts from her thesis, which focused on HIV on South African television, have been published in the *Social History of Medicine* and *The Culture of AIDS in Africa* (Oxford University Press). During 2009, Hodes was the manager of policy, communications and research at the Treatment Action Campaign. Her current research focuses on the responses of HIV activists to the global economic crisis. She is also the co-founder of the Students HIV/AIDS Resistance Campaign (Rhodes University).

Simonne Horwitz graduated with a DPhil from the University of Oxford in 2007. She is currently an assistant professor of History at the University of Saskatchewan, where her major teaching, supervision and research areas are in African History and the History of Medicine. She has published on nursing history in *Social History of Medicine,* as well as on the history of leprosy in *African Studies.* Her current research focuses on comparative histories and on the history of HIV/AIDS.

Genevieve Klein was awarded a DPhil from the University of Oxford in 2007 for her thesis, 'The Anti-Apartheid Movement (AAM) in Britain and support for the African National Congress (ANC), 1976–1990'. Her honours and master's studies were completed at the University of Pretoria with dissertations on Dutch-South African relations during apartheid and the Dutch anti-apartheid movements, respectively. She has published articles on this research in the *Journal of Southern African Studies, South African Diaspora Review,* and *Journal for Contemporary History.* Klein is currently a research collaborator at the Department of Historical and Heritage Studies, University of Pretoria.

Mandisa Mbali is a post-doctoral associate in the History of Medicine at Yale University. She obtained her DPhil in Modern History at the University of Oxford in 2009. She has published articles on the political history of AIDS activism in South

Africa, AIDS denialism and AIDS policymaking. Mbali is conducting ongoing research on the history of AIDS activism, health activism, public health policy and ethics, migration and health, and the politics of gender and sexuality in Southern Africa.

Kelly Rosenthal completed her undergraduate and honours degrees in Social Anthropology at the University of Cape Town, before moving to Oxford to pursue a master's in African Studies. She is currently completing her doctorate at Oxford in Social Anthropology. Her research focuses on socio-economic rights in post-apartheid South Africa, activism and citizenship.

Chizuko Sato is a research fellow at the Institute of Developing Economies, a parastatal research institute in Chiba, Japan. She obtained a DPhil in politics from the University of Oxford in 2007. Her doctoral dissertation examined the development of land struggles in late twentieth-century KwaZulu-Natal, South Africa, focusing on the interactions between liberal activists and black community leaders. She is currently working on a comparative research project on the international migration of nurses from Asia and Africa.

Mfaniseni Fana Sihlongonyane is an associate professor at the School of Architecture and Planning at the University of the Witwatersrand. He obtained a DPhil from Oxford in 2009. His interests are spread over a wide range of theoretical, applied and policy arenas in the global as well as African realms of development. His work encompasses the interface between development and urban studies, largely within the context of the dynamics of the political economy in Africa. He has researched and published in the areas of land reform, housing, planning, gender, spatial development, urban politics, local economic development, community development, political culture and African cities. His insights into the exploration of these areas come from his experience as a GlobalAfrican.

Thula Simpson received his DPhil from Birkbeck College, University of London, in 2007 for a dissertation on the ANC's armed struggle. He completed a two-year post-doctoral fellowship at the University of Pretoria between 2007 and 2009, and is currently senior lecturer in the Historical and Heritage Studies Department at the University of Pretoria. He has published articles based on his research in the *South African Historical Journal, Journal of Southern African Studies, Social Dynamics* and *African Historical Review.*

List of Abbreviations and Acronyms

AAC	Alexandra Action Committee
AAM	Anti-Apartheid Movement
ACT UP	AIDS Coalition to Unleash Power
AFRA	Association for Rural Advancement
ALP	AIDS Law Project
ANC	African National Congress
APF	Anti-Privatisation Forum
ARP	Alexandra Renewal Programme
BBC	British Broadcasting Corporation
BWP	Black Workers' Project
CANSA	Campaign Against Neoliberalism in South Africa
CAP	Church Agricultural Project
CLAAG	City of London Anti-Apartheid Group
COPE	Congress of the People
COSAS	Congress of South African Students
COSATU	Congress of South African Trade Unions
CP	Conservative Party
DALA	Department of Agriculture and Land Affairs
DIVA	Damned Interfering Video Activists
DLA	Department of Land Affairs
EPG	Eminent Persons' Group
FCWU	Food and Canning Workers Union
GEAR	Growth, Employment and Redistribution
GTA	Gauteng Tourism Authority
HOSPERSA	Health and Other Service Personnel Trade Union of South Africa
IDAF	International Defence and Aid Fund for Southern Africa
IIE	Institute for Industrial Education
IFP	Inkatha Freedom Party
KZN	KwaZulu-Natal
MK	Umkhonto we Sizwe
MP	member of parliament
MRC	Medical Research Council
MSF	Médecins Sans Frontières
NACOSA	National AIDS Convention of South Africa
NAPWA	National Association of People Living with HIV/AIDS
NCGLE	National Coalition for Gay and Lesbian Equality
NEC	National Executive Committee
NEHAWU	National Education, Health and Allied Workers' Union

NGO	non-governmental organisation
NP	National Party
NPA	Natal Provincial Administration
NUSAS	National Union of South African Students
OWCC	Orange Farm Water Crisis Committee
PEBCO	Port Elizabeth Black Civic Association
PMTCT	prevention of mother-to-child transmission
PWA	People with HIV/AIDS
RDP	Reconstruction and Development Programme
SABC	South African Broadcasting Corporation
SACP	South African Communist Party
SAMWU	South African Municipal Workers' Union
SANA	South African Nursing Association
SANC	South African Nursing Council
SASO	South African Students Organisation
SATIS	Southern Africa: The Imprisoned Society
SCA	Soweto Civic Association
SECC	Soweto Electricity Crisis Committee
SRC	Students Representative Council
TAC	Treatment Action Campaign
TBDA	Tugela Basin Development Association
TPA	Transvaal Provincial Administration
TRACOR	Transkei Agricultural Corporation
TUCSA	Trade Union Council of South Africa
UCT	University of Cape Town
UDF	United Democratic Front
UN	United Nations
UNAIDS	Joint UN Action Plan on HIV/AIDS
UWC	University of the Western Cape
WCTA	Western Cape Traders' Association
WECOP	Weenen Community Project
WEPCOP	Western Province African Chamber of Commerce
WPDC	Weenen Peace and Development Committee

1 Popular politics and resistance movements in South Africa, 1970-2008

William Beinart

Introduction

South Africa has achieved political liberation, a measure of democracy and significant deracialisation since 1994. The country has opened up to the world and is experiencing rapid social change. Yet more than 15 years after the transition, deep inequalities remain. The excitement and optimism of reconstruction have been tempered by the intractability of social problems and the difficulties of formulating effective policies to combat them. Poverty, violence, unemployment, crime and HIV/AIDS gnaw at the fabric of society.

One symptom of social division is that, within a decade of the exhilarating election of 1994 and the coming to power of a democratically elected government, some South Africans were back protesting on the streets. South Africans waged a long political struggle internally and externally to achieve liberation and democracy. Grassroots, workplace and insurrectionary political protest rocked the old apartheid order in the 1970s and 1980s. Many of these movements fed into the African National Congress (ANC) alliance,[1] which since 1994 has been overwhelmingly successful at the polls. The re-emergence of popular protest, of 'street sociology and pavement politics', was not generally foreseen.[2] Is this a new form of politics, or does it stand as a direct descendent of the insurrectionary impulses of the late apartheid era? The chapters in this volume explore some of the key features of popular politics and resistance before and after 1994. They aim to explore continuities and changes in the forms of struggle and ideologies involved, as well as the significance of post-apartheid grassroots politics.

The passionate political disputes of the last few decades are everywhere reflected in these pages. South Africa does not at first glance appear to have a heterodox political tradition. Apartheid and Afrikaner nationalism seemed so dominant for so long, suppressing other voices. Since it was unbanned in 1990, the ANC, with all the legitimacy of a national liberation movement, has flexed its political muscles and dwarfed other parties. Yet even in the apartheid era a multitude of political positions were offered and debated. There were deep splits about appropriate ideologies and strategies both within the dominant white minority and within the opposition. In some ways, political suppression and racial division nurtured diverse political consciousness. Class divisions, fragmented rural movements and ethnic expressions all added layers to the multi-vocal political realm. While the ANC-led alliance emerged as the first fully legitimate government in South African history, there is every sign that it cannot relax in the knowledge that it has achieved a stable ideological hegemony. In addition to the resurfacing of popular movements outside of the tripartite alliance, Jacob Zuma's victory over Thabo Mbeki in the 2007 leadership election at Polokwane indicated deep divisions within the ruling party, and Mosiuoa Lekota's breakaway Congress of the People (COPE) in 2008 suggests that a new political alignment is possible. There are signs that a post-national liberation politics could emerge and that South African politics is evincing a new fluidity.

The roots of this collection lie in postgraduate student research conducted at the University of Oxford in the early twenty-first century. Papers were presented at two workshops; one held at St Antony's College, Oxford in November 2006 and the other at the University of Johannesburg in December 2007.[3] The majority of this generation of Oxford doctoral students researching South Africa has been deeply absorbed by the country's recent political history. On the one hand, the achievements and details of South Africa's liberation struggle, both internal and external, continue to transfix a new group of historians and social scientists, and it is all the more important for students to understand the political traditions of South Africa's black majority, because they are now dominant. On the other hand, the re-emergence of popular protest after 1994 has been an equally compelling social phenomenon. As Hakan Thorn remarked in his keynote address to the first workshop, waves of collective action tend to attract study and theory, sometimes by participants, and subsequently by academics.[4] In turn, consciousness is sometimes influenced by the language of analysis. For example, the term 'social movement' has entered the South African political vocabulary largely from external academic and public debate about a broader global political phenomenon. It is now widely used by South African movements themselves.

Pre-1994 popular politics is of interest to a new generation of researchers not only for its achievements, but also because it may illustrate alternative political traditions that have become less central to the ANC in power. Even on a global scale, the energy and diversity of mass politics in South Africa in the later decades of the twentieth century is striking. There are a range of practices and legacies to explore. This collection does not cover them all equally and omits some completely, but, clearly, this group of young scholars is fascinated by the potential of popular protest, both in the past and in the future. They have focused on such politics, rather than the realm of formal parties and institutions. While the ANC features in every chapter, most of the authors explore political organisations and responses that were not directly developed or controlled by it. They continue a tradition in South African historiography that answers back to a nationalist view of history. The problems of a new African nationalist and liberation movement historiography were extensively debated at the workshops, and in a context where biographies of key nationalist leaders dominate published analysis of recent political history, this collection helps to provide an alternative and, perhaps, less heroic perspective.[5]

The political context has changed fundamentally. Since 1994 the ANC has commanded a large electoral majority – even though its overall vote and the percentage of the electorate who voted declined.[6] Political rights and freedoms have been claimed and extended. The ANC led and oversaw the transition, which has given it enduring, though not unchallenged, legitimacy. The scale of popular protest in the 2000s does not rival that of the 1970s and 1980s, but posing questions about continuity and change before and after 1994, as some of these chapters do, in itself raises key issues concerning the nature of power and poverty in the country. Contributors suggest that expressions of popular politics are deeply set within South African political culture and still have the capacity to influence political outcomes. Central themes in the collection concern continuities and change in popular politics; the strategies, scale and influence of popular activism; the role of leadership; ideological shifts; patterns of violence across time and space; the changing relationship between state and protesters; different sites, symbols and modes of protest; newer issues such as AIDS activism; and the use of the media.

Historiography

How we analyse these developments is inevitably influenced by the comparative and conceptual framework deployed. Various strands are evident in these chapters. Firstly, the starting point for some contributors is a deep tradition within South African historiography and political writing concerned with political protest. For a generation of writers who took their primary position in opposition to white minority rule and who tried to rewrite history in the 1970s and 1980s there was a shared interest in resistance to colonialism and racial domination.[7] Some used the comparative framework of African history. South Africa shared all the forms of resistance that were so vividly covered in that flourishing sub-discipline: from wars by independent chiefdoms to millennial movements; from fragmented peasant rebellions to dramatic industrial strikes; from mass nationalist rallies to armed struggle. South African historiography was perhaps distinctive, however, in its concern to explore labour history. South Africa had a proportionately larger urban and migrant working class than any other African country. This writing also reflected the influence of socialist and neo-Marxist theories, which placed class at the heart of history, as well as the links between academics, intellectuals and the independent trade unions launched in the 1970s. Academics writing on resistance also espoused elements of the new social history – a comparative field that ranged from South Asian subaltern studies to the History Workshop in England. The interests of social historians and labour historians overlapped in many respects, but the former tended to explore the diversity of protest and social alienation, expressed, for example, by rural rebels, women's movements, gangs and urban crowds rather than social relations in the workplace. Their focus was on fragmented political responses in the streets and the slums rather than on strikes; on farms and reserves rather than in factories.

What do these analyses offer the discussion of popular protest since the 1970s? They tended to celebrate as well as analyse popular resistance, and in some cases legitimated it as a response to oppressive, racially based rule. They emphasised the importance of context and of understanding the particular economic and social position of those involved in popular movements. Thus, episodes of protest are often preceded by detailed discussion of political economy. Nevertheless, those influenced by comparative African history in particular were reluctant to read off modes of protest from the material conditions of its agents. Perhaps most importantly, they increasingly illustrated the complexities of popular consciousness, in which the old and new were intertwined – e.g. African heritages; radical Christianity; and specific concerns about land, wages and exploitation.[8] While this writing ran parallel to histories of nationalism and the ANC, it was more concerned with capturing alternative, less institutionalised, sometimes short-lived, expressions and strategies of resistance. Historians have left a detailed, carefully contextualised record of many key events and movements, drawing on both oral and documentary sources. They recognised the diversity of grassroots activism and also the critique of post-colonial nationalism in other African countries, at a time when South African movements were still engaged in national liberation struggles. As a result, they predicted or anticipated, in a sense, the continued salience of everyday struggles after apartheid and provided a longer-term narrative and analytical tradition in which to fit them. These elements in South African historiography are one inspiration for authors in this collection, although not a major influence on all of them.

A second strand of analysis draws on the leftist critique of the transition in South Africa, a materialist, and in some cases socialist, view exemplified in the writing of Hein Marais, Patrick Bond, Roger Southall, William Gumede, Dale McKinley, Ashwin Desai and others.[9] In this framework, the transition in South Africa was precisely that: it was not a revolution; nor even fully a transformation of society; but more a result of an elite pact that left property relations intact. The transition, in this analysis, made space for a black ruling group and its upwardly mobile supporters without fundamentally addressing social inequalities. Renewed mass protest is a symptom of inequality, which some argue is intensifying. They see this as a direct result of 'neoliberal' policies, to various degrees prompted either by the power of global capitalism, or economic constraints imposed by international institutions, or because the ANC has catered largely to the interests of local corporations and the emerging black middle class. They argue that such policies have done little to benefit the majority of poor people, perhaps over 50 per cent of the population, in the far-flung urban townships, in the vast informal settlements that still cling to the peripheries of major cities and in the former homelands. Many of the poor are unemployed, dependent on state benefits, or struggle to survive on meagre incomes from casual work and from the rapidly expanding informal sector.

While some argue that the tripartite alliance delivered fairly favourable labour legislation, especially in the first five years of the ANC government, critics on the left emphasise the constraints on organised labour and the government's reluctance to protect workers from the cold wind of global competition.[10] Employment in the manufacturing sector has declined and strikes have gathered momentum. Even public sector workers have come under huge pressure; the 2007 strike – the largest since the end of apartheid[11] – is a case in point. To these authors, post-1994 popular politics reveals the weaknesses of the ANC's capacity to deliver many of the improvements that seemed possible in a reconstructed South Africa. Social and economic rights apparently enshrined in the Constitution have proved difficult to realise. South Africa seems to have achieved only a 'fragile stability',[12] or what others have referred to as a 'low-intensity democracy'.[13] As a result, the South African masses (as they are sometimes conceived) remain, metaphorically speaking, bolshie. This critique of the transition has helped some of the contributors to this collection contextualise past and present protest – although it is not shared by all.

Thirdly, some contributors draw on social movement theory. One variant is North American resource mobilisation theory, which sought to portray the efforts of social movements as 'rational, institutionally rooted, political challenges by aggrieved groups.'[14] It pays particular attention to the political resources available for effective mobilisation and sees social movements as '*political* actors that operate side by side – sometimes in competition, sometimes in collaboration – with traditional political institutions.'[15] The idea that such political activism potentially broadens the scope of meaningful, participatory democracy informs some of the contributions to this volume.

European scholars developing 'new social movement theory' drew on literature about pressure groups in the post-war Western world and noted the emergence of mass movements that were based not in the politics of the old left or labour, but evolved around specific issues.[16] These, such as the peace movement, the green movement or the women's movement, were essentially oppositional, but called forth cross-class and cross-cultural alliances that did not necessarily find their way into stable political parties or organisations. These scholars related them to the relative decline of industrial production in Western capitalist countries. As a corollary, conflict has shifted away from the factory. In this analysis, post-industrial struggles have diverse sites: they address consumption and relative poverty, as well as global, cultural, moral and charitable issues, rather than issues defined by the interests of class. Globally oriented non-governmental organisations (NGOs), debt relief and climate change are examples. New social movement paradigms explore the shared meanings, experiences, identity and values that inform such mobilisation. Melucci sees new social movements as essentially diverse and inchoate – collectively they offer new identities and can change the focus of debate, but less so the structure of society.[17]

Clearly there are problems in applying this body of theory – diverse though it is – to non-Western contexts. Hakan Thorn has argued that the global anti-apartheid struggle was a significant example of a new social movement.[18] This is a valuable analysis with respect to the international dimensions of the struggle. But South Africa's late twentieth-century mass movements centred particularly around the trade unions and the national liberation movements. In many senses these were older forms of political organisation and it is inappropriate to apply the term 'new social movements' to them. The ANC and labour movement remain central in a post-apartheid context, but now, of course, as part of a dominant alliance rather than oppositional social movement. The term seems most useful within South Africa, as in other non-Western countries, for the struggles of poorer communities, especially in rapidly expanding cities, around such social problems as services and housing.[19] However, these new social movements in South Africa are by no means restricted to specific issue-based politics. They see themselves as offering continuity for class-based politics and broader ideologies of social transformation.[20] Theoretical literature on social movements, sometimes focusing on culture, symbolism and identity, and relegating political activism to the realm of pressure group or civil society, can obscure the overarching political ambition of some new social movements.[21]

As mentioned, the term 'social movement' has not only been applied by analysts to post-apartheid popular politics, but has been adopted by some activists, or at least the intellectual leaders among them. In contrast to approaches based on radical historiography, new social movement theory – as applied to South Africa – tends to stress the novelty of these political impulses and opens the way to analysing recent popular politics as part of a global phenomenon with its own recent history.[22] Some movements explicitly share the rhetoric and mobilisation of the loose coalition of global justice activists, coordinated in the World Social Forums. The demonstrations against the World Summit for Sustainable Development in Johannesburg in 2002 were an important marker in the consolidation of political protest critical of the ANC government.

Activists and researchers alike have analysed developments in South Africa through the lens of a critique of globalisation. This has been a widely shared political discourse since 1994: Mbeki himself called for a reordering of global relations at the 2002 summit, particularly in relation to trade. Anti-globalisation rhetoric resounds across the African continent. There is self-conscious identification with a supportive international context – a new internationalism calling for political renewal that is not limited to South Africa's gnarled traditions of protest. Social movement theory encourages scholars to ask comparative questions across time and place. The idea of being identified as a new social movement can also be attractive to older political parties and organisations, because it signifies vitality, international connectedness and a pro-poor orientation. The South African National Civic Organisation, the ANC-aligned umbrella for civics, now 'a patient in intensive care' that has struggled to maintain a political presence, has on occasion adopted this language, and ANC members frequently identify themselves as part of a movement rather than a political party.[23]

New social movement theory also emphasises the significance of knowledge and information as sites of struggle and the media as central to mass action. Activists link service provision, wage demands or refusals to pay rent with debates around international trade and global warming, the costs of providing reticulated water, and the epidemiology and treatment of diseases such as HIV/AIDS. Such developments are, of course, not entirely new in popular politics. The independent union movement in the apartheid era developed an impressive range of industrial and financial expertise, and intellectuals associated with the civics and NGOs became experts in such fields as land reform and health. Yet recent debates around services, the environment, health and culture place a premium on knowledge-based politics. Ultimately, the Treatment Action Campaign (TAC) has scored its successes through the effective mobilisation of scientific knowledge around the treatment of HIV/AIDS as much as its street protests and media-friendly approach. The literature has important points to make about the centrality of media for mass action and creating communities of identity. The success of direct action is partly achieved through its reporting in a wide range of media, particularly television. Movements can also self-mobilise through the Internet and cellphones.

An awareness of international linkages was not absent from earlier labour or social history, and radical historiography always had a strong comparative dimension, but social movement theory in the hands of comparatively oriented scholars suggests a different and more global dynamic to political protest. Unlike many earlier popular leaders, Zackie Achmat, leader of the TAC, and Trevor Ngwane, the leader of the Soweto Electricity Crisis Committee (SECC), could connect internationally. As noted in the title of Ben Cashdan's documentary film, the 'two Trevors' (Ngwane and Manuel) could both 'go to Washington'.[24]

In sum, analyses based in African and social history emphasise the specific material context of political action, the diversity of the legacy of protest, and the complexity of political consciousness; critiques of the transition emphasise the structural continuities in South African society, and hence the logic of continued popular action; and social movement theory captures the international influences and comparisons, as well as new repertoires of resistance.

While there are some differences in the analytical tools used by the contributors to this collection and different political sympathies among them, there is a degree of unity in their approaches. All of them share a methodological commitment to a form of contemporary history. The chapters all develop detailed narratives as a means of explaining and assessing popular politics. All discuss case studies as a route towards expanding our knowledge and analytical capacity. This is a particularly appropriate approach for popular movements and organisations. The tools that may be useful for discussion of elections, party politics or attitudes are of limited value in this sphere.

At a time when quantitative material is being deployed more extensively to survey attitudes and political loyalty, these chapters raise implicit questions about the relationship of this data to the issues of power and political mobilisation. As an analogy, it is worth noting that even at the time of the formation of the Congress of South African Trade Unions (COSATU), in 1985, the majority of workers remained outside of the independent unions – yet the political significance of this movement is not in question. The chapters express a collective confidence in the value of historical methods in grappling with these issues of mobilisation, changing ideologies and consciousness, and their implications for political analysis.

Ideologies

Can we find continuities in the ideology of pre-and post-1994 popular movements, or do the latter represent new and distinctive phases of organisation? Chapters in this collection reflect on the views of only a limited number of activists and groupings, but they suggest a radicalisation of ideologies and a shift from nationalist and anti-racist to socialist positions. Kelly Rosenthal compares the pre-1994 Soweto Civic Association (SCA), in particular its highly influential leader Dr Nthatho Motlana, with the SECC and its spokesperson, Trevor Ngwane. Even during the 1970s and early 1980s, Motlana articulated the SCA's commitment to private property and disdained socialism. He was a medical practitioner and businessman as well as a politician and became Nelson Mandela's personal doctor. Rosenthal argues that the SCA aimed to empower the masses politically and to develop strong grassroots organisation so that the movement could not easily be crushed. Soweto-based groups focused initially on local issues such as rents and services, but the SCA's ambitions soon transcended these: people's power implied displacing the local state, and in the longer term aimed to be part of the transformation of the national state. Certainly, its ideology included participatory democracy, although it was then led by a largely self-selected leadership. But as Rosenthal points out, the SCA 'was not actually prescriptive in terms of economic ideology'.

By the late 1970s Motlana was increasingly espousing ideas about the value of entrepreneurship and homeownership. The latter was all the more important because black people could not own urban property. It was only after the 1976 Soweto uprising that the state began to allow longer-term leases. Before 1990 few could own rural property either, as the great bulk of land in the homelands was held under communal or customary forms of tenure. While lack of title did not prevent investment in homes, it greatly discouraged it. Rosenthal argues that civic action encouraged entrepreneurialism and self-organisation rather than dependence on the state. In the post-apartheid period, some of the leaders of the SCA moved into the private sector or government. Amos Masondo, mayor of Johannesburg since 2001, became a particular target of the new social movements.

By contrast, both Rosenthal and Dawson argue that the new social movements have, to varying degrees, espoused explicitly socialist positions and participatory democracy since the late 1990s. Rosenthal uses Ngwane and the SECC as her model, while Dawson draws on interviews with key figures in the Anti-Privatisation Forum (APF) in Gauteng. The ANC's failure to provide adequate services for poor people has been central to recent mobilisation. In the APF's view private ownership of utilities such as water and electricity companies or public–private partnerships pursued by the ANC inevitably introduced a profit motive; corporations and suppliers have prioritised shareholders over and above the people's needs. A corollary of this position is that services should, as far as possible, be provided free. Dawson illustrates that the case is made most strongly for water, as a basic human right and necessity. Access to such services is presented as a constitutional right and the implication of this position is that if services were publicly owned, the state would underwrite universal access and halt service cut-offs. As Ngwane argued, 'calling for free basic services is an attack on commodification; we try to attack the capitalist method of making profit from services'.[25]

At the level of leadership, socialism is explicitly articulated as an ideology, and this does to some degree permeate more generally. Dawson notes that the song 'That's why I am a socialist' was sung regularly on marches and at meetings, and signifies a desire for a more 'egalitarian society governed and controlled by producers of wealth'.[26] In the song, the International Monetary Fund, as much as South Africa's Growth, Employment and Redistribution (GEAR) strategy, is the enemy. The APF thus locates its struggle over services in South Africa within the context of the spread of global multinationals and aligns itself with those in poorer countries subject to crushing debt burdens. The collapse of communism in Eastern Europe and Asia and that of African socialism removed old external solidarities. But anti-American nationalist versions of socialism in Cuba, Venezuela and other parts of Latin America provided an alternative point of reference – certainly more so than African governments. New social movements seek their alliances with global justice activists, whether in the West or in non-aligned, developing countries. They see the South African Constitution as a potential guarantor of socio-economic rights, and particularly the right to receive services. For some activists, gaining piecemeal improvements is insufficient. They are calling for radically different forms of ownership, at least of services, and also worker self-management, as well as participatory democracy.

The notion of a transition in the ideology of protest movements should, however, be qualified both by an examination of political ideas in the 1970s and 1980s, and of the limits to socialism in the twenty-first century. Socialist ideas and rhetoric can be found in the Freedom Charter and were ubiquitous in the language of the exiled liberation movements, and some of this language permeated into the internally based civics. We can also discern a gradual transition in the influence of socialist ideas in the independent trade unions. In this volume, Julian Brown illustrates the limits of workers' ambitions in the 1973 Durban strike. The strikers focused primarily on wage demands. But the unions emerging after the strike in the 1970s drew on the legacy of the South African Congress of Trade Unions and the South African Communist Party and imbibed neo-Marxist writings. Activists schooled in these political traditions remained, as Suttner shows, underground, but not entirely silenced.[27] Although both organisations were banned, Tracy Carson illustrates how individuals such as Oscar Mphetha in Cape Town bridged the old and new unions; others brought alternative strands of socialist analysis from the Unity Movement. Neo-Marxist ideas, which also linked apartheid with capitalism, were espoused by academics and activists in reaction to the limits of South African liberalism.[28] White radicals were touched by the ideas that rippled out from Europe in the wake of the 1968 student rebellions, which attempted to link student and worker action. These approaches straddled the interconnected worlds of academic study (both in South Africa and among expatriates 'overseas'), the independent trade unions and some of the emergent black-led civics.

The independent trade union movement did not, however, become specifically socialist, nor did it adopt strategies narrowly tied to the industrial working class. By the late 1970s trade unionists and community activists, especially in the Cape, attempted to weld their struggles together. Boycotts were a well-established political tool in South Africa, and the anti-apartheid movement internationalised them. Workers in the Food and Canning Workers' Union struck at the Fatti's & Moni's food plant in Cape Town in 1979. As Carson demonstrates, unionists were able to work closely with community activists and black traders to organise a widespread boycott of pasta and other products made by the company. On this occasion the strategy was successful and workers were reinstated with a pay rise. Replication of this alliance in subsequent strikes did not always result in victory, and some unions, especially in the Federation of South African Trade Unions, felt it wiser to limit their ambitions to factory floor issues. By contrast, the South African Allied Workers' Union, which launched the Wilson Rowntree strike and boycott in East London in 1981, aimed not only to mobilise the wider community, but to further the ANC's struggle.

A striking feature of this key period (from 1976 to 1983) in the building of internal opposition was the flexibility in ideology and alliance building. Carson illustrates that at the height of apartheid, the Fatti's & Moni's strike and boycott brought together white and black organisers, coloured women workers, and African migrant men. They were able to forge links with coloured and African traders, with black and white students, and with activists from a Unity Movement tradition. There was a freshness and fluidity to this popular politics as it began to penetrate the armour of the apartheid state. Many Black Consciousness thinkers and activists who played a central role in urban and student mobilisation were moving towards the Congress, or charterist, positions. Shared antipathy to white minority rule facilitated alliance building and the emergence of the United Democratic Front (UDF), but the movements had not yet been subjected to the ideological discipline of the ANC. After the formation of the UDF in 1983 and COSATU in 1985, activists increasingly worked within the framework of a national liberation struggle. The ideas of freedom and unity became increasingly important, the latter seen as essential in negotiating an end to apartheid. In sum, socialist ideas were thus present – often in diffuse form – although not dominant in the unions and civics at the time. Rosenthal and Dawson may underestimate this strand in popular ideologies during the apartheid period.

The other element in their argument concerns the degree to which new social movements in the early twenty-first century are attempting to formulate an explicitly socialist ideology. As Dawson notes, leaders of the APF place great emphasis on the idea that they rather than the ANC are bearers of key redistributive traditions in the national liberation struggle, as embodied in the Freedom Charter and exemplified in the Reconstruction and Development Programme. However, recent popular activism has been equally diverse. The TAC, one of the most successful of the new movements, has tried to represent a broad front, arguing for empowerment, expanded rights and new notions of health citizenship. Some of its key leaders were steeled in the civic struggles of the 1980s and are effective in using new media. But the TAC has limited the range of issues on which it campaigns and has worked to influence government policy. In advocating access to antiretroviral treatment for HIV/AIDS, it emphasises individual rights and opportunity to live a fuller life in the face of a potentially devastating disease. Simonne Horwitz's chapter on nurses also illustrates the ambiguous political position of public sector workers in the early twenty-first century.

Popular struggles in recent years have evinced diverse and heterodox political thinking that often espoused radical democratic ideas in principle and highlighted the division of wealth in the society, but were not framed by a socialist ideology and rhetoric. In this sense, there are significant continuities, before and after 1994, in the complicated and layered ideological strands of popular protest

Diversity and alliances

The diversity of political expression is even more apparent if we move our view beyond worker organisation and urban civics (before 1994) and social movements (after 1994) to focus on particular groups of employees and rural communities. In this volume, Simonne Horwitz examines the long history of political action by nurses at Baragwanath Hospital and Chizuko Sato discusses rural struggles over land in KwaZulu-Natal. Together with other contributors, they raise another important issue: the capacity for alliances among organisations with differing political priorities, and differing social and ideological positions. Studies of rural political protests in twentieth-century southern Africa have made claims for their national significance, at least up to the 1950s; they have also taken issue with the idea that such struggles were predominantly 'isolated, covert and often passive'.[29] However, while rural protest could be triggered by broader political upheavals, it did not always run parallel with urban movements. The literature records the tensions between rural and nationalist struggles and also elements of popular politics that could be explicitly divisive, such as ethnicity and violence. Tim Gibbs, who explores populist politics in the largely rural Transkei before and after 1994, develops this point.

The position of public sector workers has been particularly important in the last couple of decades. While manufacturing employment declined, that in the public and service sectors expanded. Horwitz's chapter on strike action by nurses at Baragwanath hospital is an instructive example of the broadening of ideologies of protest. It focuses on one group of women workers at one institution over a 60-year period. Until the last few decades, nursing, alongside teaching, was one of the two major opportunities available to African women for professional careers. Baragwanath, serving Soweto, was the largest hospital in South Africa, and possibly in the southern hemisphere.[30]

Nurses were powerfully discouraged from striking, both by their profession and the hospital authorities, but they did so nonetheless. In the 1948 strike, their concerns were shaped by conditions at the hospital and by the tightness of discipline imposed on them. As the struggle against apartheid intensified, later strikes reflected broader political mobilisation, notably in 1985, when they joined with non-professional staff to close down the hospital. In the late 1980s and early 1990s they unionised and identified themselves as 'black, oppressed and underpaid'. Post-1994, it may have been predicted that nurses and public sector workers would become depoliticised, but the transition opened the way for public sector workers to use strikes more freely. The South African Municipal Workers' Union (SAMWU) was one of the most militant within COSATU and argued vociferously against GEAR. It was involved in the founding of the APF in the late 1990s. SAMWU and other public sector unions experienced substantial growth in the face of declining membership of unions as a whole and by the early twenty-first century COSATU became dominated by public sector workers.[31] By 2007 some nurses were prepared briefly to join in mass action against the failure of public services; their conditions and wages had improved little since 1994.

Although nurses were politicised, Horwitz brings out two key features of their struggles. Firstly, black nursing organisations were not directly part of the liberation movement before 1994, nor social movements or radical unions afterwards. Their activism was part of popular struggles, but had its own momentum and dynamic. Secondly, nurses were often torn between their professional duties and self-image, on the one hand, and their role as workers in an under-funded public sector institution, on the other. Many also sought upward social mobility. As individuals, a number of nurses became important political actors, but as a group of employees they had specific institutional and professional interests and did not easily join broader alliances.

The same may apply, in a very different context, to many rural communities. Sato draws her chapter on Weenen district from her thesis on land struggles in rural KwaZulu-Natal.[32] In Weenen the majority of Africans were tenants and workers on white-owned land who were removed from farms by the termination of labour tenancy. They had no rights under the Restitution Act of 1994, but formed an effective political front demanding the restoration of rural resources.

Tenants and workers in Weenen formed a community organisation as early as 1980, at a time when urban civics were also emerging. The Weenen Community Project (WECOP) was led by Johannes Sosibo, who linked the Weenen struggle first to Inkatha and then increasingly to radical NGOs such as the Association for Rural Advancement (AFRA), which was later a key component of the National Land Committee. It is interesting to note that Sosibo recognised the significance of media exposure for his movement in the 1980s and that AFRA was an important channel for this purpose. WECOP was able to make some headway in a rapidly changing political context, where both the central and local state were increasingly uneasy about implementing forced removals without adequate compensation. WECOP mobilised a strike on white-owned farms in 1992 – a particularly difficult form of action in this decentralised and hierarchical world. This sharply signalled the transition from a politics of begging and imprecation to one of militancy and demand.[33]

The process of transition from protest against forced removals to demands for the acquisition of land, however, involved tortuous negotiation with many different stakeholders. By 1994 the Weenen case had become of national importance and the new land affairs minister, Derek Hanekom, attempted to broker a solution. The district was a core area for the land reform pilot scheme in the province. As in other cases, determined and persistent organisation around land demands, together with strikes and threats of land invasion, won some priority for this particular rural community. Mandela himself briefly visited the district. But just as gains materialised in the shape of white-owned farms, the claimants split. There were rivalries between local ethnic communities that identified different segments of the farmlands as their historical territories. Community leaders competed for support in the local elections in 1996. The Department of Land Affairs found it very difficult to determine who should be the beneficiaries and, by 1998, the trusts that were established to take ownership of the land and manage the new settlements were bankrupt and families were moving onto the newly acquired farms without authority.

Land activism and land reform proved to be a divisive process, reinforcing prior identities as much as forging new movements. Tenants and agricultural workers became increasingly militant during the 1980s and some were beneficiaries of the transition. But 'the logic of tribal politics', Sato notes, 'became … an indispensable feature in implementing land reform'. Moreover, the central aim of organised groups of tenants in Weenen during this period was to acquire land. Their demands were different from those of urban social movements, who were focusing on wages and services. A national Landless People's Movement did emerge in the post-apartheid period, aligned with other new social movements, but it was unable to engage with many of the key local rural communities.[34] The Weenen struggle, although it had moments of regional and even national prominence, was essentially shaped by local priorities and its own specific dynamics. Sato alerts us to the significance of divisive identities and suppressed ethnicity in South African popular politics.

Tim Gibbs focuses on the former homeland of Transkei. He argues that regional politics after Transkeian self-government in 1963 became less focused around the struggle for rural resources and more around the patronage available from the state. As bureaucratic effectiveness diminished, so the language of politics became increasingly populist and personal. Gibbs differs from Mamdani and others who have seen in the homelands an intractable traditionalism built around reactionary tribal authorities. Populist politics allowed a voice for the people. It greatly limited what the state could do – for example a near rebellion in Mpondoland in 1977 completely undermined the government's attempt to introduce a new tax on livestock. Increasingly, the political leadership in the homeland attempted to act as intermediaries to provide access to and distribute state resources.

Strikingly, Gibbs argues that such forces persisted beyond 1994. Many Transkeian politicians, including key chieftaincies, swung behind the ANC in the late 1980s and early 1990s. The Eastern Cape, an ANC stronghold, demanded considerable resources from the central state. And the form of populist politics that evolved in the homeland era influenced regional and national politics – it became absorbed in the divisions within the ANC over leadership from 2005 to 2007. Rural Transkeians very largely backed Zuma, who spent far more time campaigning in rural districts than Mbeki and seemed more in tune with rural demands. He explicitly noted that 'somehow we in the ANC have messed up when it comes to the rural areas. It's place like this, Nkandla, and others that we have not reached, and we should have.'[35]

What are the implications of such diversity for alliance building outside of the ANC? In the 1980s the centrality of national liberation and the fluidity of opposition politics opened the way to an overarching political alliance under the umbrella of the UDF.[36] This has been difficult in the shadow of a democratically elected ANC government since 1994. Those who challenged the ANC's legitimacy or were excluded by the tripartite alliance were depicted as disloyal. While new social movement strategies were attractive to some of those who benefitted little from the political transition, and the struggle for urban services provided some unity, disparate political views and issues diminished opportunities for broader ideological assonance. Not least for this reason, COSATU, the South African Communist Party and ANC populists – who feared being isolated from the mainstream of national politics in a left-of-centre grouping – stayed within the ruling alliance. Under Mbeki's presidency, there were rumours that they would break away. Instead, they succeeded in taking over leadership of the alliance during the 2007 Polokwane conference. Zwelinzima Vavi, COSATU leader, repositioned himself as leading the opposition within the ruling alliance: 'perhaps others have arrived in the Promised Land', he said, 'but the working class and the poor have yet to make it there.'

The leadership conflict in the ANC and the outcome of the Polokwane conference signalled a new fluidity in South African politics. In some respects, however, the victory by Zuma and the more populist wing of the ANC has diminished the scope for any alliance of popular forces outside of the ruling party. The breakaway by Lekota in 2008, and, the formation of COPE as an alternative centrist party claiming the traditions of the ANC did create new possibilities for oppositional alliance building, but after early successes in the Western Cape by-elections of December 2008, popular support for COPE diminished. It is difficult to see how it could unite with radical social movements or find an alternative mass base.

Structural and social fault lines tend to reinforce organisational differences. Sharper class disparities within the black population and divisions between the employed and the many unemployed tend to fragment radical political expression. Nattrass and Seekings demonstrate that organised employees have been significant beneficiaries of the transition in respect of wages, job security, pensions and affirmative action.[37] COSATU represents the organised working class in mines, factories, and increasingly in the public sector and white-collar jobs. COSATU and the ANC have been able to appeal to those with ambitions for upward mobility. By contrast, the new social movements with their roots among the unemployed in the townships and in the shack settlements, together with a sprinkling of activist intellectuals, have found it difficult to penetrate the mainstream political movements and to build bridges to rural areas. In this context, social movements that address a more limited range of issues and with more fluid ideological positions, such as the TAC, have found it easier to expand support. The potential for ideological assonance and alliances is there, but it has not been realised in the manner of the early 1980s when the struggle against apartheid provided a cause for unity.

In a stimulating analysis, Michael Neocosmos sees 1984–86 as a watershed for a new mode of popular politics different from the national liberation struggle, which was reaching fruition in the mass protests of the early twenty-first century and providing renewed impulses for a fully participatory democracy.[38] But there are problems with his periodisation and his characterisation of mass mobilisation in the late apartheid years. Firstly, as illustrated above, the key period in the formulation of new ideologies and political practices was probably earlier, in the late 1970s and early 1980s. Secondly, the period from 1984 to 1994 also witnessed the rise of popular participation in ethnic conflicts and violence within divided communities. Thirdly, as suggested in this section, he underestimates the diversity of popular politics and perhaps overestimates the potential for a single movement outside of the ANC.

Yet there are signs in South Africa of a post-national liberation politics – a politics that can free itself from explaining all social problems with reference to the evils of apartheid era, and one that can challenge the moral and political hegemony of the liberation movement. The scope for heterodoxy, never repressed, is broadening again within the ANC and in popular movements. This is of great importance if South Africa is to become a mature democracy and escape the trap of creeping authoritarianism and corruption around an immovable national liberation movement in power. Southern African countries as a whole, where five national liberation movements still hold power, and Zimbabwe in particular, provide salutary cases in point. The record in government of Southern African liberation movements has not encouraged participatory democracy. South Africa, of course, has a different history and the strength of popular politics is one important element of its particular trajectory. For all their fragmentation, popular organisations and new social movements in the post-apartheid era, drawing on earlier traditions of mobilisation, have contributed to frame key social and economic issues, put pressure on the ANC and nurtured political fluidity. Even if opposition political alliances prove elusive, popular resistance has shown itself as a distinctive and persistent element of South African political culture.

Violence, repression and direct action

Violence has stalked South African history, and South Africans have experienced a relatively high level of both political and personal violence over two centuries. The Union of South Africa, established in 1910, presided over a period of about 70 years, until the 1980s, in which public political violence was constrained. The Union faced regular and intense flourishes of resistance from its earliest years, and even in these decades, popular protest sometimes contained the potential for violence. More frequently, violence was meted out by the state, its antennae always alert to immanent rebellion. In the 1906 Bambatha rebellion rumours of a Zulu uprising against the poll tax prompted reprisal killings of about 4,000 people.[39] This scale of slaughter was not repeated until the mid-1980s insurrection, and even then not by the police and military. The National Party government after 1948 initially relied on overwhelming policing, bureaucratic power and court-based proceedings under laws that greatly restricted both political rights and free expression. The shooting of urban pass protesters at Sharpeville, near Vereeniging, and rural rebels at Ngquza Hill, Mpondoland, in 1960, together with many smaller incidents, signalled that the state would resort to punitive violence when the police felt threatened. Soweto in 1976 confirmed this. By unleashing superior force at moments of confrontation, the state was generally able to exert its authority before any sustained armed rebellion or violent resistance could take shape.

The great majority of opposition political movements in South Africa between the end of conquest in the late nineteenth century and 1960 explicitly renounced violence as an instrument of struggle – whether because of the asymmetry of power relations or because of a commitment to constitutional methods. Where violence accompanied protest, it was often a by-product of crowd dynamics or police overreaction. After 1960, when the state banned key liberation movements, several groupings resorted to armed struggle. Even then, opposition groups, with the partial exception of Poqo, were cautious about such strategies and could find little foothold in the country. The ANC in particular tried to limit its actions to sabotage against property rather than warfare against the state's agents. As Julian Brown notes, between Sharpeville (1960) and Soweto (1976), neither of which was the direct result of the armed struggle, popular protest was characterised by relatively low levels of violence. Violence is often part of a reactive process, and the limits of the armed struggle, in practice if not always in rhetoric, constrained this dynamic and doused the flames of political violence. Internally, this was a period of transition and renewal in the shape of political struggle. The ANC had to remain underground, and new impulses and ideologies – such as student groups, radical Christianity, Black Consciousness and the independent unions – took shape between 1968 and 1973. None of these espoused the armed struggle.

The Durban strikes in January and February 1973, when over 100,000 African workers staged a series of 160 short stoppages, perhaps represented the most dramatic mass action in the years before the Soweto uprising. Brown's chapter on the management of the strikes, and also Carson's on the Fatti's & Moni's boycott, is a reminder of the scope for popular protest during the apartheid period. In view of the state's approach to nationalist protest in the 1950s and to the challenges it faced at Sharpeville and Soweto, Brown argues that violence was surprisingly absent from the Durban strikes – all the more so because workers were not unionised, the strikes were illegal and there were no formal structures for negotiation. The state could have broken the strikes up quickly. Brown sees constraint as arising from both sides. Employers and the local state in Natal were prepared to recognise some of the workers' demands; and they were keen to see the strikes as expressing narrow economic grievances and reluctant to call in the full repressive apparatus of the central government. The workers were cautious about challenging the police openly, and although they did march through the streets, they largely confined their rallies to places where they did not directly threaten property or public order. Traditional Zulu weapons were in evidence, but were seldom used to threaten strike breakers or opponents of the strike.

The strikes were not simultaneous and most were settled within a week. By and large, employers did not lose production and workers did not lose jobs. Whatever their larger political affiliations, workers limited their demands to those that could be translated into a framework acceptable to employers and the state, and to some degree could be met. A reactive process of violence was always possible, but it was avoided. The strikes set the pattern for a decade of highly disciplined worker action. Those involved in worker mobilisation were fully conscious of the broader political potential of workers. Their analysis, as noted above, placed workers at the heart of the South African struggle. But they saw political liberation as a long game, for which discipline and organisation were essential. It could also be argued that over the longer term, the 1973 strikes signalled that the state approached industrial action more cautiously than mass protest in the townships.

The significance of direct action and violence in popular politics, and its influence on the political process in South Africa, changed fundamentally during the 1980s. Thula Simpson examines the links between external armed struggle and internal politics in this period. On the one hand, cadres trained by the liberation movements managed to find a slender foothold in the country and to stage some dramatic incidents. On the other, internal insurrectionary forces threw off the shackles of political constraint and the comrades movement began systematically to target state property, those seen as collaborators with apartheid and even the white agents of the state. While the ANC was cautious in calling for outright rebellion, its invocation of ungovernability set the scene for a series of confrontations. In turn, the state ratcheted up the levels of retaliation, both internally and externally, as it conceived itself to be facing a far more threatening challenge.

External armed struggle, Simpson argues, was of far greater rhetorical than military importance to the ANC: 'its material weakness … was belied by its immense symbolic strength'. From the mid-1980s, most of those sent by Umkhonto we Sizwe (MK) into South Africa were killed or arrested. Of the approximatedly 240 MK cadres deployed from Zambia in 1989 for Operation Vula, a third were captured, a third defected and few of the others could remain effectively in touch with headquarters. It was an irony that at the very moment when the ANC needed the threat of armed struggle most in order to secure the most favourable negotiating terms with the National Party, it was increasingly ineffective.

Yet Simpson argues that the rhetoric was important. The ANC had to show its commitment to violence and capacity occasionally to mobilise it in order to retain popular support and its vanguard role. Chris Hani was a highly skilled publicist in this regard. The ANC, through the medium of the UDF and Mass Democratic Movement, was restoring its leadership internally, and as political killings by agents and allies of the state multiplied, the legitimacy of opposition violence seemed unanswerable.

While armed struggle was faltering, with the front line being driven further and further north from Zambia and Angola to Tanzania, its potential hovered over South Africa. Critically, the ANC had shown that internal fuses could be lit. Armed struggle gained its potential through the comrades movement in the townships, although it was not fully controlled or marshalled. The militant *toyi-toyi*, the carved wooden guns, and the slogans celebrating the AK[40] accompanied ANC colours at an increasing number of meetings and funerals. There was a growing sense of political fearlessness inside the country. At the first mass rally addressed by the newly released political prisoners in 1989 and attended by 70,000 people, Sisulu and his colleagues were escorted by 20 young militants dressed in military style, symbolic of MK. Throughout the negotiations (1990–94), ANC supporters were able to retaliate when the state, Inkatha, or vigilantes mobilised violence; they were also able to initiate violence and undoubtedly contributed to the ANC's negotiating strength.

The failure of MK to develop a large army perhaps had an unexpected impact on post-1994 South African politics. In some countries where there had been extended liberation or civil wars, ex-soldiers had an explosive potential, lying like social land mines in the post-conflict political environment. While soldiers initially seemed to be a vanguard for social transformation and their generals often took power, their potential for destabilisation also became apparent. Dealing with demobilised liberation movement fighters was a major feature of Mozambican and Zimbabwean politics. In Zimbabwe especially, the dissatisfaction of war veterans in the late 1990s, coinciding as it did with economic problems and the ruling party's political insecurity, triggered the complex and dismal trajectory of current Zimbabwean politics. South Africa did not have to deal with the threat of so large a group of liberation fighters, and it had more space in its regular army. In this sense, the weakness of the armed struggle may ironically have helped to ease the post-apartheid transition.

Although violence ebbed quickly as a feature of popular politics after 1994, political tensions were still played out on the streets of South Africa. Direct action – rooted in the strategy and style of the 1980s insurrection – has been evident in the early twenty-first century. Social movement activists invoke the idea that the state represses popular organisation. Visually, the confrontations between protesters and the state have echoed those in the apartheid years.[41] Police seemed to use unnecessary force with similar kinds of uniforms, riot gear and vehicles. The relative freedom of movement and meeting enabled protesters to choose highly sensitive symbolic spots, easily accessible to the media, such as the World Social Forum or Constitution Hill. A heavy police presence surrounded a number of protests and activists have pushed the limits of legal civil action. Dawson notes that the Orange Farm Water Crisis Committee, affiliated to the APF, explicitly advocated the destruction of state property: 'Destroy the meter, enjoy the water' became their rallying cry. In an echo of the 1980s they organised several marches, involving thousands of residents, to the homes of councillors and to local Eskom offices,[42] demanding an end to cut-offs. In 2003 a group of 15,000 blocked the Golden Highway skirting Soweto. Police dispersed the crowd. The highway was blockaded again twice in 2006, to the slogan of 'No freedom without basic services!' Police arrested 18 people and injured some with rubber bullets.

Violence skirted a wave of protests about service delivery, unemployment and housing in the Free State. In 2004 the Greater Harrismith Concerned Residents group burnt T-shirts emblazoned with Thabo Mbeki's face, as well as ANC membership cards. A 17-year old demonstrator was killed and others injured when the police opened fire. In 2005 angry residents at Kgotsong, near Bothaville, looted shops, disrupted schools, blocked roads with burning tyres, damaged councillors' homes and stoned police officers. Television news reports reminiscent of the anti-apartheid struggles showed sequences of conflict, including youths making petrol bombs in full view of the cameras.[43] The capacity for violent direct action was chillingly evident during the 2008 killings of immigrants, mostly in Gauteng.

South African radical political traditions have embraced direct action, with a veiled threat of violence, and post-1994 policing has been erratic. The government had legitimacy on its side and allowed relative freedom of protest. But it was difficult for the ANC to defend itself against the visual images created of police action, or the fact that protesters were clearly poor and black. Violence has an emotional impact and, as in the anti-apartheid struggle, evoked moral debates over governance. South African popular struggles have drawn on strategies of direct action that still contain a potential for violence. Direct action of this kind starkly reveals social problems and has helped to create a new sense of political urgency.

Icons and iconoclasts

The South African struggle created a powerful set of visual images, conveyed by a multitude of different media, from posters to film.[44] From the 1980s popular protest was widely associated with the ANC's flag, the *toyi-toyi* and resistance songs. As the popular movements began to find their feet during the 1980s, Mandela, Tambo and others were constantly invoked in mass rallies, accompanied by resounding cries of, 'long live!' (*viva!*) Images of Mandela circulated, although there were no recent photographs of him. They were printed on T-shirts and posters, and the names of struggle heroes were memorialised in streets, informal settlements and shanty towns such as Tamboville and Chris Hani. After 1994 museums, memorials, renamings and heritage sites have fixed – with visual displays – the great tradition of South African resistance.[45]

ANC leaders, especially those in prison, were central symbols of resistance. Mandela was always part of the pantheon of remembered leaders and had a particularly charismatic role before he was tried and imprisoned.[46] Winnie Mandela, equally charismatic, worked hard to keep him in the public eye. He was a key figure of authority on Robben Island, and this trickled through to ANC structures, but Genevieve Klein suggests that his stature could have languished, chiselled down over the hard prison years.

Klein shows how the Anti-Apartheid Movement (AAM) in Britain decided to focus on political prisoners from 1976 and developed the SATIS – Southern Africa: The Imprisoned Society – campaign. In part, this was because of requests it received for international support for prisoners; arrests and trials intensified in the post-1976 political turmoil. Prisoners were a particular concern of well-organised British-based support movements such as Defence and Aid, which cooperated in the campaign. Focusing on political prisoners also enabled the AAM to concentrate on human rights and de-emphasise the armed struggle. Western governments, still broadly tolerant of the South African regime, were uneasy about imprisonment without trial, and a campaign based on rights and justice offered the possibility of broadening support. As the campaign matured, it proved useful to highlight specific prisoners, particularly the long-serving leaders of the ANC. The ANC and AAM wanted to resist a cult of personality, but they realised the value of humanising the abstract issues of the struggle and elevating recognisable personalities. An iconography of Mandela was produced with busts, photographs and posters displayed at meetings, rallies, cycle rides and tribute events. AAM officers worked with students and other groups in Britain on projects named after Mandela. Mandela could not be besmirched by the realities of power or actual involvement in commanding violent armed struggle. So Mandela's name boomeranged back and forth from South Africa to Europe, gaining recognition, adherents and moral force as his story was told. Sacrifice was important in struggle; the capacity to forgive emerged gradually as a parallel virtue.

It is difficult to know how important these campaigns were, but they surely contributed to Mandela's authority and moral stature.[47] This was assured by the time he emerged from prison, and for nine years he bestrode South African politics as the symbol of legitimacy, leader of the liberation struggle and protector of the ANC's commitment to non-racialism, reconciliation and a rainbow nation. He was certainly able to weather the tensions over economic and social policy and the gravy train that accumulated during his government. He provided a sense of unity and optimism about the future, including the possibility of achieving major social gains for poor people. His standing was such that there were many attempts to cement his legacy, in which Mandela was often a willing participant. Aside from lending his name and authority to a multitude of good – and not so good – causes and institutions, and building his own charity, he was the subject of memorials and museums in his honour.

Despite the power of this heritage, some of these symbols and iconography are being contested. Sihlongonyane's chapter focuses on the Mandela Museum project in Alexandra township, Johannesburg. Apartheid left South African cities fragmented. The project aimed to lend profile to an impoverished, densely settled and socially divided township, which had nevertheless been a crucible of political activism.[48] A Mandela museum would add lustre, give a specifically African character and identity to Johannesburg, and promote nation building and a shared sense of the past. But a project conceived to create consensus by honouring a national hero in a marginalised township also prompted discordant views among the Alexandra residents.

Located close to a house where Mandela lived temporarily in the 1940s, the museum was initiated by the Gauteng Tourism Authority in 2003 as part of the R1.3 billion Alexandra Renewal Programme. The problem for the local community was that construction of the museum displaced 48 families. A complicated politics emerged over where they would be relocated. Some refused to go and mounted a series of protests about removal to an area named after another liberation hero: 'We said, "*Asiyi* eBram Fischer! Bram Fischer no!"' The council brought bulldozers; the people armed themselves with sticks and petrol bombs. Those forced to move named their new site Baghdad as a metaphor of devastation. Local people accused the ANC of appropriating the memory of the struggle for its own purposes. Mandela was certainly a hero of the struggle in 1980s Alexandra, but complaints were articulated about his government's record by the end of his presidency: in a poll, 74 per cent of people in Alexandra thought crime and violence had worsened.[49] By 2000 school students were *toyi-toy*-ing in the streets against the government. For most in Alexandra, Mandela was a distant figure and there were more immediate, vivid local heroes such as Moses Mayekiso.[50] In the Mandela Museum, the diverse local memories, experiences and dramas of the struggle were not mapped; the information board told a national story. Local families were displaced and the potential for tourism revenue had yet to be realised. Sihlongonyane argues that national heritage policy, teaming up with globalising forces, acted as a cultural bulldozer capable of flattening marginal cultural expressions.

Parallel processes can be found in other parts of the country, although the lines of political loyalty were different. The old Bhunga building in Umtata, borrowing from the style of Herbert Baker, had been the site of the Transkeian Territories General Council and the Transkeian Legislative Assembly and parliament. A symbol of apartheid's homelands policy, which attempted to make Transkei an independent country, the Bhunga building was also converted into a Mandela museum, as one of three sites to honour his association with his home region of the Transkei. The Mandela Museum has been a significant tourist attraction and local educational site in a town that has neglected its older buildings and has little else to offer the tourist. But the Bhunga's wooden interior was removed, and the Transkeian Territories General Council archive was packed up and moved into an unsafe house where it could not be effectively used. The conversion of the building caused a ripple of dissent among a few academics and members of the Transkeian elite, some of whom at that time were lending their support to Bantu Holomisa's United Democratic Movement. They felt that the Transkei's local history could have been given greater emphasis.

We must be careful about assuming from the case of the Alexandra museum that popular protest has emerged against Mandela. After 1999 Mandela in some respects distanced himself from Mbeki and tried to retain an all-embracing fatherhood of the nation, espousing causes that the government neglected. In particular, he focused on poverty, on children and on destigmatising HIV/AIDS. He stood for the more universal, humanist, non-racial face of the ANC at a time when Mbeki projected a sterner Africanist, centralising and technocratic face.[51] But both the construction of Mandela's iconic status and its maintenance celebrate a particular version of history with emphasis on the grand narrative of the struggle and particularly the centrality of the national leadership. His status lends the ANC enduring legitimacy and reminds the nation of the leaders' sacrifices at a time when there are murmurings of opposition not only from the minorities, but also from the masses and within the ANC itself.

Hidden issues and new repertoires

Knowledge and media have been important for movements. Social movement theory is not the first to tell us this, although it does sharpen questions about the changing nature of media and their impact. Photographs of Sharpeville and Soweto had a stunning potential to mobilise opposition locally and globally, and helped to delegitimise the apartheid regime. Unions and civics in the 1970s and 1980s spread their message with leaflets and theatre, and through mainstream newspaper reports. There is little doubt that the increased level of literacy achieved through Bantu education was a double-edged sword for the government.[52] Boycotts, as Carson shows, could be quickly globalised through international support networks in the late 1970s.[53] Television helped to create the images that won the world over to the insurrection in 1984–86.

Attempts to conceptualise recent social movements alert us to the importance of symbolic terrain and new media. New movements and interest groups, jostling for attention and legitimacy in the post-apartheid context, also draw on elements of the symbolic traditions of pre-1994 struggles. Some see themselves as its bearers. Post-1994 popular opposition groups have also diversified their tactics, connected with international networks, and exploited the possibilities of television and the Internet. This section illustrates these developments in the politics surrounding HIV/AIDS.[54]

The South African Constitution greatly expanded the notion of rights and citizenship for all of the country's people. Yet extending rights, and especially socio-economic rights, has been particularly difficult. Rights to health and treatment have rocketed up the political agenda because of the centrality of HIV/AIDS. Both the white government and the liberation movements were tardy in recognising the devastating potential of the epidemic in the 1980s and early 1990s. For the ANC, Mandisa Mbali argues, there were other pressing priorities. Although the disease was identified in South Africa by the early 1980s, it was seen, as in the West, to be largely a problem of homosexual men. Even when its potential for spread among heterosexual people was evident by the late 1980s, rates of reported infection remained low and it was difficult to imagine how quickly it would take hold. The Chamber of Mines, for example, alerted to the possible susceptibility of migrant men, was resistant to the idea that the miners could spread AIDS, and the National Union of Mineworkers denied the idea that African miners' sexuality might be characterised as profligate. There were, however, groups of activists, some associated with the UDF and unions, who did take the disease seriously at this time. Gay and lesbian activists were at the forefront, although they were organisationally fragmented and found it difficult to overcome internal racial divisions. Medical professionals and those associated with industrial health issues provided another node of AIDS activism and helped to organise two major regional conferences in the early 1990s.

In the mid-1990s it seemed that HIV/AIDS prevention and treatment might receive strong backing from the government. A new director general of health, Quarraisha Abdool Karim, was sensitive to the destructive potential of the disease and attuned to professional concerns. Nkosazana Zuma, minister of health in Mandela's government, also seemed sympathetic to organised action. As in other ministries, such as Land Affairs, the potential for joint action among ANC politicians, activists and professionals involved in the UDF and NGOs seemed considerable. In the sphere of HIV/AIDS, knowledge-based activism rather than direct action was of particular importance. Those concerned about the disease saw their priorities as understanding its complex epidemiology, informing government and politicians, and spreading knowledge about prevention to the public. It was necessary to keep in touch with a rapidly growing science, statistical debates and attempts at public education in other parts of the world.

Mbali illustrates how the state and activists moved apart during the next few years. The government's own publicity campaign, initially focused around the musical *Sarafina*, came under intense criticism for cutting corners in commissioning, for overspending and for its quality. The critiques, if justified, were counterproductive. They embarrassed the government and were interpreted to have racial overtones. The ANC's involvement in the Virodene scandal also distanced the politicians from the activists and professionals.[55] The coincidence of this set of forces, together with Mbeki's particular take on the disease, fed the state's reluctance to recognise the scale of the crisis and the possibilities for treatment. As a reaction, health activists and gay activists, including people who had cut their teeth in the pre-1994 UDF, such as Zackie Achmat, explored new ways of mobilising. As treatment became available, so too the political focus changed and activists founded the TAC in 1998.[56] The TAC aimed both to build grassroots support and to change government policy through campaigning.

HIV/AIDS campaigners certainly staged marches and explored direct action. But in a battle over information and interpretation they put access to the media at the heart of their strategy. Hodes analyses the links between the TAC and *Beat It!* – a series on South African television that powerfully articulated an activist view of the treatability of AIDS. First screened in 1999, the series was guided by Jack Lewis, a close associate of Achmat, and co-produced by Mercy Makhalemele, a founder member of the TAC. *Beat It!* and the TAC aimed primarily to remove the stigma surrounding AIDS, to provide a vehicle for people to disclose that they were HIV-positive, to discuss the disease openly and to stress that they were 'living positively with AIDS'.

Beat It! aimed at creating a positive community of sufferers and securing the right to treatment. The programme makers initially shared the government's critique of multinational pharmaceutical corporations over the pricing of drugs. However, they became increasingly critical of Mbeki and Health Minister Manto Tshabalala-Msimang when their denialism became more patent. The government's reluctance to roll out antiretroviral drugs was a repeated theme, pivotal to the series. The TAC and *Beat It!* aimed to move beyond this single issue and discuss rights more generally, dispense advice and create a new form of health citizenship. There was particular emphasis on empowering women, on non-racialism and on the lifestyle of HIV-positive participants. Audiences reached an estimated four million during the early 2000s.

Television has the potential to reach a wider audience than street protests and socialist songs. The TAC saw itself as a social movement based among the largest group of sufferers – the African poor; Lewis portrayed *Beat It!* as 'amplifying and echoing a mass movement on the ground'. This may have been soft activism, but it dispensed knowledge and information very effectively. The programme's content producer saw continuities with pre-1994 civic struggles: it 'was like plugging back into a vein of popular politics'. Both Dawson and Hodes distinguish the TAC from other new social movements in that it singled out a particular issue to mobilise around – albeit one that ricocheted through the social fabric of South Africa in a multitude of directions. Yet it developed as a vehicle for popular protest against the government and multinationals, it invoked the spirit and strategies of the civics, and it has probably been the most significant movement in creating a new visual language of struggle. There is a disturbing continuity, also, in the politicisation of funerals.

While breaking new ground in the use of television, the TAC and other movements also echoed earlier struggle repertoires by using the courts. Radical lawyers, some in the Legal Resources Centre, proved critical in chipping away at the edifice of the apartheid state in the 1980s, for example in cases challenging the legality of the pass laws.[57] One of these was Geoff Budlender, who went into government as director of land affairs in 1994. Sacked in 1999, he returned to the Legal Resources Centre and led the successful Constitutional Court case challenging the government's refusal to distribute antiretrovirals to pregnant women. In 2008 residents of Phiri were successful in their High Court battle against the City of Johannesburg, Johannesburg Water, and the Department of Water Affairs and Forestry. Pre-paid water meters were declared unconstitutional and the amount of free basic water was increased to 50 litres per person per day.[58]

Continuity and change

Elements of post-1994 popular politics echoed apartheid era mass mobilisation, and in that sense we can see the significance of popular protest in South African political culture. Intellectuals and activists challenged the ANC government in a multitude of contexts. New movements struck roots among poorer communities in the townships and had particular success in winning the support of women. They sustained the culture of discussion, of participation, and of the link between politics and community activity that characterised anti-apartheid mobilisation. But the new social movements and similar organisations were different in significant ways. They operated in a transformed context, were beneficiaries of democratisation, had more freedom of organisation and were smaller in scale. They also found it more difficult to build alliances across a range of organisations and communities, more particularly with organised workers.

While there were incidents where public protest was constrained by police or where the state over-reacted, the ANC government has largely tolerated protest. The ANC itself has deep roots in townships and rural districts and on some issues remained responsive to demands that emanated from them. The sea change in leadership at Polokwane demonstrated a measure of internal democracy, flexibility and a capacity to respond to popular concerns. Zuma acted as a lightning rod for a range of popular forces in the tripartite alliance. Although the ANC's legitimacy was to some degree challenged by grassroots mobilisation, it has so far shown the capacity to secure electoral support.

Most of the chapters in this collection implicitly or explicitly argue for the value of protest in extending democracy and expressing diverse political views. But some also accept that popular politics displayed a dark side and on occasion demonstrated the potential for violence within divided communities. Recent xenophobic attacks and ethnically based dissension have been major cases in point, and were potentially dangerous for the body politic. Liz Gunner argues that the celebrated singing of 'Umshini wami' (My machine gun) by Zuma's supporters was more about collective memory of the struggle than a renewal of Kalashnikov culture.[59] But it was also a reminder that the bloodshed of the past is not entirely dead and buried, and that levels of violence in South African society remain high.

The chapters in this collection do not draw on comparisons with other African countries. They focus on popular political movements that largely articulate an ideologically based opposition susceptible to political solutions rather than ethnic separatism, traditional authority, pentacostalism and millennialism. The chapters understand popular struggles since the 1970s largely as modern (and in this case mostly urban) movements, responding to material concerns such as poor wages, high rents and the lack of services, or as competing for national political power. There are clearly alternative strands of consciousness to examine, but these are essentially modernist essays that shy away from such issues as witchcraft, neopatrimonialism or ethnic violence and see these as less central in the South African national political context.

In many respects the flourishing of new social movements and the increased fluidity of politics have been a sign of healthy democracy. It is surely valuable that the movements considered here were fundamentally concerned with ideological and policy debates and advocated a broadening of citizenship, civic rights and democratisation that impacted on the lives of the majority of South Africans. They have succeeded in forcing key issues, such as urban services and the right to antiretrovirals, onto the political agenda. The re-emergence of popular politics has not threatened the ANC's political control, but it has influenced political debate, reframed issues and contributed to changing policy priorities. These movements, as well as more formal parliamentary political opposition, may help to prevent the gradual fusion of party and the state – a baleful tendency in many African countries. Grassroots politics have undoubtedly shaped the leadership changes within the ANC.

The studies in this book focus on the diversity of popular politics since the 1970s. They discuss an exciting range of political ideologies and repertoires. It is important to study and analyse the anatomy of protest and the rich texture of popular political expressions. This collection of essays shows something of both the continuities and changes in the character of protest and makes an argument for a distinctive tradition, as well as continuing strength, of grassroots mobilisation. It also suggests the salience of popular politics in shaping the broader political culture of the country.

2 The Durban strikes of 1973: Political identities and the management of protest

Julian Brown

Introduction and context

Labour mobilisation, work stoppages and strikes have often been central elements in popular protest in South Africa, both before and after 1994. This chapter is the first of three that focus on workers and protest; it examines the Durban strikes of 1973 – a series of labour actions that preceded the rise of independent trade unions in the course of the 1970s. These strikes provide an important window through which to examine not only labour activism, but also the roles played by the state and company managers in the containment of protest; beyond this, they also provide an insight into the complexities of the relationship between protest and violence in this period. In this chapter I argue that – somewhat surprisingly – the state and employers did not automatically use violence to repress the strikes in Durban; in turn, workers were not provoked into retaliation. This suggests that – in analysing continuities and changes in the potential for popular mobilisation and protest in the apartheid era – it is necessary to consider the rare moments in which the state hesitated to close down political space. This theme is pursued further in the next chapter.

Between 9 January and 31 March 1973 approximately 61,410 black workers in Durban embarked on strikes in their various industries and companies.[1] This made the Durban strikes the largest labour protest since the 1948 election win of the National Party. Indeed, more black workers were on strike in Durban in these months than during the whole of the 1960s: according to figures gathered by the South African Institute of Race Relations, an average of 2,000 black workers had embarked on strikes for each year of that decade.[2] The first two years of the 1970s had seen an increase in both the intensity and frequency of strikes: at the end of 1971, for example, 13,000 Ovambo workers had taken part in a work stoppage in South West Africa.[3]

It is notable, however, that these earlier strikes rarely involved more than 2,000 workers at a time; likewise, they were isolated within individual industries and did not threaten either to combine into a general strike or invade the central spaces of the affected cities themselves. The Durban strikes, by contrast, not only involved tens of thousands of workers across all of the city's industries, but also developed from the various workplaces and compounds to spill out early in February onto the city streets. The strike wave thus became visible within the ordinary experience of the white citizens of the city. Through their unprecedented scale and the very public nature of their spread and development, the Durban strikes entered into the public sphere in a way that recent labour protests had not been able to do.

And yet the state did not consider these strikes as a form of public political protest. Instead, it described them as resulting from economic grievances and delegated the responsibility for resolving them to employers. In contrast, this chapter considers these protests as bound up in the development of public forms of protest in the 1970s. It does not aim to consider how they fit into the development of trade unionisation in the course of this decade, but focuses instead on attempting to understand both why these strikes were allowed to develop and how they were resolved. Their successes expanded the space available for public protest – and pointed to ways in which such protests could develop.

It is worth noting at the outset that the Durban strikes are frequently mentioned in the historiography of the South African labour movement, but discussion is generally underdeveloped. Much of the literature focuses on the later 1970s and early 1980s, on the emergence of local and national coordinating organisations, and on their movement towards public political engagement.[4] In this context, the spontaneous protests of 1973 are only interpretable either as preliminary indications of the potential that would be activated by later organisations or as catalytic events that helped lead to these organisations being formed. In neither approach are the strikes seen as interesting in themselves, and in neither approach is it asked why the workers did not become more confrontational.

Some of the detail missing from much of these accounts can be found in the small number of articles directly addressing the Durban strikes.[5] The major account was compiled at the time of the strikes themselves under the name of the Institute for Industrial Education (IEE) and published in 1974 as *The Durban Strikes 1973: Human Beings with Souls*.[6] The IEE – centred around Rick Turner, who, being banned at the time, could not take credit for having written the book – used this publication to set out an argument for the formal recognition of African trade unions and advocated for the adoption of a specific labour policy. This may help explain why this work focuses little on the potential political conflict between the workers and their managers, and puts its emphasis instead on the economic rationale of the strikes. This was also a source of some of the later criticism the book received, most notably from Johan Maree.[7]

This chapter concerns the quotidian details of the strikes themselves and uses the IIE's *The Durban Strikes* as a guide. The daily accounts published in Durban's two local newspapers provide a broader focus on employers' reactions, public space and confrontations. I have also been able to use the notes collected by Gerry Mare, one of the IIE's researchers, which are housed at the University of KwaZulu-Natal's Alan Paton Centre. The archives of the Federation of South African Trade Unions – the first major African trade union federation to emerge after the strikes – also contain records of the IIE, including additional details on the events of 1973 and their consequences.

The decade preceding the Durban strikes was marked by the apparent consolidation of the apartheid order. In political terms, the state appeared strong: the banning and repression of the African National Congress, the Pan Africanist Congress and their allies in the early 1960s seemed to have been successful. The underground operations of these movements – while exciting the imagination of politicians – rarely had an impact on the white public. Extra-parliamentary white opposition groups were also restricted. Although several groups – including the National Union of South African Students (NUSAS) and the Black Sash – sought to protest against apartheid policies, they struggled to find an audience. Meanwhile, the parliamentary opposition was weak: the United Party, the official opposition, did not challenge the fundamentals of state policy, the Liberal Party collapsed, and a white liberal opposition was largely restricted to the voice of the lone representative of the Progressive Party in parliament, Helen Suzman. Indeed, conservative Afrikaner breakaways could seem a more pressing electoral threat.

In economic terms the apartheid order seemed equally strong. The country's economy had continued to grow since the end of the Second World War; in particular, its manufacturing, commerce and finance sectors all continued to boom throughout the 1960s. (The textile industry, for example, almost doubled in size in this period – being recorded as employing 50,000 workers in 1962 and 90,000 by the mid-1970s.) The mining sector, too, grew substantially. Notably, gold production doubled between 1955 and 1970 – in time to catch the sudden wave of profit associated with the deregulation of the international gold price in 1968. Throughout this decade the country's gross domestic product grew at an annual rate of 6.2 per cent, while employment grew at an annual rate of 3.2 per cent.[8] The South African economy expanded despite the imposition of sanctions and trade restrictions – a fact that was noted at the time, and that influenced both public and academic debates.[9]

The country's economic strength was reflected in the significant improvements in living standards for South Africa's white citizens. According to Beinart's survey, contemporary commentators suggested that white South Africans enjoyed a standard of living comparable to that of the richest developed countries in Europe and the Americas. And although – as Beinart suggests – there may be some difficulties with this direct comparison, it is nonetheless easy to share the conclusion that in the period leading up to the early 1970s (and to the Durban strikes) 'white South Africans had never had it so good'.[10]

For black South Africans – and, most obviously in the context of this chapter, black South African workers – the effects of the economic boom of this period were, however, more ambiguous. The total size of the urban black labour force increased dramatically throughout this period, with the number of African employees in the manufacturing sector doubling between 1960 and 1980.[11] The growth in the country's manufacturing sectors also produced shifts in the types of labour demanded; Lambert notes that there was 'an *increasing* demand ... for workers who were sufficiently trained and prepared for semi-skilled operative functions'.[12] He points to the metal industry, in which the percentage of semi-skilled black employees rose from 23 per cent of the total in 1968 to 29 per cent in 1974; this expansion of the semi-skilled sector of the industry was replicated unevenly across the country.

However, African labour remained heavily regulated by the state. Influx control remained a pervasive element in workers' lives throughout this period. In addition, the ability of black workers to organise in any formal fashion was severely limited. Some unions did exist, operating at variable levels of effectiveness: the South African Congress of Trade Unions, for example, was largely moribund by the middle of the 1960s. The Trade Union Council of South Africa (TUCSA) continued to operate – in Durban, most notably through the textile industry – but was recognised to be fundamentally 'ineffectual and schizophrenic'.[13] Generally, African workers were excluded from the unions active in Durban at the start of the 1970s; Indian and coloured textile workers were partially represented, but African workers were not, despite occasional efforts to extend the unions.[14]

The absence of African labour organisation was once again becoming a key political issue. In 1971 NUSAS resolved to form wages committees on each of its affiliated campuses; by the end of the next year these committees existed in Cape Town, Johannesburg, Grahamstown, Pietermaritzburg and Durban. In 1972 the South African

Students Organisation (SASO) called for the formation of the Black Workers' Project (BWP) and the eventual formation of the Black Allied Workers' Union – a general union open to all black workers. Although there is little evidence to suggest that any of these organisations played an active role in the labour disputes in Durban in 1973, nonetheless their formation signalled an increasing focus on workers by white and black activists.

The first strikes

The first of the Durban strikes began on the morning of 9 January 1973 at the Coronation Brick and Tile works. Before dawn, workers moved through the company's hostels spreading word of a strike. Instead of moving to their workplace, 2,000 black workers marched from the hostels to a nearby football field. They demanded that the company's management increase their weekly wages; but they refused to elect representatives to lead negotiations, fearing that these representatives would inevitably be victimised. The provincial Department of Labour sent a spokesperson to the field in an attempt to mediate between the company and its workers; this spokesperson was, however, unsuccessful in engaging the workers and was forced to retreat from the field to the sound of the crowd's jeers. The day ended in a stalemate, with neither the workers nor the company's managers any closer to reaching an agreement. The next morning, the paramount chief of the Zulu nation, Goodwill Zwelithini, arrived at the football field promising to negotiate on behalf of the workers. After a representative had announced his imminent arrival, he then kept the workers waiting for several hours while he consulted with the company's management; after this wait, the workers were at first reluctant to allow him to take on their cause. One worker was heard to call out during Zwelithini's speech: 'We've heard this all before!'[15] It was only after they were told by one his representatives – that in refusing to accept Zwelithini's authority they were impugning the honour of the royal house that the workers finally agreed to cede responsibility for the negotiations to the paramount chief.

A farcical sequence of events then followed, as Zwelithini was taken to task by Chief Mangosuthu Buthelezi, the KwaZulu Authority's prime minister. He insisted that the paramount chief had no authority to embark on negotiations; he also suggested that such an endeavour might negatively impact on the prestige of the paramount chief.[16] Zwelithini then chose to withdraw from the negotiations, leaving the workers to finally choose to appoint their own representatives – ordinary workers, although they were in fact at first misidentified by the local press as being themselves members of the Zulu royal house.[17]

Meanwhile, strikes began to spread across Durban. On 10 January – the day that Zwelithini spoke at Coronation Brick – a group of workers at A. J. Keeler, a transport firm based on Durban's Point Road, downed their tools.[18] Over the next week, several hundred workers at six different companies – primarily in the transport and marine sectors – initiated their own strikes and pickets.[19] By Thursday, 18 January the workers at Coronation Brick had resolved their strike and returned to their workplace. In the last week of January the textile industry in Durban became the focus of the strikes. On Thursday, 25 January hundreds of workers at the Frametex factory – located in the New Germany industrial area in the southern reaches of Durban – downed their tools; on Friday this strike spread to the other four textile mills owned by the Frame Group in New Germany. At first 1,000 workers were said to be taking part in the strike; then, as the strike stretched on over the weekend and into the first days of the following week, the number of participating workers rose to between 6,000 and 7,000.[20] These strikes continued to grow and spread.

Thus, by the end of the month dozens of companies had experienced strikes and the police expected a transport boycott on 1 February. This boycott never occurred; nonetheless, in the following weeks the action spread. On 6 February over 6,000 municipal workers went on strike; the city's vital services were halted and newspaper images showed white volunteers distributing food and clearing refuse from the streets.[21] Over 7,000 workers on the city's industrial periphery also embarked on a mass strike over these same days.

● ● ●

Despite the scale of these strikes, however – and despite the expectations of observers at the time – they were notably non-violent. Although previous governments had never hesitated to suppress labour strikes with brutal force, in 1973 the apartheid government did not do so. The National Party had not dealt with sustained and significant labour protests for many years and appeared uncertain in its response. Two aspects of the state's approach are addressed in this chapter: firstly, uncertainty as to the political identities and motives of the striking workers, and, secondly, uncertainty as to how to manage and control the strikes.

In regard to the first issue, while the national minister for labour hinted darkly that 'agitators' were manipulating the workers into protests, the local business community and media rubbished these claims. Instead, they emphasised the economic causes of the strikes and the essentialised ethnic Zulu identities of the striking workers. I suggest that both sets of claims worked to depoliticise interpretations of the protesting strikers:

if the minister was right, then the workers were naïve and manipulated – and if he was wrong, and the local elite right, then the workers were simply concerned with bread-and-butter issues. They were only able to organise themselves through the shared habits of their ethnic identity.

In addition, I suggest – with regard to the second point – that one of the reasons for the relative absence of violence (and the often-noted 'restraint' of the police) in this strike was the acceptance by the state of this economic interpretation. The minister of labour's attempts to identify politicised agitators were dismissed; the prime minister instead accepted that economic need explained the workers' actions. He therefore displaced responsibility for controlling the striking workers from the state and onto their employers.

Political identities and agency

Political discourse blaming agitators was ubiquitous at the time. On 10 January – the second day of the strike wave, before the eventual scale of the strikes was even suspected – the managing director of A. J. Keeler told the press that agitators had caused the strike: 'it was always the same, the ringleaders had intimidated the others into taking the action they had.'[22] Selwyn Lurie, financial director of the Frame Group, presented a similar argument at the end of the month. Not only did he announce to the press that 'a small group of agitators' had started the strike at Natal Canvas Rubber Manufacturers, but that they had 'threatened to kill' worker representatives on the negotiating council. The company then invited the police into its premises to break up the strike, with the result that 'the police saw that the workers left the factory in an orderly manner.'[23] Notably, these 'agitators' and 'ringleaders' came from within the workforces themselves: they supposedly aimed at causing trouble for their employers and fellow workers rather than representing economic hardship.

Three weeks after the first strike at the Coronation Brick and Tile works the national minister for labour, Marais Viljoen, released a statement in which he too suggested that the strikes in Durban were neither spontaneous nor innocent. Viljoen attributed them to scheming political activists from outside the workforce who were following a broader, vastly more threatening, agenda: 'the strikes in Natal follow a pattern from which it is clear that it is not merely a question of higher wages.' This was evidenced, he said, by the fact that while 'there were cases where existing works committee in factories hit by strikes regarded the workers' wage demands as unreasonable and urged them to return to work', in these cases 'this advice was ignored by workers'. To Viljoen, the 'unwillingness of the workers concerned to negotiate shows undoubtedly that the agitation for trade unions is not the solution, and is merely a smoke screen behind which other motives are hidden', notably 'to bring about disorderliness prejudicial to the order of the state'.[24] Looking forward, he suggested also that 'the agitators behind the strikes must ask themselves what the position of the workers will be once they lose their jobs and find themselves without any income'.[25] Viljoen did not need to flesh out the identity of these figures; vague allegations about agitators were a part of the period's political vocabulary. Durban's mayor also believed in agitators, but admitted that 'obviously nobody can prove this'.[26]

In some hands ideas about agitators were linked to prejudiced stereotypes of black workers. P. R. de Jager, a member of parliament, claimed of the striking workers:

> I know them and I am convinced, as regards the labour done by the Bantu in Natal and the level at which they move, they that do not have it in them to come together and agree that a thousand of them should strike. There are other influences in this strike.[27]

This crude statement renders clear the unspoken sub-text to the assertions of agitators: how else were the strikes to be explained? The agitator hypothesis solved these problems without requiring its exponents to reconsider their assumptions about the capabilities of the workers.

It is thus particularly interesting that many Durban employers and other commentators took a different view. A spokesperson for the United Party told the press that 'once before the Government thought grievances among the black workers were artificially created by agitators. The Government did not act in time and the result was the disaster of Sharpeville'.[28] Viljoen was incensed, claiming that this statement was 'the height of irresponsibility' and also, perhaps more seriously, 'un-South African'.[29] The reference to Sharpeville – less, perhaps, a direct reference to the sequence of events than a rhetorical shorthand for the government's past embarrassment – stung the minister into a more specific response. Viljoen defended his characterisation of the strikes by naming the organisations and bodies that he believed were sponsoring the unrest. These included NUSAS, the BWP and the 'pro-Leftist Trade Union Council of South Africa'.[30] He made a definite link between the student protests and the strikes, and suggested that these students 'see Black unrest as the only remaining way to bring the Government to a fall'.[31] The security police did raid SASO's Durban offices at the end of January – but allegedly no warrants were issued for this raid, and certainly no arrests resulted from it.[32] Beyond this, little effort seems to have been made by either the police or the local political authorities to discover the identity of these supposed agitators.

In fact, one of the clearest refutations of the agitator hypothesis came from Brigadier H. J. Schroeder, the divisional commander of the Port Natal police, who told the *Sunday Times* that 'there was still no definite proof that agitators were behind the stoppages'. He added that 'had there been we would have taken action'.[33] While members of the police may have believed that agitators were lurking in the shadows of the strikes, the inability of the force to obtain any evidence that might identify these figures meant that – to all intents and purposes – the police remained distanced from the minister of labour's statements.[34] Without any potential evidence, it was impossible for the police to address his allegations.

Durban's white newspaper editors, meanwhile, were deeply sceptical of the minister's claims, the *Daily News* being particularly so. An early February editorial dismissed the minister's 'tired old clichés about agitators and hidden forces' as the 'obligatory political noises' that he was expected to make.[35] Later in the month – after Viljoen had accused NUSAS, TUCSA and the BWP of agitating the workers – a further editorial referred to the minister's 'white-tinted spectacles' and hoped that if the minister ever acknowledged the humanity of the workers involved, he would be 'less disposed to regard an eight-rand a week striker as a political agitator'.[36] This tendency to dismiss the minister's claims ran through both local newspapers' reporting. They emphasised three aspects of the strikes instead: the economic hardships suffered by the workers, the apparent absence of political rhetoric and the apparent ethnic homogeneity of the striking workers themselves.

The newspapers frequently presented the strikes as a natural – and pre-political – response to significant increases in material hardship suffered by these workers. In an article on 12 January, the *Daily News* noted that 'to exist on R40 a month undoubtedly accelerates frustration. These workers get R8,97 a week. For those who support a family on this wage it means they are doing so with R43 a month less than the poverty datum line'. These figures were then contrasted with the profits made by Coronation Brick at the time: in 1969 – 'admittedly a boom year' – the company made a profit of R2,196,000. Since then, the company had merged with 'the giant Tongaat Group, which had a turnover of R14.5 million'.[37] This juxtaposition clearly showed sympathy for the workers, as did an editorial that called wages 'a pittance for existence'. The minimum wage for brick workers bore a 'relationship to increases in the cost of living' that was described as 'remote, to say the least'.[38]

In addition to emphasising the possible economic causes of the strikes, the local press also seized on any indication that the workers were acting independently of a political programme. On the first day of the strike at Coronation Brick, for example, it was reported that – according to the striking workers – one of the immediate causes of the strike had been a pamphlet issued by the company's management. This apparently stated that the company was aware that some workers were considering a strike and that any such action could only be undertaken at the instigation of 'communist agitators'. This touched a chord among the workers: a 'workers' spokesman' was quoted as saying: 'We would not have gone on strike if this notice had not called us communists.'[39] The workers were regularly quoted as calling for higher wages, but never for any political cause. Even the Zulu paramount chief was treated with relative disrespect when he addressed the striking workers at Coronation Brick. The workers were portrayed as being without external organisation or order – and as being reluctant to submit their demands to any legal or illegal political authority for ratification.

The presence of the Zulu paramount chief at Coronation Brick played a role in cementing the local media image of the striking workers as ethnically and linguistically homogeneous. The workers were referred to in formulaic terms as 'African workers' during the day before the paramount chief's arrival; after this, however, they were more regularly described in specifically Zulu terms – as forming an 'impi' and chanting in Zulu, 'Hobe Usuthu' (Zulu warrior) and 'Asiyi' (We are not going). This terminology was strengthened by the attempts of the Zulu royal house to mediate in this early strike.[40] The default assumption in the local press throughout was that the striking workers at any given firm were African and, more particularly, Zulu. A speaker at a meeting of a local employers' association claimed that in India and in other parts of Africa, such organisation was unheard of: as far as he was concerned, the strikes 'just could not have happened, except with the Zulu'.[41]

The demographic make-up of Durban's workforce at the time suggests that although African workers were in the majority and although workers identifying with the Zulu culture constituted the majority of those workers, there nonetheless remained very large groups of workers not included in this category. These included workers of other African backgrounds – notably from Pondoland – and, most significantly, Indian workers.[42]

The assumption of ethnic homogeneity helped the local press to convince themselves that there was no direct political motivation behind the strikes nor a potential threat of violence against the white population and company managers. A precedent for this diversion can be found in the speech given by the Zulu paramount chief on the second day of the strike at Coronation Brick. Among other statements, he told the gathered workers that he understood that 'they were not treated like human beings, yet another race is given respect'. Nonetheless, he told the group, he 'would not like to see a repetition of the racial incidents of 1949'.[43] These statements referred to workplace tensions between African labourers and Indian overseers at Coronation Brick; the monarch's statements, however, went beyond the workplace by suggesting that these tensions might result in anti-Indian violence similar to that in 1949.[44] The press took up these tensions and generalised them across the various strikes, referring to anti-Indian tensions not only at Coronation Brick, but also in the textile industry and during the municipal workers' strike. In each of these, the racial make-up of the workplaces differed from that at Coronation Brick, and other sources indicate that Indian and African labourers were protesting side by side – most notably, during the municipal workers' strike. In at least one case, the potential conflict between a white employer and a group of African workers was explicitly diverted into an account of the terror felt by Indian workers in that workplace.[45]

In sum, the striking workers were portrayed as traditionalist. They bowed to traditional leadership, displayed traditional modes of military organisation and were in danger of allowing traditional antipathies to inflame their valid workplace grievances. Their protests were thus conceived as being essentially pre-political, motivated by material hardship and economic necessity and not by any intention to engage with a broader political agenda. This portrayal also allowed the press to respond critically to the agitator hypothesis. Why were the workers striking? Because of economic hardship. How were the workers organising themselves? By following age-old cultural patterns of military association.

This approach was not confined to the press. The Durban Chamber of Commerce subscribed to a similar understanding of the strikes, outlined in a confidential memorandum circulated to its members on 9 February.[46] The strike wave was growing at this point, as the municipal workers' strike brought workers out onto the city streets for the first time. This memo was thus intended in part as a reflection on the first series of strikes, at the same time as preparing its readers for the possibility of further action. The second part of the memo addressed this concern with a list suggesting ways of preventing further strikes.

Three prime causes were listed: firstly, the low wages that the workers had been receiving – 'in many cases without review or appreciable revision for a number of years'; secondly, a substantial rise of as much as 11 per cent in the cost of living in the past year; and, thirdly, 'the recent 16% increase in rail fares'. The memo argued that an average 'Bantu family of 5' would need 'in terms of absolute minimum categories of expenditure' an income of R85.15 per month. Assuming that the main (male) earner contributed two-thirds of the family's income, then his weekly wage would have to be at least R14.74.[47] The average striking worker at Coronation Brick was earning R8.97 a week before the strike; after the successful negotiations, this was raised to R11.50 a week – a figure closer to but still below the national poverty datum line.[48]

The Chamber of Commerce hesitated to expand its explanation for the strikes in Durban far beyond the obvious economic rationale for local labour discontent.[49] The memo was reluctant to support the minister of labour's statement widely publicised in the press a week earlier. In the place of the agitator hypothesis, the memo offered tentative indications of an alternate explanation. It emphasised that 'the local Bantu labour force is drawn predominantly from the Zulu and is, in this way, more ethnically homogeneous than the labour force on the Reef'. And it suggested that 'the large and better skilled Indian community has also served to limit wage and job opportunities' for African workers.[50] This document does not discuss the organisational strategies of the striking workers. The similarity of these explanations to those offered in the local press is obvious: both assume the ethnic homogeneity of the striking workers and exclude non-Zulu and Indian workers from their analyses.

The workers themselves did not agree with this ethnic explanation for their strikes. Academics and students affiliated with the IIE conducted interviews in Durban in the aftermath of the strikes and recorded the responses of several workers. None of these interviews contains any declaration of ethnic solidarity and – in at least one case – the suggestion that traditional Zulu authorities played any role in inciting or organising the strikes was rejected, as a worker argued that '[t]hese people who say that it was Gatsha Buthelezi or the Paramount Chief who encouraged people to strike are still encouraging more trouble because I do not think two people can decide for so many people to do what they have done'.[51]

This same worker went on to suggest that 'these two men have nothing to do with the strikes but it was our empty stomachs'. This was a common note in these interviews, suggesting an unlikely agreement between workers and the Chamber of Commerce. Another worker expressed his belief that 'African workers have decided to strike because of the working conditions and because of a very low wage'. A third expressed himself in poetic rhetoric, explaining that the strikes had occurred because 'the child that does not cry dies' and, therefore, 'we should cry for ourselves for working hungry'.[52] The economic causes of the strikes were thus eloquently expressed in terms of material deprivation and poor pay.

These workers explicitly rejected the idea that outsiders were behind the strikes. One dismissed the minister's notion that student groups – such as SASO and NUSAS – had incited the strikes, saying: 'It is not true that university students encouraged African people to strike because first of all we do not know them.'[53] Most workers quoted in the press and interviewed by the IIE appear to have rejected any suggestion of explicit political influence or intention. They articulated an interpretation that shared some of the assumptions apparent in the press coverage, notably that the principal cause of the strikes was economic. There seems to have been little need to discuss how they organised themselves – perhaps because, unlike the minister of labour, the white press or their employers, the workers themselves were not surprised by their ability to act rationally and in unison.

On the same day that the Durban Chamber of Commerce released its memo, the prime minister, John Vorster, made a lengthy speech in which he distanced himself from his minister's allegations. He did not mention the word 'agitator' in his speech. Instead, he said:

> in the past there have unfortunately been too many employers who saw only the mote in the Government's eye and failed completely to see the beam in their own. Now I am looking past all party affiliations and past all employers, and experience tells me this, that employers, whoever they may be, should not only see in their workers a unit for producing for them so many hours of service a day; they should also see them as human beings with souls.[54]

Vorster emphasised the autonomy and agency of the employers and distanced his government from both the causes of and possible solutions to the strikes. It was not political agitation that had caused the strikes, but economic hardships; therefore, it was not political solutions that would resolve the strikes, but economic ones. These were now the responsibility of employers. Vorster thus adopted a position that supported that of the Durban Chamber of Commerce and white press and not that of his minister of labour.

It is notable, however, that in neither of these positions were the striking workers themselves conceived of as political agents. For many contemporary commentators it was impossible to imagine African labourers as possessing political consciousness, let alone agency. Even for those who were sceptical about the agitator theory did not suggest that the workers had chosen to strike out of political discontent: rather, they believed workers were driven by economic necessity and hardship. Even the workers themselves denied acting out of political considerations. And thus, for Vorster, the workers themselves could be understood as essentially apolitical – or pre-political – men: 'human beings with souls'.

This idea that the striking workers were not politically aware shaped how both employers and the police in Durban responded to the strikes and the workers. If the workers were politically innocent, then any improvement in their conditions depended on those with consciences. By de-emphasising the political possibilities of the strike wave the government was delegating responsibility for the strikes to employers, who were conceiving of the protests as soluble within the current political context of South Africa.

This had several different implications. For example, the IIE took Vorster's quote for the title of the study it published soon after the end of the strike wave.[55] The quote played an unambiguous role in its argument, marshalling the prime minister in support of its primary contention – that the presence of 'agitators' was not necessary to explain these strikes. It too agreed that material hardship had driven workers to strike, and alleviation of their economic position – and the legalisation of protest and trade unions for African workers – would help prevent further unrest. The study was criticised for focusing too heavily on disproving the presence of agitators and thus sidelining possible explanations of worker organisation and activism.[56] Neither that study nor its critics, however, remarked on this partial consensus of views on the strike. Nor did they consider how this consensus on the non-political natures of the striking workers might have affected the local responses to the strikes. Instead, the IIE wrote its account of the businessmen's responses to the strikes from within a similar conceptual paradigm.

Managing the strikes

When the researchers affiliated to the IIE came to prepare their initial analyses of the Durban strikes, they turned to a central theoretical text: Gouldner's 1955 sociological study, *Wildcat Strike*.[57] This provided an insight into how the management of a strike-struck company in the United States had responded to its workers' non-union strike. In this book, Gouldner describes how – in the case of spontaneous 'wildcat' strikes – managers 'tended to conceive of the strike as a *struggle for control*' between the workers and the company management itself. Understanding the strike in this way encouraged company managers to concentrate on the efficient administration of the progress of the strike – negotiations, offers and counter-offers – rather than on addressing the fundamental causes of the strike. The IIE suggested, then, that this approach described the ways in which various company managers in Durban attempted to control and contain their striking work forces; it is also possible to extend this description beyond the IIE's initial remit and include in it the actions of the South African police and local magistracy as well.

The Durban Chamber of Commerce memo was remarkable because its final pages acknowledged that the ability to resolve the strikes lay in the hands of employers.[58] It presumed that, in the average case, employers not only had the ability to resolve these strikes through increasing inadequate wages, but also had the responsibility to do so. The list of suggested actions that closed the chamber's memorandum all follow from this: after a perfunctory instruction to 'notify' the Department of Labour, all further suggestions presumed the autonomous action of a company manager. This manager was instructed to first attempt to control the strikes by warning the workers that they would not be paid for the time that they were on strike and by advising them that their demands would only be considered 'on the condition that they return to work'. At this point, it was up to the manager himself to decide whether or not his current rates of pay were 'fully justifiable':

5. If you feel an increase in minimum wage is necessary, determine this increase and tell them of your decision. Thereafter stand by your decision.

6. Do not attempt to bargain as this will only encourage the Bantu to escalate his demands. Action must be positive, definite and final.[59]

The manager should not surrender initiative, but could choose to recognise the validity of workers' claims. This approach thus allowed employers to bypass 'the ethical facet of the conflict' and to do 'whatever is necessary in order to "handle" or control the situation'. This approach, Gouldner suggested, was 'peculiarly useful to those who require some escape from a moral crisis' and bolstered a public defence of technical and managerial solutions to the strike.[60] Local business in Durban was determined to take the strikes – and their own responses to the strikes – out of the political realm and into their own control.

In reality, however, employers were often unable to reclaim the initiative from their striking workers. Many managers were unsurprisingly unable to project a firm façade of authority when faced with several thousand striking workers: the city engineer, for example, was forced to retreat when he sought to address striking municipal workers.[61] Likewise, employers and managers were forced into negotiations with their workers in several cases; in many others, they were faced with large crowds of workers chanting demands for R10, R20 or R30 a week. Nonetheless, this scenario provides an insight into how local management sought to control and contain the impact of the strikes on their companies: they saw the strikes as unfortunate but unavoidable events that must be managed and not as calamities that had to be immediately suppressed.

The autonomy of employers and company managers was also emphasised in the Chamber of Commerce's approach to the policing of the strikes. Labour stoppages and strikes by African workers were illegal at the time, and an employer in Durban would thus have been more than justified in calling the police to the scene of a strike. In theory, at least, all the strikers could have been arrested for contravening the law. Police action could be used to break strikes – the dockworkers' strikes in Durban and Cape Town in 1972 provided a recent example of police intervention.[62] Nonetheless, the chamber advised its members to call the police only after the employers had done 'everything possible to avoid violence'.[63]

Employers were reminded that 'stoppages to date have been mainly good natured' and that it was 'tactful police action' that had 'contributed greatly to this'. The relative peacefulness of the strikes, despite large crowds of armed and unhappy workers, was seen as a significant factor supporting the managerial approach to the strikes. (This was in implied contrast, perhaps, to the dockworkers' strikes of some months before.) The employers and company managers in charge of negotiations – and in charge of deciding whether to call in the police or not – were sternly advised by the Chamber of Commerce to acknowledge this relative peacefulness and to '[m]ake every effort to keep it this way'.[64]

The reluctance of employers to see the striking workers as political agents also contributed to their general reluctance to see the strikes as needing forcible suppression. Very few employers did in fact call the police onto their properties – the notable exception here being the Frame Group's textile mills.[65] No charges appear to have been laid against workers as a result of their striking. Neither do charges appear to have resulted from the workers' own – sometimes threatening – behaviour while within their actual workplaces.

Indeed, this suggests that a particular pattern can be discerned in the policing of these workplace-based strikes. The police would gather in force outside the site of a strike; but they would remain on the periphery of the site, only rarely entering into the spaces occupied by the workers, and even then, only on the explicit invitation of employers. They would not interfere with the progress of the strike and would allow the workers to enter and to leave the site of their strikes individually and disperse without interference. The workers would, however, be discouraged from leaving their workplaces en masse.

In the IIE's brief analysis of the policing of the strikes, it noted that 'apparently acting on higher authority, the police acted with restraint in the situation'. Thus, although noting that 'from the worker's perspective' the very presence of 'armed police, often with dogs, could only have been seen as a form of intimidation', this analysis emphasised again the absence of violence in the actual conduct of the police.[66] This characterisation of police action as 'restrained' found echoes in newspaper reports and editorials: in the *Daily News*, for example, the police were described as 'exemplary' due to the 'presence, the diplomacy and the quiet efficiency' that they had displayed 'in their true role as the protector of the innocent'. Even this praise, however, was tempered with the recognition on the part of the writers that, in the past, criticism of the police's brutality, 'sometimes justifiably', was common. Nonetheless, they noted, at present the police had not yet 'lost their cool'.[67]

A consideration of the tension between the apparent 'restraint' and 'diplomacy' of the police and the recognition of their potential for brutal violence may provide an interpretation of the police's actual actions that was neither made at the time nor appeared in the literature that followed. The display of police force seems to have been central to the practice of policing these strikes and closely connected to the police's apparent reluctance to engage the strikers directly. At one level, this connection is simple: the display of potential force may act as a powerful preventative. The presence of 'truck-loads' of policemen accompanied by dogs and armed with batons, automatic rifles and tear gas would certainly have caused workers to reconsider the wisdom of acting violently. Even the workers at the Frame Group's mills in the most violent of the early strikes did no more than jeer at the nearby policemen.[68]

But at another level, the spatial relations between the striking workers and watching policemen assume prominence: rather than focus, as observers at the time did, on the police force's positioning of its men away from the workers, it is useful to focus instead on the resultant positioning of the striking workers themselves. Workers were gathered in clearly demarcated spaces – a football stadium in one case, and the factories and compounds in which they lived and worked in most other cases. These spaces were demarcated both by their ordinary boundaries of fences, walls and gates and also by the cordons of patrolling policemen. The strikes were thus contained within the physically delimited spaces of factory grounds and compounds. While the participating workers went unmolested within these spaces, they were not permitted to breach their boundaries. The police stood by at the entrances and exits, allowing marching workers to enter, but ensuring that they remained within these spaces. Workers were only permitted to leave these grounds in small groups or individually when finally dispersing homeward at the end of the day.

Early in February, before the municipal workers went on strike, a spokesperson told the press that the police would only act if the striking workers committed one of the following four offences: 'striking; holding a public meeting without a permit; carrying dangerous weapons; and creating a disturbance'.[69] Of these four, the first and the third were clearly the most significant; nonetheless, when the group of over 100 striking workers were arrested on Umgeni Road after a police baton charge, they were not charged with these offences, despite being in contravention of both. Instead, they were charged with and convicted of 'causing a public disturbance' – a charge that carried a sentence of either 30 days imprisonment or a fine of R30. The presiding magistrate, however, suspended either 25 of the 30 days, or R25 of the R30, for those convicted on the condition that they did not commit another offence involving violence 'to persons or property' in the following 12 months.[70] Judicial restraint was analogous to police action. It is not so much the conviction but the lenience of sentence that is extraordinary. The workers were not prosecuted for the serious offences of striking or carrying dangerous weapons, despite the availability of such charges: instead, they were given light (largely suspended) sentences and instructed not to strike again.

Whether explicitly agreed or not, the actions of the police and judiciary operated within a shared field to ensure the preservation of local public order. By containing the striking workers within the physical spaces of their factories in the majority of the strikes, the police not only acted to ensure that the strikes could be controlled and resolved, but also to ensure that the communities outside of these factories would be insulated from disruption and potential violence. When in the case of the rumoured transport boycott the police protected the train stations against expected protesters, they acted also to insulate the central city and its working areas from potential disorder. When in the course of the municipal workers' strike the police disarmed and shepherded workers through the town, they were acting both to minimise the actual violence caused by those striking workers and to reduce their potential for violence. Police practice therefore emphasised control and constraint, containment rather than engagement and disarmament rather than confrontation. It was neither philanthropic nor accidental, but in a context of some uncertainty of interpretation and strategy by the state, which was confronting a mass withdrawal of labour for the first time in many years, it was designed to maintain public order.

It is important to note, however, that this pattern of police restraint and disengagement was occasionally broken in the course of the strikes. In the case of the municipal workers' strike, for example, the spatial containment that marked the earlier attempts to police the strikes broke down. Unlike the workers in the earlier strikes, the municipal workers were not used to spending their days within a demarcated workspace: the first groups of striking workers were street cleaners, refuse collectors and other labourers employed by the City Engineer's Department.[71] Their workplaces were not factory floors, but the city's streets. When they marched in protest, they did not congregate in one central space and the police could not contain them. This spatial freedom was sometimes connected to an increased public awareness of their violent potential. On 6 February, the first day of their strike, a large group of workers congregated outside the offices of the City Engineer's Department and demanded that the African clerks still working inside the building leave their desks. If they did not, the striking workers were alleged to have threatened that they would burn down the building.[72] The same day, a group of African refuse workers were reported to have been 'chased several blocks by the strikers who brandished knobkerries'.[73] And on the following day, another group of striking workers invaded a local golf course, crossed its greens, and confronted its white secretary and his staff.[74]

These encounters took place in notably public settings: in the city streets and outside the municipality's offices among others. The police concentrated on disarming the strikers and then on ensuring that they caused the minimum possible disruption while progressing through the city itself. Rather than try to break strikes, they set out to shepherd strikers. Most workers complied with police demands: they neither protested against nor resisted the instruction to break into smaller groups, nor did they resist the police as they were disarmed. Some of this compliance may have been associated with the police's superior force. Not only were the police fully armed with riot control gear, including rifles and tear gas, but two army helicopters were also patrolling the skies above Durban.[75] When one group of strikers moving down Alice Street refused to follow these instructions, they were assaulted by the police, arrested and charged with disturbing the public peace.[76] But clearly the majority of strikers were content to restrict their engagement to orderly marches.

Conclusion

The decision to treat these strikes, despite their illegality and scale, as essentially ordinary labour disputes that could be resolved through standard managerial techniques emphasised the agency and ability of individual employers and their managers. It also emphasised their autonomy. In one of the rare cases in which a representative from the provincial Department of Labour was called in to assist in resolving a strike, he was humiliated by the gathered workers. The eventual resolution of the strike at Coronation Brick was then effected without the department's aid. This example would have given little encouragement to the idea that provincial or national structures set up to resolve and contain such labour disputes would be effective. Employers preferred, instead, to trust in their own ability to manage the strikes and to communicate with the workers, contain their protests and resolve their grievances.

One consequence of this approach was that in the rush to resolve strikes before they became entrenched, most of the strikes resulted in an increase in wages. Out of approximately 160 strikes and work stoppages, 70 lasted for a day or less. A further 24 went on into a second day before being resolved, meaning that the majority of the strikes in Durban were resolved in under two days. The remaining 70 strikes lasted for more than two days, but less than seven days; no individual strike lasted for more than a week. Of these 160 short-lived strikes and stoppages, 118, or over 70 per cent, resulted in a wage increase for the workers involved. These increases were not overly generous (and fell far short of the sums being called for by the workers), but nonetheless represented a significant addition to the average worker's weekly wage. The majority of these increases ranged between R1 and R2 per week – which represented an increase of between 10 and 20 per cent on the average weekly wage at Coronation Brick and Tile, for example.[77]

Employers were thus largely convinced that economic grievances lay at the root of the strike and acceded in part to workers' demands. The apparent economic strength of the country at the time – as well as the increasing need for semi-skilled black labour – may have also made these small wage increases seem commercially justifiable. Vorster's utilitarian approach to the strikes was thus confirmed and the state did not seek to suppress the strikes.

The Durban strikes and these responses to them helped set the framework for labour relations in subsequent years. Some opposition commentators saw in the strikes the rebirth of mass opposition to the apartheid regime. Although I cannot analyse labour activism here, it is clear that many of those engaged in the resurgence of trade unionism had broader political aims, and many would come to experience personal retribution from the state. But the pattern of the labour disputes in 1973 enabled them to be seen – at least at first – as largely non-political. The workers themselves were largely seen to be lacking political identity and agency. This view facilitated, as Friedman and Lodge demonstrate,[78] a relatively flexible approach that culminated in the Wiehahn Commission of 1979 and the rebirth of legal labour organisation and unionisation among black workers in South Africa.

The government thus inadvertently created an ambiguously non-political space within which further activism could take place. The immediate result of the Durban strikes was the increasing scale and recognition of black labour mobilisation. This helped to open up a space not only for economic protests, but also for the organisation of unions and, post-Soweto, associated civic movements. Tracy Carson's chapter – immediately following this one – illustrates the scale of such mobilisation in Cape Town in the late 1970s. The Durban strikes were by no means the only example of popular protest in the early 1970s, but as the largest strike wave in the course of the decade, they helped shape the contours of an emerging political map, detailing the relations between sometimes-protesting workers, employers and the state.

3 'There's more to it than slurp and burp': The Fatti's & Moni's strike and the use of boycotts in mass resistance in Cape Town

Tracy Carson

Introduction

Mass resistance in the Western Cape gained momentum in 1979 after workers at the Fatti's & Moni's pasta and bread factory in Cape Town stopped work and organised a boycott of the company's products. Yet this was not the first boycott initiated by a trade union during this period. Five months earlier, the National Union of Motor Assembly and Rubber Workers of South Africa launched a consumer boycott against Eveready South Africa, a battery-manufacturing company, after its management dismissed 230 coloured female workers for striking at its Port Elizabeth factory. While the Eveready boycott garnered an extensive international following, it failed to force the company to settle the dispute – neither receiving the widespread national publicity nor generating the momentum that followed the Fatti's & Moni's campaign.

The Fatti's & Moni's protest marked a watershed in the history of South African labour protests, highlighted the strategic viability of boycotting as a tool to challenge state dominance and created the impetus for anti-apartheid organisational development in South Africa during the early 1980s. At the time, Ian Morgan, an investigative journalist, argued that 'not since the Potato Boycott of the Fifties had war been waged against a company's products and its image for so long and so successfully'.[1] While Morgan is inaccurate in his analysis of the boycott's relative length – the Eveready boycott, for example, lasted more than eight months – he is precise in his assessment of the boycott's achievement. The Fatti's & Moni's protest formed part of a larger debate concerning the desirability of trade unions linking shop-floor protests to other community struggles. In the early years of their growth, from around 1972, the new independent black unions had limited legal recognition and were subject to state repression and employer hostility. They often decided to build shop-floor organisation before considering broader political struggles. Political activity was seen by some unionists to endanger still-fragile organisations and to expose leaders to retribution by the state. The Fatti's & Moni's strike, however, led by the Food and Canning Workers Union (FCWU), used the consumer boycott as a vehicle to forge crucial alliances between trade unions and burgeoning community groups. This helped to ignite a robust debate within the labour movement over its role in the broader liberation struggle.

The Fatti's & Moni's campaign coincided with broader initiatives within opposition forces. The strike overlapped with the release of the Wiehahn report, which called for the official recognition of black trade unions. This report formed the basis for the Industrial Conciliation Amendment Acts of 1979 and 1981, which enabled registered black trade unions to engage in limited collective bargaining with employers and to strike. The Federation of South African Trade Unions was established in the same year to develop a national union strategy, expand factory organisation and promote working-class consciousness. Although the FCWU did not join the federation, the Fatti's & Moni's boycott in tandem with these other processes helped to create a national and increasingly confident union organisation. Immediately following the dispute's settlement, other unions adopted the boycott strategy. This is most prominently observed in the Cape strikes and boycotts of red meat (1980) and sweets (1981).

Background to the dispute

The FCWU was a former South African Congress of Trade Unions stronghold that was decimated during the state's crackdown on labour organisations in the early 1960s. As unions found a new impetus, it sought to re-establish itself around the country. In 1976 the union was under the leadership of Jan Theron, a radical white law graduate from the University of Cape Town (UCT), who was the son of a judge. According to Peter Moni, Theron was 'young, dedicated, and paid a pittance'.[2] Morgan claimed that Theron was 'fast developing a reputation as a force to be reckoned with, and one quick to seize any opportunity to press home wage claims'.[3]

In Cape Town Theron received support from Athalie Crawford, his girlfriend at the time, who had become politically radicalised during her time as a student at UCT. Crawford was working as a teacher at a coloured school, Grassy Park High School, when she was asked to help to reorganise the Cape Town branch of the union in 1978, together with Virginia Engel, another former teacher. Engel joined the Cape Town branch as a volunteer, after being kicked out of the teaching profession in 1974 for publicly criticising the apartheid government.[4] She was involved in Black

Consciousness student politics at the University of the Western Cape (UWC). Norma Gabriel, who had links with the Unity Movement, helped with administration.

Theron also solicited support from two FCWU veterans: Liz Abrahams and Oscar Mpetha. Abrahams helped the younger organisers in an advisory role. Mpetha, who had been imprisoned on Robben Island, was almost 70 years old; a Xhosa speaker from the Eastern Cape, he was integral in helping the union organise African workers. These unionists sought to reorganise Western Cape factories that were once union strongholds and eventually to spread this infrastructure throughout the region. In August 1978 they approached workers in Fatti's & Moni's, Bellville; the factory had been organised by the FCWU in the 1950s.[5]

Fatti's & Moni's was established by two Italian immigrant families, initially involved in the South African liquor trade. In 1927 they sold the liquor company and embarked on pasta production. In 1930 they established their principle subsidiary, United Macaroni Group, which managed wheat mills, and produced a number of products, most notably pasta and bread.[6] Fatti's & Moni's was a small pasta and milling company with a turnover of R24 million by 1978, compared to milling industry giants Premier Milling and Tiger Oats, with more than R1,000 million in turnover.[7]

By the time of the strike, the group was in its third generation of family management and possessed a board 'consisting entirely of sons and grandsons of the founders'.[8] John Moni was the company's biggest single shareholder. According to his son, Peter, who served as the company's managing director, John '*was* the business', as he oversaw all of the company's decisions.[9] John also received support from his other sons: Adrian, who controlled human relations, and John Jr, the operations director. The Fatti's & Moni's headquarters were in the Transvaal, although the company was also well established in the Western Cape. The family owned a number of bakeries and a large plant in southern Bellville, which is where the dispute occurred.

Fatti's & Moni's was divided into three primary sections – the flour milling section, the manufactured flour (pasta) section, and the ice cream cone and wafer section. The plant employed 247 black workers (114 African and 133 coloured) and 49 whites. This was a not a particularly large food processing factory; the Australian-owned H. Jones & Co. had more than 4,000 workers in its canning section alone. Because the Bellville plant produced products across industries, some of the workers were allowed to affiliate with various unions, which could represent them, while others were not. The Biscuit Industry Union, connected with the Trade Union Council of South Africa, organised the ice cream cone and wafer section of the factory, and the FCWU's registered union supported workers in the manufactured flour and macaroni section of the factory.

Immediately before the strike, the FCWU attempted to organise workers in the milling section of the factory.[10]

Workers in the milling section included both coloured women, who were responsible for filling bags with flour and closing them, and African men, who carried the bags to storage areas for long hours.[11] A small number of younger coloured men, largely from Elsie's River and commonly referred to as 'the boys', performed non-strenuous physical labour and had a high turnover rate.[12] Management believed that women were 'delicate enough to not break the bags'. The company was also subject to the Coloured Labour Preference Policy, which prohibited employers from hiring African workers in the Western Cape unless coloured labour was unavailable.[13] African men were, however, racially stereotyped by the company as suitable for arduous labour. Peter Moni remembered:

> we had a really large Xhosa, black, element working there and I remember under the old system, you had to, in the Western Cape, offer the jobs first to the Cape coloured, and if they weren't prepared to do the job, they [the state] would allow you to bring in contract labour. Now, the kind of work that the Xhosas were brought in for were to carry bags of flour, and to move stock. It was all done physically, and they were good at that.[14]

The factory's Xhosa employees were predominantly migrant workers with one-year contracts. After one year, the workers were obliged to return to their homes until they received new or renewed contracts. One such worker, Friday Mabikwe, joined Fatti's & Moni's in 1963 as a dayshift dispatcher after one of the company's foremen, Mr Mosca, travelled to King William's Town to select 30 men to work for the company. According to Mabikwe, all men seeking employment with the company were required to 'put a bag of flour on a shoulder to show that they could walk a long distance'.[15] Once in Cape Town, the men lived four workers per room in a hostel provided by Fatti's & Moni's on the outskirts of Nyanga township – but if found in Cape Town after their contracts expired, Mabikwe maintains they would be 'chased out by police dogs'.[16]

African workers comprised a majority in the milling section. However, they were legally barred from joining the FCWU, which could only represent the factory's coloured workers. Theron insists that coloured workers 'could do nothing on their own' because 'the industry was dependent on migrant labourers, so to organise the workforce one had to organise the African labourers'.[17] However, if migrant workers were to join the union, and especially if they took strike action, they risked violating their contracts with the Department of Labour and could be expelled from the city.

The company actively cultivated divisions within the factory by separating workers along racial lines. Devan Pillay notes in his examination of the union that the workers had 'different lunch hours, cloakrooms and wage rates'.[18] Because contract labourers performed more physically strenuous tasks, the African workers earned an average rate of R32 per week, while coloured workers received on average between R19 and R25. Language differences presented an exceptionally daunting problem for organisers – most coloured workers were Afrikaans speakers, whereas African workers spoke Xhosa. The company exploited these geographic, gender and racial divisions among workers and this undermined effective organisation in the factory.

Despite these divisions, African workers joined the FCWU when Mpetha helped win compensation for a worker who was denied damages after he became paralysed from breaking his neck in the factory. Mabikwe was among the first to join and recruited a number of people into the union.[19] According to Crawford, 'Friday [Mabikwe] was the workers' undisputed leader and they took his joining as a sign of safety'.[20] Mabikwe was 44 years old at the time, older than many of the African workers, a preacher in King William's Town, well established and well respected within the factory. He received strong support from Julius Kota, Galisile Ditala and Council Sinuka, who were also from the Eastern Cape.[21] They joined those coloured workers in the milling section who were already registered members of the FCWU.

The Fatti's & Moni's strike

Early in 1979, 42 African and coloured workers from the milling and flour-manufacturing sections of the factory signed a petition indicating their desire to be represented by the FCWU.[22] Although the African workers were not legally recognised as members of the FCWU, they used this petition to give power of attorney to the union, which they hoped would enable it to legally act on their behalf.[23] The FCWU approached Fatti's & Moni's for a R40 per week minimum wage, an eight-hour work day, tea and lunch breaks, and annual leave of three weeks.[24] The company, however, insisted the African workers negotiate via a liaison committee.[25] According to Peter Moni, 'we [Fatti's & Moni's] were not supposed to recognise [unregistered] unions; they were not supposed to be unions according to the then situation'.[26]

Nevertheless, workers in the milling section unequivocally refused to negotiate via a liaison committee. In view of the impasse, on 12 April the FCWU applied to the Department of Labour for a conciliation board to force Fatti's & Moni's to meet with union leaders about the workers' grievances. However, this was difficult for all workers at Fatti's & Moni's, because only coloured people were allowed to obtain official representation.[27] The company argued that the union did not represent a majority of the company's 272 employees in the milling and pasta-manufacturing sections of the factory.[28] On 19 April Tony Terblanche, manager of Fatti's & Moni's, requested a meeting with the coloured workers involved in the petition. The content of this meeting became the focus of a debate between the union and the company. Theron contends that Terblanche summoned the workers and advised them that there would be 'moeilike tye' (difficult times) for them if they refused to be represented by the liaison committee.[29] Four days later Terblanche dismissed five coloured workers without an explanation and paid them a week's wages. Terblanche maintained that the company had been introducing mechanisation and reorganising so that it was overstaffed.[30]

Theron insisted that workers throughout the factory would have been aware of any restructuring.[31] Rather, he believed the workers were dismissed because they participated in drawing up the petition seeking higher wages and that the company fired the coloured workers because they 'wanted African workers to get the message'.[32] The following day, ten coloured workers refused to work until they knew the reason for the dismissals. They also demanded that the dismissed workers be reinstated. After the ten workers refused the management's request for them to return to work, Terblanche called in the Department of Labour, as the action of the workers constituted a strike; five then returned to work, but the others walked out.[33] According to the union, the officials from the Labour Department used intimidation to force the strikers to return to work. On 25 April 78 more African and coloured workers struck in solidarity with the five workers who were initially fired and the five additional workers who refused to work. Officials from the Labour Department were called in again by management and insisted on speaking exclusively to the striking coloured workers.[34] The department official told the Africans to stand on one side of the factory and coloureds on the other side. The workers, however, refused to do this, despite threats of fines and prison. One worker shouted at the Labour Department official: 'We are all there for the same purpose.'[35] Both African and coloured strikers stood firm in refusing to work without an explanation as to why their colleagues were dismissed.

The strikers' solidarity was complemented by efficient and effective organisation. Instead of reporting to work, the workers gathered every day in the Lyric Theatre in Bellville South, near the factory. They established a strike committee, formed on the basis of an existing shop stewards' committee that was organised by the FCWU. The strike committee worked with union organisers to coordinate meetings and make all decisions regarding the strike. The meetings were essential to sustaining morale. Many of the workers – both African and coloured – were expected to send money home to their families, and the strike placed them in a desperate position where they could not receive a regular income.[36] During the meetings the workers were offered daily meals and general encouragement. For example, Mabikwe led prayers and provided the workers with spiritual guidance; while Crawford, a trained vocalist, led other workers in freedom songs such as 'Senzeni na'; and others enthusiastically toyi-toy-ed (danced) and chanted;[37] see figures 3.1 and 3.2).

Daily meetings forced the workers and unionists to rapidly bridge some of their cultural divides. Crawford remembers:

> The strike happened and it really speeded things up. There was a group of young coloured guys from Elsie's River who could speak a bit of Xhosa, and if they didn't turn up to the strike meeting, which was often because they were quite young and the least reliable, then we were in a bit of difficulty because the coloured workers spoke Afrikaans and the black workers spoke Xhosa. We only had a few translators, so if Oscar Mpetha wasn't there, then I or Jan would have to try to translate. Eventually, we all had to learn really fast.[38]

Crawford, who was already part of a Xhosa study group with Theron, and David Lewis and Judy Favish of the Cape Town-based Western Province General Workers' Union became proficient in Xhosa following the strike.[39] Similarly, Mabikwe recalls that the meetings helped him to improve his English.[40] Beyond language training, the meetings became a vehicle for the workers and organisers to discuss political issues, conduct literacy classes, and coordinate community projects.[41]

Nonetheless, Devan Pillay contends that by June the strikers seemed to be in an 'unwinnable position'.[42] The FCWU was unable to negotiate the workers' reinstatement before new workers were hired. Only one-third of the work force participated in the strike and Fatti's & Moni's insisted that they had been replaced on 25 April.[43] Terblanche maintained that 'the 88 workers had dismissed themselves by their own action' and 'the strike ended on 25 April after the mill had been out of operation for 24 hours'.[44]

The organisers' worries were further complicated on 26 June when Fatti's & Moni's offered to place 23 of the striking coloured workers in its Good Hope Bakery factory. The strikers unanimously refused. After receiving the company's offer, Theron announced to the Cape Argus, 'not one coloured worker is prepared to take a job while the African workers who stood by them are without work'.[45] This persistence did

Figure 3.1: Fatti's & Moni's employees singing 'Senzeni na' at a meeting in Bellville during the strike

Source: A. Salle, *Muslim News*, 19, 12 (June 1979)

Figure 3.2: Striking Fatti's & Moni's workers eating meals provided by the FCWU during a strike meeting

Source: 'Projects Committee: CPU University of Witwatersrand', 1979, FCWU Collection, BC721:M

59

not come without consequence: the *Cape Argus* reported that Matthews Sokupha's three-year old daughter Francis died in the Eastern Cape because her father could not pay for her health care.[46] Although the union offered the workers R15 in weekly strike pay – costing the union approximately R1,000 per week – this was half the amount contract workers made from the company and did not leave much room for workers to send money home.

The 88 striking contract workers – the majority of whom were migrant labourers from the Ciskei – faced additional worries the same month when a representative of the Ciskei government visited their hostel and openly informed them that 'if they didn't want jobs, there were one million Ciskeians awaiting work contracts who did.'[47] Mabikwe recalls telling the representative in Xhosa: 'We're sitting down here; we are not coming back; we are not giving you an answer, and you know why!'[48] Nevertheless, 31 strikers returned to work after the visit, leaving 57 on strike (20 coloured and 37 African workers).[49] Many of the remaining contract workers faced legal troubles. Twenty police officers attended one of the strikers' daily meetings in July and inquired about the workers' contracts. Western Cape Administration Board inspectors began raiding Fatti's & Moni's hostels. During one raid at 3:30 a.m. the inspectors read from a list of names that they were given by Terblanche and informed the workers to report to the Administration Board's chief superintendent, P. U. Schellhause, because they had been 'causing trouble' at the hostel. The strikers and the union seemed to have limited political muscle themselves. But by this time the boycott was in full swing and added a major new dimension to their action.

The community boycott

The Fatti's & Moni's boycott influenced contentious debates within the labour movement concerning the appropriate role of unions in the broader struggle against apartheid. Some unions during this period prioritised their obligations to build factory-floor structures over mobilisation against the apartheid state. Members of this grouping, sometimes called 'workerist' at the time, believed that increased politicisation within organised labour would enable the national struggle to overwhelm working class interests and solicit state repression. Their politics diverged from 'populist' unions, which feared that an exclusively shop-floor-based labour movement risked relegating unions to 'small plant-based organisations' incapable of exercising significant political might.[50] The FCWU forged an independent position near the centre of these polarities. Its organisers saw their union as possessing a small, but potentially expanding, class-based leadership role in the liberation struggle, a stance derived in part from the union's historical ties to the Congress movement, with Mpetha and Abrahams, for example, coming from the political union tradition of the African National Congress (ANC). Nonetheless, the union still valued strong shop-floor organisation grounded in structures of democratic accountability. In her research on the FCWU during this period, Riyaad Schroeder concludes that the FCWU 'represented the best marriage of what were to become two traditions in the trade union (and indeed broader political) movement, workerism and populism'.[51] The union's successful boycott of Fatti's & Moni's helped to pioneer new forms of alliance politics; the protest demonstrated the value of cooperation between the labour movement and community organisations and served as a model. In the months after the dispute, unions around the country launch similar boycott campaigns against recalcitrant companies.[52]

There has been much debate over how the idea to boycott surfaced and when the tactic began to play a crucial role in the Fatti's & Moni's campaign. Virginia Engel claims that the idea for a boycott came from community activists during a 'closed house meeting' of union and community leaders. John Issel, a student activist-turned-community-organiser, maintains that he 'had gone into a supermarket near the union's offices to see what Fatti's & Moni's products it stocked' and it 'set this discussion going in the office about the consumer boycott'.[53] Theron argues that the idea emerged from Kassiem Allie and other members of the Western Cape Traders' Association (WCTA) who were not largely involved in civic organisations:

> The idea came from coloured traders who approached me … we were at Greenmarket Square and they were fired up. We didn't know the things they knew because they were traders and they bought bread from Fatti's & Moni's. We knew about pasta and flour, but we didn't know about the bread. Flour was going to a bakery that made bread. The bread was sold in a few coloured townships.[54]

Theron's view is particularly compelling. By the mid-1970s small-scale traders were beginning to feel the economic effects of the expansion of major supermarkets. In the Western Cape, as in most other areas, national chains such as Pick 'n Pay and Checkers had a marked advantage over small and medium-sized businesses because they could generate capital via financial institutions, purchase in bulk and sell more cheaply. Many of these disadvantaged traders, who were mostly Muslim, came together to form the WCTA in the latter half of 1976, which soon represented about 400 traders.[55] African traders in the area aligned themselves separately under the Western Province African Chamber of Commerce (WEPCOC), which was affiliated to the National

61

African Federated Chambers of Commerce, an organisation that included 15 regional organisations.

Prior to the Fatti's & Moni's campaign, the WCTA had already become familiar with the strength of a boycott. Many of the traders believed they had a responsibility to help the strikers. Sharief Hassan, WCTA chairperson, reflected:

> We felt that we are part of a community of oppressed people and on one side we had a relationship with the company because we are buying their products, we are marketing and buying their products. We also had the association with the consumer. They come and buy it off our shelf. We could approach our supplier and say the consumers are the workers who work in your factory. They are aggrieved and we feel like we should do something about it. It was only right of us to apply whatever type of pressure possible.[56]

Five months before the Fatti's & Moni's dispute, these same traders supported a boycott of Eveready batteries. Other black traders' associations in the Cape were also becoming politicised. For example, the Amalgamated Automobile Spares Association, which represented 30 dealers in the Cape Peninsula, had recently used a boycott to force a firm to change its policy – in their case, the organisation defended a woman who was fired over the issue of separate toilet facilities.[57] While boycotts had frequently been used in earlier political actions in South Africa, the black traders associations in the Western Cape had been directly involved in such actions in the previous year.

FCWU organisers were closely informed about the boycott, but not publicly involved. According to Theron, this was intentional; while the union 'grabbed on to the idea and started promoting it', the organisation explicitly distanced itself from the boycott's implementation and insisted that the community spearhead the boycott campaign, not the union.[58] Aware of the state's use of repression to prohibit the FCWU's overt involvement in politics in the 1960s, Engel recalled that the union 'had to make sure it did not get banned, so that it could function as an organisation.'[59] Engel further reflected:

> There was a big political debate over whether unions and political organisations should work together. I remember we came up with a slogan for the stickers that we would put on cars everywhere and initially it was: 'We don't buy Fatti's & Moni's', and that became such a big debate. The union feared that we could be arrested for

saying 'we'. Who is we? Is it an organisation? We finally had to use: 'I don't buy Fatti's and Moni's' (see figures 3.3 and 3.4).[60]

Figure 3.3: Original Fatti's & Moni's sticker

Source: 'Fatti's & Moni's publicity', 1979, South African History Archive, William Cullen Library, University of the Witwatersrand, AL2457, box M: Labour, file 6, Worker/Community Strike Support Committees folder

Figure 3.4: Revised Fatti's & Moni's sticker

The union thus possessed a fragile embryonic relationship with newly emerging community organisations. While some older organisers were involved in and influenced by underground South African political movements, such as the ANC, the independent unions that emerged after the Durban strikes had limited experience of working with a new generation of community activists and sought to avoid state repression. As a result, much of the boycott's planning occurred surreptitiously, without union involvement.

According to Virginia Engel, a small vanguard group of coloured community activists and union organisers covertly planned much of the boycott. The group's members, who included Engel and Norma Gabriel on the union's side, commonly described themselves as 'the think tank'. Other core members included Virginia's cousin, Ferdie Engel, who worked with her in youth organisations while they were both students at UWC, and John Issel, who came from a Black Consciousness background at UWC, where he served as the Western Cape regional secretary for the South African Students' Organisation (SASO) and helped the FCWU with its medical section.[61] Additional activists who participated in the meetings were Peter Gabriel, Norma's husband; Desmond Engel, Virginia's husband; and Marcus and Theresa Solomon. Ferdie Engel maintains that 'Virginia and Norma would take the decisions back to the union', while he reported to other community activists.[62]

The apartheid state's widespread ban on political organisations during the 1960s and 1970s created a severe lull in mobilisation in the Cape during this period. Ferdie Engel remembers:

Community organisations weren't very strong. A year before, the Black Consciousness Movement had been banned and there was a real decrease in community organisations ... school organisations were largely banned; SASO was banned and COSAS [Congress of South African Students] was only starting to form; there were very few women's organisations and there were no civic organisations.[63]

Ideological disparities further weakened the potential for community activism. Some Black Consciousness activists prioritised other forms of struggle and conscientisation. And although many of the boycott organisers were influenced by Unity Movement writings, the remnants of this organisation opposed the ANC's multi-class and non-racial nationalist struggle. According to Virginia Engel, 'we got many of our ideas about the value of the boycott' from the Unity Movement, yet 'we were sceptical of them because they were so anti-ANC'.[64] Many union organisers, such as Mpetha and Abrahams, were ANC stalwarts. Community support for the boycott had to overcome these obstacles.

The expansion of public support

As early as mid-April members of the 'think tank' produced an extensive list of all products marked, produced or packed by United Macaroni Factories Ltd and its subsidiaries. They began to hold meetings, distribute pamphlets and visit door to door around Cape Town.[65] Small activist groupings around the Western Cape, including students, women's organisations and political leaders, took up the boycott call. Women regularly cooked and sold soup in the townships to fundraise, while medicine and food donations poured in for the strikers and their families.[66] Virginia Engel remembers, 'even the most ordinary person identified with the plight of the workers and the need to do something at the time'.[67] By mid-May, local newspapers began publishing regular rosters of boycott supporters, and Peter Moni recalled that he 'had to read the newspaper in order to keep track of what was happening, and who joined in'.[68]

In early June the Community Action Support Committee was created to coordinate community support for the boycott. Thirteen organisations joined the committee and Ferdie Engel was elected chairperson.[69] The committee's primary task was to raise funds. McGregor estimates that it ultimately cost about R3,000 to maintain the strike, most going towards the worker's R15 weekly strike pay. The largest source of financial assistance came from church organisations and non-governmental organisations internationally, primarily in Germany.[70] Robert Krieger, from Cape Town, co-ordinated support campaigns among students in West Germany. Two key local support groups were students from high schools and universities around the Western Cape and the traders.

Students

Students were among the strongest forces mobilising support for the boycott and sustaining its momentum. By the time of the Fatti's & Moni's strike, many of these activists had become profoundly interested in political philosophy; they studied Marxist literature to theorise the liberation struggle and socialist ideas. Zackie Achmat, a student activist during this period, states, 'around [19]78 and [19]79, we started reading *Work in Progress,* the Wits student journal, *Communist Manifesto,* and Trotsky's *1905*'.[71] From these reading groups and students representative councils (SRCs) in secondary schools and universities, a new generation of student activists surfaced during the Fatti's & Moni's boycott, which endeavoured to link education concerns with the labour movement and expand on the developing class-based critique of apartheid. High school students joined the boycott through the Inter School Magazine Committee, formed in 1979 in order to connect matriculation students across Cape Town and increase their participation in youth movements. Many coloured students were drawn into politics by their exposure to Unity Movement literature, such as *Discussion* and the *Educational Journal of the Teachers' League of South Africa,* which they obtained from their secondary school teachers.[72]

By 1979 ideological transformations were taking place within the forces of the liberation struggle, as activists began to make the transition from Black Consciousness politics. In the Cape, the labour movement provided space for non-racial alliances to be formed. Coloured high school students forged relationships with students from the UWC who had previously taken part in the protests of 1976. Both established links with activists from UCT involved in the Wages Commission and the National Union of South African Students. Student groupings joined the boycott in early April after Virginia Engel and Issel approached a group of student leaders. On 10 May nearly 500 students from UWC, Bellville Teachers' Training College, Bellville College for Advanced Technical Education and Hewat Teachers' Training College pledged their support for the workers.[73] Days later, students from UCT took up the call to boycott. UCT's SRC eventually linked with 17 student bodies on campus and sold 'strike lunches' where all the proceeds were donated to the workers.[74] Pamphlets produced by the SRC's projects committee were distributed in shops and on message boards all around Cape Town.[75]

Student activists linked the Fatti's & Moni's protest to a more comprehensive critique of apartheid. A speaker during a student meeting on 16 May argued:

'The student movement should be linked to the forces of change in South Africa'.[76] By late 1979 students at UCT and UWC were promoting boycotts to demand nutritional improvements in school lunches, changes to the school curriculum and labour rights for school custodial workers.[77] Mass meetings on university campuses drew these struggles together and denounced 'transparent attempts to divide workers on the basis of colour' because this 'has no place in the South Africa of today'.[78] Student publicity highlighted Fatti's & Moni's use of racial divisions to undermine the workers' cohesion (figure 3.5).

Figure 3.5: A flyer distributed by the UCT Wages Commission highlighting the company's attempt to racially divide the workers

Source: 'UCT Wages Commission', 1979, FCWU Collection, BC721:M

These students also espoused critiques of apartheid laws that were commonplace among activists in the labour movement concerning South Africa's collective bargaining system, especially the denial of African workers' right to strike, the racist nature of influx control laws and the contract labour system (figure 3.6). Sustained connections were being made which identified apartheid with capitalism, and the trade union with the student movement.[79]

Figure 3.6: A flyer produced by students connecting the boycott to the broader struggle against capitalism and worker exploitation

Source: 'Projects Committee: CPU University of Witwatersrand', FCWU Collection, BC721:M

Student publicity often took on a creative dimension of its own. High school students were integral to these publicity campaigns, which sought to besmirch the company's image. To generate publicity, students would frequently run into the Fatti's & Moni's factory posting 'I don't eat Fattis & Monis' stickers and generally irritating the company's management. For a number of months the students would enter supermarkets and pierce holes in Fatti's & Moni's flour packs. In September 1979 more than 100 students from UCT, UWC and black high schools began a campaign to enter crowded supermarkets on Saturdays to promote the boycott. They placed stickers on Fatti's & Moni's products, and left trolleys filled with pasta in the aisles and refused to pay for them.[80] These students greatly inconvenienced the company. Peter Moni remembers: 'It was a simple exercise that was very effective because [they] had to repack all the shelves and it was continuously being done to shops very near our factories in the Bellville area.'[81] This tactic began to worry the company, which feared that coloured checkout women would support the boycott and refuse to handle Fatti's & Moni's products.

The message of the boycott spread across the country and in Isando, an industrial area of Johannesburg, student sympathisers picketed John Moni's Catholic church, which eventually announced its support for the boycott. Peter Moni claims that Father Thomas Kelly, the pastor of his father's church, was 'preaching anti-Fatti's & Moni's, right there from the pulpit with my father there'.[82] Pamphlets and flyers ridiculed the company. For example, slogans like 'Fatti's & Moni's: There's more to it than slurp and burp' were widely distributed by students (see figures 3.7 and 3.8).[83] The students' publicity not only helped to decrease the company's sales, but also dented its image.

The company responded to these publicity stunts with media tactics of their own. Fatti's & Moni's changed the names of some of its products, offered free T-shirts as a prize for purchasing its products, and hired sales people to travel around and announce that the boycott was over.[84] However, much of the damage to its image had already been done. Concerned about negative publicity, the company hired a public relations consultant, Patrick Taylor, but 'he soon concluded that it was the company's policies, not the way in which it handled the media that was the problem'.[85] Friedman contends that the students' publicity campaign proved that the fear of public embarrassment could, in this case, force corporate compliance 'in the most hostile of climates'.[86]

The publicity generated by students and community organisations was aided by a series of political victories in favour of trade union rights. Theron maintains that 'the boycott could not have come at a worse time for the company'.[87] The week following the walkout the Wiehahn Commission report was tabled in parliament, which kept the public focused on trade union rights. Additionally, it was seen as a rare occurrence for African workers to unite behind coloured workers, despite the threat of forced removal. The Community Action Support Committee had good access to sympathetic journalists such as Tony Weaver and Pippa Green.[88] These concurrent events pushed the dispute to the front page of three major Cape Town newspapers: the *Cape Argus*, *Cape Times* and *Burger*. Theron contends: 'Every day there was something in the newspaper', so 'the company could not start packing people into buses'.[89] Retaliation would have damaged Fatti's & Moni's further.

Traders

While students were eager to launch a publicity campaign, the traders were more apprehensive about boycotting – yet ultimately they were very effective in forcing the company to negotiate. The traders' boycott differed from the general community's

There's more to it than slurp and burp

Fatti's & Moni's strike

Five workers were dismissed from the Fattis and Monis factory in Belville South on April 23. All were active members of the Food and Canning Workers Union. Five more workers were "retrenched" after demanding reasons for the dismissals. Seventy-eight workers came out on strike the following day, demanding the re-instatement of the dismissed workers.

The strike follows a year long struggle by the Food and Canning Worker Union to negotiate a draft agreement with the management, calling for inter alia a minimum weekly wage of R40 and a 40 hour week. At present some workers receive only R23 a week and workers in low pay categories earn below the poverty datum line. Secretary of the union, Jan Theron said the Union represents workers at the factory. He said the five dismissed had sign a power of attorney instrument in connection with the draft agreement.

forced ethnic discrimination and wor ing class solidarity was cited as salient points for supporting the strike. UCT SRC Projects Officer Steve Bow said by showing solidarity with workers "we are linking the student movement to the real forces of change in South Africa."

Arising out of a SRC motion the Refectories have pledged to stop selling F & M products at canteens.

F & M have a ninety per cent monopoly on the pasta industry in South Africa. Furthermore, they have a considerable stake in the milling, baking and confectionery industry. Ironically many workers cannot afford the staple food the factory produces. F & M market under the names Fatti's and Ultra and control Hope and Wrench factories.

UCT's rightist Conservative Alliance has called the support for the strike and said th be harmful, causing rising unemployment and more potential recruits for

Figure 3.7: A flyer produced by students that capitalised on pasta as a product to generate publicity

Source: 'UCT Wages Commission', 1979, FCWU Collection, BC721:M

Support Fattis and Monis Boycott

Figure 3.8: A flyer produced by students ridiculing the company and its products

Source: 'Projects Committee: CPU University of Witwatersrand', FCWU Collection, BC721:M

boycott. While the latter asked individuals throughout the community not to purchase a company's products, the former encouraged shops not to stock the products. Fatti's & Moni's products were disbursed to black traders that were part the WCTA and WEPCOC. In the Western Cape, local traders had instituted a zoning policy in order to avoid competition. WEPCOC traders sold products in the African townships of Nyanga, Langa and Gugulethu. The widest distribution of Fatti's & Moni's products was from the Good Hope Bakery to these townships, which made African traders integral to the boycott's success.

Although the WCTA had experience using boycotts in disputes with Eveready and Coca-Cola, the association was ineffective in securing compliance by its members during the Fatti's & Moni's boycott. Crawford maintains: 'There was never really a proper boycott, and we were often involved in useless discussion with the officials of WCTA.'[90] She suggests that it became clear that the organisation was unable to control its membership. John Issel contends that students were often brought in as 'shock troops' to force traders to comply with the boycott.[91] This came in the form of students visiting stores to check shelves, questioning shop owners about where they purchased products and convincing reluctant traders to join the boycott. Members of the Community Action Support Committee also patrolled the township to enforce the boycott. Ferdie Engel remembers:

If I saw a Fatti's & Moni's truck in my area with the flour and the packets and the boxes, and I knew that these were scab labourers, I followed the truck and it stopped. One time, I went to one particular small shop. I got out of my car and I said to the trader (I didn't interfere with the workers), 'Are you a member of the Traders Association?' are you aware that there's a boycott of this company's products? He said, 'Yes, but oh, oh I didn't realise it ...' and then he was forced to tell the guy to take the product back to the truck. So, the truck moves on to the next delivery point, and the next, and I followed him to each stop.[92]

In general, WCTA members observed the boycott in areas of Cape Town where they risked strong moral pressure from the community, such as the outer reaches of the Cape Flats. However, the boycott was often ignored by most traders outside of these areas.[93]

WEPCOC, on the other hand, was successful in controlling its membership. African traders felt discriminated against as Africans and they were more likely to be under physical threat in African townships. They were also responding to outside economic pressures. According to Roger Southall's research on African traders during this period, white commercial interests were 'impatient to enter the black areas'.[94] WEPCOC traders helped force Fatti's & Moni's to the negotiating table. Theron recalls that once traders stopped selling bread produced by the Good Hope Bakery, 'it changed the entire context of the boycott; the effect was immediately felt'.[95] A director of the firm expressed his worries about a boycott of the company's products in African communities, because 'much of the factory's trade is with blacks'.[96]

In August 1979 the union capitalised on its highly organised FCWU branch in Johannesburg under the leadership of Neil Aggett to spread the boycott outside of the Cape. Aggett was the Transvaal regional secretary and the primary organiser for Fatti's & Moni's workers in Isando and Tembisa. He was also a part-time physician at Baragwanath hospital and forged alliances with a number of trade unions and community groups in the Transvaal.[97] According to Peter Moni, 'Aggett was doing here [in Johannesburg], what Theron was doing in Cape Town'.[98] Members of the University of Witwatersrand's SRC had been publishing material on the boycott since June, and in early August sent student activists to meet with other university students in Johannesburg.[99] The company feared that the boycott could do serious damage on the Witwatersrand, where it owned a number of bakeries.[100] As a result of this combined pressure, Fatti's & Moni's contacted the union to arrange talks in August.

Peter Moni remembers:

It was hugely politically motivated ... we were approached by Allan Boesak, Desmond Tutu, later on Frank Chikane, and Albertina Sisulu, and you name it. ... We had a string of guys, most of them we had never paid attention to in the process, all of a sudden trucking across the scene, inviting us to meetings that we would never attend.[101]

Moni recruited a team of consultants, led by an up-and-coming labour relations expert, Andrew Levy, and the company entered talks on 5 October. The South African Council of Churches appointed UCT academic Dr James Leatt to serve as the mediator. After the company tried to negotiate with workers individually and bypass the union, the talks temporarily collapsed.[102] However, after a month of negotiations, a settlement was announced on 12 November and included the re-employment of the striking workers in their original jobs at the same wages that they were paid prior to the strike.

Analysis of the boycott's impact

There is considerable debate over why Fatti's & Moni's agreed to negotiate with the union. According to Pillay, 'Moni began to express real concern about the effects of the boycott, which was reflected in the company's falling share price'.[103] However, Peter Moni later suggested during an interview that the situation was much more complicated. Political, economic and public relations concerns stemming from the boycott forced the company to negotiate. Levy and other labour consultants advised Moni that he could no longer 'sweep the problem under the rug', because major chains, such as Shoprite, were threatening to discontinue Fatti's & Moni's products if protests continued to disrupt their stores' operations.[104] These same consultants directed the company's campaign to restore its public image following the boycott.

Nonetheless, there is reason to believe that the company's profits decreased as a result of the boycott. Fatti's & Moni's taxed profit was nearly halved for the first six months of 1979.[105] G. Bijsters, head of the company's Johannesburg office, confessed that the company's profits for January to July 1979 were R186,000, compared to R363,000 for the same period in 1978.[106] A *Financial Mail* economics report determined a year after the boycott that '1979 was probably the worst year ever' for Fatti's & Moni's. It suggested that the main causes of the poor performance were losses in the bakery division and trading loses in the Cape Province, where the consumer boycott was the most successful.[107] John Moni accepted a year after the dispute that the protest 'affected productivity and damaged the group's image' and 'demonstrated the need to improve employee relations and introduce more appropriate communication methods'.[108] Moreover, Peter Moni admits that some of the company's bakeries were 'absolutely ground to a halt', as the company 'couldn't dispose of products in the townships'.[109]

Fatti's & Moni's was especially susceptible to a consumer boycott for two reasons: its size and the nature of its product. Compared to industry leaders like Premier Milling and Tiger Oats, Fatti's & Moni's was a fairly small company and likely to lose sales to larger companies that were capable of filling any void left in townships. Moreover, the company's limited resources reduced its capacity to engage in the publicity battle and deal with the union. Fatti's & Moni's was one of the last family-owned pasta companies in South Africa and was purchased by Tiger Oats less than a decade after the boycott.

The nature of Fatti's & Moni's products created a different set of issues for the company. While canned fruits and vegetables were not easily vulnerable to a boycott because they were partly produced for export, bread and flour produced by the milling section were susceptible to consumers wielding their buying power because the two products were sold locally in large quantities. Moreover, unlike ice cream cones and wafers, bread, flour and mealie meal (maize flour) were 'staples in the African diet', so the products were particularly vulnerable to a boycott by African consumers. The shelf lives of these products were also more limited than, for example, that of canned fruit.[110] In general, boycotts of consumer products with shorter shelf lives tended to be more effective than those of durables. Boycotts of commodities such as minerals and engineering products, which were not purchased by black communities, were also less likely to have immediate effect.

In fact, the boycott of Fatti's & Moni's helped the union to start organising in the milling industry, where unions were largely opposed. Theron noted: 'Prior to the Fatti's & Moni's strike, there was really no [trade union] organisation in the milling and baking industry.'[111] The union's ability to penetrate the industry presented problems for larger companies such as Tiger Oats and Premier Milling, who feared boycotts of maize meal in their primary market – African townships. In retrospect, Peter Moni believes that Theron 'did his homework before entering the dispute' and strategically targeted Fatti's & Moni's in order to challenge the entire milling industry.[112] Theron later acknowledged that the union used the boycott to 'get into a new sector of the economy with national importance'.[113] Following the dispute, larger milling companies increased their cooperation with the union. Premier Milling, for example, signed a recognition agreement with the FCWU two years later that contained unprecedented procedures for addressing strikes caused by controversial dismissals.[114]

By 1979 support was broadening for the ANC's non-racial agenda. During this year, Black Consciousness Movement exiles Barney Pityana and Tenjiwe Mtintso publicly announced their support for the ANC.[115] In the Western Cape it seems as if the Fatti's & Moni's boycott established a foundation for non-racial activism. The boycott brought individuals from different racial, class, political and geographical backgrounds together, foreshadowing the UDF's multi-layered attack against apartheid. During the boycott, Cape Town residents were willing to support workers who were legally unable to reside in the area; white middle-class students attended meetings with African traders from the Cape flats; and African workers were willing to risk being evicted from Cape Town to stand in solidarity with their coloured colleagues. Theron maintains that it was common to hear four different languages spoken during meetings.[116] While many of the workers at the factory were illiterate, some student and community leaders were part of Marx reading groups and immersed in socialist literature. White activists were experiencing a transition and coming to terms with the

Black Consciousness leaders, while some of the latter endorsed a white- and coloured-led trade union and organisation across race and class lines.

Other unions throughout the Cape immediately replicated the boycott strategy. In May 1980 the Western Province General Workers' Union helped to coordinate a nationwide boycott of red meat after 800 workers throughout the industry were dismissed for participating in a solidarity strike on behalf of workers from Table Bay Cold Storage. The boycott lasted for three months and cut red meat sales in Cape Town nearly in half. However, the strategy that was developed differed from the Fatti's & Moni's dispute; this boycott was aimed at all red meat, which made it more difficult to isolate an individual company and win specific demands. The union was forced to deal with the industry as a whole, because the boycott did not leave room for other companies to compete and sell red meat. The Fatti's & Moni's protest, by contrast, allowed competition to ensure consumers had access to these products while the boycott was still being observed.

The effects of boycotts were not only felt in the Western Cape region. In March 1981, 500 African workers from the Wilson Rowntree sweet factory in East London mobilised community activists to support a strike. The sweet workers were organised by the South African Allied Workers' Union, which had been launched two years earlier by a group of young African men who joined the union movement as former factory workers. Their boycott lasted for nearly a year, yet, like the red meat employees, none of the sweet workers was reinstated. This boycott showed the limits of the strategy in another way. Unlike bread or red meat, sweets are not a key food. As a result, the company was not as vulnerable to a consumer boycott.

Trade unions were not alone in intensifying boycotts following the Fatti's & Moni's protest. Students employed the tactic to protest educational inequality. Only one year after the Fatti's & Moni's dispute, COSAS, for elementary and high school students, and the Azanian Students' Organisation, for university students, initiated a massive school boycott in the Cape. During these protests, approximately one hundred thousand students throughout the Western Cape boycotted classes between April 1980 and January 1981.[117]

Conclusion

The Fatti's & Moni's boycott commenced a phase in South African history in which unions began to shift their focus from the factory floor and link with their broader communities. Although the Fatti's & Moni's campaign was not the first trade union-linked boycott, it helped to popularise the tactic. Steven Friedman, a South African labour journalist at the time, argues, 'in 1980, the new union movement arrived: in 1982, it came to stay'.[118] Boycotts of red meat and sweets demonstrate that other unions were looking to the Fatti's & Moni's dispute for inspiration and guidance.

The impact of boycotts spread as South Africans became aware of their political and economic power, and withdrawal-based strategies swept through the country. The insurrections of the 1980s are often linked with direct action, confrontation and violence. Yet youth and community organisations regularly employed boycotts and withdrawals to challenge the application of apartheid in many contexts; these various strategies were juxtaposed. The period following trade union revitalisation was dominated by student and consumer boycotts. By the mid-1980s the boycott formed an integral part of popular opposition that challenged the state from a variety of angles.[119] In many ways the Fatti's & Moni's protest laid the groundwork for the resurgence of boycotts as a mode of resistance in the Western Cape.

4 The role of the African National Congress in popular protest during the township uprisings, 1984-1989

Thula Simpson

Introduction

Mass protest against the apartheid system reached unprecedented levels during the 1980s as acts of resistance ranging from school and rent boycotts to strikes and open violence became commonplace. From September 1984 the scale of protest escalated when insurrection commenced in the townships. The South African government maintained that the crisis was largely of foreign provenance, and particularly that the banned liberation movement, the African National Congress (ANC), was responsible for orchestrating events from beyond the country's borders. Although unsustainable, this contention nevertheless does raise the question of the precise extent of the ANC's contribution to the progress of internal events. The issue of the reciprocal influence between internal popular protest and the external liberation movement forms the subject of this chapter (see also Klein's chapter in this volume). I focus on the period between September 1984 and September 1989, which corresponds with the tenure of the last South African parliament to sit before the commencement of formal negotiations between the National Party (NP) government and the ANC. The chapter therefore encompasses a period in which popular protest rose and was beaten back, only for it to re-emerge stronger than before, contributing to the state seeking a negotiated settlement.

The Vaal uprising

Throughout 1984 school boycotts and protests against high rents were endemic within South Africa's black townships. In many areas an underground war waged by township youths against local authorities had been in progress since council elections in November and December 1983. On 3 September 1984 riots in Sharpeville, Sebokeng and Evaton, three townships in the Vaal Triangle to the south of Johannesburg, heralded the onset of the most sustained mass urban revolt in South African history.

At the time, the ANC was reeling from the Nkomati Accord, a non-aggression pact signed by the South African and Mozambican governments in March 1984 that committed both countries to cease support for organisations engaged in armed struggle against the other. This affected the ANC's military wing, Umkhonto we Sizwe (MK), because the route from Mozambique via Swaziland had hitherto been the movement's principal means of infiltrating its guerrillas into South Africa. After Nkomati, Mozambican government leaders planned to expel MK cadres in their territory to Tanzania, a country that had no common border with South Africa. Instead, the ANC shifted over 100 of its members, the majority of whom were MK operatives, from Mozambique to Swaziland with the aim of building new external bases in rural areas there. However, these plans were undermined after the South African government announced late in March 1984 that it had reached an agreement with the Swazi government two years previously that contained terms similar to those of the Nkomati Accord. Following this announcement, Swazi police staged a number of raids on ANC hideouts in Swaziland.[1]

This pressure contributed to the ANC's decision to rush a large number of its guerrillas into South Africa, both to show that the armed struggle had not been crippled and also to find an outlet for its cadres based in Swaziland and Mozambique. The South African police estimated that around 50 MK fighters were part of this influx. Due to the actions of these guerrillas, MK operations within South Africa rose sharply between April and August 1984, only to fall rapidly thereafter. Figures released by Pretoria University's Institute for Strategic Studies estimated that of around 44 MK attacks in 1984, most occurred between April and August, with only nine coming in the final four months of the year. By September a large number of those infiltrated in the post-Nkomati surge had either been captured or killed, and the ANC proved to be unable to replenish these losses or construct alternative logistical lines through other countries to replace the Mozambique–Swaziland route.[2] The ANC's 1984 military offensive therefore faded just as the Vaal uprisings commenced.

The ANC's difficulties in establishing its political and military structures within South Africa limited the organisation's direct contact with the population within the country. The ANC tried to guide the course of the insurrection through the alternative means of its broadcasting station, Radio Freedom. Senior ANC member Ronnie Kasrils compared the situation to the Iranian revolution of 1979. He recalled that by the mid-1980s the ANC felt that people within South Africa were looking to the organisation's headquarters in Lusaka for guidance and inspiration in a manner similar to the Iranian masses that tuned in to the Ayatollah Khomeini's weekly broadcasts from France during the struggle against the shah of Iran. The ANC believed that its calls to the people from exile helped activists overcome their disorganisation by enabling them to view their local acts of resistance as part of a coordinated revolutionary strategy spearheaded by the external movement.[3]

In the wake of the Vaal uprisings the ANC's instructions to the masses restated a demand initially made by the organisation's president, Oliver Tambo, in January 1984, when he called on the masses to act in unity to render South Africa ungovernable. Throughout September 1984 the ANC transmitted this message into South Africa via Radio Freedom, as well as pamphlets mailed to the addresses of prominent activists, organisations and random individuals picked out from telephone directories. The campaign was coordinated by the ANC's Department of Information and Publicity, which was led at the time by Thabo Mbeki.[4]

For its own reasons, the South African government sought to stress the ANC's direct control over events. However, when asked, ANC spokespeople emphasised the agency of the people based within the country. When a journalist put the government's claims of external instigation to him in October 1984, the ANC's secretary general, Alfred Nzo, speaking from Lusaka, replied:

One thing the ANC over the years of its existence can be said to be guilty of is its ability to make the people conscious of their own oppression, and [to] show them that it is necessary for them to do something about their own oppression. ... If they say it is the ANC [behind the unrest] because of that history, we plead guilty.

Meanwhile, Thabo Mbeki replied similarly, saying:

Of course the people will respond [if] you shoot at them. Such is the determination to be free. The people will fight back with whatever they have .... And of course the ANC is continuously saying, let's fight them with what we have. But we're not going and standing around saying, now is the time to throw stones.[5]

The ANC was nonetheless unsatisfied with its limited political and military contribution to the rising. It sought to reach a position where its operational structures could contribute more actively to events unfolding on the ground. The ANC viewed its objective as being to establish links with groups fighting the state security forces in the townships. Oliver Tambo articulated this priority on 8 January 1985 when he delivered a speech on behalf of the ANC's National Executive Committee (NEC), marking the

73rd anniversary of the organisation's founding. There he called for the 'mass combat forces' engaging the state security forces in the townships to be armed and trained as part of MK, and for areas affected by unrest to become 'mass revolutionary bases, from which Umkhonto we Sizwe must grow as an army of the people'.[6]

However, the progress of the uprising highlighted a substantial obstacle hindering the realisation of this goal. This was that the state had spent heavily during the previous four decades in ensuring its security forces' ability to control black urban areas. Government investments during that period had succeeded in creating townships that were mostly far from white areas and whose few access roads were monitored by army camps and police stations. Any attempt to break out of these areas – whether to seize power, join up with protesters in other zones or threaten white residential areas – could be met by an overwhelming armed response. Meanwhile, housing units in the townships were almost always single storey and detached, thus offering little concealment for rebels and a clear line of fire for the security forces. Additionally, the government's control of South Africa's internal transport network meant that it could rush sufficient manpower wherever it was required and quash resistance whenever it arose in any particular township. Usually the suppression of revolt was accomplished at little human cost to the security forces. It was not until January 1986 that the first white security officer was killed in an incident of unrest.[7]

Guerrillas, meanwhile, found it difficult to operate in the affected areas. MK conducted virtually no military actions in the townships most affected by violence in the months following September 1984, while in general MK's armed operations in townships formed a small fraction of its total military effort. Tom Lodge notes that no attacks were attributed to MK in the Vaal Triangle and Eastern Cape townships, and only a few in those in the East Rand in the period leading to the government's July 1985 declaration of a state of emergency. These had been the main centres of the insurrection. Lodge does not record the location of all 78 attacks attributed to the MK between 1 January 1984 and 30 June 1985, but 37 were in business districts or industrial areas of towns, as opposed to 13 in townships.[8]

While the protests were not able to extend beyond the communities in which they originated, they were able to reach black members of the police force and community councillors resident in those townships, who were the local organs upon which white domination of black urban areas rested. In the words of General Johan Van der Merwe, who in 1985 was the head of the Security Branch, the police 'knew [that] if we could not succeed in protecting our Black members ... the whole system would collapse and that we in no way would be able to defend ourselves against the onslaught'. By mid-1985, the police's ability to control black areas in the East Rand and Vaal Triangle in particular was diminishing. In June of that year, after receiving news that a group of activists were planning to launch armed attacks on black policemen in East Rand townships, Security Branch headquarters authorised an initiative to penetrate the group and kill its members. According to Van der Merwe, the police leadership decided that arrests would be pointless in the existing circumstances because witnesses would be unlikely to come forward because of the high levels of intimidation that they would encounter, while any informers' lives would be in grave danger.[9]

The task of infiltrating the group was given to Sergeant Joe Mamasela, a police agent who had years before received training and a supply of hand grenades from the ANC in Botswana. Early in June 1985 Mamasela arrived in Duduza township in the East Rand, saying he had come 'from Lusaka' looking to arm the leadership of the Congress of South African Students (COSAS). The COSAS executive refused to take part in the operation as a body for fear that if the enterprise went awry the entire leadership would be eliminated. Instead, its members nominated deputies. This proved a wise move because when the squads went into action on 25 June, eight activists were killed when their booby-trapped weapons exploded prematurely. In the aftermath of the incident, government spokesmen alleged that incompetent ANC terrorists had supplied the victims with dud weapons and thereby caused the deaths; the ANC asserted that police agents posing as guerrillas were responsible.[10]

Taking the struggle to white areas

The police operation against the COSAS members was codenamed Operation Zero Zero and it coincided with a consultative conference held by the ANC in Kabwe, Zambia, on 16–23 June 1985. At the conference, which was attended by around 250 delegates, MK's record, which featured some 30 attacks in the first five months of 1985, following nine between September and December 1984, came in for criticism from some of those present. The conference agreed on two main recommendations regarding the future prosecution of the armed struggle. The first, as Tambo announced at a press conference held in Lusaka on 25 June, was that the ANC must 'intensify the struggle at any cost' and that this would necessarily entail the relaxation of many restrictions that had hitherto been imposed on MK units. Previously the ANC had urged its guerrillas to only attack 'hard' military and government targets, and to avoid inflicting civilian casualties. When journalists asked Tambo whether this meant the ANC would now authorise attacks on 'soft' civilian targets, he replied that 'the distinction between soft and hard targets is going to disappear in an intensified conflict'.[11]

The second resolution was for the ANC to 'take the struggle to the white areas'.[12] The ANC was aware, as Thabo Mbeki stated in an interview a few months later, that people within South Africa were complaining, 'Why is it that it's always the black mothers who are crying for their children who have been killed? When are the white mothers going to cry for their own children?'[13] Other ANC leaders confided to journalists that they feared that if the movement did not respond to popular demands for a more aggressive prosecution of the armed struggle, it could begin to haemorrhage support to rival organisations prepared to countenance bolder forms of violence. Such concerns had to be reconciled with other strategic concerns pressing on the ANC leadership, most notably the priority of isolating the government from its main bases of support within South Africa and abroad. By the time of the Kabwe conference, increasing numbers of South African whites and Western governments that had previously been hostile to the ANC recognised that no lasting solution to the conflict could be found without the latter's involvement. Although they neither subscribed to all the ANC's positions nor sought revolutionary transformation, they nonetheless realised that apartheid had no long-term future and sought peaceful change. From late 1985 a series of meetings were held between the ANC and delegations of white South Africans and Western governments.[14] An intensified armed struggle that targeted white areas could, if handled incorrectly, contribute to racial polarisation and jeopardise these gains.

The slogan of taking the struggle to white areas was first articulated publicly by the ANC on 22 July 1985 in a statement calling for 'all areas' of the country to 'join in the general offensive to make the apartheid system unworkable and South Africa ungovernable', while adding that in the process the 'struggle will also spread to the white areas of our country regardless of enemy efforts to confine it to the black townships'. The statement was issued in response to the South African government's declaration of a state of emergency the previous day.[15]

At the time, the ANC did not have a clearly defined strategy of how it would expand the struggle to white areas. All the while, the disparity between the levels of violence in black and white areas inflamed black sentiment both within and outside the ANC. By September 1985, a year into the uprising, of the 700-plus people killed in political violence, only seven were white and none of the whites was killed in officially designated white areas.[16] In the absence of clearly drawn lines from the ANC leadership entailing what its policy for expanding the armed struggle to white areas meant, incendiary statements at odds with the existing parameters of military operations emerged from sections of the movement. For example, Radio Freedom's broadcast on 3 September 1985 marking the one-year anniversary of the Vaal uprising declared:

Throughout this period, the majority of the white population have learned of the bitter confrontation only through their television screens while sipping their drinks comfortably in their cosy homes. The whites of this country now have to be rudely awakened from the dreamland that they have closed themselves into. We have now to take the battle right into their homes, into their kitchens and bedrooms.[17]

Such calls for whites to be attacked in their homes played into the hands of the beleaguered South African government by providing apparent credence to their long-standing claims of the ANC's involvement in terrorism. As Genevieve Klein notes in her chapter in this book, the ANC was always at pains to present its armed struggle to Western audiences as a defensive and 'just' war against apartheid. Tambo sought to reassure Western journalists that the ANC remained committed to these values. In an interview published in the *New York Times* on 7 September 1985 he emphasised that the focus of ANC armed attacks remained targeting military installations, institutions and personnel. However, he added, in the process of 'attacking military targets', it was 'quite unavoidable' that 'all sorts of people will be hit', and he clarified that it was only 'in this context', i.e. of striking at military targets, but knowing that civilian casualties would be an inevitable by-product, 'that white areas will come to know what is happening in the country'.[18] To *Newsweek* magazine he added that whereas in the past MK operatives were under strict orders 'when planning attacks on police and military installations' to consider 'whether civilians would die', that stipulation had been relaxed. Henceforth, 'whether civilians are likely to die will not be a consideration'.[19]

A discrepancy remained between such statements to the Western media and some of the messages that the ANC was broadcasting to South Africa's black population. For example, in an October 1985 message, Radio Freedom urged attacks on white soldiers and policemen operating in black townships. Within the ANC the argument had often been made that owing to the institution of compulsory military service for white South African males, MK should consider all white males legitimate military targets. While the issue of conscription raised valid questions about the boundaries between civilian and military targets, the Radio Freedom broadcast then advocated that attacks on white security force members be conducted as follows:

We must attack them at their homes and holiday resorts just as we have been attacking black boot-lickers at their homes. ... All along it has only been black mothers who have been mourning. ... The time has come when all of us must mourn.[20]

It must be remembered that most attacks on black collaborators occurred in the dead of night when petrol bombs were thrown through their bedroom windows while they and their families slept. The suggestion that this tactic, along with bombing holiday resorts, should be the focus of intensified struggle in white areas again raised the question of where the limits were to be drawn post-Kabwe. The ANC was communicating different messages to different audiences.

Some clarity on the issue was provided late in 1985 when the ANC distributed a pamphlet within South Africa entitled 'Take the struggle to the white areas'. Although the document echoed the sentiment that 'white South Africa cannot be at peace while the Black townships are in flames', the six recommendations made on how the struggle could be spread to white areas eschewed attacks on soft targets and advocated restraint in methods to be employed. The first recommendation was to strengthen the workers' movement to the point where industrial action in factories, mines, farms and suburbs could commence; the second called for extending consumer boycotts beyond the townships; the third was for well-planned demonstrations in white suburbs and central business districts; the fourth was for the establishment of clandestine military groups in workplaces so as to disrupt oil, energy, transport, communications and other crucial systems; the fifth called for attacks on the army and police; while the last recommended raids on arms dumps and armouries so as to procure arms for ANC military units.[21]

The problem with the restrained measures advocated in this document was that they did not speak to the demand among many blacks for reprisals to be inflicted on whites as revenge for massacres in the townships. This desire for revenge was the sentiment underpinning the popular, clamorous calls among radicals within the black community for the struggle to be taken into white areas. As repression intensified, leading in turn to increased calls for revenge, it would prove impossible for the ANC to maintain the line of military restraint advanced in the document.

Intensifying the struggle at all costs

In the meantime, the ANC continued with its attempts to infiltrate its cadres into the country. At Kabwe, the delegates felt that stepping up the number of MK attacks was an imperative necessity. As in the period following the Nkomati Accord, the method adopted to achieve this was a mass surge of MK cadres into South Africa. The name given to the enterprise was Operation Zikoma. The wisdom of the move was widely disputed within the ranks of the ANC leadership, with critics pointing to the lack of structures within South Africa capable of accommodating the cadres upon their arrival, as well as the very vague briefings given to those infiltrated, which did not go much beyond recommendations that they should integrate themselves into revolutionary struggles within the townships as best they could. Such objections were ultimately overruled and hundreds of MK cadres were poured into the country as part of the operation. As with the surge of the previous year, the initial results seemed positive. There was a rapid increase in armed activity and by the end of the year MK had recorded 136 attacks, more than any previous year, while only 31 guerrillas were killed or captured. This represented the best ratio of operations launched versus casualties suffered in the history of the armed struggle.[22]

However, in 1986 the numbers captured and killed increased rapidly. Howard Barrell estimates that MK casualties at the hands of the security forces rose by 500 per cent, while the ratio of guerrilla actions to security force neutralisations shifted from 13 attacks for every three guerrillas neutralised in 1985 to five attacks for four neutralisations in 1986. The continued deployment of large numbers of MK cadres in 1986 meant that MK actions increased by 70 per cent, but the same cycle repeated itself and the number of casualties again rose dramatically the following year.[23]

The ANC also endeavoured to build internal leadership structures within South Africa in the post-Kabwe period. In late 1985 Sibosiso Ndlasi (also known as Sihle Mbongwa), one of MK's most senior cadres, was sent into South Africa to take command of Operation Butterfly. His task was to oversee the creation of politico-military leadership structures in the Durban area. He succeeded in forming a training base inside the country that instructed people on how to use small arms, explosives and other weapons. However, the mission was short lived. Immediately upon their entry into South Africa, the group made contact with Vejanand Ramlakan, the head of an MK unit in Durban. At that time Ramlakan was under police surveillance and he inadvertently facilitated the police's task by maintaining telephone communication with other members of the internal underground from his house. The security forces were aware of their movements throughout and waited for an opportune moment to destroy Operation Butterfly. This came on 24 December 1985 in a raid launched in response to a bombing at a shopping centre in Amanzimtoti, near Durban, the previous day.[24]

As 1986 began the news for the ANC's NEC regarding progress made towards building political and military structures within South Africa was discouraging. At the Kabwe conference an agreement was reached that the NEC would meet every two months to monitor developments. After three or four unfruitful meetings, a small group of senior leaders decided during a tea break at one such meeting in early 1986 on a new initiative. During the break Mac Maharaj circulated an idea to Oliver Tambo, Joe

Slovo, Chris Hani and Jacob Zuma proposing that top ANC leaders be sent into South Africa to combine with the internal leadership that had emerged during the upsurge of resistance. The aim was to develop an integrated politico-military leadership structure within South Africa that would coordinate all facets of the struggle. Maharaj's idea was accepted during the informal caucus and the five decided to put the matter before the full NEC. The proposal was rapidly accepted and was the genesis of what later became known as Operation Vula.[25]

The second state of emergency

The first Operation Vula operatives only entered South Africa in 1988. By that time resistance within the country was at its lowest ebb since 1984. The whole internal movement was rocked by the state of emergency introduced by the government on 12 June 1986, which was much more comprehensive than the previous imposition of martial law between July 1985 and March 1986.

Among the groups most affected by emergency restrictions were the two key internal ANC aligned organisations, the United Democratic Front (UDF) and the Congress of South African Trade Unions (COSATU). ANC concerns over developments within these two organisations were voiced in a document titled '1987: What is to be done?' distributed by its Politico-Military Council to regional command centres in October 1986. The document emphasised the UDF's pivotal role in ensuring the success of the 'mass work' that the ANC considered essential for the success of its 'revolutionary perspective'. However, the document continued, 'major problems' had emerged in this sphere, owing to 'sharp divisions and conflict within the UDF leadership [and] the failure of the UDF to work out a programme of action and a set of strategic and tactical objectives'. Disquiet was also voiced about divisions within COSATU. Meanwhile, all was not well within the ANC itself, which had 'not come anywhere near' realising the objectives it had set, owing to the fact that the internal underground remained weak and unable to support guerrillas infiltrated from abroad, while MK largely remained unable to integrate its actions with those of the 'mass combat groups' in the townships. Additionally, the ANC was on the retreat in the region, as it had recently been forced to withdraw personnel and organisational structures from Lesotho and Botswana under South African pressure. The South African security forces captured copies of the document and released information from it to the media in December 1986.[26]

A further setback came with the all-white general election of May 1987. In these elections, which provided the first major test of white opinion since the Vaal uprisings, the reactionary Conservative Party (CP) ousted the liberal Progressive Federal Party as the official opposition, while the NP, which campaigned on a tough national security stance, was returned with a large majority. It was a watershed moment. Two years previously the ANC leadership had resisted calls from within the movement to cause mayhem in white areas and had opted instead for a restrained mixture of mass protest, economic sabotage, and attacks on army and police personnel. However, this moderation had been answered by a ferocious campaign by the state designed to eliminate black resistance. The 1987 general election results indicated that a majority of the white electorate approved of this repression and, to judge by the swing to the right, felt that the government was not being ruthless enough in dealing with resistance. In an interview with the South African newspaper the *Star* the following year, ANC leaders stated that the lesson they took from the 1987 elections was that whites would only stop supporting repression when it became clear that the government was no longer able to physically protect them. From that point onwards the twin objectives guiding military policy were to convince whites that the government could not protect them and to boost the black population's morale.[27]

The 1988 municipal elections

In 1988 nationwide municipal elections scheduled for 10–26 October, when South Africans of all racial groups were to vote for segregated town councils, took centre stage in the political agenda. The elections were crucial for the state's counter-revolutionary campaign. After the 1984–86 insurrection the government acknowledged that unless blacks were involved in decision making at the national level, violence would be a permanent fixture in South Africa's political life. However, it wanted to reform without having whites surrender power. Initially it attempted to impose a solution unilaterally, but found that not even conservative blacks were willing to participate due to the perception that the process was being imposed from above. In response, the government adopted a 'bottom-up' policy in which the first stage was to neutralise those perceived as political agitators. By 1988 the state of emergency had largely achieved this. The next stage was to rehabilitate the township councils in the minds of the local populations and co-opt a critical number of blacks into participating in them. Millions of rands were poured into improving conditions in the townships to ensure the success of this stage and the council elections were viewed as a defining moment in the progress of the plan. In their comments in the build-up to the voting, government officials did not state specifically what figures they would consider a successful turnout. Government's objectives were instead to get the structures up and running, to improve on the 21 per cent turnout recorded in 1983 when the town councils were established, and to achieve a vaguely defined critical mass of support that would confer legitimacy on the process. If things went according to plan, the elected township councillors would meet in nine regional electoral colleges and choose representatives for a multiracial constitutional council in which delegates from the Bantustan administrations and the white, Asian and coloured municipalities would also be represented. The process would culminate with the establishment of a multiracial council that would write a new constitution establishing a new power-sharing system.[28]

The ANC's overriding objective was to do everything in its power to abort the elections. Its campaign was launched under a new military command structure announced in October 1987, in which Chris Hani was promoted to MK chief of staff, thereby becoming deputy commander, while Steve Tshwete replaced him as MK political commissar, becoming number three in the chain of command. On 3 June 1988 the pair held a joint interview with the journalist John Battersby in Lusaka, from which excerpts were published in the *Times* of London and the *New York Times* between 5 June and 12 June 1988.

The issue of the October elections was discussed. Hani said that the ANC viewed the elections as an attempt by an emboldened government to strengthen its position in the townships by reinstalling the 'traitors' and restoring the 'system of puppet administration' that the 'people had destroyed three years ago'. He said the ANC was committed to ensuring a 'massive and resounding boycott … we won't be satisfied even with a 6% poll. We don't want them even to get 10% or 8%'. This would render the procedure a farce in the eyes of domestic South African and international opinion. This end would be accomplished through a mixture of political and military methods. The people would first be mobilised in order to dissuade candidates from running. But if this political persuasion did not suffice, then 'revolutionary violence or forceful persuasion' would be employed, as candidates who defied the warnings would be 'dealt with' and election meetings 'disrupted and broken down'.[29]

The interview became controversial for the views the two expressed on the subject of white civilian casualties. Hani prefaced his comments with the statement that white civilian deaths incurred 'in the course of this confrontation between us and the forces of the regime' would be 'regretted' and that he did not think the ANC had 'any interest in the death of white civilians', but he then detailed at length the strategic value that he felt such casualties would yield the ANC:

I don't think most whites want to die for apartheid ... our intention is to make them see, so that when they are maimed and they are in hospital, others will go there to visit them and will say: this is the price of apartheid.

'How long' he asked, 'are they going to sacrifice loss of limb to maintain a system that deprives the overwhelming majority of the right to vote, the right to a proper house, to proper medical attention, to education?' White South Africans had been 'complacent' for a long time, he declared, but the ANC now wanted to provoke 'some soul-searching' among them. The hope was that the fear created by MK's actions would cause panicked whites to pressurise the government to shift its course. In Tshwete's words, once whites realised that '[a]partheid is now no longer protecting us. Apartheid is killing us', they would then 'nudge' the government to reform.[30]

Oliver Tambo distanced the ANC from these statements in an interview he conducted with the British *Independent* newspaper shortly afterwards. He stated that Hani's comments were made as an individual and added that 'even the chief of staff is subject to the political control of the ANC'.[31] In another interview with the *Times* of London, published on 14 June, he stated again that the ANC had no intention of 'increasing its attacks on civilians or of targeting whites specifically'.[32]

Despite these reassurances, a bombing campaign by MK cadres was under way in South Africa's city centres. On 22 June a lunch hour bomb blast in an amusement centre in Johannesburg injured ten people and caused extensive damage. Two days later a limpet mine shattered the interior of a seaside restaurant moments after nearly 100 diners had been evacuated. The South African press was almost universally hostile, including newspapers normally sympathetic to the ANC. The *Sowetan*, then South Africa's only daily newspaper for blacks, denounced the 'horrific acts', declaring: 'This descent into hell must be stopped', while *City Press*, another black paper, emphasised that the clientele at the amusement centre was 'almost exclusively black'. Meanwhile, the *Star* protested: 'No cause, however just, can be served by such evil means.'[33]

These negative responses placed the ANC on the defensive. The organisation denied claims it had shifted its focus to attacks on soft targets: 'All military cadres are trained in such a way that purely civilian targets must be avoided at all times' and there were 'clear indications that a large number of [recent explosions] were aimed at government and state infrastructure, railway stations and lines and South African Police and South African Defence Force personnel' it declared in a statement on 30 June.[34] However, two days later, on 2 July, an MK unit detonated a 100 kilogram car bomb outside Ellis Park Stadium in Johannesburg as the first fans left a rugby match between Transvaal and the Free State. The bomb killed two people and injured 37 others. The attack brought the number of people killed in bomb attacks since the start of 1988 to 21, of whom ten died in June 1988.[35]

MK's Special Operations Unit, commanded by Lester Dumakude, planted the Ellis Park bomb. As Special Operations Unit commander, Dumakude reported directly to Chris Hani, and part of his job was to impart the directives of the external movement to units operating inside South Africa. The Ellis Park bombing corresponded fully with the guidelines for MK's bombing campaign articulated by Hani and Tshwete in their 3 June interview. In his amnesty application before the Truth and Reconciliation Commission nine years later, Dumakude said that those in the stadium 'were the people who had the vote to make a change in this country'. The aim was to 'bring that struggle closer to the white community, to dispel the belief that they were immune from change' and 'to emphasise to them that it was better to change now rather than later .... Let them use the vote, let them start to query the government'. Harold Matshididi, a member of the unit, explained in his testimony that in planting the bomb they did not seek to kill people, adding that Dumakude informed them that the idea was to 'set the bomb so that the people ... still in the stadium can hear it [and afterwards] intervene and talk to their leaders warning them against the anger of the blacks', with the aim of sending 'a message to the whites that we can also do a bad thing of killing them'.[36]

Further negative publicity caused the ANC's NEC to release another statement on the subject of civilian casualties on 17 August. The statement declared that while the ANC welcomed the general upsurge of guerrilla activity, MK cadres had launched attacks on civilian targets against official policy. The statement added that attacks on purely civilian targets were counterproductive and warned MK members who ignored directives that they could face punishment. There was also another reshuffle of the command structure. Tshwete's brief career as political commissar ended as he was redeployed to the NEC. Chris Hani retained his post.[37]

Despite the statement the ANC's bombing campaign continued unabated. On 23 August a bomb exploded at a Wimpy restaurant in a downtown thoroughfare in East London, wounding at least 25 people, followed the next day by a bomb at a Wimpy in Standerton that exploded without inflicting casualties.[38] During September 1988, 29 bombings were attributed to MK, leaving one person dead and 38 injured. This was the largest number of attacks ever recorded by MK in any single month. There were a further 22 blasts in October. The government introduced a number of measures to counteract those determined to impede the election process. It offered rewards for information leading to the arrest of MK guerrillas, it staggered the vote over two weeks in order to be able to exhaust any boycott actions and it made it a crime to call for people not to vote. In the run-up to the elections a number of activists were detained, while the police estimated that from 1 September they arrested around 50 MK cadres, 'neutralised' 36 guerrillas in the four weeks directly preceding the opening of the polls and seized a large quantity of arms.[39] The state also invested $2 million in a drive to get the voters to the polls – at the time a huge sum for a South African election campaign. State planners were also anxious to persuade the black electorate that there was no connection between the act of voting and support for the apartheid policy. The South African Bureau of Information chose two talking squirrels by the names of 'Nut' and 'But' to be the stars of its media effort, reasoning that for black voters the rodents would be less controversial than human figures who would inevitably display racial characteristics.[40]

Stalemate

MK made a large commitment to the 1988 military campaign. Speaking in September 1988, Tshwete claimed that since the beginning of the year over 400 trained MK guerrillas had been infiltrated into South Africa, with a similar number of recruits having been trained clandestinely within the country.[41]

As the first results from the elections came in, senior NP leaders expressed their delight with the outcome. In their worst-case scenario, a CP victory in the whites-only polls would have been accompanied by a massive election boycott by blacks. However neither materialised. The government claimed that around 30 per cent of the approximately 1.5 million registered black voters turned out nationwide, marking a significant increase from the 1983 polls. Meanwhile, the NP won the white elections and prevented the CP from obtaining control of a single city. Minister of Constitutional Planning and Development Chris Heunis, who was responsible for overseeing the government's reform programme, declared the vote a victory for 'peace, prosperity and democracy' over 'revolution, violence and poverty', and pledged to plough on with the reform agenda, asserting that the elections would 'give greater momentum to the process of constitutional development'.[42]

However, the fact remained that almost half the 1,839 black council seats went uncontested and the 400,000 blacks that voted formed a small proportion of the overall black population.[43] In a Radio Freedom broadcast the day after the polling stations closed, Thabo Mbeki branded Heunis's claims to be satisfied with the turnout as 'face-saving bravado'. The ANC's assertion was that among blacks, less than 2 per cent of registered voters and fewer than 10 per cent of the entire electorate had cast their ballots. The movement felt that this figure was sufficiently low to prevent the government from being able to credibly claim before the wider world that the process had seen the black population confer 'approval and support' on its planned changes. However, the ANC also stated in the broadcast that the government's post-election claims to have received such a mandate represented more than just an attempt to save face and that it indicated a desire to persist with the reform programme, albeit with minority support. Given this determination, the movement articulated its intent to continue the political and military methods of resistance employed during the elections, but this time aimed at ensuring that the 'puppet councils' never saw the light of day.[44]

The elections had shown that the government could withstand such pressures and implement its policies, and that the military balance was sufficiently in its favour for it to be able to do so for the foreseeable future. The government therefore possessed the option of imposing its reform programme, although without domestic and international support. This was the option that the so-called 'securocrats' in the cabinet sought to exercise. In their eyes, mass popular enthusiasm was not essential; acquiescence was sufficient. They felt adequate support had been garnered to enable them to push through the constitutional development programme. They were also sure of their capacity to 'neutralise' the 'radicals'. However, by late 1988 their perspective was being challenged within the NP by reformers who viewed the course the securocrats were advocating as a recipe for further polarisation and violence. These reformers called for talks with the banned movements, above all the ANC, in the belief that without their involvement militant resistance would inevitably resume.[45]

For the time being the existing state of affairs persisted. On 8 January 1989 Oliver Tambo delivered his customary speech on the occasion of the anniversary of the ANC's founding. He called for the ANC and its supporters to launch their 'biggest offensive at all levels to smash the local authorities, regional services councils and the so-called National Council' that the South African government had committed itself to establish in pursuance of its reform agenda, despite the low participation recorded in the October 1988 poll.[46] After a meeting with more than 60 representatives of black town councils on 16 January 1989, Chris Heunis announced the creation of a 'National Forum' for urban blacks that would enable them to take part in a 'negotiating process' together with other groups. Heunis added that a steering committee had been appointed to draft a constitution for the National Forum and that the committee would report back before the end of March. The objective was to identify urban leaders to serve in a 'National Statutory Council', which would consist of delegates from the

Bantustans and representatives of whites, coloureds and Indians, and would negotiate a new constitution.[47]

However, two days later, on 18 January 1989, President P. W. Botha suffered a stroke. He chose to resign as NP leader, but tried to cling on to the state presidency, thus creating a power struggle with F. W. de Klerk, his successor as NP leader. Meanwhile, hopes that the black population would acquiesce in the reform process were dealt a blow when – as the reformers within the NP had predicted – popular resistance revived during 1989, reaching a crescendo in the weeks leading to the whites-only general elections in September of that year. The upsurge made it clear that the state of emergency had failed to eradicate mass protest and undermined the position of the securocrats. After a NP victory in the September elections De Klerk began dismantling the national security system and moved towards talks with the ANC.

As for the ANC, in 1989 it launched another military surge. Its political leadership pressed the MK command to step up attacks at all costs so as to support the impression that the armed struggle was not losing momentum. Once again, cadres were rushed towards South Africa without proper preparation or adequate structures to receive them. The effects were ruinous. Bill Anderson, an ANC military intelligence officer based in Lusaka at the time, estimated that of about 240 MK cadres deployed to infiltrate South Africa in 1989, a third defected, a third were captured or killed by the enemy, while a third remained 'in place, whether active or drifting'.[48]

Conclusion

A constant theme in black protest in South Africa during the apartheid era was its invisibility to the white population at large. This is hardly surprising, since achieving racial segregation had always been a fundamental objective of apartheid. As a consequence, black protest remained largely out of sight and out of mind for most whites. Events following the Vaal uprising highlighted this social distance: black communities were afflicted by unprecedented levels of political violence, but most whites had no comprehension of what was going on and their lives were mostly unaffected. The security forces proved largely successful in their policy of preventing the violence from crossing over from black to white areas.

Frustrations over the ANC's failure to redress the unequal combat taking place within the country sparked criticisms of the movement's policy at the Kabwe conference. The critics' two main demands were for the struggle to be intensified at all costs and for it to be spread to white areas. These latter calls were motivated by two considerations. The first was to exact revenge for security force violence, but the second was to awaken whites to the reality that the country was in conflict and to conscientise them about conditions in black areas. For a while the ANC leadership managed to resist the most radical formulations of this call, but after a turn to the right among the white electorate in 1987 the ANC came to the conclusion that only when whites felt that their physical safety was under threat would they feel induced to reform. This, and raising the morale of blacks, became the dominant objectives of the ANC's military strategy from that point onwards. It is interesting to ask whether the ANC's attempts to conscientise whites about the predicaments of the black majority were successful and whether this factor had an influence in enabling the relatively 'peaceful' transition of the early 1990s, in which whites voluntarily surrendered their power without the levels of bloodshed many had long predicted.

5 Strategies of struggle: The Nelson Mandela campaign

Genevieve Klein

Introduction

Popular politics has crossed international boundaries, and Hakan Thorn analyses the international anti-apartheid struggle as a significant modern international social movement linked to the internal struggle.[1] Chapters in this book explore these connections, illustrating interactions between global and local political ideologies and strategies. The struggle against apartheid took various forms and utilised different techniques. This paper considers one such technique – the focus on Nelson Mandela as a symbol of struggle. The focus on Mandela played a role in both the internal and external struggle and Mandela was instilled with a multitude of meanings. In the post-apartheid period Mandela was again adopted by a range of political groups to highlight aspects of the transition to post-apartheid South Africa. Some of the conflicting ways in which Mandela's name and image were appropriated are elaborated in chapters by Fana Sihlongonyane and Rebecca Hodes. This chapter focuses on how Mandela was used in international anti-apartheid campaigns in order to attract support for and solidarity with the struggle against apartheid. In Britain the Anti-Apartheid Movement (AAM), an organisation formed in 1960 consisting of both British citizens and South African exiles, ran an impressive campaign centring on Mandela and making him better known to the British public.[2] Wole Soyinka commented that Mandela's individual identity was subsumed by the many campaigns that made him into a struggle symbol.[3] I discuss the importance of the Mandela Campaign internationally and comment on some simultaneous developments within South Africa.

A central argument concerns the attempts by the AAM to broaden international support by emphasising human rights and de-emphasising the armed struggle. Political prisoners made Western governments, still tolerant of the South African regime, uneasy and a campaign based on rights and justice offered the possibility of broadening support. The African National Congress (ANC) and AAM were concerned about a cult of personality, but realised the value of humanising the abstract issues of the struggle and elevating recognisable personalities. In this way, they contributed to the iconography of Mandela as a central element of popular politics. Mandela's name boomeranged back and forth from South Africa to Europe, gaining recognition, adherents and moral force as his story was told.

The origins of the Mandela Campaign

Despite numerous studies analysing Mandela's rise to prominence, there is no clear consensus on either when or why he became a focal point of the struggle against apartheid.[4] However, a study of the AAM archives reveals that its focus on him only developed in the mid-1970s. The movement began to highlight political trials and prisoners in August 1962, when Mandela was arrested, and this strategy intensified during the Rivonia trial of 1963–64. In October 1963 members of the AAM, International Defence and Aid Fund (IDAF), Africa Bureau and Christian Action met to discuss a campaign around the Rivonia trial. They formed the World Campaign for the Release of South African Political Prisoners. A petition, organised to try and save the lives of the Rivonia accused, was handed to the United Nations (UN) with over 180,000 signatures. The committee succeeded in raising the profile of the trial and arguably played a role in saving the lives of the accused by internationalising the issue.[5] The World Campaign focused on all of the Rivonia accused, and while Mandela was publicised, especially as a result of his speech from the dock in which he explained the ANC's standpoints, he was not the sole concern of international activists.[6] After the conclusion of the Rivonia trial the World Campaign committee took up other political trials, but by the end of the decade it had all but ceased to exist, despite various attempts at its revival. AAM executive member Alan Brooks commented that he could not remember a single action for Mandela when he worked for the AAM from 1967 to 1970.[7]

Evidence obtained from scanning prominent newspapers affirms the view that initially Mandela received little international exposure. Anthony Sampson points out that while Mandela was mentioned 24 times in the *New York Times* of 1964, he then disappeared from the paper for the rest of the decade, except for 1967, when Winnie Mandela was mentioned.[8] According to the *Times* Digital Archive, that newspaper mentioned him 37 times in 1964, only five times in 1965 and twice in 1966. The number declined further in the early 1970s. A marked increase is clear in the 1980s, with 27 mentions of Mandela in 1980, 160 in 1985 and over 200 by the end of the decade. Furthermore, the publication of books with Mandela as the subject also suggests this shift in focus. The first two publications, both collections of Mandela's speeches, appeared in 1965 and 1978, i.e. over a decade apart.[9] It was only in the 1980s that full biographies were authored by Mary Benson and Fatima Meer.[10] Finally, the list of honours bestowed on Mandela again shows that he initially fell from the spotlight after Rivonia. In the 1960s and 1970s fewer than ten honours were bestowed on him, while in the 1980s the number rose rapidly with new honours accorded annually. In 1983 alone he received over 20.[11]

The revival of the international focus on South African political prisoners in general began in 1973. The impetus came from the ANC secretary general, Alfred Nzo, who approached E. S. Reddy, secretary of the UN Special Committee Against Apartheid, and suggested that the anniversary of the Rivonia arrests be observed. Reddy deemed it better to celebrate the tenth anniversary of the 11 October UN resolution – a more positive event that covered all the Rivonia accused. The UN General Assembly resolution, adopted in 1963, called on the South African government to abandon the Rivonia trial and to grant unconditional release to all political prisoners and other persons restricted for opposing apartheid.[12] The renewed focus on political prisoners in 1973 was also influenced by the trial of six ANC men for terrorist activity; a resolution at the International Trade Union Conference Against Apartheid; and a call by the UN Special Committee chairperson, Edwin Ogebe Ogbu.[13] The Durban strikes (see Brown's chapter in this volume) signalled a new urgency in internal protests.

The British AAM organised a conference on 8 December 1973 entitled Southern Africa: The Imprisoned Society, which in turn led to the formation of SATIS, a group focusing on political prisoners run under the auspices of the AAM with members from other interested groups.[14] Although SATIS focused on political prisoners in general, its formation led to increased concern about Mandela as an individual. The AAM found that student and local groups were particularly interested in his plight. Howard Smith, a student AAM member, explained how in the early 1970s, before the AAM and ANC elevated Mandela symbolically, there were moves among students to honour him.[15] The AAM's executive secretary, Mike Terry, remembered:

The first discussion I ever had about a campaign for Mandela's release was with two NUSAS [National Union of South African Students] leaders, Paul Pretorius and Neville Curtis, who came to London in 1971. Their idea was that NUSAS should try to do something on the primarily English-speaking campuses in South Africa, for the tenth anniversary of Mandela's arrest.[16]

This once again points to the prominent role initiatives from inside South Africa had on the international solidarity movement.

It was, however, only in the late 1970s that AAM political prisoner campaigns shifted towards Mandela. The call for his freedom came to symbolise the call for the release of all political prisoners.[17] The Soweto uprising and internal political developments again played a major role. Ellis and Sechaba suggest that the ANC emphasised Mandela (and the Freedom Charter) after 1976 in an attempt to re-establish itself internally in a period when the Black Consciousness Movement was winning widespread support.[18] Sampson argues that after Steve Biko's death in 1977 the international spotlight on Mandela increased from a human rights perspective.[19] Terry notes that the ANC and AAM realised that Black Consciousness could provide a rival opposition force and that by publicising Mandela's plight, the ANC could be placed centre stage.[20] The timing of the international Mandela Campaign supports this interpretation. The ANC and AAM felt it was more productive to work around one central figure than to try and explain ANC ideology and focus on all prisoners. Paradoxically, it was also at this point that internally Mandela and his colleagues received criticism. Many youths saw 'Mandela as respected but outdated, [Robert] Sobukwe as moderate, and [Oliver] Tambo as "exiled and irrelevant"'.[21] This analysis is supported by evidence of disagreements that occurred on Robben Island when the imprisoned Soweto youth arrived and by a 1978 West German survey that found that there was only 18 per cent support for Mandela in the country at that time.[22] The campaign never received support from all ANC elements. Some were concerned about highlighting one person when the ANC was a collective organisation; others viewed Mandela as insufficiently militant or worried about him selling out to the apartheid government.[23] The Mandela Campaign began at a juncture when the ANC needed to regain its prominence as the leading anti-apartheid movement. It was well aware of the importance of media in increasing its support base. The call for Mandela's release was neither radical nor contentious, and therefore attracted broad support, both inside South Africa and internationally. As the campaign for Mandela's release gained momentum inside South Africa, international solidarity increased.[24] The importance of the Mandela Campaign was its broad impact. Attempts at keeping the issue of apartheid and the name of the ANC alive in the period after the ANC was banned were not always successful, but the AAM soon realised that the Mandela Campaign was capturing international public interest in a sustained way. In the mid-1970s many international politicians, fearing the consequences of radical change in South Africa, were hostile to the ANC and the armed struggle. The Mandela Campaign effectively dealt with these fears by giving the ANC a moderate face. The campaign explained the movement's initial preference for peaceful protest and the limits on violence. It showed Mandela as intelligent, rational and moral rather than a terrorist, and publicised the ideals and aspirations of the ANC, thus providing assurance regarding the future of South Africa should the ANC come to power.

The Mandela Campaign also impacted on those inside South Africa. Political prisoners' morale was strengthened and the South African government recognised that it was losing the battle over international reputation. Gerald Kraak, a member of the group South African War Resisters, explained that

> with it you had the whole highlighting of the ANC ... starting off with the non-violent approach and being forced into an armed struggle [and] ... the non-racialism of the ANC, especially when the UDF [United Democratic Front] was formed – you know, the broader support for the ANC. So... Mandela [was used] as an emblem, as a symbol of the essence of what the ANC was about. It was a very powerful campaign.[25]

The start of the campaign, 1976-80

The change to the focus on Mandela, rather than prisoners in general, was gradual. ANC member and ex-Robben Island prisoner Mac Maharaj remembers that when he was in Britain in 1977 the focus was still 'all political prisoners'.[26] He also recalled suspicion among ANC exiles regarding Mandela selling out to the government, which he refuted at the time. These rumours persisted throughout the struggle and were not limited to people in exile.[27] It is difficult to understand why the Mandela Campaign was developed to such a large extent internationally, despite these views, although internally it was not as much of a systematic focus. By 1978, when the AAM organised celebrations for Mandela's 60th birthday, it was evident that he had become the focus of international prisoner campaigns. The initiative for the 1978 birthday celebrations came from Reddy, who discussed the idea with both Maharaj and ANC President Oliver Tambo. On Robben Island Walter Sisulu and Ahmed Kathrada encouraged this strategy.[28]

To publicise Mandela's birthday the AAM produced a pamphlet discussing Mandela's lifelong struggle to liberate South Africa and calling on British people to join the celebrations. The AAM stated that the international community should see the day as symbolising 'the courage and determination of the black people of South Africa to overthrow apartheid', making it clear that Mandela was being used to represent all those fighting apartheid. The AAM called Mandela the 'leader of South Africa's liberation movement', not only suggesting that the ANC was the only liberation movement, but assigning him a position that he did not formally hold.[29]

The 1978 campaign dwelt on Mandela's personal life and his leadership qualities. Pamphlets centred on his education, royal stature, profession and marriage to Winnie Mandela (who also played an important anti-apartheid role).[30] The AAM emphasised Mandela's importance by discussing his role in the formation of the ANC Youth League and in the ANC prior to its banning and his imprisonment. The Rivonia trial and the international attention it attracted were publicised along with Mandela's role in the formation of Umkhonto we Sizwe, although the armed struggle did not receive much attention. At the centre of the campaign was Mandela's picture. Nobody had up-to-date photos of him, and for this reason he became known, visually, through a few older images. Stylised images were also popularised.[31] Rob Nixon suggests that the South African government's attempt at making Mandela 'invisible' actually aided the Mandela Campaign. In the absence of new images, a few photos were reproduced continually and these, together with stylised imagery, created the iconic representations of an unchanging and rather youthful Mandela. The classic images of Che Guevara provide an analogy. The pictures provided a powerful visual reminder.[32]

The 60th birthday campaign aimed at broad, public support across the political divide. Over three thousand birthday cards were sent to Mandela, a sign of his growing prominence (see figure 5.1). A birthday card was signed by British cabinet members, and when the South African embassy refused to accept it, Labour Prime Minister James Callaghan sent greetings to Mandela from the floor of the House of Commons. This was the first instance of such an action and it was a major achievement for the AAM. The campaign also attracted media attention and the *Times* carried a report calling Mandela 'the colossus of African nationalism', reflecting a marked change to a few years earlier when he was all but forgotten or condemned as a terrorist.[33]

Figure 5.1: Birthday card using image from the IDAF publication

Source: 'Mandela Campaign, 1983, MSSAAM1910

Broadening the campaign, 1980-88

In the period 1980–82 the Mandela Campaign took form as one of the most important aspects of international anti-apartheid activism. On 9 March 1980 the Johannesburg newspaper the *Sunday Post*, catering primarily for a black readership, began a petition to free Mandela under the front-page headline 'South Africa's black spokesmen welcome convention call, but say first "Free Mandela"'. 'Free Mandela' was in large, bold print. The article was in reaction to two Afrikaans newspapers calling for a national convention in the wake of Robert Mugabe's election victory in Zimbabwe. Nthato Motlana, founding member of the Soweto Committee of Ten, and Inkatha leader Mangosuthu Buthelezi both replied that they welcomed a national convention, but only if it included leaders on Robben Island. Further preconditions were to allow all exiles to return unconditionally, to lift the bans on the ANC and Pan Africanist Congress, and to scrap apartheid. The men warned that with Zimbabwe's independence the liberation struggle would escalate. Other black commentators added their support to this view and Wilson Skosana of the Port Elizabeth Black Civic Association (PEBCO) stated that '[t]here are many black spokesmen who do not represent our aspirations and the only person we can be confident in is Nelson Mandela and other leaders imprisoned with him.'[34]

Alongside the article was a call from the *Sunday Post* to sign its petition. The call stated that 'Nelson Mandela commands a following that is unheard of in this land'. Editor Percy Qoboza stated that 'surveys have shown beyond any shadow of doubt that by far the largest percentage of our people still regard Nelson Mandela as the number one leader of our people'. The newspaper stressed the need for all political prisoners, not only those in the ANC, to be released.[35] Sampson and Mandela both describe the *Sunday Post* campaign as initiated by the ANC in Lusaka.[36] Nevertheless, it had the effect of placing Mandela centre stage in the internal media.

The *Sunday Post* continued the focus on Mandela in its following issue and carried a barometer showing that 1,225 signatures in support of the petition were received in the first five days. It followed up with an article where Zinzi Mandela called for the release of her father, another editorial on Mandela and a feature on 'The struggle is his life'. This coverage correlated closely with similar publicity by the AAM.[37] By 23 March 13,113 signatures had been collected and the International Commission of Jurists sent a cable to President P. W. Botha asking him to release Mandela. Qoboza noted that support also came from white South Africans, with about 140 posting petitions and others demonstrating their support as signatories during street collections. The petition received coverage, some critical, in the white press.[38]

By 30 March 1980 support for the petition stood at 21,890, according to the front-page barometer. The paper reported support from Transkei leader George Matanzima and the British Labour Party. Qoboza warned that some people might use the petition to publicise their own importance and he called for a focus on the real issues.[39] On 6 April the paper welcomed the revival of guerrilla actions inside the country. A front-page article reported that '[t]he ANC assault on the Booysens police station on Friday was the biggest since the movement's guerrillas began operations in this country … [they] left behind leaflets demanding the release of Nelson Mandela and Walter Sisulu'. The paper commented that the police were linking the newspaper's Free Mandela campaign with the attack on the police station, a link that Qoboza considered tenuous. The newspaper faced increased government persecution as a result of its coverage.[40] By June the barometer stood at 59,029 signatures.[41]

It is clear that the *Sunday Post* campaign attracted widespread support inside South Africa. Mandela committees were formed across the country and endorsement came from various political persuasions, including the South African Council of Churches and Allan Boesak, PEBCO, the coloured Labour Party, Desmond Tutu (black Anglican archbishop of Cape Town) and prominent white figures.[42] The *Sunday Post* call provided the unique opportunity for international action in support of an internal campaign. The UN Special Committee issued a press statement supporting Mandela's release and the issue was brought before the UN. Both the Security Council and General Assembly specifically mentioned Mandela in their calls for the release of political prisoners in June and December 1980, respectively.[43] The issue was raised in the British House of Commons in April, and while the new Margaret Thatcher government, which assumed power in May 1979, welcomed his release, it rejected pressuring Pretoria.[44]

The AAM believed that support for the Mandela Campaign from outside of South Africa was of the utmost importance. Mike Terry met with, among others, John Collins (IDAF) and Yeyedwa Zungu (ANC) in April to discuss a short, intensive campaign for May and June 1980. He proposed that the AAM and IDAF work together to publicise Mandela's plight and increase international support for the internal campaign.[45] In May SATIS forwarded a memorandum to the ANC proposing prolonged international mobilisation with an official launch on 11 October. The ANC responded positively and, after Tambo gave his support, the campaign grew quickly in size and stature. The ANC, AAM, IDAF and SATIS discussed in detail what actions each organisation should coordinate.[46] Further meetings were organised with the UN Special Committee and an initial launch took place in August with Yusuff Maitama-Sule, the UN Special Committee chairperson (1981–83). The UN and AAM worked closely, recognising the need for the use of similar logos across different nations (see figure 5.2). The involvement of the UN Committee was of particular importance due to its international links and access to finance. Terry and Reddy were in frequent contact and on occasion the AAM received financial support from the UN.[47]

In 1982 Mandela and some of his colleagues were transferred from Robben Island to Pollsmoor Prison in Cape Town without warning. This was considered a sign of the success of the Mandela Campaign, which had made Robben Island another symbol of apartheid oppression. The AAM began to publicise the conditions in Pollsmoor Prison and objected to Mandela's loss of certain privileges.[48]

Following the success of using Mandela's birthday in raising awareness, the AAM and ANC coordinated celebrations of his 65th birthday in 1983. Two points of focus

Figure 5.2: AAM Mandela logo for correspondence/merchandise
Source: 'Mandela Campaign, 1983', MSSAAM1910.

were the Festival of African Sounds on 17 June and the Free Mandela Concert at
Queen Elizabeth Hall, London on 26 June (see figure 5.3), both organised with outside
assistance. The Festival of African Sounds was reviewed in the *New Musical Express*,
a breakthrough for the AAM in reaching a new popular audience. Hugh Masekela
performed at the concert and later wrote of Tambo's desire to promote Mandela
internationally as a symbol.[49] Mandela's birthday was commemorated in the House of
Commons with a motion calling for his release and conveying greetings to him. Local
AAM groups arranged activities and the Camden Council in London proposed and set
in motion the renaming of Selous Street, where the AAM office was located, to Mandela
Street, which was finalised in 1984.[50]

Figure 5.3: Poster for the 1983 Mandela birthday concert
Source: *Anti-Apartheid News,* June 1983

The AAM became increasingly aware that British popular culture was receptive to its Mandela Campaign. A high point in 1984 was the release of the single 'Nelson Mandela' by the Two-Tone/Ska Punk group The Specials. While the AAM did not suggest this initiative, it provided its address and information about apartheid, Mandela and the ANC to use on the record sleeve. The song reached an impressive number nine on the British charts, prompting hundreds of letters from young people who bought the record and wanted to become involved with the struggle. The AAM prepared an information pack for all respondents. Most requests came from Britain, although there were also international requests. The majority of these came from the United States, where many complained about apathy regarding apartheid. The release of the single emphasised the effect of popular music in extending awareness to the younger generation. This was important for the AAM, which sought to gain support from those beyond organised politics. Both the ANC and UN Special Committee congratulated The Specials and songwriter Jerry Dammers.[51]

Another achievement in 1984 was the South African government's offer to Mandela of conditional release. The condition was that he accept citizenship of the Xhosa homeland, Transkei. This would, in effect, show his acceptance of the Bantustan system, which the ANC rejected. Mandela refused release. The AAM interpreted the offer as a sign of the impact of the campaign. It began to focus on unconditional release and increased pressure on the British government. Further success was achieved when Thatcher raised Mandela's release with Botha during his visit to Britain, but she refused to announce his response.[52] A second offer of conditional release was made the following year. This time Botha called on Mandela to renounce violence, hoping to regain the moral high ground by publicising the fact that Mandela and the ANC propagated an armed struggle. He believed it would either destroy Mandela's image internationally if he did not reject violence or separate him from the ANC if he did. Botha made the offer publicly, and Mandela reacted with a public statement. Zinzi read his response at a UDF rally in Soweto on 10 February 1985. Mandela called on Botha to renounce violence first, and called for the unbanning of the ANC and dismantling of apartheid. His response received the support of the masses, was circulated by the AAM and clearly linked Mandela to the ANC.[53] Botha's attempt to destroy Mandela's image failed and instead support for his release increased. By mid-1985 the international community was almost unanimous in its support for Mandela's release, and even Thatcher indicated her support for his unconditional release in a letter to the AAM president, Trevor Huddleston.[54] The UN Security Council, the European Economic Community and South African business leaders all expressed support for Mandela.[55]

Despite Mandela's refusal of Botha's 1985 offer, the year also witnessed the start of the process to initiate talks between the government and Mandela. While Mandela was in hospital, he was visited by Minister of Justice Kobie Coetsee. Mandela had previously sent a letter to Coetsee suggesting a meeting, but had received no response. After Mandela left hospital he was returned to Pollsmoor Prison, but was placed in a separate section. He saw this as an opportunity for contact with the government.[56] Faced with a more general insurrection (see Simpson's chapter in this volume) the government began real discussions with Mandela in 1987. Before taking this step, Mandela informed his imprisoned colleagues and Tambo in Lusaka. He also made direct contact with Botha, sending him a memorandum on his views and those of the ANC.[57]

Meanwhile, action in support of Mandela continued both internationally and inside South Africa. The Eminent Persons' Group (EPG) was formed by the Commonwealth heads of state at the Nassau summit in October 1985 as a compromise with Thatcher, who rejected sanctions. The group visited South Africa in mid-1986, aiming to bring about dialogue. After its visit to South Africa the EPG released a report stating that it had met with Mandela and found he was a 'unifying, commanding and popular leader' and an 'essential and heroic figure in any political settlement in South Africa'.[58] In August 1986 Boesak organised a march to Pollsmoor Prison. He was arrested before the march and demonstrators were attacked by police. In the following year the South African National Free Mandela organisation was established with support from civics, students and trade unions. Police repression of activities related to Mandela continued.[59]

Thus, by the end of 1987 the international and internal Mandela campaigns were well developed and many more people were aware of and understood the plight of political prisoners. World leaders lent their support to the campaign and bodies across the world began to offer their support to Mandela and the ANC. The campaign succeeded in giving the ANC a human face. However, while support for Mandela was considerable, it was only in 1988 that mass mobilisation was achieved internationally.

Freedom at Seventy Campaign: A tribute to Nelson Mandela

The Freedom at Seventy Campaign, so called in the hope that Mandela would be free by his 70th birthday, mobilised British youth on a scale previously unrivalled. Its impact reverberated beyond Britain, even into South Africa. The campaign failed in its basic aim – to free Mandela by his 70th birthday – but succeeded on a deeper level in attracting mass support from new sectors of the population for the struggle against apartheid and for the ANC.[60]

Planning began in 1987, and decisions were made in close consultation with the ANC and the Mandela family, largely through Mandela's lawyer, Ismail Ayob.[61] The campaign consisted of four key elements, and while these remained in place throughout the year, they were adapted and supplemented as necessary. The first was the Tribute Concert at Wembley Stadium on 11 June, followed by a Glasgow rally on 12 June that launched the Mandela Freedom March. The Freedom March proceeded from Glasgow to London and ended with a rally on 17 July in Hyde Park. Mandela's birthday on 18 July was celebrated with local events across the country.[62] Merchandising was recognised as an important aspect of the campaign and had the dual function of increasing awareness about Mandela and the AAM, while also raising funds for the AAM. The AAM brought in external support for the funding, design and sale of Mandela tribute merchandise and used mainstream sales techniques such as mail order and placing products in retail outlets, including Virgin Stores. The AAM recognised that the more interest generated in Mandela, the more effective these sales would be and understood the potential of penetrating the fashion industry. Merchandise included the concert programme, T-shirts (see figure 5.4), badges, posters and pamphlets. The choice of merchandise shows the focus on attracting the youth – especially badges, which were very popular at the time and which the AAM even gave away. Shirts with Mandela's image became fashion items.[63]

Figure 5.4: Design of the Mandela T-shirt sold at the concert

Source: Mandela souvenir programme

In order to ascertain the overall effect of the campaign on the British population, the AAM commissioned a Gallup poll conducted from 29 June to 5 July 1988. A total of 1,929 people were questioned, of whom 797 were Conservative Party supporters,

673 Labour supporters and 147 Liberals. The poll asked questions on British government policy, Thatcher's stance in respect of South Africa, and Mandela. Of those asked, 92 per cent knew who Mandela was, and of these 77 per cent knew about his prison conditions and that he came from South Africa and 70 per cent supported his release, while only 10 per cent opposed it. Only 3 per cent of Labourites opposed his release, while 59 per cent of Conservatives supported it. In the age group 16–24 years, 76 per cent supported his release.[64] This suggests the broad political support the campaign attracted, as well as its success in generating support from the youth.

The Tribute Concert

The concert was initially the idea of Artists Against Apartheid, a group formed in 1986 by Dammers and Oliver Tambo's son, Dali. Dammers approached Tony Hollingsworth of Elephant House Productions (which worked on producing Glastonbury festivals) in late 1986 to plan a concert the following summer. The concert never materialised, but some artists expressed a willingness to participate. In October 1987 Huddleston and Terry said they were 'enthusiastic [about] and grateful' for the initiative and would like to go ahead with the event. Simple Minds expressed its commitment as long as no money went towards armaments. In November Huddleston wrote to Peter Gabriel and Sting explaining the concert.[65] The AAM was confident that the concert would go ahead, considering it had guaranteed backing from one big name.

The AAM chose 11 June (as the stadium was already booked for 18 July) to mark 25 years in prison for those convicted at Rivonia. It was the first major activity in its Freedom at Seventy Campaign. The concert was a 'tribute' and not a 'Free Mandela' concert in order to attract broader political support.[66] Money was to be divided between agencies in southern Africa and the AAM, and Huddleston supervised the allocation and selected the recipients. Laister Dickson, an international press and public relations firm that specialised in the entertainment industry, was chosen as the public relations company. The AAM aimed to make the concert as professional as possible.[67] After the line-up was announced the British Broadcasting Corporation (BBC) expressed an interest in broadcasting the event. The AAM realised that television and radio coverage would transform its capacity to reach an international audience. The AAM entered into negotiations with international stations and the scale of the event grew. Hollingsworth explained that

> 67 countries, on main broadcasters, watched an event around the Anti-Apartheid issue for 11 and a half hours. Amongst those countries were some very large ones

– the USSR ... India. That broadcast, still to this day, holds the ratings record for any, in television terms, entertainment event. The ratings for that show are only superseded, nowadays, by the collective mass of the Olympics on their opening ceremony.[68]

The planned BBC broadcast was criticised by the likes of Conservative MP John Carlisle as a political event that exceeded the organisation's remit. The South African government issued a statement and the South African embassy approached the BBC about the broadcast and the use of funds raised. The government commented on a series of car bomb atrocities by the ANC and linked the concert with the armed struggle.[69] The BBC's response emphasised that the broadcast was for musical and not political reasons.[70] If anything, the controversy led to greater media coverage.

The line-up for the concert was impressive and at the time of the launch included Simple Minds, Dire Straits, Sly and Robbie, Whitney Houston, Hugh Masekela, Miriam Makeba and Harry Belafonte.[71] It included black artists renowned for their anti-apartheid views, such as the latter four, and more-mainstream English and American stars who appealed to a wider audience. As momentum grew other big names joined, including the Eurythmics, Tracy Chapman, Chrissie Hynde, Billy Connolly, Joan Armatrading, UB40, George Michael, the Bee Gees, Phil Collins, Midge Ure, Paul Young, Jessye Norman and Whoopi Goldberg. This made it the largest international television and radio event since Live Aid, exceeding ten hours.[72] The Tribute Concert was to some extent fashioned on Live Aid – staged at Wembley and simultaneously in Philadelphia in the United States in 1985. The main difference was that Live Aid aimed at raising money for famine relief in Africa, while the Mandela concert aimed at mobilisation and political awareness.[73] The organisers wanted to demonstrate to the South African government the level of international support for the struggle. The AAM measured its success by the number of people who knew about Mandela rather than the amount of money raised.[74] It is interesting to note that Live8, held in 2005, also aimed at awareness and tickets were given away. The tradition of Mandela's image being used in combination with music to generate both popular and financial support continues today as seen in the 4664 concerts to raise awareness about HIV/AIDS and the Make Poverty History Campaign.

The Tribute Concert was generally popular, and the AAM received hundreds of letters of congratulations and support from organisations and people who attended or watched the concert on television. However, there was also some criticism. One problem was a lack of time. The concert ran over time and addresses by Huddleston and Winnie Mandela were cut short. People interpreted this as the AAM reducing political content due to BBC interference. There were also rumours, denied by the AAM, that it asked entertainers not to make political comments.[75] Criticism of the event also came from the City of London Anti-Apartheid Group (CLAAG), a London-based group that disagreed with some of the tactics of the AAM and complained that the AAM stifled debate and ignored opposing views. CLAAG was not the only anti-apartheid grouping in Britain that found the AAM to be sectarian and opposed to debate, and there was also tension regarding support for non-aligned South African trade unions.[76] In this instance CLAAG complained that the AAM dropped a profile of Mandela from the design for political reasons, while the AAM explained that it was due to space constraints.[77] It seems unlikely in this case that the move was political, considering the focus of the concert was Mandela and the plethora of Mandela images at the concert.[78]

A significant achievement was coverage in a wide range of newspapers, most commenting positively on the concert. Articles appeared in, among others, the *Guardian, Sun, Evening Telegraph, Sounds, Daily Post, Star, Time Out, Evening Post, Tribune, New Musical Express, Daily Mirror, Herald Tribune*, and local and regional papers. Articles also appeared in international papers and magazines such as *Newsweek* and in South African newspapers. This suggests that the concert also impacted on those inside South Africa fighting apartheid.[79]

The Mandela Freedom March

The Mandela Freedom March consisted of 25 marchers, representing 25 years in prison, and stretched from Glasgow to London. It took the Freedom at Seventy Campaign to different parts of Britain, visiting over 40 towns and cities, and involving local groups. The march was the longest political march in Britain at the time, covering 590 miles in five weeks.[80]

Glasgow was selected as the starting point because it was the first city to offer Mandela freedom of the city and Glasgow University had elected Winnie Mandela as its rector. The march began the day after the Wembley concert with a rally attracting 15,000 supporters. Tambo attended the rally and personally greeted each of the marchers.[81] The AAM aimed to generate wide support by focusing on less controversial issues.[82] Support for the ANC was, however, expressed through the portrayal of Mandela, speakers, the ANC flag, and selected songs such as '*Nkosi sikelel' iAfrika*'. Events along the route of the march were arranged in cooperation with local anti-apartheid groups. The AAM encouraged local councils and influential people to participate in sections of the march or to appear in press reports and photos. Numerous schools got involved and in Manchester 100 school children sang the ANC anthem. Public participation along the way and the many requests for information reflected growing support for the AAM in new areas. A 'freedom bus' accompanied marchers along the route and provided both a visible advertisement for the AAM and transport for merchandise, first aid and necessities.[83]

There were no major problems along the route and in most areas marchers were well received. At Rochdale there were some protesters, but more often there was spontaneous support. The AAM viewed the march as a success, although internal discussions revealed criticism over the limited number of places visited. Winnie Mandela wrote:

> We greatly appreciate and are extremely proud of the marchers who have identified themselves with our struggle. I think it is extremely significant for them to identify and isolate the twenty five years of the imprisonment of our leaders: that is a gesture which puts not only the African National Congress on the international map, but the cause of our people and what the African National Congress stands for and what is embodied in that sacrosanct document the Freedom Charter ... Mandela stands out as a symbol of resistance and stands out as that symbol which each and every one of us who believes in our freedom identifies with.[84]

The 17 July Hyde Park rally

The height of the campaign was the rally at Hyde Park, which was the final point on the Mandela March and a Mandela Cycle was organised to coincide with the end of the march. It consisted of 11 cyclists cycling 400 miles from Lands End, the southernmost tip of the British Isles, to London. Thousands of supporters joined the marchers and cyclists for the last leg of the march from Finsbury Park to Hyde Park. The AAM publicised this rather than the concert as the focal event because it was more political, catered for more people and was free.[85]

The Finsbury Park rally was a short event where the crowd was encouraged to march towards Hyde Park. Bernie Grant (one of three black British MPs at the time) addressed the crowd. The AAM ran an information stall and collected money at the gates to cover costs and expand membership. Badges and placards were available, and people were encouraged to buy what they wanted, as no stalls were allowed at Hyde Park. On entering Hyde Park police ensured the lowering of banners and placards, which caused some problems, as AAM supporters complained that other demonstrations were allowed placards.[86] The Mandela marchers, followed by representatives from the liberation movements, led the procession, followed by local anti-apartheid groups, black and ethnic minority groups, trade unions, women's movements, student unions, and, finally, political party representatives.[87]

Robert Hughes, AAM chairperson and Labour MP (who was later appointed to the House of Lords), chaired the Hyde Park rally, which began with a video on apartheid. Addresses and performances at the rally tried to combine the political and popular. Messages by prominent people were interspersed with performances by Jonas Gwangwa, Jerry Dammers and Simple Minds. Aside from speeches by AAM executive members Abdul Minty (honorary secretary) and Huddleston, political messages came from Desmond Tutu, Shridath Ramphal (Commonwealth secretary general), Toivo ja Toivo (South West Africa Peoples' Organisation leader previously imprisoned on Robben Island) and the ANC chief representative in Britain, Mendi Msimang. Video messages from Winnie and Zinzi Mandela were broadcast and the day ended with the singing of 'Nkosi Sikelel' iAfrika'.[88]

The day ran smoothly, despite logistical problems. It was the biggest political rally ever organised by the AAM and numbers at Hyde Park exceeded expectations, with about 250,000 at its height. There was wide international press coverage. The rally was followed by a late night vigil outside the South African embassy to mark the start of Mandela's birthday. By midnight there were a few hundred supporters and the ANC choir sang, while a banner saying 'Happy birthday Nelson Mandela' was displayed.[89] However, while feedback regarding the event as a whole was positive, there were complaints about the vigil. Jennifer Smith of Battersea complained that when she arrived at South Africa House there were no AAM representatives. CLAAG was demonstrating outside the embassy, as they had been non-stop for 821 days. Smith joined the demonstration, which she felt had a good atmosphere of unity and understanding with songs, different speakers and people listening to each other with respect. She complained that things changed when AAM representatives arrived, who tried to take over the vigil and drown out CLAAG. They sang over everybody else, demanded that CLAAG stop making speeches and eventually asked for a police barrier dividing the groups. Smith was disappointed by this division within the struggle. A similar letter of complaint came from Debbie McConnell, who felt the AAM representatives were only at the vigil for a short period. The CLAAG non-stop picket of South Africa House began in April 1986 and was criticised by the AAM for its confrontational approach, which, it argued, caused problems for both the AAM and ANC.[90]

Figure 5.5: Mandela 70th birthday memento card distributed in Britain by the ANC

Final campaigning for Mandela's release, 1988-90

By the end of the Freedom at Seventy Campaign, support for Mandela's release had increased considerably. The AAM stated in its annual report that the campaign 'demonstrated the capacity of the worldwide anti-apartheid movement to determine the international agenda and thereby demonstrably influence the politics of governments throughout the world'.[91] In May 1988 Mandela met with a government committee, and meetings continued on an irregular basis over the next months, normally at the government's initiative, but sometimes at Mandela's request. In these meetings issues such as the ANC's history, the armed struggle, relations with the Communist Party and majority rule were discussed. Preparations were made for Mandela to meet with Botha, but after Mandela fell ill talks were delayed.[92]

In October 1988 the AAM began a campaign sparked off by reports that Mandela had tuberculosis and was in danger of dying. The AAM arranged an emergency advertisement in the *Observer* calling for his immediate release and emphasising the need for extra pressure on the South African government. The AAM called on Thatcher to intervene and asked people to add their names to a second advertisement in the *Observer*. Over 400 influential leaders and organisations responded. A second petition for 27 November was organised with an alternative text, as the AAM expected Mandela to be released before then. A similar declaration was translated into other languages and the AAM received over 10,000 signatures. British MPs from all political parties drew up their own petition expressing alarm at Mandela's illness, their belief in the humanitarian and political urgency for Mandela's release, and their opposition to apartheid. They called on Thatcher to act immediately to ensure the release of South African political prisoners.[93]

The AAM began preparations for Mandela's release and the South African government announced that Mandela would not return to Pollsmoor after his hospitalisation, fanning rumours of his planned release. Instead he was moved to Victor Verster Prison in Paarl.[94] Discussions between Mandela and the government continued and Mandela met with colleagues and UDF members. It was, however, not until July 1989 that he met with Botha. The following month Botha stepped down as president and was replaced by F. W. de Klerk.[95] In the wake of rumours of Mandela's imminent release, Huddleston suggested forming a Nelson Mandela International Reception Committee to cooperate with the internal National Reception Committee. He suggested membership of prominent African leaders, including Kenneth Kaunda, Robert Mugabe, Julius Nyerere and Olusegun Obasanjo. The formation was coordinated by, among others, Tambo and Cyril Ramaphosa (general secretary of the National Union of Mineworkers, who was prominent in the internal reception committee).[96] The international committee was formed in January 1990, followed by similar groups in 27 countries, and the British branch remained closely linked to the AAM.[97]

On 2 February 1990 De Klerk announced the unbanning of the ANC and other movements; the imminent release of political prisoners, including Mandela; and the end of the state of emergency. This marked a major turning point in the struggle for democracy in South Africa. Mandela was released on 11 February. Wide media coverage meant that people worldwide watched him walking, together with Winnie Mandela, out of Victor Verster Prison. He proceeded to a huge rally at the Grand Parade, Cape Town, where thousands of supporters awaited him. Over the next months Mandela addressed crowds across South Africa and across the world as his release was celebrated and steps were taken to bring about an end to apartheid.[98] In a telephone call he expressed his gratitude to the AAM:

Friends, the solid support we have received from the AAM throughout the years has not only been a source of real inspiration to us all but has also put the struggle for a non-racial South Africa on a level never seen before. My release was the direct result of the people inside and outside South Africa. It was a result of the immense pressure exerted against the South African government by the international community in particular from the people of the UK.[99]

Conclusion

In post-apartheid South Africa Mandela's image continues to be recreated. In the transition and its immediate aftermath he came to represent the new nation and embody reconciliation. Due to the role he played in South Africa's transition he came to be seen as a mediator for other conflicts. Despite problems in his ANC-led government, Mandela's messianic image remained largely intact. While he did come under criticism from some quarters, especially as a result of slow change, criticism was more often directed at the government.[100] However, as problems continue to plague South Africa, growing concern around the extent and nature of change brought about in the 1990s is once again drawing the focus to Mandela. In this context his image needs further analysis and more critical consideration, and the symbolic and cultural contestations generated by his representation are explored at greater length in the chapters by Hodes and Sihlongonyane in this volume. Most recently, the ANC recognised how it could use Mandela's 90th birthday 'to reconnect with the masses' before the 2009 election.[101] In the lead-up to the 2009 election Mandela was again used by the ANC, now led by Jacob Zuma, to garner mass support and to try and dispel any allegations that the ANC had changed from the days when it was led by Tambo or Mandela. Once again, Mandela was used to try and quell fears of what to expect from the ANC-led government.

The campaign around Mandela was effective in increasing international support for his release and in making South Africa and apartheid more topical internationally. The campaign helped to establish Mandela internationally as a leader and important figure in the future of South Africa. This led to international leaders feeling more certain about what to expect regarding a change of government in South Africa. The image of the ANC, in turn, changed as Mandela was portrayed as a rational, forgiving figure, a man of royal lineage with a degree in law, as well as a family man. His image was thus recreated and reworked while he was in prison, and his legitimacy as leader of South Africa established. This was achieved despite the fact that he was unable to develop this image himself, while the fact that he was out of the public eye may have aided the campaign. As international pressure increased, the South African government realised that its propaganda had failed. Mandela's release became a necessary prelude to real change in South Africa. At the same time, the government made use of his influential position to initiate discussions.

Internally, the Free Mandela Campaign also attracted broad support and provided a vehicle to unite different political groupings. As demonstrated, critical initiatives in the call for his release were taken within South Africa and some of the images of Mandela travelled across international boundaries. However, the campaign never became as integral a part of the struggle inside the country and some people harboured suspicions about Mandela selling out. There was always some tension over Mandela's position, especially during the negotiations and after he acceded to political power. Mandela meant different things to different people. To some he signified armed struggle, to others an option for peaceful change, and to others a voice of reason in the ANC leadership. The campaign not only elevated Mandela, but played a role in legitimising the ANC as representative of the majority of the people of South Africa, justifying armed struggle, and thus helping to bring about an end to apartheid.

From removals to reform: Land struggles in Weenen in KwaZulu-Natal, South Africa

Chizuko Sato

Introduction

Land activism and land reform were key sites of struggle during the years of transition in South Africa. Segregation and apartheid had barred land ownership by black people in many parts of the country and had gradually eroded their access to rural resources. While South Africa's liberation movements were not primarily rooted in the rural areas, many activists came from this background and rural politics and non-governmental organisations (NGOs) produced important popular leaders. New local struggles gave voice to communities that had been politically marginalised. But land struggles sometimes proved to be divisive, reinforcing old conflicts as much as creating new movements. Sustained regional organisation on the land was often more difficult than in the townships.

This chapter discusses the quest for land reform by African farm tenants and labourers in the district of Weenen in mid-western KwaZulu-Natal (KZN). Weenen is a small district of 628 square kilometres and had a total population of 14,000 in 1980.[1] Unfavourable agricultural conditions in the area, together with its location off major highways, limited the development of modern commercial farming and irrigation. Most farms in Weenen were white owned, but many historically accommodated a large number of African tenant families. Under the labour tenancy system, African tenants worked for farmers for six months of the year in exchange for their right to reside, cultivate certain plots and graze their livestock on the farms of their employers. This system, originating in the nineteenth-century colonial period, was associated with less-intensive agricultural practices and ran counter to the ideology and policy of apartheid. It was finally outlawed in the district in 1969 and an estimated 10,000 people were evicted from farms in the next few years. The majority of them were relocated to closer settlement villages at Tugela Estates on land administered by the South African Development Trust, adjoining the KwaZulu district of Msinga.[2] The abolition of labour tenancy, however, did not completely eradicate African farm tenancy, nor did it stop farm evictions. Sporadic evictions continued and racial tension over land increased in many parts of this district after 1969.

The deeply rooted struggles by African labour tenants to stay on the land during the apartheid era were quickly transformed into overt land demands after 1994. Local communities in Weenen actively lobbied the new government and its minister of land affairs, Derek Hanekom. Their land struggles bore fruit in the form of a land reform pilot programme under the post-apartheid government: within KZN as a whole, Weenen was an initial focus area for the land redistribution programme. This is one reason why it is important to study popular protest and land reform in the district.

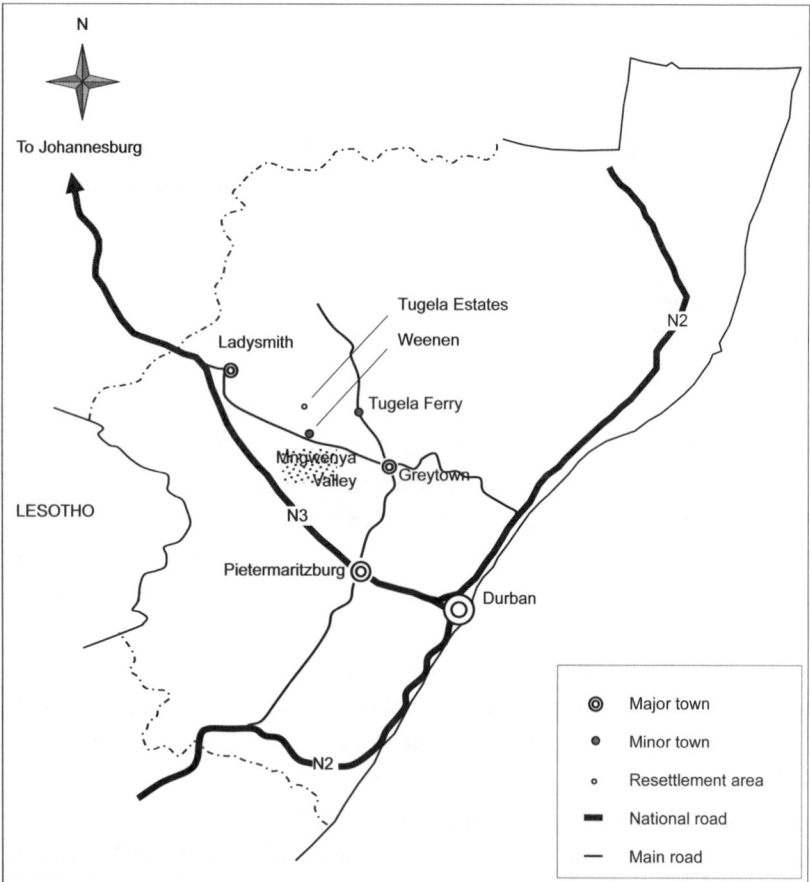

Map 1: KwaZulu-Natal

The principal focus of this chapter is to describe local struggles over land in Weenen district from the early 1980s. It seeks to examine the nature of land demands and the characteristics of local leaders, as well as their interaction with outside organisations. I will show that the tenacity of ingenious local leaders, together with their connections to white liberal groups and NGOs, combined to make land reform in Weenen possible in the very early stages of the political transition in South Africa. Liberal organisations were not deeply embedded in rural African communities in Weenen, nor were they directly involved in mobilising farm tenants. But their assistance in providing legal help, publicity and visibility was important in making the tenants' case heard. This case study points again to the complexity and potential significance of political alliances between grassroots organisations and activists engaging at the national level.

The early cases of land reform in KZN were driven by committed local leadership with a strong sense of justice and entitlement to land. Historical grievances and animosities felt by black communities in Weenen towards white farmers underlay their actions. However, their success was soon followed by division. Land reform revealed diverse economic and political aspirations among new local leaders. Some saw land reform as an opportunity to enhance their status and influence within the community. While old conflicts between white farmers and African farm tenants eased, new conflicts surfaced between African politicians that threatened the progress of land reform. In the latter part of the chapter, I will shed some light on the question of the sustainability and viability of land reform policies that principally aimed to redress past injustice.

Seeking local solutions in the late apartheid period

Farm tenants and labourers in Weenen had long attempted to defend their position on the land. This discussion begins in the early 1980s when the government introduced stricter conservation measures on certain farms in the district. It resulted in a new spate of farm evictions that heightened local tension between white and black communities. By this time key local leaders and supporting organisations were already involved in land conflicts in the district. They pressurised the Natal Provincial Administration (NPA), which was known as a conservative institution, to look for an alternative to farm evictions in the district. This section discusses the emergence of different local forces that paved a way to local negotiations for land reform in Weenen.

The enactment of the Conservation of Agricultural Resources Act in 1983 put renewed pressure on white farmers in the Weenen district to comply with conservation measures. Tenants and their livestock made compliance very difficult. This in practice meant that farmers who accommodated a large number of African tenants as a labour force had to evict them so that the veld could recover. The main target of the Act was the Mngwenya valley in the south-east of Weenen, where a large number of African tenants lived on 'labour farms'. The valley was also the base of a local community organisation called the Weenen Community Project (WECOP), founded in about 1979–80. The identity of the original founder of WECOP is uncertain, but it was led for 20 years by Johannes Mbuso Sosibo, who was born and grew up on a farm in the Mngwenya valley.[3] According to Sosibo, he was inspired by Neil Alcock to form a self-help organisation fighting against evictions of African farm tenants in his area. Alcock was a liberal activist who ran an agricultural development project called the Church Agricultural Project (CAP) in Weenen from 1975. After setting up the CAP on highly eroded, white-owned farms in the north-eastern corner of the Weenen district bordering Msinga, Alcock began holding informal meetings with African communities about local agricultural problems. Sosibo was one of the first participants at these meetings.

Sosibo was an authentic local leader. At the same time he was always eager to seek assistance from outside organisations and was very flexible in choosing whom to work with. He sought support from Inkatha, as well as from the Association for Rural Advancement (AFRA), a Pietermaritzburg-based NGO supporting rural communities threatened by removals. This makes it difficult to analyse his ideological standpoint. In the early 1980s he acted as a regional secretary of Inkatha in the area, hoping that the KwaZulu homeland government might be able to help in the fight against evictions. However, the amicable relationship with Inkatha did not last long.[4] Sosibo believes that this was due to his increasing appearances in newspaper articles and his blunt criticism of farm evictions. His interactions with Alcock and activists in AFRA gave him increasing opportunities to speak to journalists about the hardships of farm tenants in Weenen and he enjoyed the publicity.[5] This style of protest through the media was not welcomed by the KwaZulu government, who told him to 'go on proper channels, not on newspapers'.[6]

Sosibo's working relationship with AFRA started soon after it was formed in 1979. In fact, the formation of AFRA by activists in Pietermaritzburg was a response to the alarm raised by Alcock about the escalating farm evictions in Weenen. The provision of assistance to African tenants in Weenen who were threatened with immediate evictions was the initial focus of AFRA's activity. By the mid-1980s Sosibo and AFRA became important partners. AFRA tried to formalise WECOP by assisting Sosibo to draft a constitution for the organisation.[7] Sosibo was one of the very few labour tenants of his generation in Weenen who had received a relatively good education. His fluency in English was a great advantage for both him and AFRA. For a decade both sides offered each other mutual benefits. Sosibo provided an entry point for AFRA into the labour tenant community in the Mngwenya valley, while AFRA increased Sosibo's credentials as a community leader and his capacity to publicise the tenants' plight.

Sosibo's ambition did not stop at being a local leader for a self-help organisation like WECOP, nor at seeking assistance from outside organisations to stop farm evictions. From the early 1980s he wrote a series of essays on the state of farm evictions in the Mngwenya valley and in some of them recollected his meetings with Weenen government commissioners.[8] He later sent his handwritten essays to AFRA and a Johannesburg-based publisher, requesting that they be published.[9] His essays included truth and rumour, historical material from books and newspapers combined with his own memory, and evaluation of the events and allegations. Historical events and fictitious incidents are mixed in his writings, but they are valuable in telling us about his perception of what was happening on the Weenen farms. One persistent argument in his writings was that the ultimate solution for the African tenants in the Mngwenya valley lay in the valley itself. Sosibo repeatedly refers to 'the promised 24 farms'. According to him, in September 1976 the then commissioner of Weenen promised to give African tenants 24 farms in the district and that these would 'end all kind of misery and grievances'.[10] Five years later Sosibo wrote a letter to the Weenen commissioner reminding him of this promise. His letter was read out at a regular quarterly meeting with the commissioner, attended by an unusually high number of about 370 people. Those who were present at the meeting unanimously supported the letter, and *indunas*, representing three chieftaincy groups in the district, corroborated the old promise of 24 farms.[11] Although the 24 farms never materialised, this promise became a basis for the black community's request for specific white-owned labour farms to be transferred to them.

In the late 1980s, when, in accordance with the new Conservation Act, farmers began evicting African tenants in the Mngwenya valley, Sosibo sought AFRA's intervention. In addition to providing legal help for individual tenant families who were charged with squatting, AFRA launched a publicity campaign and successfully increased media attention. This in turn precipitated the intervention of various new parties and stimulated debates on the future of the district. One such organisation was the Tugela Basin Development Association (TBDA), which represented the interests of various local white pressure groups in mid-western Natal.[12] Through a local National Party MP, the TBDA lobbied the NPA and advocated the expansion and upgrading of the Weenen emergency camp to receive tenants. The TBDA argued that this should be developed as a township that would not only accommodate the displaced people in the district, but also prevent the influx of evicted farm tenants into mushrooming informal settlements around the cities.[13]

The TBDA's proposal was intended as an intervention to provide some resources to displaced people, but it was nonetheless unacceptable to Sosibo, who firmly believed that the expropriation of white-owned farms and a rural future was the solution for Weenen tenants. As a counter-argument to the TBDA's proposal, WECOP and AFRA requested the NPA to consider the purchase of 11 farms, owned by white absentee landlords but occupied by black people, in the Mngwenya valley.[14] The contrasting views of farmers and tenants in Weenen developed into a public debate in a local newspaper, the *Natal Witness*. The TBDA's commitment to urbanisation was taken up by Graham McIntosh, MP for the Progressive Federal Party, who owned a farm in Weenen and became an eloquent critic of the Sosibo-AFRA proposal.

At first the NPA was more sympathetic to the white farmers. In early 1988 NPA officials met the Weenen Farmers' Association and the TBDA and they agreed to resettle the evicted families in the emergency camp. The Weenen Town Board endorsed this decision and agreed to donate extra land for this purpose.[15] Three months later the NPA convened a meeting of farm tenants and informed them of its plan to upgrade the camp into a township. Six hundred farm dwellers attended this meeting, at which Sosibo publicly requested that people be allowed to stay on farms. Following this, people queued in front of the NPA officials and lodged complaints about ongoing farm evictions and harassment by farmers. Faced with quiet but determined protest by African tenants, the NPA had to back off and suggested the formation of a committee in order to continue discussing the matter.[16] In the late apartheid period, amid national urban insurrection, both central and local government in South Africa were more cautious than they had been before about forced removals of African people.

While the debate over the future of farm tenants in Weenen raged on, sporadic farm evictions continued. In late 1988 the *Natal Witness* reported that about 200 former tenants were living in tents outside the emergency camp, as the latter was full.[17] Eight months later a second tent town was created. Some Mngwenya tenants refused to leave their area and 30 families settled by the side of the road, just outside the boundary of the farm they had lived on. However, in spite of people's determination to stay on the roadside and despite wide newspaper coverage, they were eventually pushed into buses and taken to a tent town by NPA officials and the police.[18] The two tent towns created by the evictions in late 1988 and 1989 came to be called Lindelani and Thandanani.

At this time, the cooperative relationship between AFRA and WECOP began to sour. The first incident had happened two years previously. In 1987, 15 members of WECOP hired a kombi (van), travelled to the AFRA office in Pietermaritzburg and demanded that AFRA send its lawyer to help them in court cases.[19] In the background there was a growing misunderstanding over the effectiveness of legal intervention between Sosibo and AFRA. Whereas Sosibo believed that AFRA lawyers could get a court order to stop farm evictions, AFRA was beginning to feel that the legal help it could offer to farm tenants was severely limited. Farm workers were still among the least protected people in law and AFRA's legal intervention was only able to delay the enforcement of eviction and earn an extension of time for threatened families, but not to stop evictions. Gradually AFRA diverted its resources into publicity and negotiation rather than legal assistance.[20] Without fully understanding the changes in AFRA's focus on anti-eviction work, Sosibo was bitterly disappointed with AFRA's inability to stop evictions. At a meeting between the two organisations in late 1989 Sosibo criticised a lawyer associated with AFRA. An AFRA fieldworker defended the lawyer and called WECOP 'disorganised' and its chairman a 'big shot', according to Sosibo.[21] By then AFRA, strongly committed at least in principle to a participatory approach, was beginning to see Sosibo as an autocratic leader.[22]

The NPA and negotiations in the political transition

With the beginning of political transition in the country in February 1990 the political climate surrounding negotiations in Weenen changed and political spaces opened up for popular leaders. Three distinctive local groups representing farm tenants emerged and local mass action by these groups increased, as did their capacity to pressurise the NPA. The first group were residents of the now-upgraded township of KwaNobamba (formally Weenen emergency camp) and Lindelani tent town. In early 1990 residents in KwaNobamba marched to the offices in the township and handed over written grievances and demands for the extension of their land to accommodate their expanding families. This march, organised by the youth, was the first organised protest by KwaNobamba residents.[23] At first the NPA completely ignored their demands and attempted to resettle the residents of Lindelani tent town in the township. Representatives of both Lindelani and KwaNobamba firmly rejected this policy and demanded separate land for each group. An *induna* for KwaNobamba warned the NPA officials that resettling Lindelani residents in KwaNobamba might result in violence between these two communities.[24]

The second group was AFRA and the residents of Thandanani tent town. Even

123

after falling out with Sosibo in 1989, AFRA tried to maintain its liaison with farm tenants in the Mngwenya valley. Sosibo went to Johannesburg and WECOP lost some of its momentum, but AFRA maintained its commitment to a rural solution and worked with the Thandanani residents to find space for settlement in the valley. Evicted tenants living in Thandanani maintained their social ties with people living on farms in the valley and occasionally attended Saturday meetings previously organised by WECOP. Ex-tenants in Thandanani were excited with the idea of 'going back to the farms', but those still living on farms were reluctant to endorse this idea without Sosibo's approval.[25] Sosibo retained wider support than AFRA had originally thought and people in the valley highly valued both his local connections and his ability to communicate with government officials.[26]

In late 1990 Sosibo wrote a letter to Patrick Lekota and Harry Gwala, well-known ANC figures, and asked them to make formal representations to the De Klerk government for the expropriation of farms in the Mngwenya valley. In this letter he criticised AFRA as 'undemocratic' and working 'without consulting with the community'.[27] AFRA received a copy from Sosibo and was infuriated.[28] Nonetheless, the change in the external environment made it necessary for both parties to attempt reconciliation. When the White Paper on Land Policy was published by the De Klerk government in early 1991, Sosibo approached AFRA and proposed that they resume their cooperative relationship in order to respond to favourable policy changes. Having realised Sosibo's popularity among tenants in the Mngwenya valley, AFRA decided to re-engage with him.[29]

The third group lobbying the NPA was CAP and its surrounding communities in north Weenen and Tugela Estates. By then Alcock's two sons, Marc and Rauri, had taken over the management of CAP and they saw securing the land rights of African tenants as a priority.[30] CAP's local ties were much deeper than AFRA's. Under CAP's coordination various communities on farms in north Weenen and in resettlement villages in Tugela Estates drafted a joint demand for land. Each community identified particular farms where they hoped to make a living based on livestock and crop production. Some evicted tenant groups requested to be allowed to return to their original farms. Some asked for low-interest loans to purchase farms from their current owners, while others asked the government to purchase the farms for them. Either way, their bottom line was to live on farms rather than to move to a township. They wanted to remain 'on the land of their forefathers' or to be given opportunities for farming nearby.[31]

Under pressure to act, the NPA eventually called a meeting in 1991 of various stakeholders, including local farmers, the Weenen Town Board, and representatives from KwaNobamba and the two tent towns. At this stage, the NPA still considered the expansion of the township as the best solution and the meeting formed a working group to pursue this possibility. However, the white farmers, who had previously favoured this strategy, were split. A few farmers who owned farms next to the township opposed its expansion unless a new bridge over the Bushmans River was constructed. Without the bridge, they would have to drive through the township in order to get to town – an idea that some farmers could not accept.[32]

Two NPA documents of this period – *Weenen Development Strategy* (1989) and *Weenen: Expansion Proposals for Entokozweni* (1990) – considered other possibilities. They acknowledged that African tenant families relied on various sources of income for their survival and that they desired to have a rural life. The importance of cattle for African culture was recognised, as were the African tenants' links to land. The NPA identified six different scenarios for African settlement in the district, varying from the acquisition of white farms in the Mngwenya valley by the government in order to settle Africans to the resettlement of evicted tenants in townships outside the district.[33]

The different options attracted different supporters. When these reports were made public in early 1992, Sosibo immediately expressed his support for the Mngwenya valley scenario at the NPA working group meeting.[34] McIntosh, the local MP for the Progressive Federal Party, attended the working group meetings as a representative of absentee farmers and argued that tenants in the valley could not be a good farming community.[35] Deadlock ensued. In response CAP facilitated direct action. In late 1992 the leadership of various black communities organised a two-day strike of casual labourers on white farms. CAP claimed that the strike achieved an 80 per cent stayaway of farm workers in Weenen and Msinga. Worried by this new form of mass action, the farmers requested another meeting. However, the meeting was fruitless, as both black leaders and white farmers ended up accusing each other of bad faith.[36] Although farmers were still uncompromising, a new militancy had manifested itself in the strike action – always difficult to organise in dispersed rural settings. In a broader context, farm murders were affecting the outlook of white landowners and KZN as a whole was being destabilised by violence. The tone of black representatives was changing from begging to asserting as they gained confidence from the broader political transition across the country.

Act No. 126 of 1993 and the Thuthuka Mngwenya land purchase

The persistence of rural demands for land, as opposed to new urban sites for settlement, also bore fruit in 1993. The NPA was changing its position. There was new urgency for a solution in Weenen, partly prompted by the militancy of former tenants and partly due to the necessity of restructuring local government. In an era of transition, municipalities were being deracialised. The Weenen Town Board insisted that Thandanani residents had to be removed before any agreement would be made for the establishment of a joint local authority between the white municipality of Weenen and the black township of KwaNobamba.[37] Thandanani residents were adamant that they would not accept anything less than resettlement on farms in the Mngwenya valley.[38] The new Provision of Certain Land for Settlement Act No. 126 of 1993 provided a legal mechanism for governmental assistance to communities that wished to purchase farms.[39]

The NPA opened a negotiation forum for Thandanani residents, who were represented by two local leaders – Sosibo and Elias Bheki Nyawo, new *induna* for the KwaNobamba township. The NPA entrusted Nyawo with two crucial jobs in transferring land from white farmers to black people in Weenen. Firstly, he was to inform Thandanani residents of the procedures and obligations for purchasing land through Act No. 126 of 1993. Secondly, he was to identify both purchasing families and farms for sale in the Mngwenya valley. Nyawo managed to find three farms, in total about 3,000 hectares, in the valley whose white owners agreed to sell their farms to the African communities.[40] Once surrounding white landowners knew that neighbouring farms were going to be owned by Africans, they also put their farms on the market, because they perceived that they could not farm adjacent to African settlements. The farmers' perceptions therefore directly influenced which farms were available for land reform.

Identifying purchasing families was a more complicated and demanding task. Nyawo and Sosibo separately prepared a list of people who wanted to settle on the newly purchased farms. The attempt to combine the two separate lists into one never succeeded and subsequently Sosibo resigned from the Mngwenya land purchase meeting and came to distance himself from Nyawo. One of the difficulties in finalising the list of purchasing families was the continuation of sporadic farm evictions in the district, even while the Mngwenya land purchase was being discussed at NPA meetings. The issue of ongoing evictions was taken up at the meetings several times, but with no result.[41]

Another critical issue concerned the number of families who would settle on the newly purchased farms. Here there was a major contradiction. The Act stipulated that the community had to bear 20 per cent of the purchase price of the farm, while the government would pay the remaining 80 per cent. Thus, the more families who settled, the less the contribution for each family. However, if there were too many purchasing families, they would find it difficult to gain much supplementary income from the farms. The investigation of the Department of Agriculture about the carrying capacity of these three farms found serious soil erosion and limited arable land, which implied rather bleak prospects for agriculture.[42]

Local farmers criticised the proposed land transaction on the grounds that the farms were not suitable for community agriculture. McIntosh, a persistent advocate of the urbanisation of farm tenants in Weenen, predicted a gloomy picture for the resettled community and argued that the NPA was setting an undesirable precedent in a new South Africa:

They wish to create a rural village in the Mngwenya valley where there is no water, no services but only dry thorn bush … Apart from the costs, I am unconvinced about the economic feasibility. It will end up by being nothing more than the lower end of the time share market located in a drought stricken, eroded and overgrazed environment with miserable crops of sorghum and maize and gardens of dagga tucked away wherever possible.[43]

Paradoxically, McIntosh owned one of the three farms intended for purchase by the community and he eventually agreed to sell it. The chairman of the Weenen Farmers' Association did not think community members were serious about farming the land, arguing that they 'simply [felt] that they [were] entitled to the land because they claim[ed] that it once belonged to them'.[44]

As it was, even white farmers were giving up cattle farming in the district. Since the early 1990s a group of local farmers had been contemplating converting their land into game farms and developing a new conservancy. They thought that this could attract ecotourism by linking it to the existing Weenen Game Reserve. Historically, the development of conservancies among white farmers in Natal originated from their concern to secure their land and, where they had introduced wildlife, to curb poaching by black people through jointly employing game guards. The changing political environment in the country, however, began to make farmers realise the necessity of involving African communities in their conservancy projects. Thus, Weenen farmers claimed that the new biosphere reserve could provide new job opportunities for local African communities.[45] The idea was not popular among black activists, who saw the biosphere reserve as a pre-emptive measure by white farmers to prevent transfer of land. In the end the biosphere reserve was developed in a much smaller area than originally envisaged.[46]

In spite of the opposition from local farmers, the NPA and the Department of Regional and Land Affairs proceeded to finalise the purchase of the three farms by the community. Nyawo submitted a list of 159 families as collective purchasers.[47] By mid-1994 he had established the Thuthuka Mngwenya Community Trust[48] and started to collect the necessary 5 per cent deposit from families in order to pay for the farms. The proposed purchase of three farms by the Thuthuka Mngwenya Trust was the only land reform project in the district that preceded the installation of the new government. From mid-1994 the change in government caused delay and disruption in implementing the project, which was further complicated by the emergence of personal rivalries among local leaders.

Post-apartheid: The land reform pilot programme

In early 1994 African residents on Weenen farms and Tugela Estates staged another strike. Their mass action lasted for two weeks and resulted in the formation of a local conflict resolution committee consisting of representatives of the police, white farmers and the community.[49] Six months later another mass march was carried out from a local farm in nearby Muden, east of Weenen, to the community hall in Weenen. A Muden farmer complained to the new Department of Land Affairs (DLA) that his workers withdrew their labour after this incident, that his house was vandalised and that several deliberate fires were set on his farms.[50] The official ending of apartheid was the signal for the unleashing of anger among African farm tenants and workers in the deeply rural area of KZN. How well did the post-apartheid government handle their land demands?

Local mass actions in the first half of 1994 produced a new leadership in the shape of the Weenen Peace and Development Committee (WPDC). Representatives from different farms in Weenen gathered under the WPDC, but the dominant figure was Stanley Bonginkosi Dladla, the principal of a school in Tugela Estates. CAP was part of the WPDC and attended its meetings as an observer.[51] A separate group was formed in nearby Muden by Jotham Hlalefuneka Myaka, who in his youth had worked with Neil Alcock at CAP. Both Dladla and Myaka studied at the University of Zululand and became teachers. In the early 1990s Myaka obtained a scholarship from the South

Africa Institute of Race Relations and studied for an MA degree at the University of Reading in Britain. Dladla and Myaka led two separate groups, but jointly pressurised the new minister of land affairs in Mandela's government, Derek Hanekom, for the urgent implementation of land reform in the area. They had an effective knowledge of the changing national context and were skilled negotiators.

In September 1994 the WPDC threatened to initiate an occupation of the Weenen Townlands and white farms on 1 October unless the minister met them.[52] Hanekom flew to Weenen and promised a formal meeting.[53] It was held at the end of September at the Weenen farmers' hall, which was packed with approximately 400 Africans. Representatives of the WPDC and Muden showered Hanekom with numerous stories of hardships that had been inflicted on people as a result of evictions and the impounding of livestock. They made it clear that they were no longer prepared to tolerate these conditions. Their narratives were enormously effective in moving the mind of the new minister,[54] but although Hanekom's sympathy lay with the African communities, he could not go back to Pretoria without talking to the local whites. On the same afternoon he held a separate meeting with about 50 Weenen farmers and three African representatives. Here an agreement was made to form another joint local committee between African communities and white farmers.[55] According to the *Natal Witness* reporter who was present at this meeting, the minister 'defused a tense situation' and 'averted possible bloodshed.'[56]

Subsequently, the Weenen joint committee met twice with Hanekom. The *Star* reporter depicted the confrontational atmosphere at the beginning of the first meeting:

> 'We are bitter', says man after man, bitter about past evictions, bitter about continuing evictions, bitter about the ancestral land, bitter in particular about the new 'Biosphere'. ... 'The animals roam our father's graves freely', says one, 'and we can't go near.' ... It sounds so clear, what the Zulus are saying. 'You have plenty (and what is more it was once our forebears), now give us some.' ... The Zulus are talking invasion; the whites are talking resistance, and there are real signs that tomorrow morning there'll be blood.[57]

However, both the African representatives and white farmers welcomed Hanekom's arbitration and the tone gradually changed. According to the same reporter, 'Zulu speeches were suddenly about appreciation for the farmers. Mark Winter [a farmer] spoke with tears in his eyes about everyone paddling the joint canoe together.'[58]

Committees were set up to deal with the problem of continued evictions and to identify farms for purchase.

Meanwhile, the basic components of the land reform policy of the post-apartheid government were beginning to be disclosed. Black owners who lost land after 1913 through racial laws or measures were entitled to lodge claims under the Restitution of Land Rights Act. The land demands of other communities were to be met by a land redistribution programme to be implemented on the basis of the 'willing-seller willing-buyer' principle. Land redistribution was initiated in pilot programmes within chosen districts in each province. The new KZN Provincial Administration chose Estcourt and Weenen, including Muden. The selection of Weenen as the pilot district was a direct result of long-term conflict over the land in the area, as well as community mobilisation.[59] By the end of 1994, when the official announcement about the pilot programme was made, the local committee of Weenen had made up a list of 19 farms that white farmers were willing to sell for the settlement of black communities.[60]

The official launch of the pilot programme took place in Weenen in early 1995. It was a memorable event at which President Nelson Mandela made a brief appearance, accompanied by ministers and officials of both the ANC and the Inkatha Freedom Party (IFP).[61] Three months later, the pilot programme office was opened in Estcourt. In the meantime, the Weenen committee instructed the Department of Agriculture to evaluate the 19 farms and compiled a list of families who wanted to share in the purchase.[62] A local agricultural extension officer noted:

> The communities are under the impression that the Government will purchase all available land that they consider suitable. ... the expectations among the buyers and sellers is extremely high. A number of options have already been signed and sellers are expecting payment within 90 days. The Black communities are positive that they will not have to contribute towards the purchase price of the land.[63]

There was a time lag between the official announcement of the pilot programme and the date on which the mechanism of land transfers was made public. The changes in government officials and policies affected most severely the proposed purchase of three farms by the Thuthuka Mngwenya Trust headed by Nyawo, which was the only land purchase project in the district that preceded the launch of the pilot programme. At the meetings with Hanekom in 1994 Nyawo understood that he could set up a sub-committee under the WPDC and proceed with the pending purchase.[64] Nyawo informed the DLA at the end of 1994 that he had collected the necessary deposit for the purchase of farms.[65] Nyawo and three trustees persistently lobbied the DLA, arguing that their land purchase should be finalised as soon as possible, regardless of the development of the pilot programme. The DLA explained the advantages of its incorporation into the pilot programme, most notably financial flexibility, including a subsidy per household and an additional budget for development planning. The DLA also raised its concern that purchasing families might not be able to pay the monthly instalments.

Nyawo was adamant that the Thuthuka Mngwenya land purchase should be done outside the framework of the pilot programme.[66] He was concerned about further delays.[67] Moreover, an investigation by Harold Riversage, a consultant appointed by the DLA who used to work for AFRA, suggested personal and political rivalries within the local leadership as a reason for Nyawo's sense of urgency. Some local leaders, including Nyawo, began to see land reform as a means to establish their political patronage. On the one hand, Nyawo needed to consolidate his support base by successfully finalising the land purchase. Some of the prospective purchasers in Thandanani tent town refused to make financial contributions until the purchase was finalised. Nyawo blamed the WPDC for telling residents of Thandanani not to pay for land, as the government was going to provide land for free. On the other hand, the WPDC disputed the legitimacy of Nyawo as a representative of the purchasers, alleging that he did not have majority support.[68] Riversage also found that no one had verified information on the intended purchasers; the list of 146 families was never produced by Nyawo nor the DLA. It was generally assumed that the purchasers were either ex-farm tenants living in Thandanani or farm tenants currently facing eviction in the Mngwenya valley. Nyawo claimed that he could produce a record of people who had paid a deposit, but this information was never disclosed.[69]

In spite of local confusion, the KZN Land Reform Steering Committee, which administered the pilot programme, recommended at the end of 1995 that the Thuthuka Mngwenya purchase receive ministerial approval. Accordingly, government funds totalling R2,190,000 (R15,000 per household for 146 families) were released to purchase the farms.[70] The DLA was fully aware of local frustration about the delay and knew that some people had already illegally moved on to one of the farms identified for purchase. It was worried about setting a precedent in the pilot area by allowing the illegal occupation of a farm intended for land reform. Moreover, an owner of a nearby farm had been threatening to evict his tenants and the DLA wanted to expedite the purchase so that evicted tenants could move to Thuthuka Mngwenya farms without becoming temporarily homeless. Both black and white communities were putting pressure on the DLA by threatening illegal occupation and eviction.[71] In early 1996 the purchase of two farms, in total about 2,450 hectares, was finalised. The owner of the third farm refused to agree to a price and the purchase of this farm was cancelled.[72]

The DLA wished to sort out problems of identifying beneficiaries and their representation before initiating development plans for these farms. In the process, it discovered that 'tribal differences' between local leaders were causing difficulties at the grassroots level.[73] The Weenen area is dominated by two strong chieftaincy groups – Mchunu and Mthembu – whose chiefs reside in the Msinga district. Elderly members of both groups were aware of the geographical boundaries between them even on white-owned farms. These 'phantom' boundaries coexisted with the district boundaries drawn by the colonial authority and they were sometimes fiercely contested during the twentieth century.[74] *Indunas* of chieftaincy groups who were chosen within the community also acted as their representatives to the Weenen commissioner. Even in white farming districts the apartheid government relied on traditional structures when it came to governing black communities. The resilience of traditional identities and structures among black communities in Weenen was in part related to the way that the white governments administered rural black communities.

Local leaders who negotiated with the minister were cautiously coordinating the identification and allocation of farms and people according to tribal boundaries and affiliations so that the two groups would purchase and settle land separately. The WPDC was dominated by the Mthembu group, while Myaka was like 'a land minister' of the Mchunu group.[75] Negotiators did not discuss their tribal differences overtly with Hanekom, but this did not mean that they did not matter. According to Sosibo, the agreed boundary between the Mthembu group and the Mchunu group in the Mngwenya valley was the Mngwenya River. The Mthembu group occupied the land north of the river, while the Mchunu lived to the south. The groups, however, did not live in complete separation. They had long lived on the same farms in the valley and intermingled both socially and through marriage. Sosibo identified himself as Mchunu, but his mother came from the Mthembu group.[76]

Nyawo belonged to a third group known as the Mbhele, who also believed they had legitimate claims to some parts of Weenen. Nyawo was from Durban and therefore did not belong to any of these groups, but he married a local Mbhele woman and apparently *khonza*-ed (meaning joined a group by paying tribal allegiance) to the Mbhele chief. When a chief *induna* to the Mbhele died, he succeeded to this position.[77] The WPDC suspected that Nyawo was trying to create a Mbhele zone through land reform in the area that was traditionally considered to belong to the Mthembu.[78]

Local leaders brought in tribal politics in identifying who should be the beneficiaries of the Thuthuka Mngwenya land purchase. At the very beginning this land purchase was planned for the residents of Thandanani tent town who had been evicted from the Mngwenya valley in 1989. However, Riversage's investigation in 1996 found that 'a large portion, if not a majority' of the Thandanani residents did not intend to move to the purchased farms. Through the WPDC, Thandanani residents expressed their desire to move to two other farms in the valley.[79] The Mthembu in Thandanani opposed the idea of a Mbhele land purchase in Mthembu territory, and the Mchunu in Thandanani refused to move to the area regarded as Mthembu land. Ignoring the mediation efforts of the DLA among the three groups, Nyawo and other trustees encouraged people to move on to one of the farms owned by the Thuthuka Mngwenya Trust.[80] The new occupants built their huts, despite the DLA's warnings to restrict people from moving on to farms until the detailed settlement planning was complete.[81]

In addition to local tribal politics, personal ambitions and rivalries among the local leaders were also having an impact on land reform in Weenen. Riversage noted in his confidential report to the DLA:

> The principal leadership all want to be seen to have done something for 'their people' and seen to be co-operating in the run up to the local elections. All three core leaders are candidates for the election. Rewards for this patronage seem to vary between the different leaders, there is circumstantial evidence that Mr Nyawo has expected and received financial rewards whilst the other leaders appear to be driven more by political rewards and social commitment.[82]

The first local government election in a democratic South Africa took place in KZN in 1996. All three key leaders in Weenen, i.e. Nyawo, Dladla and Myaka, stood for election and won seats in the local government. While Nyawo and Dladla represented the IFP, Myaka stood as an independent representing his community-based organisation, Zibambeleni. Subsequently, Nyawo was elected mayor of the Weenen Town Council and Dladla became mayor of the wider Uthukela Regional Council.[83] Political advancement had been long denied to Africans in apartheid South Africa outside of the homelands and it is no surprise that capable local politicians emerged when the opportunities opened up. Furthermore, these men were the ones who were able to deliver concrete benefits such as land and water to the rural communities where basic services and needs had long been ignored and denied.

After failed attempts by the DLA to broker agreements about the beneficiaries of the Thuthuka Mngwenya project, it temporarily came to a halt. By late 1998, when the DLA decided to sort out the project once again, both the financial position of the Thuthuka Mngwenya Trust and the settlement of beneficiaries were in a complete mess.[84] A legal investigation found that the trust's bank account did not have any cash and Nyawo could not produce the records of financial transactions. While about 80 families illegally occupied the two farms, a similar number from the Thandanani tent town had moved off due to conflict. Neither the DLA nor the trust could stop people moving on to the farms.[85] It appears that those who had fled the farms were mainly Mchunu people, who subsequently moved to another farm in the Mngwenya valley traditionally considered to be within Mchunu territory.[86]

Sustainability of land reform

Apart from the Thuthuka Mngwenya project, the DLA initiated about eight land reform projects in the Weenen area during the pilot programme stage. The number of beneficiaries in each project differed, and so did the complexities. However, all in all, these projects originally identified and assisted by the WPDC, and sometimes by CAP, seemed to be less complicated than the Thuthuka Mngwenya project and proceeded smoothly from the transfer of land to planning and settlement.[87] By 2002 the immediate land needs of black communities in Weenen seemed to have been met. A report compiled by CAP in that year confirmed this and further identified a new challenge of making better use of land.[88]

This does not mean that these projects were without problems, while the question of whether living conditions were dramatically improved by land reform or not is a different matter. The sustainability and viability of agricultural production comprise a sensitive but crucial issue in evaluating the results of land reform in a long-term perspective. But black demands for land reform in the district were based on the desire for historical justice, and although the DLA was concerned about agriculture, it prioritised settlement.

Although it is beyond the scope of this chapter to discuss in detail the question of the sustainability of land reform, I would like to briefly touch on it here.

Two inseparable questions have to be posed with regard to the results of land reform in Weenen. Are land reform pilot projects in KZN economically sustainable? And then, are they ecologically sustainable? One major reason for difficulties in enhancing the livelihoods of black communities who benefitted from the pilot programme was the lack of post-settlement support.[89] At the end of 2000 an official of the KZN Department of Agriculture admitted that 'there [was] a lack of will to act within the Department as far as addressing the problem of land reform projects [was] concerned'. His department did not have a sense of ownership of land reform projects, nor was it interested in subsistence farming.[90] The Department of Agriculture that had catered for the needs of white farmers during the apartheid era had to transform itself in order to cater for the different needs of African communal farmers. This was especially so in Weenen, where agricultural resources were very limited. The fact that generally the carrying capacity of these farms was low demanded that purchasers reduce the number of livestock they could keep. This was not easy and in many cases the purchasers failed to reduce their livestock. Moreover, in some cases they became victims of illegal grazing by their black neighbours in Tugela Estates and Msinga.

It gradually became apparent that not all the beneficiaries of the land reform projects in the district moved back from their resettlement villages to farms, where basic services and facilities such as water and schools were lacking. In contrast, the provision of basic services was improved in the resettlement villages after 1994. When Dladla became mayor of the Uthukela Regional Council, he installed communal tap water facilities for the first time in Tugela Estates. Some families in Tugela Estates who contributed to the purchase of farms in Weenen therefore did not move. They were also reluctant or unable to bear the cost of transporting their belongings and building new houses. However, the farms provided them with secure access to pasture land, and many of them began to graze cattle on the purchased farms.[91]

Despite such problems, the pilot programme satisfied the most pressing land demands of black communities in the area, provided security of tenure for those who moved and increased the opportunity for livestock ownership. As a member of the WPDC repeatedly emphasised: 'You need to have land first before you talk about development. You can't talk about development if you don't have land.'[92] Land invasions did take place in Weenen, but were largely limited to the Townlands, and only happened after the initial land demands of the black community were met. Three separate groups belonging to the Mthembu, Mchunu and Mbhele, respectively, occupied different portions of the Townlands. The Umtshezi District Council, which incorporated the former Weenen Town Board after the 2000 local election, acquiesced to this occupation. Faced with death threats, even elected black councillors were unable to remove people who occupied the Townlands.[93]

The end of the pilot programme was not the end of land reform in the Weenen district.[94] After the WPDC ceased to function, several groups of labour tenants who still resided on farms in the Mngwenya valley lodged their labour tenant claims with the DLA in accordance with the Labour Tenant Act of 1996. Moreover, separate groups of former tenants who were evicted from farms in the valley during the apartheid period lodged restitution claims with the Land Commission in accordance with the Restitution of Land Rights Act of 1994 before the deadline of the 31 December 1998. Sosibo was one of the restitution claimants and acted as their representative. Some local farmers sold their farms to a business company that proposed to set up a huge game reserve containing the big five. The Gongolo Wildlife Reserve was to encompass 37,000 hectares of land stretching from the southern part of the Weenen district to the northern part of the Estcourt district. Land claims by labour tenants, as well as restitution claims amounting to 18,000 hectares, fell in the proposed reserve. This clash of interests brought the DLA and the Land Commission into negotiations between representatives of the Gongolo company and black claimants. The company emphasised the prospect of local economic development and employment opportunities once the game reserve was established. It suggested settling the claims in such a way that the community become a legal owner of some of the land and leased it to the company for its management. Labour tenant and restitution claimants on the other hand were sceptical about the proposed game reserve and its economic benefits to them. In particular, they insisted on finalising land transfers before they began talking about the game reserve. It did not help when the DLA and the Land Commission insisted on setting up one trust among claimants in order to settle these separate land claims. Some suspected that perhaps the DLA and the Land Commission wanted to facilitate the negotiation in favour of the Gongolo company by setting up just one representative body for local communities.

Lack of trust between different race groups was not the only factor in complicating the negotiations for the Gongolo land claims. Originally the black community insisted on setting up seven separate trusts for seven *izigodi* (tribal wards/neighbourhoods) on the claimed land. The DLA came up with a compromise of setting up two trusts – one for the Mthembu and one for the Mchunu – thus formally acknowledging the different chieftaincy groups. The negotiations had not yet been finalised at the time of writing.

Conclusion

This chapter has discussed continuity and change in three distinctive phases of black community struggles over land in Weenen. In the 1980s, when farm evictions were still common in the district, a black community organisation was formed through interaction with white liberal groups. Johannes Sosibo emerged as a key local leader with assistance from CAP and AFRA. He was a well-respected figure and had wide support among farm tenants in the Mngwenya valley. He persistently argued for the transfer of land from white farmers to the black community and succeeded in developing an organisation with clear local aims that was a popular movement of a kind, although it did not articulate a broader ideology. Like many such rural movements it was relatively short lived, but its institutional continuity was assisted by NGOs. In the 1970s and 1980s Sosibo's strategy seemed impossibly optimistic. By the early 1990s, however, the prospects of acquiring land improved greatly. The demand for land remained a priority for many former tenants and workers, although some chose eventually to stay within closer, more urban settlements where services were better.

The real negotiations regarding the land needs of evicted labour tenants in Weenen only started after the 1994 election. However, much of the groundwork had been done in earlier discussions involving tenant communities, land NGOs and the NPA. These meetings paved the way for the emergence of new and better-educated local leaders. Expectations were undoubtedly increased through discussion with government officials. Popular politics in the shape of local mass action, as well as persistent participation in meetings, played a significant role in the move towards land reform. In this case, as in others, complex alliances at the local level facilitated real political gains. By 1994 the WPDC became the most powerful representative body in Weenen, drawing support from Tugela Estates, where most of the former Weenen farm tenants were relocated, as well as other settlements. However, the WPDC did not succeed in involving all the local strongmen, which resulted in a power struggle among themselves, with a destructive effect on the community. Local leaders had complex, multiple identities and aspirations stretching into both the tribal and modern political spheres.

In the post-apartheid implementation of land reform in Weenen the logic of tribal politics became prominent. After the difficulties of the Ihuthuka Mngwenya land purchase project, even the DLA admitted the importance of tribal boundaries in the district and took this element into consideration when facilitating land transfers. Another interesting feature of land reform in Weenen was the political inclination of its black leadership. Local leaders saw new opportunities in local politics. The WPDC was not keen to get involved in the development process of individual land reform projects after the transfer of land to the black community and it ceased to exist soon after the pilot programme was closed. The focus of local leaders in Weenen was not narrowly limited to land reform per se, although it was important. The immediate purpose of the WPDC was to meet the land needs of local African communities in the areas in which they were still largely based. However, its underlying purpose was ultimately to change power relations.

It should be noted that this process, contrary to what was described by Jonny Steinberg in his book *Midlands*, did not include violent confrontation between the white and black communities. Land invasions in the district were very limited. While the African community talked about the reoccupation of farmland, this was more of a rhetorical and verbal threat, i.e. a tactic of negotiation. The reoccupation of Townlands took place after land reform had been implemented through the pilot programme and was carried out by different groups. Steinberg describes how deep antagonism between farmers and their tenants/workers turned into violence by the latter against farmers when they realised that the end of apartheid did not bring the results for which they had long hoped.[95] In Weenen, the African community grabbed the new opportunities presented to them and opted for direct action and negotiations rather than violence.

Figure 6.1: Sosibo and his family and friends at his home in the Mngwenya valley. He lives on top of the hill at one of the farms in the Mngwenya valley. (August 2008)

Figure 6.2: Sosibo's cattle kraal (August 2008).

Figure 6.3: A family who returned to a farm in the Mngwenya valley. Friends and neighbours gathered to hold a function (August 2008).

Figure 6.4: Ukusiza (literally meaning 'to help', it refers to a Zulu custom of 'loaning/ lending out cattle') system is still prevalent in the Mngwenya valley (August 2009).

7 From popular resistance to populist politics in the Transkei

Tim Gibbs

Introduction

Of all the rural rebellions that broke out in South Africa in the middle of the twentieth century, the 1960 Pondoland revolt was the largest and most celebrated. Like the Sekhukhuneland rebellion, it was in part a 'last ditch defence of land and cattle' – arguably the end of a sequence of popular struggles by rurally based peasants and migrants against state intervention into their land and livelihoods.[1] The revolts had been provoked by the apartheid government's so-called Betterment or Rehabilitation policies of the 1940s and 1950s that attempted to induce economic development by forcibly reordering rural society.[2] Equally contentious were the state's attempts to reshape and control chieftaincy in the Bantu authorities system. Historians have recognised that traditional authorities did not die in twentieth-century South Africa, despite the long history of colonisation. Rural resistance reflected the still 'pulsating remains of African kingdoms'.[3] In some contexts there were direct connections between rural revolts and nationalist movements. But there were also tensions: rural resistance could be mobilised around local interests and ethnic identities that were uncomfortable for more modernising nationalists.[4]

The historiography on the rebellions is growing. Yet the question remains: what happened afterwards, when rural communities were more fully incorporated into the state, as peasant production eroded and the grasp of government extended over rural regions? The overwhelming answer by historians has been that the homeland governments in South Africa were essentially dependent on Pretoria, which devolved power to reactionary, government-appointed chiefs as the basis for the fiction of homeland independence. Furthermore, the growth of the homeland state crystallised class divisions – the fault line lying between increasingly impoverished rural communities and the corrupt, comprador elite, centred round the chieftaincy, who enjoyed access to the goods of government. The 1980s saw anomic, runaway youth revolts in rural areas against the collaborating chiefs and Bantustan establishment, but the African National Congress (ANC) leadership negotiated with the pillars of the old, corrupted regimes in the 1990s.[5] This account resonates with Mamdani's analysis of the legacy of late colonialism in Africa. In an argument that draws on Ranger's ideas about the 'invention of tribalism', Mamdani suggests that the authority of the colonial/apartheid state was extended through its alliance with the local chieftaincy.[6] This left a legacy of decentralised despotism – a mode of rule that has remained unbroken, despite the best attempts of post-colonial governments.

This chapter, however, suggests an alternative interpretation of homeland politics in Transkei. It extends the idea that popular political impulses remained significant in the rural areas and draws on recent academic literature that argues for a mutually constitutive relationship between state and society.[7] Questions of political culture – how rural communities and the Bantustan state were constructed in relation to each other, the manner and idiom in which the state worked, and the language by which people made claims on the state – are emphasised in my account. In brief, I suggest that the driver of rural politics in Transkei was the consumption of state resources by impoverished local communities, who accessed Bantustan development projects through local brokers and patrons. Thus, ideas of local and ethnic identity, once centred around peasant production and access to land, were increasingly focused around a locality's relation to the state. This new pattern of politics was dramatically seen in a second bout of smothered, explosive unrest in Transkei militating *for* state support of rural livelihoods in the late 1970s, less than two decades after the celebrated 1960 revolt *against* state intervention. Finally, in an extended conclusion, I tentatively trace a link between this pattern of protest and the populist discontents that have re-emerged in South Africa in the twenty-first century – political forces that have been drawn into the coalition of malcontents who supported Jacob Zuma's successful leadership bid to become president of the ANC. As in the case of some other chapters in this book, I explore continuities as well as change in local popular protest and suggest that they still impact on South Africa's provincial and national political processes.

Land rehabilitation abandoned

The 1960 Mpondo revolt was shattered – a dozen shot dead on Ngquza Hill, scores condemned to death and many more tortured at temporary police detention camps – but on its accession to power in 1963, Kaiser Matanzima's Bantustan government, although supported by the might of the apartheid state, hardly acted as if it had won a resounding victory over the Transkeian peasantry. On the contrary, rumours swept the territory that Betterment measures had been suspended and that a commission of inquiry was to visit all districts to hear the complaints of rural communities.[8] Members of the official opposition, the Democratic Party, toured the countryside holding report-back meetings and drumming up popular anger against Betterment in their stump speeches.[9] While government-backed Betterment policies continued in many rural localities, the intensity of forcible state intervention decreased in many aspects. Instead, economic planners threw their weight behind a series of government-sponsored, local development schemes. The effect of this was to create a political culture centred on the consumption of state resources by rural communities.

In 1964 Kaiser Matanzima announced that 25 per cent of the total area of Transkei had either reached the first stage of planning or was in the course of being 'rehabilitated'. By the end of apartheid, 25 years later, Betterment planning had been implemented in perhaps 566 (55 per cent) of the 1,014 localities that made up Transkei.[10] Nevertheless, Betterment policies were not rigorously pursued, nor backed to the hilt by the full force of the state during the Bantustan era. Increasingly, Betterment was 'loosely' planned in an effort to speed it up and diminish the cost. In many locations, stock culling was suspended in order to minimise opposition, in spite of official 'doubts about whether rehabilitation could actually succeed without the limitation of stock numbers and the control on grazing'.[11]

The Transkei government increasingly made a virtue of this retreat. Again and again the minister of agriculture, Columbus Madikizela, stood up in the Transkei Legislative Assembly to announce the relaxation of a raft of laws, regulations and circulars. In 1964, for instance, he relaxed the laws governing the movement of livestock. Previously, livestock owners' herds were depleted under rules that allowed them only to buy in one head of cattle for every two that that they sold; now the laws allowed a fair exchange. He then authorised the introduction of 100,000 more cattle into the Transkei.[12] In 1965 he announced that government agricultural officers would no longer castrate bulls. Not even Tribal Authorities, under government-appointed chiefs, were given these powers; the responsibility went all the way down to local committees and headmen. 'Now the duty devolves to you and the Department [of Agriculture] has nothing to do with it', he said. 'You can keep all the beasts you want, you can have ten bulls to one cow' – a nonsensical and abject proposition.[13]

When a chieftainess complained that one of her locations had not received new boreholes or windmills, she was told:

The people of the Administrative Area [i.e. the location] made it impossible for the work [of Betterment planning] to be executed. They slashed the tyres of the drilling machine; they attempted to burn out the machine ... Fences were destroyed and lives of officials threatened ... It was unsafe and meant the expenditure of funds fruitlessly.[14]

By the admission of government officials, the Betterment policy had failed. In 1972 a Department of Agriculture survey found that three districts that had supposedly been planned only had 40 per cent of the number of selected bulls that would be necessary to improve the quality of livestock.[15] A few years earlier officials had admitted that

there are no areas where the Betterment scheme has been carried out to the complete satisfaction of the department ... Some of the most important aspects depend on the co-operation of the people, such as strict and voluntary grazing control. No scheme will be completely satisfactory until the residents apply themselves energetically.[16]

Having retreated from Betterment planning, the Transkei government pumped resources into stock improvement and agricultural development schemes that were, in turn, financed by Pretoria, which was also anxious that the apartheid project should succeed. Two debacles, above all, came to epitomise the runaway politics of this type of economic development. One large rural cooperatives scheme, which had 30,000 members, received millions of rand of government loans, ostensibly to improve agricultural production. But hardly a cent was paid back; the money disappeared into rural communities. In 1980, with the collapse of many cooperatives, the Transkei government was forced to send a grovelling letter to Pretoria detailing the outstanding loans that it had been forced to write off.[17] A ploughing scheme supposed to boost arable yields was even more disastrous. In the late 1970s the Transkei government devised a complicated scheme to increase maize and sorghum production in which hundreds of government tractors would increase agricultural efficiency by offering ploughing at subsidised rates. Yet the scheme was rolled out even before the pilot project had been evaluated, with R4.5 million spent in the first year alone.[18] Predictably, it failed. Later investigations reported that there had been 'a great deal of political interference and poor technical control' and included allegations of corruption that went all the way to the doors of the prime minister of Transkei.[19]

The effect of the provision of these economic development projects was to create a political culture centred on the consumption of state resources by rural communities. Certainly, the Transkei government ruthlessly played this card, favouring friends and punishing enemies, consolidating its wealth and power. But this did not simply create a parasitic state bourgeoisie that was engaged in a top-down politics of neopatrimonialism.[20] Instead, influential chiefs, government officials and other notable figures of all political stripes positioned themselves as regional brokers, channelling state resources into their localities. This was, firstly, because the politics of economic patronage was the only game in town. The stagnation of peasant production and the failure of rural economic development schemes meant that the state was an increasingly important source of sustenance. Ideas of community and ethnic identity that had once been rooted in relation to land, livelihoods and locality were now reorientated in relation to the state. Secondly, the language of community was important because so many projects – not only agricultural development projects, but also infrastructure such as schools and clinics – were goods given by the state not to individuals, but to a locality.

This pattern of economic development projects had a couple of long-lasting consequences that would continue beyond the end of apartheid. Firstly, even if there were occasional economic successes – the development of tea plantations at Magwa in Pondoland and the Ncora irrigation scheme in western Thembuland, for example – most development projects failed. These schemes supposed to spark economic growth instead became social welfare handouts of a sort. Secondly, South Africans in rural areas reworked ideas of locality, ethnicity, and social rights and obligations to make sense of their new relationship with the state. Stalwart Bantustan opponents and ANC sympathisers, such as Alfred Xobololo and Chief Ntsikayizwe Sigcau, would complain:

> There is undue enrichment … Moneys that come from South Africa are exploited by our own Government to the disadvantage of our lower ranks … We see farmers on the northern side [i.e. in K. D. Matanzima's region] developing well … but the implements are not well distributed … There is no fair economic distribution here.[21]

Government officials and community leaders

The provision of economic development projects was one means by which local and ethnic identities were reworked rather than obliterated by the extension of the state into rural communities. A second means by which the ideas of ethnicity were perpetuated

145

was the political culture of the bureaucracy: authority was understood in intimate terms and regional brokers accessed state power on behalf of their communities. These ideas of power and authority flourished in the rottenness and factionalism within the Transkeian Department of Agriculture. Indeed, this factionalism had been written into the foundations of the Bantustan state, which was, from the outset, riven by racist hierarchies. In 1963 one bemused observer explained:

> It is difficult to say just how much control is exercised over each [African] minister [in the Transkei government] by their secretaries [seconded from Pretoria]. It appears the minister's ... authority [is confined] to areas of policy, drawing very liberally on the advice of top [white] civil servants ... Although some Africans fill very senior posts, none is closer than about 3 steps from the top post ... and an African cannot be promoted until all the posts subordinate to the one he could fill are in African hands.[22]

The desire for African advancement in the face of racist intransigence quickly led to the balkanisation of the bureaucracy, riven by cliques, mistrust and suspicions. Black officials' promotion was held back by lack of training and opportunity – a legacy of white rule that continued throughout the Bantustan era.[23] As late as 1981, Tsolo College of Agriculture in Transkei, the main educational institution producing agricultural officers, could only accommodate 10 per cent of its total applicants. Transkei only had 11 university graduates in Agricultural Sciences and related subjects.[24] The agriculture minister admitted, 'because of the acute shortage of essential skills and professions', his department was 'heavily dependent on seconded and contract staff'.[25] Under these tense circumstances, African politicians across political divides insisted on the dignity and status of African officials, especially when compared to their white counterparts. 'It is not proper that a promoted officer should shiver on a motorcycle everyday, no matter what the weather is like', complained one member of the legislature.[26] Another asked that African stock inspectors be given housing, just like their European counterparts: 'the Transkei is their homeland where they should be privileged to have all the rights.'[27]

From there, it was only a small step for junior officials to refuse orders – particularly from white superiors. 'Mr Pienaar's authority [Pienaar was the secretary of the Department of Agriculture] only goes as far as Umtata', claimed one agriculture officer, insisting that he alone had the power to close down dipping tanks in his locality.[28] As early as 1975 the minister of agriculture worried that 'a tendency seems to be developing where everybody expects to be the boss. Productivity is in decline and authority is not freely accepted … A stable and competent civil service cannot develop under such conditions'.[29] A detailed study into this problem made troubling reading:

> There is a chronic shortage of graduate specialists and field workers … [and] extension staff are relatively young and inexperienced, and generally have limited formal education, low morale and motivation … Problems of salary, short length of service in work areas, transport, housing, office accommodation, record and reporting systems place constraints on efficiency.[30]

As a result, there was widespread mistrust of officials in the Department of Agriculture. Allegations of corruption and malfeasance were endemic. One study suggested that only 14 per cent of senior agriculture extension officers and 24 per cent of other officers 'feel they know exactly what is expected of them', and half were not happy in their job.[31] In turn, less than a third of villagers surveyed in three localities could either name their local agricultural extension officer or explain his function. And during an outbreak of cattle disease, rumours were spread that bureaucrats had profited through 'sweet-heart' agreements with the pharmaceutical companies: 'While our stock is perishing, these officials are merely thinking about their personal gains.'[32] 'The young agricultural officers are continually causing confusion', complained another chief, 'because they maintain they are the bosses … We are then ruled by these boys.'[33]

Facing a bureaucracy that did not operate through formal procedures, many people instead accessed state resources by drawing on personal connections. Thus, ideas about personal authority associated with chieftainship became central in the processes of officialdom and bureaucracy. It was the idiom of complaint: 'The day when control was removed from the magistrates and handed over to these extension officers, who go by different names, is the day when everything went wrong', argued one local community leader.[34] Others suggested that local agricultural officials charged with enforcing government regulations were 'in danger of being molested by the local people' as 'they are unknown either to the people'. Instead, it would be better for a local community to choose these officials just as they would select a headman.[35] But a sense of personal connection was also the idiom of accountability in a dysfunctional state when official channels were often blocked and had to be bypassed. One location appealed for the return of two much-loved agricultural officers, who 'were of great assistance to our people'. Such personal connections went all the way to the top. One ANC supporter was 'left in tears' by the departure of the secretary (i.e. the top official) in the Department of Agriculture who had protected his locality from government harassment:

There was a complaint from the Thembu people that their cattle were not being allowed to graze on the commonage ... It was the Secretary who gave relief to the people of Engcobo ... He showed us respect as ... he would personally go to Engcobo to see that the cattle should be allowed to graze on the commonage.[36]

Thus, local officials reinvented themselves as both community leaders and local brokers able to access the power of the state. Some chiefs complained that fowls were slaughtered and beer brewed in extension officers' honour whenever they provided services in local communities.[37] Another explained:

The dipping labourer whose duty it is to fill the [cattle dipping] tank [with water] goes about his duties in this way. He brews beer and invites people to assist him in emptying the tank; then he fetches water to refill the tank. In order to do this he runs a furrow towards the tank, but moles and frogs sometimes block the furrow so that the water does not run freely. In the meantime [while the celebrations were being held], he expects the tank to be full by morning, but instead it is empty.[38]

The cattle-dipping crisis

The consequences of this pattern of economic development and the recalibration of the relationship between the Transkeian government and rural communities are evident in the cattle-dipping crisis of the late 1970s. An examination of this crisis also adds a significant caveat to a commonly held view that, under apartheid, chiefs became decentralised despots, i.e. the local pillars of the Bantustan state.[39] Rather, the breakdown of cattle-dipping services suggests that the Bantu Authorities system was more brutally frail than effectively authoritarian.

From the outset, the Transkei government retreated from maintaining stringent cattle-dipping regulations, just as it had backed away from fully implementing Betterment planning. It had good reason. As sites of state control where Betterment regulations were announced and cattle were counted so as to be culled, cattle dips had been one of the first symbols of apartheid to be smashed by angry protestors in the 1960 revolts. Thus, in office, with the memories of the revolt still simmering, Matanzima's government retreated from renewing its conflict with rural communities. Powers over cattle dipping were given to the nine new Regional Authorities of the Transkei chieftaincy, which had been set up under the Bantu Authorities Act. Regional Authorities were responsible for collecting the levies that paid for cattle dipping, raising the funds to build and repair dipping tanks, and employing the associated labourers and supervisors, as well as possessing significant powers to determine how often cows were dipped.[40]

These policies were designed to enhance the powers and administrative range of traditional authorities, but instead exposed their essential fragility. The reasons for this fragility are perhaps threefold. Firstly, it was a question of rural poverty: the rising dipping costs outstripped the ability of the Tribal Authorities to raise revenue. From 1966 to 1976, Transkei-wide, they were able to increase the money they raised through the dipping levy from approximately R190,000 to R430,000.[41] But this sum was a pittance, when R3 million was necessary to put dipping operations on a sound financial footing.[42] Dipping had long been a ramshackle affair run on a shoestring, and by the early 1970s some of the ticks that spread stock diseases were becoming resistant to the cheapest dip chemicals that were still used in the homeland regions.[43] The world financial crisis in the mid-1970s also raised the cost of dipping chemicals by a further 40 per cent, at a time when rural communities faced the additional strain of dipping their sheep against an outbreak of scabies.[44]

Secondly, in giving huge power to Bantu Authorities, apartheid ideologues had half-hoped to transform chiefs into administrators who could take on the functions of the state. Kaiser Matanzima made great display of being the best-schooled traditional leader in Transkei and that more should follow in his footsteps. Chiefs' salaries were restructured to reward the efficient collection of taxes. A prominent educated chief and politician, Sandy Majeke, admonished:

> Time is past when a chief has to be paid simply because he is a chief. He must be punished by low wages if he was too lazy to attend school … When a chief is in charge of an Administrative Area, he is performing a duty and should be paid on the same basis of other people performing duties. I hate the frequent talk that chiefs are always taking bribes and gifts.[45]

Yet these exhortations underlined the corruption and ineptitude of the lower reaches of the state. The language of governance within rural communities, as noted above, was becoming less bureaucratic and reflected the politics of the belly. In some ways this was literally so in that feasts sometimes went in tandem with official meetings. It was also metaphorically evident: the Public Accounts Committee noted that 'the less educated chiefs and headmen are not quite sure … what they can eat' and which receipts were to be paid into the public purse.[46] This style of governance was accentuated when power was devolved and financial accounts placed in the hands of Bantu Authorities. 'No-one understands it, the treasurers least of all ... The more sensitive keep threatening to resign because of the suspicion cast upon them through being unable what to explain what the balances are.'[47] Too often, administrative records quite literally rotted away in damp huts or were eaten by livestock who were kept in the same buildings as the files. In 1971 auditors found they could not balance any of the Tribal Authorities' financial accounts they had inspected.[48] In 1976 chiefs were required by law to both issue receipts when they demanded fines and also receive payments in cash rather than livestock.[49] There were no effective means of implementing this rule.

Thirdly, and perhaps most importantly, the very illegitimacy of the Tribal Authorities hamstrung the system. On the one hand, the Bantu Authorities system was ripe for abuse and became synonymous with local corruption and petty despotism.[50] The unelected appointment of chiefs and councillors 'deprives the great majority of taxpayers of a voice in the affairs of the district ... [and the] people of their ablest men', complained a native commissioner charged with implementing the system of government. 'The chief and his cronies are life members of the Tribal Authority. The only way to get rid of them is by murder.'[51] But chiefs were hardly firm pillars of authoritarianism, as some scholars have suggested.[52] Their very illegitimacy hampered their room for manoeuvre. And in the wake of the violent unrest against Betterment, chiefs were wary of implementing government regulations to the letter. One complained that 'I am not regarded as a headman but as a dipping foreman' and feared his people 'are conspiring to kill me.'[53] Regional Authorities often decided to reduce the regularity with which cattle were dipped, against the advice of the Department of Agriculture and scientific wisdom.[54] But conflict with government officials and the risk of an outbreak of cattle disease were preferable to facing the wrath of the people.

The result was disaster. Noxious dipping chemicals would sometimes 'overflow the banks and spread on the grass', because dip tanks were in such disrepair. In other locations, livestock died of poisoning when sheep and cattle were dipped together in an inept attempt to save costs.[55] Matters became so bad that by the mid-1970s three coastal districts were incapable of dipping their cattle during the summer months when tick-borne diseases were most virulent. 'Various districts ran out of money and so did not purchase dip or had no money to repair dip tanks leading to a breakdown of the programme', especially in Pondoland.[56]

The second Pondoland revolt

By the late 1970s many of Transkei's agricultural policies were failing – a crisis epitomised by the outbreak of livestock disease that followed from the decline in dipping. Apartheid officials had taken comparatively little interest in animal disease in Transkei since East Coast fever was brought under control, but an outbreak of sheep scab in the late 1970s brought stock dipping to the forefront of their minds once more. Pretoria threatened it would not import livestock from Transkei unless the government improved its cattle dipping. Although there was not a significant decline in stock numbers across Transkei, the state's increased spending on rural development, specifically subsidised cattle improvement schemes, was undermined by the collapse of disease control. The Transkei government-backed cattle marketing and meat company lost R92,000 worth of its stock through tick-borne diseases in 1976 alone, for instance.[57] There were complex socio-economic reasons for the failure of Transkei's rural development schemes and the commensurate stagnation of agricultural production; nevertheless, the political outcome was clear. Facing an epidemic of disease, the Transkei Department of Agriculture took over dipping operations from the Regional Authorities in the late 1970s. Within a year, there had been a 40 per cent reduction in the number of deaths caused by tick-borne disease.[58] Significantly, this transfer of power was happily conceded, even demanded – an indication of the changing relationship between rural communities and the Bantustan state.[59]

Yet in the late 1970s the Transkei state was struggling to take on additional responsibilities and financial commitments. It cost R3 million annually to put dipping operations on a sound operational footing and to give the woefully underpaid dipping staff adequate salaries.[60] This came at a time of 'Kaiser-gate', as South African journalists described 'Transkei's perilous state of near bankruptcy'. The government had run up huge deficits in the three years since Transkei's 'independence' in 1976, turning a surplus of almost R16 million into a deficit of R1.5 million. Of course, these amounts were relatively small and Umtata bitterly argued that financial transfers from Pretoria had declined.[61] Nevertheless, the system of state budgeting was in meltdown. Transkei's government departments had run up R5 million of unauthorised expenditure because of a 'general breakdown of financial administration' and 'complete disregard' of the Treasury. Transkei's civil servants were only paid in 1979 because of a last minute R70 million bail-out by Pretoria.[62] As a result, the Transkei Treasury was forced to make swingeing emergency cuts in its budget, from R328 million to R253 million, throttling the spending commitments of the other government departments.[63]

It was during this crisis that agricultural planners dusted off an old plan of introducing a livestock tax, which promised to solve the financial crisis and turn rural development around. The logic of this tax was deceptively simple. Firstly, and most immediately, when the government had taken on stock-dipping and veterinary responsibilities, it intended to claw back these costs by introducing a stock tax.[64] On top of this, additional revenues generated by the new tax would, secondly, force rural communities to pull their weight in reducing the government's debt – at a time when Pretoria was arguing that it would only give more financial aid if Transkei raised more revenue. It seemed unfair that rural communities hardly contributed to the Treasury. Indeed, the tax regime for rural areas was nonsensical: one levy had not been raised since 1925; while the revenue that was brought in was less than the cost of collection. Raising rural taxes by large amounts – the general levy and hut tax by a factor of ten, and general tax by 20 per cent – would give the government an additional R6.5 million. On top of that, a new livestock tax on cattle, sheep, goats, horses, donkeys and mules could yield an additional R28 million.[65] Together, these taxes could help plug the gap in government finances.[66]

Thirdly, and most important of all, the livestock tax promised to teach the importance of self-help to these obdurate rural communities, who irrationally kept disease-ridden cattle for no good reason and had become dependent on state handouts. It was expected that the tax would stimulate Transkei's cattle keepers to sell their stock; and by commercialising cattle keeping, rural communities would make money for themselves and the national economy. Behind this argument lay an immense frustration. Planners' calculations suggested that 80 per cent of Transkei's land was suitable for grazing and a properly managed livestock industry could make a profit of R40 million per year.[67] Yet less than 5 per cent of livestock were sold through commercial channels: in 1976, only R9 million worth of stock was slaughtered in abattoirs, when approximately R20 million worth died or was informally disposed of.[68] This was shocking when 'the number of herd sold at a single pen in one Tribal Trust Land [area in Zimbabwe] exceeded the total sold at auctions in the whole of Transkei'. Even the tiny Bantustan of Bophuthatswana was able to sell more of its herd through formal marketing channels.[69]

But when the livestock tax was introduced in the legislature on 23 March 1977 it 'was greeted with shocked whistles from members of the House, in spite of the prior warning given to them in a caucus meeting before the budget was introduced'.[70] Most fundamentally of all, most of Transkei's stock owners were simply not in a position to sell their cattle to pay for the tax. Only half of Transkeian households had cattle – the number of livestock in Transkei had dropped since its peak in the 1930s, while the population had grown more than two-fold. And of these cattle owners, almost 80 per cent had less than eight head – the minimum number considered necessary to have a surplus to sell to market.[71] The few households that had sufficient cattle to make regular sales disdained the government-run abattoir and marketing scheme. The auctions were rigged at the two stock sales pens at Cofimvaba, complained one chief. Owners were unable to get a fair price because the weighing scales were broken and there was only one buyer at the sales, who could command rock-bottom prices.[72] Ministers instead argued that prices were low because the government-backed corporation, which had the monopoly on the business of buying and slaughtering meat, had faced numerous problems: diseased and poor quality cattle; few economies of scale; even corruption and stock theft.[73]

This moment, almost as much as 1960, was a moment of crisis, as the state attempted to exert itself against rural communities and the regional powerbrokers. Tensions were particularly high in eastern Pondoland. As one of the main cattle-keeping areas in the Eastern Cape, it would be hardest hit by stock taxes, and as one of the poorest regions in Transkei, rumours persisted that Pondoland was hard done by compared to other regions. In the early 1970s, at a moment of comparative political calm, the *Daily Dispatch* newspaper reported how, 'women at Xura location [in Lusikisiki district] forced the official car of Chief Minister [K. D. Matanzima] to stop' during a time of drought. 'The women, carrying empty buckets, pleaded with Paramount Chief Matanzima to give them water to drink' and assailed the chief minister until they were driven away by security guards.[74]

Regional representatives now railed against the unfairness of the swingeing new stock taxes. They also gave dark warnings of rural uprisings. Cromwell Diko warned the government

that the 1960 disturbances were the result of an unfortunate decision made by [members of] this House … In Pondoland the ordinary man, if you have gone too far, will cut your neck … They will tell you: 'we sent you to parliament to put right our affairs and now you have decided to join Matanzima'.[75]

(Diko's warnings regarding the volatility of rural communities were personally prescient. Less than a decade later, during a local chieftaincy dispute, he was killed by a hired assassin.)[76] The Transkei government hurriedly revised its plans: less than two months later, the tax was reduced by a factor of five.[77] Yet even this was not enough. The people, particularly in Pondoland, were incensed. One member of the legislature reported:

[At the Great Place] where the Paramount Chief had called us [for a general meeting] … a discussion arose where the Honourable [government] Minister said it was essential for these taxes to be paid. When we had gone through the agenda the Pondos howled at us … We did our best … pointing out the tax [on cattle] had been lowered to R2 … We pointed out we were a free country, that if the Transkei is to be developed we would have to raise our own revenue … Even then they were not satisfied. They instructed us to come and explain the position to the House and have the taxes reduced again.[78]

Quietly, the livestock tax was abolished; a year later the much less expensive General Stock Tax was introduced. But even then it proved unpopular and tax collectors were only able to net two-thirds of the expected revenues.[79] During the 1980s the Transkei Agricultural Corporation (TRACOR) was set up and hived off from the Department of Agriculture, supposedly to reorientate agricultural policy by sustaining and supporting small-scale rural development schemes. Previous agricultural development projects had failed because 'unfortunately the people saw it as another government handout, and the net result of this attitude was that the objectives of various projects were not achieved', opined the director of TRACOR.[80] But TRACOR was tainted by the failings of its forerunners, and the old Bantustan patterns of state formation remained unbroken.[81]

Consequences and conclusions

When the ANC came to power in 1994 and incorporated Transkei into a larger, new province of the Eastern Cape, it was hampered by its inability to dismember and dispose of the remains of the Bantustan system. Many critiques of provincial government have focused on the appropriate role of the state in the economy. This debate follows the shift away from the Reconstruction and Development Programme plans and state-led economic growth to the neoliberal policies of GEAR (the Growth, Employment and Redistribution policy), in which the state prioritised welfare safety nets. Nevertheless, provincial governments have attempted to find ways to expand public works programmes and infrastructure spending. In the Eastern Cape, there have been echoes of the homeland era in that provincial government lacks capacity and has been criticised for incompetence and venality.[82] However, these issues cannot be understood without some consideration of the mutually constitutive relationship between state and society, and the difficulties the ANC government faced in building a better life for all in the ruins of the Bantustan state and apartheid system.

The provincial government inherited agricultural projects that had collapsed in the final chaotic years of apartheid, with state officials losing almost all authority. Dipping officials were no longer able to enforce the more onerous cattle-dipping regulations. When the work force employed by parastatals at Ncora irrigation scheme and Magwa tea plantation went on long strikes, agricultural operations almost completely fell apart. Even Tsolo College of Agriculture – the long-established flagship of agricultural education that pre-dated the homeland era – was thrown into a permanent state of strikes and anarchy and was looted by students and staff – an indication that government officialdom itself was in tatters.[83]

The bloated machinery of government itself faced an organisational crisis. The new provincial bureaucracy was formed out of the old Cape Province administration as well as the two overstaffed, dysfunctional Bantustan bureaucracies of Transkei and Ciskei. Creating a streamlined government machine out of three separate, mutually suspicious bureaucracies was a nightmarish task, which was compounded by the ANC's historic mistrust of these old apartheid and Bantustan administrations. More insidiously, the provincial government had inherited all of the old Bantustan development projects and corporations. In one sense their activities had provided welfare benefits of a sort – free ploughing and dipping services and the like – to marginal rural communities, but in a very ineffective way.[84] Newspapers made much of the scandal of the 15 directors general inherited from the old administrations, many of whom had been undeservedly promoted in the dying days of apartheid.[85] Yet most of the excess staff bequeathed to the new government were labourers who had been employed in the Bantustan bureaucracies on make-work schemes that paid wages of perhaps only R2,000 per month. These labourers accounted for most of the 11,800 personnel from the Transkei Department of Agriculture who were transferred into the new, 14,000 strong, Eastern Cape Department of Agriculture and Land Affairs (DALA).[86] The new provincial government hardly knew what to do with them: nine such workers sent to repair dipping tanks in an outlying district were stranded in leaking tents for three months because they had no equipment, for instance.[87] As a result, DALA spent 55 per cent of its budget on salaries.[88] And as an aggregate across all the province's departments, bureaucrats' salaries increased from 41 per cent to 45 per cent of government spending – at a time when the Ministry of Finance in Pretoria was demanding it was reduced to 35 per cent.[89]

These local crises were bound into wider debates about the role of the state in society and the economy as the ANC painfully moved from government-centred to pro-market doctrines of development. In particular, the provincial government seemed

155

at the mercy of the national Treasury, which doled out their budgets. The technocrats in Pretoria tried to use their financial clout to control the strategic direction of state spending. They squeezed DALA's spending, arguing that government resources were better directed towards social welfare rather than ineffectively subsidising economic infrastructure. Sometimes this argument was made in the neoliberal language of privatising government assets.[90] At other times, Marxist analysis was brought up to date: a parasitic bureaucratic bourgeoisie were denying destitute grandmothers their deserved pensions and social welfare grants.[91] DALA's spending demands were frequently refused, despite the protests of provincial politicians.[92] Money was taken from DALA to bail out the struggling provincial Departments of Education and Welfare.[93]

As a result, provincial governments' default mode in the late 1990s was to cut their liabilities wherever feasible. DALA announced that the government-subsidised tractor-ploughing service would come to an end. Having been advised that many plantations and irrigation schemes owned by parastatals were financially unsustainable, it tried to 'hand the projects over to the local community' – a euphemism for cutting thousands of jobs from the provincial payroll.[94] About 100 agricultural extension officers were cut, saving the province R20 million. And the 1,164 dipping assistants, whose salaries, by contrast, cost the government R28 million per annum, were dismissed from their posts and either transferred to other jobs or placed on the long supernumerary list.[95] This list was another euphemism for excess bureaucrats whose posts had been cut and who could find no other work. Under the 'sunset deal' in the national Constitution they could not be dismissed, even though this cost the provincial Department of Agriculture R44 million each year. 'They cause most trouble', fulminated the politician in charge of the department. 'They are a hell of a drain on the budget.'[96]

Despite these painful cuts, the provincial government was unable to juggle its spending priorities. It tried to pump its spare resources into more productive expenditures. The veterinary services budget was increased and personnel were given 34 bakkies (pick-up trucks) to help their work. Before that, they had 'basically been carrying cooler boxes with medicines on their heads', admitted a senior bureaucrat.[97] Nevertheless, 'animal health and vet services... were deeply affected by the budget cuts' and in 1996 animal death rates were seen to be very high.[98] Seven vets resigned or transferred to greener pastures because the department was unable to pay them salaries comparable to the private sector or other provinces. In 1999, 50 per cent of these posts were vacant and all the veterinary students from the province's universities who graduated that year immediately left the Eastern Cape.[99] And a further squeeze on spending meant that anthrax and rabies vaccination campaigns were suspended in 1997.[100] 'Cattle dipping … is the cornerstone of beef production', reported officials in one district, but the 'faltering of this service [now] results in massive economic losses'.[101]

Local officials, community leaders and NGOs sometimes moved into the space vacated by the provincial government, using the language of personal connections and status to give their work moral authority. Indeed, government policy encouraged this. For instance, it called on local communities to form dipping committees, led by chiefs and other community leaders, when dipping officials were cut from the provincial payroll. In one municipality, a well-known political activist, who worked in East London but maintained his family's rural homestead in the Transkei, organised sheep farmers to dip against scab.[102] Elsewhere, local vets made do with leftover drugs from previous vaccination campaigns.[103] In another municipality, a local government official, Kenny Jafta, helped people in the Mbashe district to negotiate the paying off of livestock loans that were suddenly called in by the Eastern Cape Development Corporation. A few years later he even managed to inspire local farmers to raise R167,000 to buy vaccinations when they were hit by an outbreak of lumpy skin disease. As a result, 'hundreds of [ordinary] people attend my meetings without [the inducement of] free food', he boasted.[104]

In one sense, there were continuities in the relationship between rural communities and the state, particularly the mediating role played by well-connected local leaders. However, the differences between the Bantustan and democratic government were immense and a much wider set of groups now came into contact with the state. For one, the ANC was supposed to be building a better life for all and government machinery was now supposed to be representative of, as well as working for, the people; many local political activists seized the opportunities available to make a mark in their localities. For another, the free-wheeling world of the new South Africa brought together a much wider set of local and national politicians and businesses in all sorts of complicated public–private partnerships. Local success and popularity could quickly lead to political prominence. Jafta, the Mbashe district government official referred to earlier, would turn up late for meetings with soil on his fingers, because he had been called at dawn – contacted on his mobile phone – by rural communities anxious that their crops might be suffering blight. He became the speaker of the assembly in his municipality, now tasked to pressurise other councillors into following his lead. His name was praised in provincial circles and the deputy president of South Africa at the time, Phumzile Mlambo-Ngcuka, even suggested she might encourage a supermarket chain to set up a vegetable-processing plant in the district. With her dismissal from office, Jafta feared that these all-important connections might be lost and the promised investment might not arrive.[105] But just a four-hour drive down the road, Mlambo-Ngcuka's husband was investing his wealth in a community dairy scheme in his home village of Middledrift in a public–private partnership also supported by the local Fort Hare University.[106]

Such local successes, however, were few and far between – the increasing incidence of animal disease and death was the most painful index of the breakdown in the relationship between rural communities and the state. In part, this was because many rural communities were too divided to work together. A local vet in Pondoland suggested that around half the local communities in his area failed to form dipping committees and many were thus unable to access free dipping chemicals. In a village on the coast where I carried out interviews, disputes between the two parts of the community disabled the dipping committee: one side accused the headmen and his associates, who controlled the committee, of keeping resources to themselves and misusing money that was collected.[107] Across the province, dipping tanks fell into disrepair and equipment was often stolen; there were even rumours that the dipping chemicals were, at times, used as poison in local murders.

Without state provision, relatively few livestock owners could afford to purchase medical supplies. 'The price of the vaccine is not affordable to the communal farmer', complained officials, particularly when the production prices of drugs increased.[108] Local leaders faced the ticklish task of collecting monies to buy medicines. Many of their neighbours and community could not pay into the communal pot, but would ask to be favoured with free veterinary treatment. The government itself felt these pressures too. The mayor of O. R. Tambo District (a new municipality formed out of half of the former Transkei) often had her skirt tugged by such supplicants when she spoke at funerals in her region. Sometimes her security guards would have to hold back the rush so that she had space to speak to one at a time.[109] In this way, the language of personal connection, obligation and shared ethnicity persisted; it simultaneously expressed relationships between political leaders and people, and marked social divides.[110]

It was in this setting that the provincial government set up a task team to bring back state support to rural communities.[111] What emerged, some years later in 2006, was the 'Green Revolution' strategy: a large-scale government infrastructure initiative for the former homeland areas. The six 'strategic pegs' of this plan essentially reintroduced the services once provided by the Bantustan government: fencing, dipping tanks and dipping material, stock water dams, tractors and farming implements, and irrigation infrastructure. Even dipping assistants were to be reintroduced.[112] These plans had the laudatory aim of turning the communal areas into a food basket – aspirations that were also recognised in national government development plans.[113] In this sense, the concerns of local politicians echoed the calls of Treasury technocrats, who were now arguing that rural agricultural development should no longer be ignored if a dent were to be made into the deep poverty in the former homelands.[114]

This expanded role promised for the state opened up more opportunities for political brokers – roles that were eagerly taken by many provincial politicians, bureaucrats and local notables. For example, the expansion of infrastructure projects created many more opportunities for local intermediaries and contractors. 'The high unemployment rate and severe poverty in the province' was a powerful impetus towards 'directing funds towards development projects' and other labour-intensive infrastructure spending projects, argued provincial officials.[115] Also, many ANC leaders understood their role in generating economic development as one of simply providing goods to rural areas. When communities claimed they could not pay back loans on tractors and other farm equipment, provincial politicians often caved in. It was very difficult to ignore these demands when, for instance, rural communities dumped their broken tractors outside the government offices in Bhisho demanding that they should be fixed.[116] Indeed, there were times when politicians used this language of politics with relish. In 1999 an ANC member of the provincial legislature, who was also a Transkei chief, was sent as an envoy to personally hand out desperately needed dipping materials to local communities.[117] DALA even faced allegations that its allocation of tractors to chiefs was simply a political gesture. 'We want Great Places to lead by example in reviving agriculture in communal areas', claimed officials in reply. [118]

Now, if anything, the pace of this pattern of politics has quickened with the election of Jacob Zuma to the presidency of the ANC, backed by a coalition of malcontents. Indeed, O. R. Tambo District, which sent a huge number of delegates to the ANC conference at Polokwane – more than the entire Western Cape – overwhelmingly voted for a change of leadership. This was in part a cry against the provincial and national politicians who had been perceived to be ignoring the plight of poor rural areas. Zuma himself adeptly uses the same language, handing out food parcels to widows in his home district of Nkandla. He has also talked about reviving institutions from the Bantustan era that brought sustenance to rural areas.[119] This language of communities consuming state resources has become an important discourse of redistribution in South Africa's highly unequal society that continues to influence the relationship between national and local politics. And it is one that follows on, at least in part, from the social identities that emerged from the transformation of rural society and its incorporation into the state.

8 'It's a beautiful struggle': *Siyayinqoba/Beat it!* and the HIV/AIDS treatment struggle on South African television[1]

Rebecca Hodes

'*Without television, contemporary humanitarianism would not exist.*'[2]
Bernard Kouchner (founder of Médecins Sans Frontières)

Introduction

Siyayinqoba/Beat It! is a television magazine show for 'everyone living with HIV, our partners, families and friends.'[3] It is screened weekly on channel 1 of the South African Broadcasting Corporation (SABC) to approximately three million viewers.[4] The audience ratings of the show have increased in correlation with HIV prevalence rates, thus signalling the increased demand for and consumption of HIV educational media in South Africa.[5] The National AIDS Helpline revealed that there was a 'dramatic increase' in the number of calls it received subsequent to the airing of *Beat It!* episodes.[6] Increased call numbers were sustained throughout the days on which episodes were screened and approximately a third of callers received the number through *Beat It!*, which includes an information bar about the helpline at the bottom of the screen. While South African television broadcasts a number of programmes that address HIV, *Beat It!* remains the only programme featuring a panel of HIV-positive participants and targeted specifically at an HIV-positive audience and, more generally, at a diverse South African public. The show is closely aligned with both the Treatment Action Campaign (TAC) and Médecins Sans Frontières (MSF), the leading HIV-focused non-governmental organisations (NGOs) in South Africa. It also has firm ties with numerous other organisations that have shaped the national response to the HIV/AIDS pandemic.

Beat It! has played a central role in public education about the struggle for access to treatment in South Africa. In late 2008 the show began its seventh series. Echoing many aspects of TAC discourse, the participants and producers of *Beat It!* have drawn frequent comparisons between the struggle for treatment access in South Africa and the anti-apartheid struggle. The treatment access movement has also been inspired by the radicalism of American AIDS activism embodied in the furious, media-savvy protests of the US-based AIDS Coalition to Unleash Power (ACT UP).

This chapter examines the historical links among ACT UP, the anti-apartheid movement and the treatment access movement in South Africa, focusing on the visual and discursive parallels that *Beat It!* draws among these three movements. It also traces the ways in which TAC and MSF involvement has influenced the show's content and presentation, as well as the composition of the programme's primary fixture – the *Beat It!* support group. The findings are based on detailed transcriptions of five series of the programme from 1999 to 2005 and interviews with the show's production staff and participants. An examination of the role of the mass media in the growth of social movements provides the historical context for this analysis.

The role of the mass media in the emergence and evolution of social movements

In a classic history of documentary film, Rotha, Road and Griffin describe the 'universal rise' of radio and cinema as representing 'the biggest revolution in instructional methods since the introduction of the printing-press'.[7] The emergence and entrenchment of globalised mass media have impacted fundamentally on the ways in which information is created and disseminated in the socio-economic, cultural and political spheres. It is one of the most prolific and powerful 'symbol-creating institutions', emulating and, in many instances, surpassing the traditional epistemological role of religion.[8]

The centrality of the mass media in democratic functioning has been widely documented as a result of the media's efficacy in the rapid and simultaneous spread of information to large groups of people as a vital means of maintaining political transparency and supplementing public education.[9] The power of the mass media is based on its ability to foreground or conceal problems, to legitimise or stigmatise groups or behaviours, to persuade and mobilise, and to entertain.[10]

Alberto Melucci acknowledges the role of the mass media in his study of contemporary social movements, citing the 'impressive development of communication technologies' as a decisive factor in the emergence of new social movements.[11] Another central strategy of these movements is their conveyance of a sense of urgency, and their insistence that action be taken and change effected without delay.[12] This sense of immediacy is also one of the most distinctive elements in the 'communication codes' of television, as is the medium's ability to convey and elicit emotion.[13]

In the emergence and consolidation of a social movement, collective action and the construction of identity are paramount processes, creating meaning and promoting group cohesion.[14] The mass media perpetuate these through their rapid, pervasive and persuasive presentation of information. In its initial stages, a social movement usually relies on the language of its predecessors, situating its new struggle within established discursive frameworks. In the case of South Africa's HIV treatment access movement, the radical protest tactics and discourses of AIDS activists in the United States provided a critical precedent. More significantly, however, the anti-apartheid struggle provided the discursive framework for *Beat It!*'s representation of the national HIV treatment struggle. *Beat It!*'s beginnings, and the programme's myriad parallels among local HIV activism, the treatment access struggle in the United States and the anti-apartheid struggle in South Africa, are discussed in the following sections.

Beat It's beginnings

The initial idea for the show pre-dated the birth of TAC in 1998, although the fissures that eventually led to the rupture of the National Association of People Living with HIV/AIDS (NAPWA) and the formation of TAC were already present. (See Mbali's chapter in this volume for a discussion of TAC's early roots in NAPWA.) The first series of *Beat It!* was screened in 1999 on the independent channel eTV and was a milestone in public disclosure as 50 HIV-positive South Africans declared their status on national television. This initial 'mass disclosure' was mounted in response to the murder of HIV activist Gugu Dlamini, who was killed near her home in a Durban township shortly after she had declared her status on a public radio broadcast.

The links between *Beat It!* and TAC are extensive, stretching from the programme's conceptualisation in 1998 to the present day. The programme was produced by the Community Health Media Trust,[15] which also produced TAC's *Treatment Literacy Project*, used in clinics across South Africa to educate people about living well with HIV, seeking correct and timely treatment for opportunistic infections, and adhering to antiretroviral regimens. The majority of *Beat It!* support group members were TAC members, and had extensive ties within both local and international HIV activist networks.[16] All support group members were self-proclaimed HIV activists. On examination of their connections to various organisations it was increasingly evident that *Beat It*'s participants were not part of an ordinary talk show, but rather the televised media wing of the treatment access movement in South Africa as led by TAC.

Protest parallels between ACT UP activists and the treatment access movement in Beat It!

In the United States, the initial response of activist groups to the emergence of AIDS was at best ambivalent.[17] Shame and stigma around gay identity and the disease itself prevented activists from mounting an organised response. Although the combination of escalating AIDS mortality, the smear campaign conducted by the moral majority against gay communities and the continuing negligence of the US government did inspire reactions by HIV-affected communities, it was the Supreme Court's *Hardwick vs. Bowers* judgement of June 1986 that catalysed the onset of radical AIDS activism. The ruling compared gay sex to 'adultery, incest and other sex crimes', and outlawed consensual sex between gay men and women.

The 'moral shock' that the ruling dealt to gay communities tapped into the vein of frustration and anger that had been mounting around the HIV epidemic. The result was a spate of protests and the rapid popularisation of a confrontational AIDS activism. The ACT UP slogan 'SILENCE = DEATH' became the mantra of the emerging movement, which employed the militant and eye-catching protest tactics of street theatre, civil disobedience, 'die-ins' and disruptions.[18] A central tenet of ACT UP's activism was its intertwining of art and politics. The organisation became renowned for its provocative demonstrations, constructed to appeal to television cameras. The use of stickers, pins, banners, posters and videos led to the emergence of a distinctive visual aesthetic and propelled ACT UP to the position of the United States' most visible social movement at the close of the 1980s.[19] The medium of video was used by DIVA (Damned Interfering Video Activists), a media offshoot of ACT UP, to publicise the movement's grievances. DIVA's establishment led to the invention of new cinematic approaches to the AIDS crisis and to the growth of new distribution networks, both of which have been consciously emulated by the producers of *Beat It!*[20] Producer Jack Lewis's account of the birth of *Beat It!* referred explicitly to the inspiration he derived from ACT UP media. Lewis recounted how he wanted to do

> something along the lines of what ACT UP had done, where we videoed the different actions that take place, and produced propaganda as well … and we were thinking of having a big screen on top of my kombi [minibus] and going to taxi ranks and other public places and playing stuff there all to generate an agitation. That was the original concept.[21]

The makers and participants of *Beat It!* have purposefully established many parallels between the treatment access struggles in the United States and South Africa. The links between the two movements are also clearly illustrated by the fact that TAC derived its name from a working group within ACT UP's structures.[22] The militancy of the latter group influenced the founding members of the South African treatment access movement, and transcontinental networks were established among activists that remained productive throughout the treatment access movement's growth and development.

While *Hardwick vs. Bowers* provided the 'moral shock' that ultimately engendered the shift towards AIDS radicalism in the United States, a corresponding example exists in the South African government's refusal in 1998 to provide public access to treatments for the prevention of mother-to-child transmission (PMTCT) of HIV. This decision radicalised South African HIV activists and resulted in increasingly overt condemnations of government negligence, which *Beat It!* broadcast. The efficacy of nevirapine and AZT in PMTCT programmes had been lauded at the Vancouver AIDS Conference in 1996 and further verified by South African doctors in public health settings shortly after. But in October 1998 Health Minister Nkosazana Zuma decided against the establishment of a national PMTCT programme. At this time in South Africa rising HIV infection rates saw approximately 70,000 babies born HIV-positive each year, and spiking infant mortality rates demonstrated the fatal effects of AIDS.[23]

TAC was galvanised into direct protests against the government's refusal to roll out a national programme of PMTCT, and the third episode of *Beat It!* was devoted largely to showcasing the efficacy of the programme and to encouraging viewers to seek PMTCT services. The documentary insert in this episode featured a young mother named Phumeza. While footage showed Phumeza engaged in domestic chores, the voice-over proclaimed: 'Phumeza is HIV-positive. She has received AZT which has prevented her from infecting her baby during pregnancy.' The viewer was then presented with images of Phumeza sterilising the teat of a bottle top and measuring out formula milk, conveying her maternal competence. A montage of newspaper headlines that delegitimised the government's initial refusal to roll out a PMTCT programme appeared on the screen. The succession of headlines read: 'Protect our children' (followed by text that stated: 'Former Pres. Nelson Mandela has called for urgent steps to protect SA's children from the HIV/AIDS scourge'), 'Govt runs out of reasons for not using drug' and 'W Cape hailed for curbing HIV in babies: Khayelitsha project "a success"'.[24]

Echoing the media of ACT UP and particularly the productions of DIVA, which often screened the personal testaments of activists, this episode of *Beat It!* drew on the power of individual experience to underscore the successes of a PMTCT pilot project. Subsequent footage of a support group for new mothers at Michael Mapongwana Hospital in Khayelitsha, Cape Town, included the following dialogue:

[Woman addressing the support group in Xhosa]: We have one of our ladies here who will further enlighten us about what AZT has done for her.

[Woman in the audience with a baby on her lap]: When I went to book at Michael Mapongwana, I was told that I would get AZT at eight months. I received AZT at eight months and my baby tested negative at nine months (see figure 8.1).

Figure 8.1: A support group for new mothers discusses the prevention-of-mother-to-child-transmission of HIV

Source: *Beat It!* series 2000, episode 3

Subsequent statements from Dr Fareed Abdullah, the chief director of support services in the Western Cape, reiterated the fiscal, moral and medical imperatives of the PMTCT programme. Abdullah stated: 'We estimate that for every rand we spend on prevention of MTCT, that we will save something like two and a half grand [thousand rand] on reduced admissions to our hospitals.'

After other interviews with MSF doctors who asserted the necessity of PMTCT programmes, viewers were again presented with footage of Phumeza and her baby girl inside her shack, conveying the message that poverty did not necessarily obstruct the efficacy of the programme. The baby was smartly dressed and seated on the bed, evidently well cared for. Phumeza handed the bottle to her and she grabbed it and put it into her mouth, a sign of vital infancy. The camera then focused on a tin of formula feed, another important aspect of the PMTCT programmes that had been discussed on the show. Phumeza picked up her daughter, placed her on her lap and kissed her while she started to drink the formula milk (see figure 8.2).

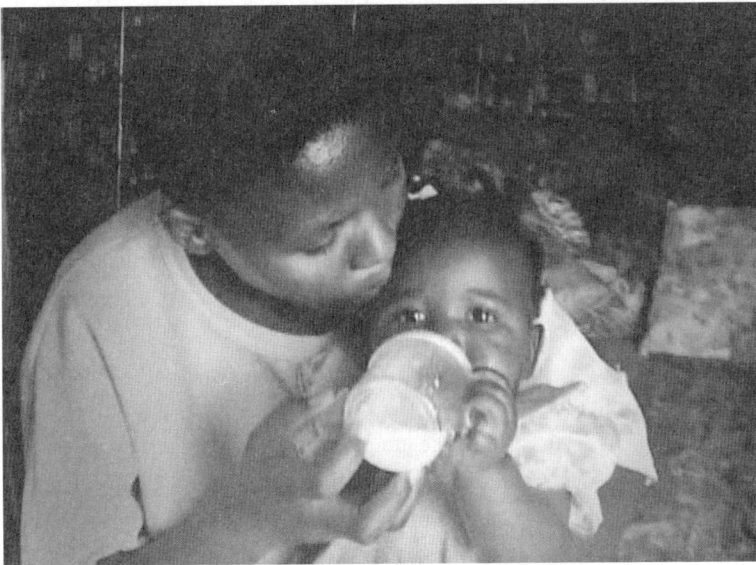

Figure 8.2: Phumeza formula feeds her baby to protect her from HIV transmission
Source: *Beat It!* series 2000, episode 3

The final images of the programme were statements of PMTCT's success and appeals to other mothers to access antiretrovirals and formula feeding to keep their babies alive and well. The episode concluded with direct statements made by the presenters about the importance of a national PMTCT programme:

Paddy Nhlapo: Hey Mercy, we really need this MTCTP programme to be introduced all over South Africa and the rest of Africa as well.

Mercy Makhalemele: It's not just words that you are saying. Seventy thousand babies are being born with HIV every year, and we could prevent most of that.

A later episode in the 2000 series opened with activists demanding free antiretrovirals for pregnant mothers. In this episode, criticism of the government was more explicit. In a documentary insert on PMTCT, TAC activist Adeline Mangcu told the audience of a World AIDS Day gathering: 'Think about this: 160 babies are born HIV-positive *every day*, and the government is saying "No" to AZT.'[25] The mobilising impact of the government's PMTCT refusal was re-emphasised later in the show, when Zackie Achmat, a TAC leader, stated at the international Durban AIDS Conference that TAC would 'commence legal proceedings' to compel the government to roll out a PMTCT programme.[26] Later footage captured Health Minister Manto Tshabalala-Msimang's recalcitrant response to activist pressure for a PMTCT programme. In addressing an audience at the Durban conference, she said: 'And in any case, we don't believe that the only way to prevent MTCT is using antiretrovirals.'[27] The show jumped directly to an interview with Achmat, wearing the HIV-positive T-shirt. He stated: 'The first reason that the government is dragging its feet is that it's found itself in an ideological muddle of whether HIV causes AIDS, and that is *completely unacceptable*' (figure 8.3).[28]

The programme then jumped back to footage of Tshabalala-Msimang on the podium. She continued her address at the conference: 'You do not have enough resources to buy drugs. We can't just be jumping on the bandwagon because we've heard that somewhere nevirapine was being administered' (figure 8.4).[29]

This statement was an example of the health minister's emphasis on the unaffordability of PMTCT drugs. The expense and harmfulness of drugs like AZT and nevirapine were misrepresented by the Department of Health under the influence of President Mbeki's AIDS denialism. *Beat It!* episodes on PMTCT often criticised governmental mishandling of PMTCT programmes and sought to dispel the confusion that had grown around antiretrovirals. After this footage of Tshabalala-Msimang, the episode cut back to the interview with Achmat, who clinched his indictment of the Minister's statement in the following way:

The second reason government is dragging its feet is because of its economic policy. Its economic strategy is one in which they are spending more money on repaying the old apartheid debt than they're spending on healthcare reform. And most important of all that the defence budget has increased by more than the rate of

Figure 8.3: Zackie Achmat condemning government's obstruction of PMTCT

Source: *Beat It!* series 2000, episode 7

Figure 8.4: Health Minister Tshabalala-Msimang arguing that PMTCT drugs are unaffordable

Source: *Beat It!* series 2000, episode 7

inflation, whereas the health budget has decreased, *per capita*, by the inflation rate and by the population growth rate. So we're in a situation where our government is spending more money on defence … than on the healthcare of its people in a situation where we have a tremendous health crisis.[30]

Achmat's comparison between government military expenditure and the health budget was a favourite staple of American AIDS activists during the 1980s. At a candlelight vigil to highlight the negligence of the US federal administration, a leading AIDS activist stated: 'Our president [Ronald Reagan] doesn't seem to know AIDS exists. He is spending more money on the paints to put American flags on his nuclear missiles than on … AIDS. That is sick.'[31]

One of ACT UP's most effective campaigning strategies captured by DIVA cameras was the accusation of genocide by governmental neglect.[32] Government officials were portrayed as murderers and people with AIDS as victims of state violence through indifference. The slogan: 'THE US GOVERNMENT HAS BLOOD IN ITS HANDS. ONE AIDS DEATH EVERY HALF HOUR', was printed on posters, T-shirts, stickers and badges. It is an example of the succinct and polemical graphic aesthetic of ACT UP, with its simple lay-out, use of stark colour (red, white and black) and bold imagery (a bloody hand print against a blank background) (figure 8.5). This slogan was copied directly by South African HIV activists protesting against the Department of Health's alignment with Matthias Rath, a controversial vitamin salesman and AIDS dissident who claimed that his products could cure the disease. In episode 15 of *Beat It!*'s 2005 series, footage of a protest against the unregulated experiments conducted by Rath in Cape Town's townships featured a poster with a big red hand emblazoned behind text stating, 'YOUR HANDS ARE BLOODY RATH! SOUTH AFRICANS WILL NOT BE RATH"S GUINEA PIGS' (figure 8.6).[33]

While TAC printed posters with the face of the Minister of Health and the slogan, 'WANTED FOR MURDER' and Achmat referred to the government's HIV policies as 'a holocaust of the poor',[34] *Beat It!* was not able to broadcast these remarks or images as the SABC forbade such direct condemnation of the government on its airwaves.[35] However, there were dozens of other instances in the programme in which the government was harshly criticised, often by guest speakers or medical experts who had joined the support group, or by footage that exposed and indicted government for neglect.

In episode 12 of the 2005 series, which examined the failures of the antiretroviral roll-out, a woman from Queenstown whose sister had died of AIDS while on the

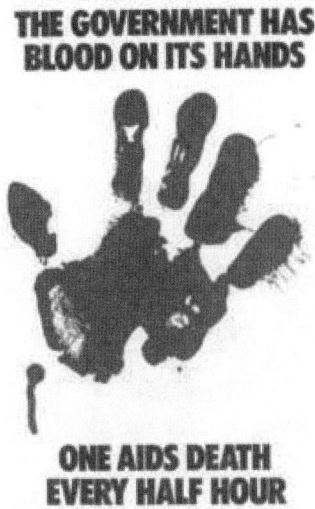

Figure 8.5: An ACT UP poster using a bold graphic condemning the response of the US government to AIDS

Source: ACT UP poster, <http://www.campusprogress.org/tools/941/out-with-the-new>

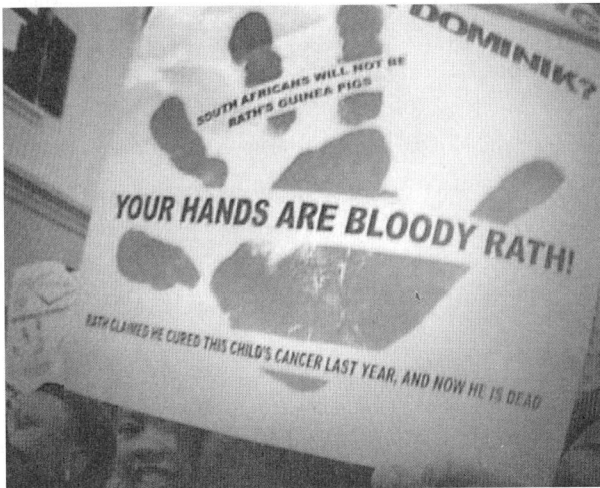

Figure 8.6: A TAC poster, borrowing an image from ACT UP, condemning the harmful and unauthorised experiments of AIDS denialist vitamin seller Matthias Rath

Source: *Beat It!* series 2005, episode 15

waiting list for antiretrovirals, made this emotional statement: 'I think the government doesn't care if people are living or dying [tears streaming down her cheeks]. They don't care about people with HIV as long as things are looking bright on their side' (figure 8.7).[36]

Figure 8.7: Caroline Songqushwa mourning her sister's death from AIDS while on the waiting list for antiretrovirals

Source: *Beat It!* series 2005, episode 12

The same episode emphasised the negligence of government when a woman with AIDS on the antiretroviral waiting list personally confronted another in-studio guest, the Director General of the Department of Health Thami Mseleku.[37] The support group's reaction was openly disdainful, and the presenter drew the discussion to a premature close as some members grew increasingly angry over the Director General's inane responses.

The fatal effects of a disinterested bureaucracy were also bemoaned by American activist Roger Lyon in his renowned statement at a 1983 congressional meeting about the inadequacy of the federal response to AIDS. The quotation was later preserved in cinematic history by its inclusion in the blockbuster film, *And the Band Played On*,[38] as well as being memorialised in a panel on the AIDS quilt (figure 8.8). Lyon, at the time suffering from Kaposi's Sarcoma,[39] had travelled from San Francisco to deliver the following plea:

We do not need infighting. This is not a political issue. This is a health issue. This is not a gay issue. This is a human issue. And I do not intend to be defeated by it. I came here today in the hope that my epitaph would not read that I died of red tape.[40]

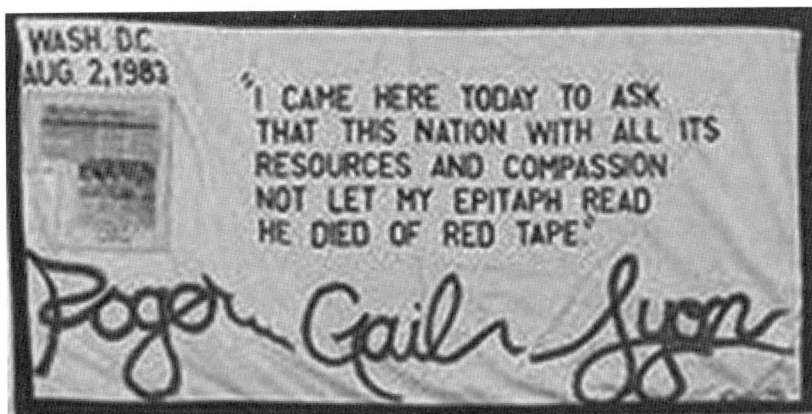

Figure 8.8: Roger Lyon's panel in the AIDS Memorial Quilt

Source: <http://home.cfl.rr.com/atbpo/>

One of the most important ideological assertions by radical AIDS activists in the United States was their refusal to term HIV-positive people 'victims' or 'sufferers'.[41] Instead, they established the moniker, 'People with AIDS', and the term 'Living with HIV' (in contrast to 'dying of AIDS'). But the information ACT UP disseminated was based on in-depth background research into the biomedical and commercial aspects of HIV treatment. Thus, these activists articulated new identities as HIV 'health citizens', equipped with the technical knowledge to compete with medical experts and pharmaceutical industry spin doctors on a more equal footing.[42]

By the end of the 1980 ACT UP's 'SILENCE = DEATH' sloganeering, in addition to medical developments and increased knowledge about the workings of HIV, resulted in the gradual erosion of the AIDS stigma in the United States.[43] By the 1990s, and especially after the emergence of highly active antiretroviral therapy in 1996, HIV/AIDS was increasingly portrayed as a chronic but manageable disease. The emergence of the new identity of the aware, empowered and motivated HIV-positive activist, initiated by the treatment access movement in the United States, greatly influenced and inspired the activist discourses of *Beat It!*[44] Like its predecessors in DIVA, the production staff of the programme realised early on the power of language

173

and naming. Therefore, the show's participants frequently asserted that they were 'living positively with HIV', and spurned the terms 'victim', 'sufferer' and even 'patient'.

The necessity of antiretroviral access and the lengths that South African AIDS activists were willing to go to procure treatment were illustrated in the 2000 series, when Zackie Achmat travelled to Thailand to procure generic fluconazole.[45] He purchased hundreds of boxes of the drug for distribution in South Africa, where its cost and lack of accessibility in public health clinics had resulted in several AIDS deaths, among them TAC activist Christopher Moraka. The point of Achmat illegally importing the generic drug was also to expose the profiteering of the pharmaceutical enterprise.

In a later episode from the 2003 series, South African HIV activists again travelled overseas to visit a generics pharmaceutical company, with *Beat It!* cameras in tow. This time they toured Farmanguinhos in Brazil, which manufactures medicines for the country's public antiretroviral treatment programme.[46] The tactic of purchasing and illegally importing HIV treatments also originated in the United States. During the 1980s a group of Californian AIDS activists, the 'Tooth Fairies', even compiled a purchase guide of experimental AIDS treatments in Mexico and gave advice on how to smuggle them through customs.[47]

Finally, what resonated between the protest actions of ACT UP and South African HIV activists on *Beat It!* were their protests and memorial ceremonies. While ACT UP demonstrators pretended to be corpses lined up on pavements outside pharmaceutical company headquarters and fertilised the lawn of the White House with the ashes of their loved ones who had died from AIDS, *Beat It!* showcased footage of a march for antiretroviral treatment in which dozens of small coffins, painted white with red crucifixes to represent AIDS deaths, were used as protest props. The programme portrayed the winner of Miss Stigma-Free, a Botswanan beauty pageant, draped in her sash while conducting an HIV awareness workshop at a primary school (figure 8.9).[48] It also recorded a meeting of HIV-positive mothers working on their memory boxes and captured the angry shouting of an activist clutching a garlic clove that was part of the South African pavilion at the Toronto AIDS Conference in 2006. Antiretroviral medications were initially absent from the display.

While *Beat It!* represented numerous parallels between American and South African HIV activism, the show made even more prominent use of the anti-apartheid struggle as a comparative framework.

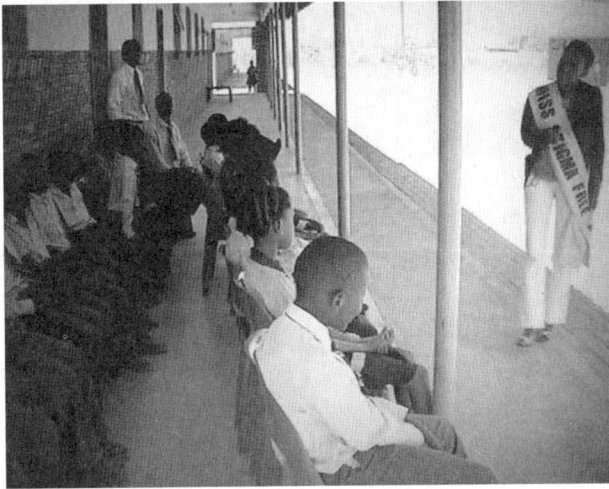

Figure 8.9: Botswana's 'Miss Stigma Free' conducting an HIV awareness workshop at a school

Source: *Beat It!* series 2005, episode 13

HIV as the 'new struggle'

The rhetoric of the anti-apartheid struggle is a trope of South African national culture, and TAC has been described as 'a stepchild of the popular struggle that brought racist rule to an end'.[49] Michael Rautenbach, *Beat It!*'s content producer, who was involved in the End Conscription Campaign during the 1980s, described the commencement of his work at *Beat It!* as follows:

> It was like plugging back into a vein of popular politics. ... It felt like I had come home again. It felt like there was something very familiar from the songs to the activism to the camaraderie.[50]

Vuyani Jacobs also referred to the experiential and iconic connections between the two struggles:

> The anti-apartheid struggle became a cornerstone of the struggle against HIV. You had a lot of beautiful white labourers who had serious communist backgrounds, people who never actually finished the old struggle, who never ended up in jail, who would have wanted to feel how it is go to jail [laughs] .... You had the fantastic

175

young people who actually wanted to feel how it is to sing *toyi-toyis* because at the time they were so young that they could not join, during the eighties. It's a beautiful struggle.[51]

Each series of *Beat It!* included portrayals of the agitprop used by South African HIV activists. The programme's representations of marches, songs, protest dances, posters, banners and T-shirts established obvious and purposeful connections between this 'beautiful struggle' and its predecessor, the anti-apartheid struggle. In an episode from the 2004 series, which focused on student-led HIV-awareness campaigns in schools, a banner proclaimed: '1976: Youth Against Apartheid, 2002: Youth Against HIV/AIDS' (figure 8.10).[52]

Another episode in this series included footage of a spirited protest with treatment activists wearing the iconic HIV-positive T-shirt. A large banner on the wall situated the struggle for access to antiretroviral treatment within the semantic mould of anti-apartheid resistance. It stated: 'FORWARD WITH THE TREATMENT PLAN!! Treat the People!' (figure 8.11).[53]

The ubiquitous HIV-positive T-shirt, worn by many of the show's participants, bears brief analysis. The T-shirt was designed subsequent to the murder of Gugu Dlamini in 1998 to oppose stigma, but it gained celebrity when Nelson Mandela wore it to his meeting with Zackie Achmat in 2002. This meeting, in which Mandela pleaded with Achmat to begin taking antiretrovirals, was widely covered by the national press. Mandela's wearing of the shirt was seen as a public statement of solidarity with the HIV-positive community, and an encouragement to disclose. The T-shirt is a well-established prop from the anti-apartheid era. It is an effective means of social movement propaganda, as it involves the body of the protester. By covering one's torso with an image or a slogan, ideological alignments are elevated to the level of the corporeal. *Beat It!*'s persistent portrayals of protesters in the HIV-positive T-shirt conveyed the message that, like the anti-apartheid resistance fighters before them, HIV activists were willing to use their whole selves – voices, movements and torsos – to achieve their goals (figures 8.12 and 8.13).

The figure of Mandela played an important role in the programme (see the articles by Klein and Sihlongonyane in this volume for a comparison of the role of Mandela iconography in the anti-apartheid struggle and South Africa's heritage industry). In every episode of the programme there was a clear image of Mandela on the walls of the lounges where the support group held its discussions. In many instances, a programme's introduction showed the presenter welcoming the viewers and outlining the topics for the day, with a clear view of Mandela's image in the background. The qualities and struggles of these two figures, the iconic statesman and the programme presenter, were thereby linked, inviting viewer identification with the show's messages (figures 8.14 and 8.15).

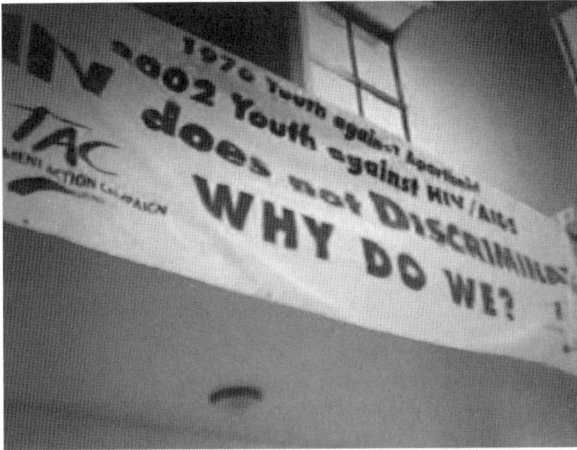

Figure 8.10: A TAC banner promoting HIV awareness among youth

Source: *Beat It!* series 2004, episode 4

Figure 8.11: A TAC banner celebrating the national roll-out of antiretrovirals

Source: *Beat It!* series 2004, episode 8

177

Figure 8.12: TAC protestors wearing the HIV-positive T-shirt

Source: *Beat It!* series 2003, episode 12

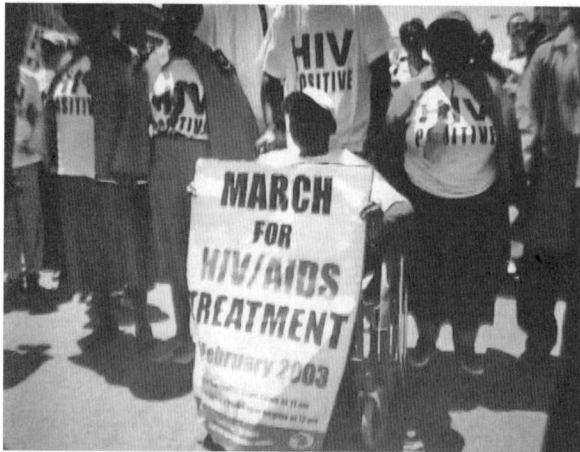

Figure 8.13: TAC protestors wearing the HIV-positive T-shirt

Source: Source: *Beat It!* series 2003, episode 12

It is notable that Peter Baker, the programme's cameraman, began his career as a documenter of the anti-apartheid struggle, filming the township uprisings of the 1980s. Much of the show's footage of marches is reminiscent of the jittery, frenetic coverage of the popular protests against apartheid. The screening of mass demonstrations calling for a public antiretroviral treatment campaign, for the availability of treatments

Figure 8.14: A Beat It! presenter addressing viewers with a clear image of Nelson Mandela in the background

Source: *Beat It!* series 2004, episode 1

for opportunistic infections and for an end to violence against women conveyed similarities between anti-apartheid activism and HIV-activism.

Beat It!'s reliance on rhetorical parallels with anti-apartheid resistance was also illustrated in its frequent footage of protest leaders and their reception by the crowd. The programme's portrayal of HIV activist marches and demonstrations uniformly included shouts of '*Amandla/Ngawethu*' and '*Viva!*' As mentioned above, T-shirts and posters emphasised the collective identity of the protesters. Movement leaders delivered impassioned statements from stages and fists were often raised. Camera angles were kept low so that the viewer watched the marchers as if he/she were on the ground, inviting solidarity with the protesters (figures 8.16 and 8.17).

Figure 8.15: A Beat It! support group discussion taking place with an image of Nelson Mandela on the set wall behind them

Source: *Beat It!* series 2005, episode 17

Figure 8.16: A TAC protest against pharmaceutical profiteering, shot at a low angle by Beat It!'s cameraman

Source: *Beat It!* series 2000, episode 2

Figure 8.17: A TAC meeting shot at a low angle by *Beat It!*'s cameraman

Source: *Beat It!* series 2003, episode 12

The visual and discursive emulation of these anti-apartheid resistance tactics was embodied in Achmat's speech at the end of the Durban AIDS Conference, captured in *Beat It!*'s 2000 series. Against the backdrop of TAC posters and wearing his HIV-positive T-shirt, he addressed the audience:

> On Sunday 9th July we mobilized a historic coalition. We led a march to demand HIV/AIDS treatment access. [Onscreen images show hundreds of demonstrators moving through a city street, their chanting and singing audible on the soundtrack, and the presence of an armoured police vehicle tracking their progress]. More than a thousand people joined the march, representing organizations with millions of members worldwide. [Like the international Anti-Apartheid Movement, the sense is of a groundswell of solidarity and support from a global activist community.] We will prepare a defiance campaign against drug companies.[54]

The National Treatment Congress in June 2002 recalled two aspects of anti-apartheid resistance. In both title and outcome it was reminiscent of the Congress of the People of the 1950s. It produced the National HIV Treatment Plan and, like the Freedom Charter, which was born out of the Congress of the People, it demanded an end to restrictions that threatened and oppressed South African citizens.

A final link among the resistance tactics of South African HIV activists, anti-apartheid activists and radical AIDS activists in the United States was in the show's politicisation of death and funeral ceremonies. Consonant with many other rhetorical parallels, Achmat explained how TAC leaders adapted the old resistance slogan, 'Mobilize! Don't Mourn' to, 'Mobilize and Mourn!'[55] Influenced by anti-apartheid resistance in South Africa, ACT UP members used the funerals of leading activists as opportunities to transform private ceremonies into angry spectacles of needless death.[56] Similarly, the last episode of *Beat It!*'s 2000 series ended with images of the funeral of activist Queenie Qiza, a long-standing TAC leader. The footage of Qiza's funeral showed her resting in her coffin surrounded by mourners (figure 8.18). The camera panned out to show a protest being held around the grave, with banners, songs, and posters demanding public antiretroviral treatment programmes (figure 8.19). Qiza's pallbearers wore HIV-positive T-shirts, and other T-shirts bearing the faces of activists who had died from AIDS. A final close-up focused on one of the shirts that read: 'Hambani Kahle! Produce Generic Antiretrovirals, Treat HIV/AIDS' (figure 8.20).[57]

Figure 8.18: Mourners at Qiza's funeral

Source: *Beat It!* series 2000, episode 13

The first series of *Beat It!* documented the beginning of the Christopher Moraka Defiance Campaign, a TAC project launched in 1999 after the death of one of its early leaders from oral thrush, a treatable and preventable opportunistic infection. In one of the earliest episodes, Moraka wore the HIV-positive T-shirt while giving evidence to the Parliamentary Portfolio Committee on Health on the high cost of Diflucan, Pfizer's patented version of fluconazole and the first-line treatment for thrush.[58] But after Moraka's appearance in parliament, the episode cut to an interview with him in bed where he was dying of AIDS. The next image showed Moraka's coffin being carried by mourners with HIV ribbons on their lapels. One of them told the camera: 'Chris was a pillar to us in the Nyanga branch and the Treatment Action Campaign, because on our way forward, in many respects, Chris strengthened us.'

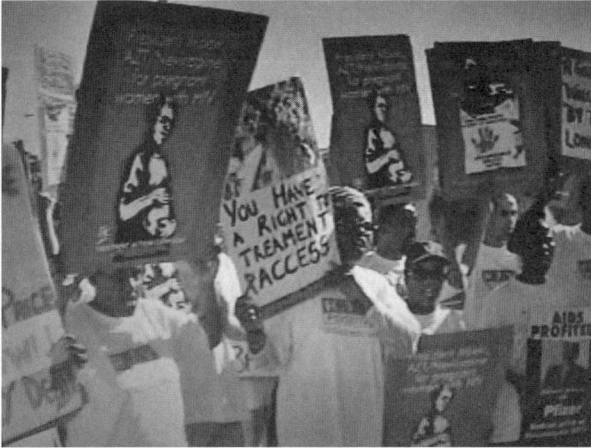

Figure 8.19: Protester's at Qiza's funeral condemning government's denial of public access to antiretrovirals

Source: *Beat It!* series 2000, episode 13

There was a clear resonance with the political funerals of anti-apartheid activists, in the sense that their deaths were regarded as part of a wider struggle. That Moraka's death had galvanised protesters into action was shown in the next image sequence of the episode, which showed a TAC march with protesters, running with raised fists and holding banners that proclaimed: 'Global March for Access to HIV/AIDS Treatment'. Placards bore the words 'AIDS PROFITEER' pasted across the image of the Pfizer CEO (see figure 8.16). Others stated, 'REDUCE PRICE OF FLUCONAZOLE NOW', and, most significantly, 'HAMBA KAHLE QABANE: "PICK UP THE FALLEN SPEAR", VIVA COMRADE CHRIS, VIVA TREATMENT ACTION CAMPAIGN' (figure 8.21). Accompanying these images, the presenter's voice intoned: 'Christopher Moraka died on the 27th July this year. His funeral took place at Nyanga on 6th August. Those present vowed to remember him for his courageous spirit in the fight against HIV and AIDS.'

Figure 8.20: Qiza's pallbearers wearing T-shirts honouring her memory and that of other TAC members who had died of AIDS, as well as promoting TAC's campaign for access to generic antiretrovirals

Source: *Beat It!* series 2000, episode 13

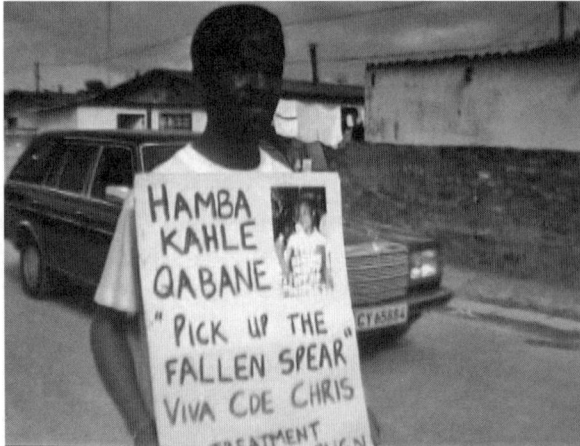

Figure 8.21: A TAC member mourning the death of Christopher Moraka

Source: *Beat It!* series 2000, episode 2

Like fallen comrades in the 'people's struggle', Moraka's death had been enshrined in the memory of the movement as it had instigated the 'defiance campaign' that bore his name. His death had not been in vain and was held up as an example of heroism to others, as well as a summons to act. The language and structure of the campaign resonated with two particular surges in the anti-apartheid resistance: the anti-dompas (pass law) Defiance Campaign of the 1950s, from which TAC's campaign drew its name, and the broad-based United Democratic Front (UDF) resistance of the 1980s, from which it drew its songs, its use of the media, its reliance on national and international activist alliances, and its grassroots mobilisation.[59] TAC's campaign garnered wide media coverage in the South African press, publicising the harmful effects of the international drugs pricing regime and global inequities in access to medicines.[60]

Divergent imagery

While *Beat It!* depicted many discursive and visual similarities between the struggle for HIV treatment in South Africa and the struggle to end apartheid, its episodes also illustrated certain important differences between these two movements. Although *Beat It!* sought to convey the universality of the HIV struggle, emphasising the UDF-like broad base of its membership through, for example, the diverse backgrounds and identities of the support group, the movement was largely constituted by black women. This was illustrated by the programme's footage from marches, in which it was apparent that women dominated the ranks of the protesters (figures 8.22 and 8.23). The great majority of studio guests who appeared on the programme to discuss the work of HIV-focused NGOs were women and the women characters in the support group were the most effusive, often directing the discussion.

In contrast, the anti-apartheid struggle, particularly within its later guise as the 'comrades' movement of the 1980s, was an overwhelmingly masculine project whose leaders today constitute an elite.[61] While women in the anti-apartheid struggle were typically relegated to supportive and domestic roles, they have played a powerful and very visible part in the HIV treatment access movement. De Waal outlines how their realities of continuing impoverishment and mounting mortality from AIDS repudiated the rhetoric of the transition and galvanised these women into action. The struggle for treatment for HIV-positive South Africans was launched as a national movement subsequent to the government's refusal of public access to PMTCT treatment. This was an issue of primary importance to poor women who are disproportionately infected by HIV/AIDS, and who depend on the public health service for medical care. The gender and economic status of the majority of South African HIV activists also contrasted with the organisational make-up of ACT UP in the United States, whose members were largely professional gay men with university qualifications. But while both ACT UP and anti-apartheid activists vilified the political regimes under which they operated, demanding drastic change and emphasising the injustices committed by the state, the HIV activists that *Beat It!* represented were more concerned with the fulfilment of political promises than their revolutionary re-evaluation.

Figure 8.22: Beat It! footage showing that TAC protests and events were dominated by women

Source: *Beat It!* series 2000, episode 2

Increasing anger over unemployment, low salaries, lack of essential amenities and continued inequality is demonstrated in the widespread 'service delivery' protests of the post-apartheid period, particularly in the large-scale public sector strikes that occurred across South Africa in mid-2007. In the latter, the previous vanguard of the resistance, the urban work force, criticised the ruling party, demanding quicker and genuine redress and more equitable economic distribution. Reflecting a similar sentiment, *Beat It!* broadcast many indictments of government negligence and inefficiency as voiced by support group members, expert guests and members of the public. However, even though these critiques were often intensified by damning visual evidence of the obstruction failure to solve social and health crises, the purpose of the programme was not to alienate the government. Rather, it aimed to ensure that the Constitution was upheld and that people could access the services to which they were entitled. For instance, in an episode from the 2005 series on the antiretroviral roll-out, a young woman named Nozuko Smile shouted to a crowd of protesters:

Figure 8.23: Beat It! footage showing that TAC protests and events were dominated by women

Source: *Beat It!* series 2000, episode 5

I want to get ARV [antiretroviral] treatment and I know that I have the right to get it. [Footage shows the disgruntled faces of the other protesters.] I don't know why I have been on the waiting list for so long. [Image of the protesters walking down the street, carrying coffins and banners. One reads: 'A people's contract for better life: MAKE HIV/AIDS TREATMENT WORK ...'] But we are here to say, 'Begin to save our lives!' It is our human right, it is in the Constitution! [The crowd roars its support.][62]

But *Beat It!* episodes also praised the government in instances in which the production staff and participants believed it had been earned. Various episodes highlighted the benefits of social grants and the freedoms guaranteed under the Constitution, including employment equity, gender equality and equal rights for people of all sexual orientations. Moreover, positive developments in the struggle for antiretroviral access were celebrated and the government was praised for honouring its constitutional commitments. However, the obstruction of public access to antiretroviral treatment until 2003 meant that state-sponsored AIDS denialism and the lack of treatment access became the primary focus of *Beat It!*'s political critique. The programme consistently conveyed the necessity of the struggle for public access to antiretrovirals.

Conclusion

The use of film as a medium to expose injustice or to promote the causes of a social movement has a long history in South Africa. Although television was only admitted to the country in 1976, once the apartheid government believed it could monitor the subversive potential of the medium, as far back as the 1920s film was being used to inspire change and galvanise action.[63] While television was used internally to bolster the credibility of the apartheid regime, some important documentaries exposed its iniquities to the international community. Similarly, while the mass media, and particularly television, played an initially harmful role in the emergence of the HIV pandemic – sowing hysteria and reinforcing stereotypes about so-called 'risk groups' – it was later used to foster awareness about both prevention and treament.

It is not the purpose of this chapter to quantify the influence of *Beat It!* on HIV activism in South Africa. However, the beliefs of the programme's participants in this regard are relevant because of how they have shaped the show's intentions. In discussing the programme's role in documenting developments relating to HIV in South Africa, Prudence Mabele stated: 'I think they played a very big role, because in every case I think Jack Lewis was there to televise it.'[64] *Beat It!* cameras sought to capture every significant development in South African HIV activism, faithful to Grierson's documentary ideal of relaying reality in the service of public betterment and social responsibility. Vuyani Jacobs reaffirmed the show's focus on the power of action and agency in his assertion that 'the leadership of people living with HIV has been one of the most important parts of democracy … and *Beat It!* has been at the forefront of that.'[65] Commenting on her role in the show, Busisiwe Maqungo asserted:

> Thousands of people's lives have changed through what I'm saying. Sometimes it's not only because you'll find that some of the people … have knowledge when it comes to HIV. It's not only about the knowledge or the information that we give, but the way we bring it to the people.[66]

By using the same discursive strategies and communication codes as its resistance forebears, *Beat It!* added weight and salience to its messages. Bringing the emotive force of television to bear, the show has documented the 'beautiful struggle' of HIV activists in South Africa.

9 The Nelson Mandela Museum and the tyranny of political symbols

Mfaniseni Fana Sihlongonyane

Introduction

Since the dawn of democracy in South Africa in 1994, the government led by the African National Congress (ANC) has used the memory of the liberation struggle in the social construction of space in several of its national development programmes. These include the Reconstruction and Development Programme (RDP), Spatial Development Initiatives, Urban Regeneration Programme and Expanded Public Works Programmes. The use of the struggle memory by the South African government is consistent with global trends whereby public memory forms part of cultural capital for promoting urban development.[1] Many emblematic buildings and projects, characterised by technological feats such as the Guggenheim Bilbao Museum, have been placed at the centre of urban regeneration practices to showcase the design styles of world-renowned architects. This is referred to as 'hard branding' and it is used to evoke reactions from citizens and the media.[2]

While hard branding based on the reputations and signature styles of global architects has become a common feature of contemporary cities, South Africa is 'iconising' its buildings and projects using the names of its struggle heroes. This process – 'soft branding' – involves the use of political and celebrated identities to steer the course of urban development in order to instantiate a particular form of nationhood. Unlike 'hard branding', which invests heavily in the physical and material development of space, 'soft branding' relies on the symbolic attachment of memory to a particular place. Whereas the former generates popular fanfare out of its aesthetic flare, the latter, as in the case of South Africa and elsewhere,[3] derives recognition from the signification of space through the personalities of individuals, in South Africa's case its struggle heroes.

This chapter focuses on the Mandela Museum project in the township of Alexandra in Johannesburg, which is part of the Presidential Urban Renewal Programme. It looks at the instrumentality of the symbolic politics of Nelson Mandela, whose support campaign is cogently discussed by Klein in this volume. The discussion explores how the ANC government uses the memory of the struggle as the official version of collective memory in the social construction of space in the township. In the process, the chapter draws out the political threads that bring together the various seams of power in the manufacturing of consensus. It also highlights the discordant views among the Alexandra residents affected by the project. The central argument of the chapter is that a particular version of South Africa's past has been carried through into the present, permitting a certain degree of continuity as far as political symbolism is concerned. Official struggle memory has become a crucial instrument in the social construction of urban spaces in South Africa due to the government's concerted effort to commemorate national heroes. These endeavours are part of an attempt to rebrand Johannesburg as a 'world-class' city, which has been motivated by the dual objectives of boosting tourism and thus the local economy in disadvantaged areas, while also projecting the city as an *African* city.

Inadvertently, however, the honouring of heroes has had dire consequences for some of the people on the margins of society, who were evicted from their homes to accommodate the construction of the Mandela Museum. While 'GlobalAfrican'[4] struggle icons – meaning people who combine international recognisability and local credibility – are promoted, the interests of some local people have been marginalised. Moreover, local township heroes and struggles have been neglected in favour of icons of the national liberation struggle, while female activists and heroes from other organisations besides the ANC have been undermined. As a result, private tourism consultants and ANC liberation aristocrats have been advantaged, while local communities continue to struggle.

Soft branding and nostalgia

Soft branding has been widely used in South Africa as a way of reinstating African heritage in cities in an attempt to create new meanings for space in the post-1994 period. It is an aspect of nation building that is underpinned by a sense of nostalgia. Svetlana Boym identifies two kinds of 'performative nostalgia': the reflective, which dwells in -*algia*, the bitter-sweet pain of longing and loss, occasioned by the 'imperfect process of remembrance'; and the restorative, signalled by *nostos*: the desire to return to the original, to rebuild the lost home and patch up memory gaps.[5] This sense of longing comes through strongly in the desire to brand Johannesburg as an African city and also through attempts to recapture the African past through the symbolic use of space. The decision to pursue soft branding, as opposed to hard branding practices, is motivated by three primary factors. Firstly, it is very expensive to acquire the services of international iconic architects or planners; secondly, there is widespread opposition among the citizens of South Africa to conspicuous spending by government; and, thirdly, the government feels politically compelled to deal with the past memories of apartheid by replacing them with new memories of the struggle.

Soft branding is central to the enactment of a new South African statehood through the prevailing norms and values of the struggle heroes. There is a perception that the deliberate use of images of these heroes advances African nationalism in order to invoke a new sense of belonging, national peculiarity and community. Struggle heroes with a 'GlobalAfrican' character tend to be favoured. Mandela is an international role model of peace and reconciliation and the concept of Mandela is widely promoted throughout the world. Much the same can be said of the Dalai Lama, Mahatma Gandhi, Martin Luther King, Jr and Dietrich Bonhoeffer. In a way, the idea of Nelson Mandela provides one of the profound compensatory subtexts that enable the ANC government to give development operations a thematic content in order to evoke restorative nostalgia.

Mandela's phantom

One of the projects to be 'soft branded' in Johannesburg is the Mandela Museum (see figure 9.1) located at the corner of 7th Avenue and Hofmyer Street in the township of Alexandra, which lies about 14 kilometres north-east of central Johannesburg. This project was initiated by the Gauteng Tourism Authority (GTA) in 2003 as part of the R1.3 billion Alexandra Renewal Programme (ARP) and was jointly funded by the GTA, the ARP and the Department of Environmental Affairs and Tourism to the tune of R6.7 million. These benefactors work in conjunction with the local Department of Arts and Culture office. According to the museum's architect, Peter Rich, the project aims to engender 'confidence, pride, hope and belief'.[6] The ARP states that the objective of the project

> is to create a vibrant, sustainable tourism industry in Alexandra that builds upon the rich resources of arts, culture and heritage to encourage entrepreneurship and to play a role in promoting civic pride to improve the quality of life of the residents of Alexandra.[7]

Figure 9.1: Mandela Museum towering above Alexandra township

The Mandela Museum is located at a site opposite the house that Nelson Mandela allegedly occupied in the 1940s. It includes the development of the Mandela Yard Interpretation Centre, which is intended to be 'an interactive exhibition telling the stories of the people, places, events and ideas that have shaped Alexandra over the last 100 years', as well as the Community Archive and Resource Centre, 'documenting the diverse aspects of Alexandra's history and heritage' (see figure 9.2).[8] As such, the museum seeks to provide leisure, education, escapism and aesthetics that evoke certain sensibilities, leading to what Dan Hill refers to as 'emotionomics', in which a profit is generated out of an emotional response to a memorable event or place.[9] For Gilmore, this marks a new stage of progression in value. He argues that

> over the last two hundred years, we have witnessed a shift from an Agrarian Economy based on extracting commodities, to an Industrial Economy based on manufacturing goods, to a Service Economy based on delivering services, and now to an Experience Economy based on staging experiences.[10]

Indeed, the experience economy is at the centre of tourism, leisure, arts, film, food and entertainment as they are promoted by the Department of Arts and Culture in South Africa.

Figure 9.2: Mandela Interpretation Centre showing 7th Avenue

The rationale behind branding the museum with Mandela's name derives from the sentiment attached to his residence in the township in the 1940s. Mandela's biography, *Long Walk to Freedom*, documents how he moved from the rural Eastern Cape to the city of Johannesburg for the first time in the 1940s, where he stayed in Alexandra Township for three years before moving to Soweto.[11] Over time, Mandela developed a towering personality as an anti-apartheid struggle hero, moving from participating in the underground struggle, to imprisonment on Robben Island, to becoming South Africa's first black president, and eventually commanding the stature of a respected world leader (see Klein, this volume).

Several artefacts, streets and buildings in Johannesburg bear the names of Mandela and other struggle heroes in politics, sports, music and academia. These include the Nelson Mandela Bridge in Braamfontein, Joe Slovo Road (which replaced Harrow Road) in Hillbrow, Beyers Naude Drive (which replaced D. F. Malan Drive) and O. R. Tambo International Airport (which replaced the already renamed Johannesburg International Airport, which was formerly known as Jan Smuts Airport). Mandela's image in particular has become a powerful site of symbolic and cultural production within the politics of the national imaginary. Indeed, Nixon has stated that the cultural cache generated by his international repute remains the ANC's best resource.[12] Since the 1990s Mandela's symbolic significance has grown and shifted from being a symbol of resistance (as highlighted in Klein's chapter) to being the prime symbolic legend that is definitive of the new optimism about Africa and its inhabitants.

The museum is intended to be one of the focal points of tourism for the township and a powerful symbol of the struggle for local residents. The presence of the museum in Alex serves to bolster township tourism and, more specifically, 'struggle tourism'. According to the project coordinator, Zodwa Tlale, who is based at the Alexandra Department of Arts and Culture office, struggle tourism involves a combination of visits to historical sites of the anti-apartheid struggle, as well as experiencing the conditions of life in the former black townships created under apartheid.[13] The building is designed so that visitors can walk through the Mandela story, pausing to look out over Alexandra at strategic intervals, relating past to present 'very directly'.[14] Just like the Hector Pieterson Museum (in Soweto) and the Apartheid Museum (in Ormonde), visitors are able to access information through interactive computers located in the exhibition space, the Community Archive and the Heritage Resource Centre. The Community Archive includes materials such as oral history interviews, photographs, newspaper articles and documents collected by the Alexandra Social History Project.

The Interpretation Centre also offers facilities such as a tourism information office, a restaurant and a range of retail outlets intended for visitors to purchase locally produced crafts and other memorabilia. The facilities are earmarked to be operated by local entrepreneurs.[15] The project forms part of a planned tourism development route (see figure 8.3) in Alex designed by a consortium of consultants, including the Heritage Resource Agency and Mafisa Research and Planning.[16] The promotion of heritage tourism has become a means by which 'management gurus', business planners and consultants convert memories of the struggle into new products that can be easily consumed by visitors. Knowledge of the struggle is packaged into commercial forms, and these products are commodified through a range of different media. The route connects with Sandton (one of the wealthiest suburbs in Johannesburg) through Grayston Drive via the Roman Catholic Church, the Mandela House and the cemetery up to the Kings Cinema area.[17] This experience is marketed under the rubric 'Heritage Route'. Other tours include: 'Intro to Alex' and 'Alex by Night'.[18]

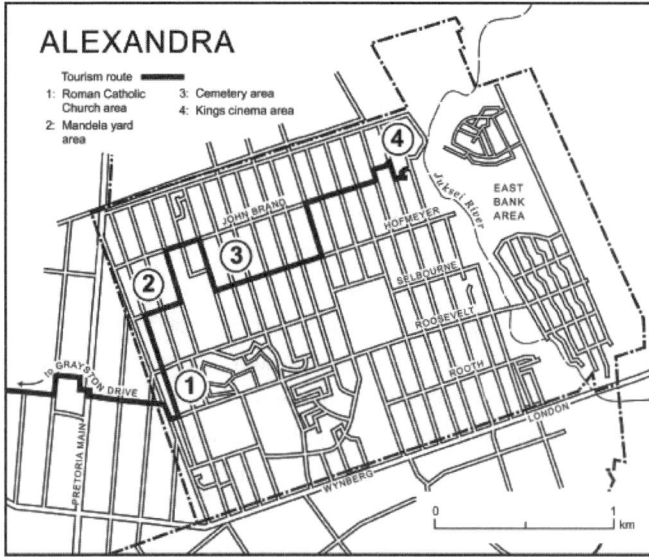

Figure 9.3: Planned tourism development route in Alexandra

Source: L. Kaplan, 'Skills development for tourism in Alexandra Township, Johannesburg', *Urban Forum*, 15, 4 (2004), p. 385

The development of this Heritage Route formed part of the GTA mission 'to stimulate, co-ordinate and facilitate sustainable tourism development and marketing of the Gauteng province', and is part of its endeavour

> to create sustainable jobs by training tour guides and hosts to welcome visitors and preserve the living history of Alex. Its objective is to create a world-class destination that will attract tourists, business people and all other visitors who will contribute to the province's economic growth and benefit the communities.[19]

Its objective resonates with the theoretical concept of the 'circle of growth',[20] whereby the promotion of tourism supposedly attracts visitors, who in turn encourage investment and economic development, which reinforces a positive image of a particular place and thus encourages tourism.[21] 'The challenge for marketers, therefore, is to be able to promote an image distinctive enough to achieve a competitive advantage.'[22] Thus, image campaigns are considered a crucial component in the circuit of cultural promotion.

Mandela's image was crucial because its various cultural ramifications were implicated in the reproduction of power relations in the township. The launch of the project was crowned by the celebration of Nelson Mandela's 85th birthday on 18 July 2003 at the house that he is believed to have inhabited in the 1940s. Mandela's symbolic signature on the project raised a profound sense of communal admiration. His presence produced a celebratory atmosphere and his struggle image created a sense of euphoria, which hid the dire implications of the project for some of the residents. Mandela's image brought with it the hope of imminent change in the urban regeneration programme. Around the township, large yellow notice boards read: 'It's happening in Alex.'[23] The boards signal areas where the ARP is under way to improve the physical, economic and social environment of the township, and the Mandela Museum is the promotional highlight for tourism in the area. Zodwa Tlale was convinced that this development would generate business opportunities for the residents of Alexandra: 'With tourists coming to Alexandra, small businesses will be able to sell their goods.'[24] Similarly, most of the Alexandra residents interviewed believed that the project would 'generate jobs'.

The critical character of this museum lies in the image conjured up by the name rather than its physical attributes. Meethan conveys this point in his claim that human-made structures can symbolise a community's shared values and experiences.[25] Knowledge of a symbol's collective meaning identifies the community that belongs to a place due to symbolic association. As noted, in Alex the local residents felt a sense of pride and optimism when this museum of significant heritage was installed in their midst. One of the local residents exclaimed: 'This is not an ordinary museum, it is a Mandela museum!'[26] Another resident stated: 'I think it will change the image of the city because it will create jobs and attract tourists.'[27] The opening of the museum, as demonstrated in the celebrations around this event, was seen as an affirmation of Alex's homeliness; 'a place I would not leave even if I were to have a lot of money'.[28]

However, branding is open to multiple interpretations. Several of the respondents harboured negative feelings towards the establishment of the museum, because people were displaced from the site where the building currently stands. When asked about the museum's contribution to Alex, an angry resident, directing his anger at Mandela, vented: 'The only thing he did is to bring his museum here and destroy our house with empty promises of payments. They promised us fifty thousand rand!'[29] Another local resident sarcastically stated: 'Hmm, yes, the museum has helped out because it has given everyday jobs to two security guards.'[30] But another resident from the same street was optimistic: 'Ja, it has made this area on 7th Avenue to be more attractive. A lot of people from outside are passing though this street now.'[31] These divergent responses suggest incongruence between creating a vibrant image to attract investment and raise Alex's profile and meeting the aspirations of the local community to improved employment prospects and social services. From a political point of view, it demonstrates that Mandela's legacy, like all historical reputations, is open to competing interpretations and constructions, even among devoted supporters.

The devil in the detail: Relocation and resistance

Forty-eight of the families that were displaced in the process of erecting the museum were interviewed for this study. An evictee, who now stays at a transit camp provided by the local authority, related her ordeal:

> Two men, named Jacob and Justice, came in October 2003 from the housing department office. They said, 'You are going to move to give way for the use of this area. *Lendawo sizoyisebenzisa* [We are going to use this place].' When we asked why, they said the Council wants to build a museum and they wanted us to take Bram Fischer [settlement].[32] This was frustrating. We asked about Extension 7 [in Alex], but they said ours is Bram Fischer.[33]

The evictee's story was ratified by her colleague, who said that the government representatives 'just came to tell us to pick up our things and go.'[34] Tales of being suddenly uprooted remind one of the forced removals that took place during the apartheid years. Authorities appeared to be no less sympathetic in present-day Alex than they would have been in the past. Jacob, the project manager from the council (who was later interviewed at the camp) was nonchalant about the evictions: '*Ja*! I told them what was going to happen in that area. We brought them here and I know each one of them.'[35]

Among the respondents who resisted eviction, there was a sense not only of material loss, but also a fear of losing the memory of being an Alex resident. While the area surrounding the museum already possessed imaginative properties of historical substance in the form of the Mandela brand, Bram Fischer settlement did not provide the same imaginary leverage for its residents. For this reason, an evictee described the removals as humiliating. She said, '*Bantu bebasihleka, bathi siyalahlwa*' (Non-displaced neighbours were laughing at us because we felt we were being thrown to an unknown place). Hence, they found it difficult to move to Bram Fischer, an unknown entity. Rather, they preferred to move to Extension 7, because it is still in Alex. However, this was not presented as an option for the uprooted residents.

Two informants, both from 6th Avenue, indicated that at first the residents were told by the officials from Region 7 that they were going to build flats in the area and that they would be compensated.[36] This official line was subsequently changed and they were told that they would be relocated to Bram Fischer to give way for the Mandela Museum. The local people formed a committee and went to assess Bram Fischer. They discovered that it did not have the promised houses and lacked amenities such as water and electricity. They informed the council that they were not leaving and a protest erupted. 'We said, *"Asiyi eBram Fischer!"* Bram Fischer no!'[37] An evictee, now at the camp, recalled: '*Kwaliwa impela* (It was a big fight). When we resisted, *umlungu weza* [the white man came], and marked the houses that were going to be removed.'[38] One respondent from 7th Avenue said: 'I don't even know when they came here. They were not negotiating. They just said the plan does not want these houses here.'[39] These comments signified the persistence of apartheid-like practices outside the ambit of the policies of the previous regime.

Faced with eviction, residents reacted with panic and anger. They held a number of meetings in which they discussed the issue and decided to get a lawyer to represent them. Each person contributed R50 (about $7), but the council came up with 'a divide and rule strategy. Jacob, the project manager, demanded permits for house ownership. This divided us in between as some of us did not have permits for shacks'.[40]

There was further division and disappointment after the court case was lost as people did not get their R50 contribution back. Some of the people (11 families in total) agreed to be taken to Bram Fischer, but others stayed put. The council brought bulldozers to flatten the houses and told the remaining residents that those who wished to concede and go to Bram Fischer would be transported to the transit camp. The rest of the group then agreed to be moved. 'As they removed their belongings from their houses the bulldozers were flattening the structures.'[41] This was undoubtedly reminiscent of the District Six and Sophiatown removals of the apartheid era, which suggests that market rationality has replaced the racist logic in the reconstruction of urban spaces, with the same pernicious consequences.

A total of 34 families were taken to the fenced Zandfontein Transit Village camp, half a kilometre from the museum (figure 9.4). These families joined others who had been removed from surrounding areas, such as those near London Road,[42] when the Earth Summit was hosted in Johannesburg in August 2002.[43] Five families remained and fought the case through their personal lawyers, but it was not long before they were also removed and taken to the camp. Three weeks later they were allocated two RDP houses in Extension 8 in Alexandra.

Figure 9.4: Zandfontein Transit Village camp/Vezunyawo

Those in the transit camp were told that they would be taken to Bram Fischer in three weeks. When the house contractors from Bram Fischer came to register them, residents protested vociferously against the planned relocation. 'We said, "*Asiyindawo! Asihambi la!*"' (We are not going anywhere! We are not leaving this place), an evictee exclaimed.[44] The protest involved everyone in the camp. Jacob, who was on leave at the time, was called in to intervene in the crisis. He described the mood as, 'very fierce' and said that 'even the public police could not come into the camp'. People armed themselves with sticks, canisters, petrol bombs and a range of other kinds of weapons. Jacob explained:

When I came here, it was tense. They almost killed him [pointing to his colleague, Colin, who was manhandled by the angry protesters, but managed to flee]. When I came, all the officials were standing outside the gate at a distance, including the police. I came in alone and spoke to the angry crowd … You see, I was straight from my church[45] [signifying that he possessed some spiritual power over the crowd]. Everyone stood still and listened to what I was saying. … The people did not want to go [to Bram Fischer] and the council decided that they cannot be moved away more than a 15-kilometre radius from Alex.[46]

The residents displaced by the museum were asked why they resisted leaving the camp. 'You know, we are not happy about this camp. As you can see, it is too small, that's why we call it Vezunyawo',[47] literally meaning 'exposing the foot'. Another camp resident claimed that the dwellings were 'too hot, too cold and too small'.[48] Other problems arising from the dwellings' small size include a lack of privacy. 'I can't have visitors here, my belongings do not fit, and there is a lot of noise', complained an informant.[49] Another lamented: 'People are really not happy about this place. Okay, it's better than nothing. But as you can see, they call it all sorts of names.'[50] Some of the monikers included 'Who's who', 'The Zoo', 'Lindelani', 'Silvertown', 'Emazenkeni' and 'Marlboro Transit Camp'.[51] Zandfontein Transit Village camp, the official name, was not used at all.

Some of the names are a clear indictment of the conditions in the area and reflect the sentiments of the people who were forced to live there. The name 'The Zoo' suggested that the camp was unfit for human occupation. 'You can't put your family here if you love it', said an evictee originally from Limpopo.[52] Another elaborated: 'This place is a "who's who". It is full of foreigners – Nigerians, Zimbabweans – our kids are not safe.'[53] Complaints about robberies, lack of security and noise were often accompanied by xenophobic sentiments. The name Lindelani comes from a Zulu word that means 'keep waiting'. It is commonly used to symbolise transitory areas. Chizuko Sato (this volume) discusses Lindelani and Thandanani (meaning 'love each other'), two 'tent towns' on a labour farm in Weenen that were established following apartheid era evictions. Lindelani is also the name given to the place of safety in Stellenbosch where children accused of committing crimes are accommodated while they await trial. The other names – Emazenkeni, Silvertown and Marlboro – draw from the descriptive character of the respective places and convey a certain social standing. The mere mention of Silvertown raised memories of apartheid removals and desperation. As one evictee stated, 'If you say you come from this area, everyone knows *uyahlupheka*' (you are in trouble because you don't have a place to stay). Similarly, *emazenkeni* in the Nguni languages is a derogatory word for poor housing. Marlboro in this specific case also has a negative connotation, since adjacent to the camp there is the old Marlboro industrial site whose factory shells are surrounded by shacks. The residents refer to it as 'Baghdad', as a metaphor for the devastation created by the war in Iraq (figure 9.5).

Figure 9.5: Shacks in the old industrial site of Marlboro next to the transit camp

Names, both official and unofficial, speak volumes as metaphors for and metonyms of space. They often reveal different mechanisms of resistance, shifting modes of protest and rearticulations of identity. They are loaded with emotion and are 'social missiles' of attack and counterattack used to contest the social construction of space. As forms of local protest, these names do not reverberate citywide or globally because they have a limited connotative effect constructed in contestation with the Mandela brand. They represent an act of insurgence since they challenge official names and evoke narratives and imagery that contest not only the official version of collective memory, but also the manufactured consensus about the present and future. While playing on words and altering official place names is by no means a new tactic in popular protest, a key difference between the apartheid and post-apartheid periods is that under the former regime there was an unmistakable enemy (as illustrated in several of the chapters in this volume). However, in the post-apartheid era, the target of popular resistance is often ambiguous. In the case of the protests against the Mandela Museum in Alexandra, the displaced people were not always clear about the target of their anger: the project leader, the council, the national government, the civics who took their money, or even Nelson Mandela himself.

Urban 'themespaces', fetishisation and 'mythscapes'

Besides the Mandela Museum, other spaces of 'GlobalAfrican' expression in the projects created by urban planners in Johannesburg include African villages, museums, heritage sites, tourist routes, fashion and entertainment hot spots, restaurants, and shopping malls, most of which are intended to valorise consumption. These themed spaces are design oriented with specific mottos, slogans and mission statements that strive to capture the mood of the new South Africa and they usually target niche markets of consumers. While the selective nature of these thematic spaces has already been acknowledged above, it is important to note that the selection of memory in the reinvention of places is also powerfully influenced by the 'anticipated interests of the tourist's gaze'[54] and 'themespaces' tend to be strategically located in areas that are unlikely to be missed by tourists. Such spaces are imbued with meanings determined by what the government or private tourism consultants deem fit for the area as an attraction. Within such imaginative spaces, consumption is based on illusory pleasures or anticipated emotions. Furnishing space with particular meanings facilitates branding and creates places of distinction that are often exclusive and expensive to access.

Branding the museum raises the issue of fetishism. For Marx, a commodity becomes a fetish when the quantification of qualitative relations allows for abstraction to take over.[55] With abstraction 'comes the danger of obscuring the nature of social reality'.[56] High prices are tagged onto the commodity's symbolic or representational value. In this process, urban imagery and narratives of the liberation struggle become 'naturalised' as though they bear an inherent value and exist independently of the people for whom the struggle was a tangible experience. Fetishised images thus emphasise the final product and not the process of production. Consequently, the human input and social power involved in this process are written out of the picture. In the case of the Mandela Museum, the diverse local memories, experiences, hardships and traumas recounted by the displaced people are not mapped and remain virtually untraceable in council reports. Fetishisation comes into play in the museum project in the magnification of the meaning of the end product, disconnecting it from its local, human processes of struggle and contestation. Everyday histories and recollections of Alex are subsequently blurred, while the deliberately selected, profitable image of Mandela is buoyed up, gradually becoming a fixture in newly manufactured memories.

However, the emphasis on the Mandela brand is problematic. While it may be true that Nelson Mandela lived in Alexandra for a while, the family who owns the so-called

'Mandela house' (see figure 9.6) claim that Mandela did not actually live there in the 1940s. A family member said:

> Nelson Mandela was brought by Mfundisi [the pastor] into our family, and he was treated as a family member when he came here. He was allocated to a backyard room and paid no rent. The house was never Mandela's ... The council also wanted to buy the house, but we refused. The ARP then put up that history board without our consent [see figure 9.7]. Visitors are coming here now and again. We feel we no longer have authority [over] the house ... Even when Mandela came here, they took photos and they told us they will bring them back up till today.[57]

Mandela himself wrote, '[Alex] was home where I had no specific house'.[58] For over 60 years now he has not had a real presence in the township. Moreover, the idea of building a museum bearing Mandela's name was not initiated by local residents, but rather by the GTA. The project was not part of the local Integrated Development Plan. Finally, the forced removal of over 50 families in order to free up sufficient land for the development of a tourist museum is questionable in a democratic society.

Figure 9.6: The 'Mandela house' in Alexandra

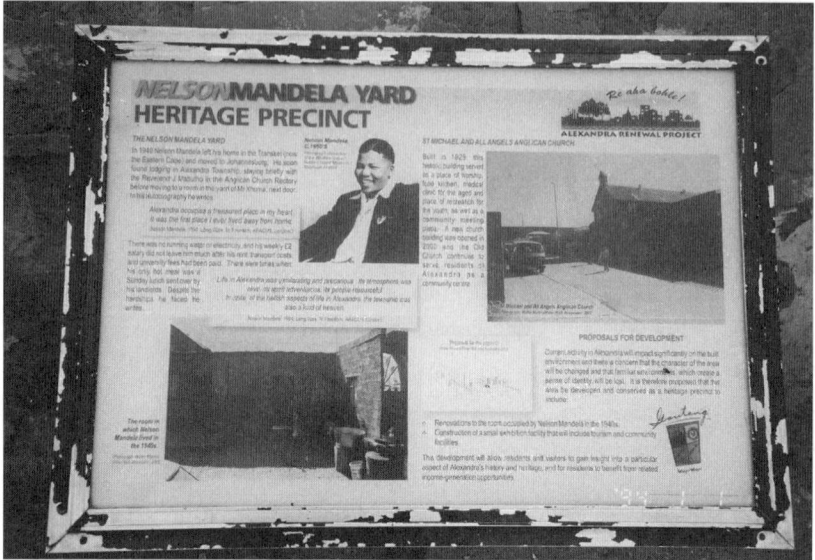

Figure 9.7: Claiming space: Nelson Mandela Yard heritage precinct

The desire to have a Mandela museum was thus initiated and sustained by the invented memory that Alex was 'home' to Mandela. Alexandra Township consequently forms part of the 'mythscapes' around which the legendary biography of Mandela was constructed to inform people's memory in order to mobilise for the development of the museum site. The branding of the museum with Mandela's name therefore demonstrates how symbolic representation is endorsed by mythical consciousness, which Cassirer defines as a process in which people become so enthralled by an imaginary tale that they are driven into action to bring the fantasy to life.[59]

The contrast between the real and the imagined reveals the tension between public memory and private memory and also between national and local claims to the space. While the project in the township was intended to generate positive developments for the local population, several residents were subjected to even worse circumstances than before the establishment of the museum. The state's heritage plans, coupled with commercial interests and the desire to satisfy the tourist gaze, silenced voices of opposition. The state thus acts as an agent of globalisation by resuscitating what seems to be latent local history into a manifest memory of rule and order. In both material and discursive ways the state influences the economic, social and imaginative geographies of the city with lasting implications for what is celebrated and what is forgotten or rendered invisible in the urban consciousness, whether it is acting on behalf of local residents or of capital.

Conclusion

In many cities in South Africa, the soft branding of memories of the struggle has become a central component of local strategies of economic development. In Johannesburg in particular, adopting images of prominent struggle heroes and, to a lesser extent, heroines has become a means of conveying to the city's citizens a positive belief in the vision of a world-class African city. It is the prominence of Mandela's image around which the powers that be are attempting to enliven Alexandra's economic potential and simultaneously build civic pride. But the way in which the Mandela brand was used in the township of Alexandra raises concerns about sincerity and social justice. Lowenthal reminds us that the past is often altered by states to make history conform to memory: 'Memory not only conserves the past, but adjusts recall to current needs ... scenes, events, persons, and things that were ambiguous or inconsistent become coherent, straightforward and clear.'[60] However, to the extent that urban memoryscapes such as Alex offer urban planners a means to recall the past, they are also sites of forgetting. In the case of the Mandela Museum, the official, manufactured memory provided for a nostalgic recollection about Mandela, while local struggle heroes faded into the background. Moreover, spatial tactics of erasure were implemented in the evictions of local residents at the site of the museum.

Through urban heritage tourism, 'sites of historic memory' are converted into 'sights of history', where the emphasis is on the consumption of the visual spectacle rather than on an in-depth understanding of local histories and geographies.[61] Memories of people, places and artefacts that are deemed unhelpful for the purpose of validating market enterprises are erased. In Alex, and elsewhere in South Africa, disenfranchised communities such as urban squatters and migrant groups have been displaced in the name of tourism through urban development and reconstruction schemes. Their dissatisfaction and anger are blanketed by an artificially created consensus about the past and by overly optimistic visions for the future.

Having one's story written out of history and replaced by an official version of events is most certainly not a new experience for some Alexandra residents. During apartheid, history was scripted and relayed largely from the perspective of prominent white men. Under the new ANC-led dispensation, official storytelling has followed the same recipe. Voices that were marginalised in the past continue to be silenced today, in order to provide an image of where the 'new' South Africa came from and where it is headed that appeals to gung-ho tourists, eager to capture and consume South Africa's much lauded 'peaceful transition'. The efforts of Alex residents to challenge fabricated histories and stamp their own memories and lived experience onto heritage plans mostly took the form of rechristening places with names that locals felt were a more accurate reflection of reality. Most of the names used in the unofficial discourse had negative connotations and reflected unpleasant experiences. While this particular mobilisation technique is not a novel feature of the post-apartheid period, the target of the residents' frustration was not as clearly defined as it was during the apartheid period. To a certain extent, these ambiguities weakened the potential of popular protest against the Mandela Museum and decreased the likelihood that the affected residents' stories would be told. This chapter is a limited, but by no means insignificant, attempt to tell the story of the tyrannical nature of political symbols largely from the viewpoint of those who are oppressed by them.

Postscript

This chapter, based on fieldwork that came to an end in 2006, captures a particular period of the heritage project in Alexandra. In 2008, after this chapter was written, the site where the Mandela Museum is situated was renamed by the community as the Alexandra Heritage Centre. The role played by the Alexandra Development Forum (ADF) in this renaming process, the internal contestations within the ADF, and the uneasy relationship between the ADF and the ARP shed interesting light on development in Alex, but such a discussion is beyond the scope of this chapter. It is, however, worth referring to the work of scholars such as Phil Bonner and Noor Nieftagodien,[62] and Luke Sinwell[63] for a critical appraisal of the role of the ADF in community development in Alexandra.

10 Black nurses' strikes at Baragwanath Hospital, Soweto, 1948-2007

Simonne Horwitz

Introduction

This chapter investigates a series of nurses' strikes that took place at Baragwanath Hospital between its opening as a provincial hospital serving black patients in 1948 through to the post-apartheid era. During this time Baragwanath experienced four major nurses' strikes in 1949, 1958, 1985 and 1995 and two major, broader civil servants' strikes in 1992 and 2007 that had significant effects on nurses.

Until the end of apartheid, nursing and teaching were the only professional options available to black women in South Africa.[1] Shula Marks, in her ground-breaking study of the nursing profession in South Africa, remarks that the number of black professional nurses far outnumbered black male elites.[2] Thus, black women nurses formed a very significant sector of the professional labour force in South Africa. Yet very little academic attention has been paid to black nurses in general or the ways in which they engaged in civil action and strikes.[3] Nursing is a gendered profession that takes place in the gendered hospital space.[4] In the hospital setting, male workers – often doctors, who are perceived as having a higher status – form the main subjects of research. Even in this collection, male workers and their actions or male protagonists are prominent. This chapter attempts to begin to fill this gap by addressing the protest actions of nurses at South Africa's largest specialist hospital serving predominantly black patients. Nurses are particularly important, not only because they are perhaps the largest group of professional black women in South Africa, but also because the history of nursing provides a good perspective on public service workers, who have become increasingly important in South Africa.

For much of the period under discussion, power at Baragwanath Hospital lay in the hands of the white, mostly male administration and the predominantly white, male doctors. Yet nurses, who were predominantly black women, were the backbone of the hospital. This gave them some power should they choose to withdraw their labour in protest. Nurses, however, belonged to a profession that frowned on such action. This left them in a somewhat ambiguous position – a central contradiction explored in this chapter. An examination of nurses' strikes shows that while the changing nature of apartheid and nursing legislation, as well as broader political shifts and the changing conditions at the hospital, had a significant effect on the nature of the nurses' actions, their underlying concern with status and professionalism tended to guide their responses. On the one hand, nurses found themselves pulled by their loyalty to the hospital and to the stereotypical image of the nurse; on the other, they experienced the contrasting reality of being black women workers in apartheid and post-apartheid South Africa. The strikes also reveal the deep social fissures at the hospital. Sweet and Digby point out that nurses' strikes – although rare – are moments of 'crisis and confrontation [that] expose issues otherwise obscured by such factors as the ordered hierarchy of a hospital, the distribution of power between White and Black, or inequalities between men and women'.[5]

1949 strike: Striking for dignity and respect

In July 1949, amid increasing unrest at medical and educational institutions around the country, a strike occurred at Baragwanath.[6] This strike, like others during the period, had its roots in mostly local, domestic grievances. The confrontation between the white nursing administration, backed by the broader hospital administration, and black staff and student nurses centred on measures taken to end the loss of cutlery from the staff kitchen. Black nurses saw these measures as an insult and refused to return to work until their grievances had been addressed. During the ensuing discussions, both sides appealed to the stereotypical nursing identity to strengthen their arguments. The black staff and student nurses complained that the actions of the administration were 'derogatory', significantly, 'to their dignity as trained nurses'.[7] The administration used an appeal to the same set of values to urge the nurses to suspend their action. Miss M. G. Borcherds, the chief matron of the Johannesburg Hospital, which had authority over Baragwanath during this period, 'expressed her surprise that persons who had undertaken training for the high calling of a nurse, should be prepared to desert their patients, for the sake of a few domestic grievances'.[8]

Jane McLarty, chief matron of Baragwanath Hospital between 1948 and 1953, who was often sympathetic to the needs of black nurses and spent much of her career fighting for their professional rights, was said to have 'dealt firmly with the situation'.[9] Staff nurses were informed that those who did not return to their duties were in danger of having their certificates of registration cancelled, thus risking their ability to continue practising as nurses. Student nurses were threatened in a similar way. The severity of the threat led to the collapse of the strike, and the nurses returned to their duties with their grievances still outstanding. McLarty's response in quelling the action could have been motivated by her desire to instil in her nurses what she saw as the correct professional ethos rather than out of a disregard for their rights.

Both black nurses and the white nursing administration appealed to the same image of the nurse as a dignified professional, although for different ends. Throughout this event, however, power lay in the hands of the white administration, which often lacked cross-cultural understanding and had little appreciation of the issues black nurses faced.[10] The black nurses had little organised support, despite the fact that others saw their action as an important part of the broader struggle. In his address to the graduating class at the University of Fort Hare in 1949, Robert Sobukwe, founder of the Pan Africanist Congress, was recorded as saying:

> the battle is on. To me the struggle at the [Baragwanath] Hospital is more than a question of 'discipline'. It is a struggle between African and European, between a twentieth century desire for self-realization and a feudal conception of authority ... the trouble at the hospital, then, I say, should be viewed as part of a broad struggle and not as an isolated incident.[11]

While Sobukwe and others might have attached broader meaning to the nurses' strike, black nurses' ability to protest was weakened by the fact that they were not represented by any black-controlled body or union. Furthermore, the nurses themselves did not seem to see their actions as part of a broader political struggle.

For much of the period under discussion the South African nursing profession was segregated, with white nurses in dominant positions in the nursing structures and hierarchies. In the early 1930s the South African Trained Nurses Association was made up of and represented white nurses, while black nurses were members of the Bantu Trained Nurses Association, which was formed in 1932. This division lasted until 1944, when Act 45 of 1944 created the South African Nursing Association (SANA), which superceded all existing organisations. The new association was, in theory at least, open to all nurses regardless of race. All nurses had the right to vote for and be elected to the nursing governing body, the South African Nursing Council (SANC). This Act was passed when the number of black nurses was relatively small and when white nurses clearly dominated the association.[12]

1958 strike: Passes and politics

These gains for black nurses were lost in the early apartheid era. As the numbers of black women entering the nursing profession began to rise in the 1950s, the Nursing Amendment Act No. 69 of 1957 introduced stricter racial segregation, and only whites could serve on the SANC. The Act empowered the SANC to implement different training programmes and separate nursing registers based on race. Although this legislation seemed to have little impact on working practices that were already de facto segregated, it sparked opposition, both locally and internationally,[13] and South Africa was finally expelled from the International Council of Nurses. Around the country there was an almost-complete boycott by black nurses of meetings called by the SANA to explain the Act. Instead, a separate meeting of black nursing representatives from around the country was held in Johannesburg. Here the Act was declared a 'gross violation of human rights, a brutal and unwarranted interference in nursing affairs, a violation of nursing ethics and traditions and an expression of racial prejudice.'[14] The response of the majority of Baragwanath nurses to the legislation is difficult to gauge. McLarty, Baragwanath's matron, was one of the few white nursing leaders who spoke out strongly against the legislation.[15]

Thus, while Baragwanath Hospital was affected by the increasing segregation enforced by apartheid legislation in the 1950s, this period also witnessed a significant change in the make-up of Baragwanath's work force. There was pressure not only to enlarge the number of black nurses in training, but to replace all white nurses serving at black hospitals with black nurses. In 1947 Baragwanath had employed 33 white and two black sisters. Ten years later there were no white and 35 black sisters at the hospital. Similar patterns can be found in all nursing categories during this period.[16] The changing social composition of the senior nurses made a significant contribution to the political balance at Baragwanath.

In 1958 the government used the Act to demand that student nurses submit identity numbers as part of their compulsory registration with the SANC. To obtain identity numbers, nurses would have to apply for a passbook or reference book – one of the most hated tools of the apartheid government, which was being extended more generally to African women. In an increasingly politicised environment, compulsory passbooks led to angry protests.[17] Helen Joseph, a founder of the Congress of Democrats and the Federation of South African Women, remembers that 'groups of black nurses in the Transvaal were holding angry protest meetings and nurses declared "our mothers were washerwomen and they educated us. We will go back to the washtubs but we will not carry passes"'.[18]

On this occasion, nurses mobilised broader support, despite the fact that many African leaders were hamstrung by detentions and the Treason Trial. The Federation of South African Women, African National Congress (ANC) Women's League, Black Sash and black nurses decided to organise a peaceful demonstration and meeting with the hospital administration at Baragwanath.[19] Baragwanath was an important hospital, and its size and location in the heart of Soweto, one of the most politicised of South Africa's townships, made it an ideal location for this kind of demonstration. Baragwanath also gained the attention of the government and the media. The demonstration was to take place on 22 March 1958 and was intended to be the culmination of the acts of individual and group resistance by nurses at various hospitals.[20]

In response, the Non-European Affairs Department set up police roadblocks to halt unauthorised traffic entering the area and cancelled all buses to the hospital. The hospital was surrounded by police armed with revolvers, stun guns and teargas.[21] The hospital administration also made emergency preparations. Martin Jarrett-Karr, Anglican chaplain to Baragwanath between 1952 and 1959, writes that before the demonstration unfounded rumours of the ferocious actions the women were planning circulated at the hospital.[22] In preparation, all ambulatory patients were sent home for the weekend and all women and non-essential staff were asked to stay at home.[23]

Facing the police on the other side of the road were a few hundred 'mothers' of the nurses, women whom Jarrett-Kerr called 'respectable, middle-class African housewives' and a few women of other races who gathered opposite the gates of the hospital.[24] A number of Baragwanath nurses joined them during their tea breaks.[25] Joseph describes the scene: 'It was a hot morning and the umbrellas were up against the sun. Perhaps the police thought the umbrellas concealed weapons. It looked a little comic from where I stood as there seemed to be more policemen than protesters.'[26] Indeed, other sources suggest that there were between 200 and 500 women at the demonstration and '400 policemen in attendance'.[27] Joseph surmises that the police feared a repeat of the huge demonstration of 9 August 1956 when about 20,000 women marched to the Union Buildings in Pretoria.[28] The security apparatus might also have used the opportunity for a show of strength to deter further action.

The demonstration was, however, peaceful. Representatives of the women, accompanied by police, were allowed to meet the superintendent, matron and principal of the nurses' training college. They presented them with a letter of protest against the introduction of passes to women and the introduction of differential standards of training.[29] Their protest won some concessions. Nurses would not have to produce identity numbers to gain registration and, while registers remained separate, certificates did not indicate race. Syllabi and examinations remained identical for all nurses. These victories, although small in the overall fight for equality within the nursing profession, were important.

Unlike the 1949 strike, the nurses' concerns could not simply be dismissed by an appeal to authority. On the surface, the nature of the protest had changed from domestic grievances to grievances linked to broader political struggles. However, central to nurses' involvement in this protest action was the perceived affront to their dignity and professional status brought about through the imposition of passes. Even for the political organisations that were in alliance with the nurses, the fact that the women were expected to carry passes was important. Their letter of protest referred to the act as 'a stain upon the nursing profession, so universally honoured' and reminded the officials that nursing was an 'honourable profession, where women of all races met and worked as nurses, united in their noble vocation'.[30] Thus, while nurses were building alliances with other organisations during the 1958 strike, they remained centrally concerned with their status and professional identity. For the political organisations, alliances with nurses were important. Nurses were a significant sector of the work force and their withdrawal of labour caused concern in a sensitive area of public service – the care of the sick. In the case of the 1958 strike, the alliance between nurses and broader political movements was mutually beneficial.

As in the previous strike, it was not only the black nurses who appealed to the traditional ideals of nursing as a dignified profession. Charlotte Searle, founding member of the SANC and SANA and long-time director of nursing services for the Transvaal Provincial Administration (TPA), gave an account of the event that also appealed to the professional identity of the nurse, but in a completely different way. In her account of the implementation of the 1957 Act, she does not record the compromises that the strike brought about. She writes:

> Despite some initial political agitation by persons who were not nurses, in most instances, the sound commonsense of the nurses has won the day and nurses of all races are working amicably together to solve the country's nursing needs and to build up the profession, working in terms of the law of the land.[31]

Here Searle puts the strike action down to outside 'political agitation' and presents both black and white nurses as unified in their goal to 'build up the profession'.

Decades without a major nurses' strike: 1960s-early 1980s

The 1960s was a particularly bleak period for urban African health services. While the state focused its funding on Bantustans and rural 'development', major black urban hospitals such as Baragwanath faced diminishing funds and increasing patient loads, making them increasingly difficult places to work. During this period potential strikes and demonstrations at hospitals were dealt with harshly by the hospital administration, supported by the state. Nurses, as public servants, faced dismissal if they took part in such activity.[32] Pressure also came from within the profession. Although some nurses dismissed the influence of the SANA and SANC, which were overwhelmingly controlled by white nurses until well into the 1990s, many had internalised the ideal of the apolitical, professional nurse that the SANA and SANC promoted.[33] In interviews, older nurses looked back to this more professional period: 'in those days no nurse would go out on the street and *toyi-toyi*'.[34] Many felt that 'nurses should not have abandoned their duty ... it was not professional'.[35] However, by the 1970s this attitude was challenged by events in Soweto. A new generation was entering nursing in the 1970s and their world, in particular, was changing rapidly. In June 1976 Soweto became the focal point of the struggle against apartheid as its schoolchildren took to the streets.[36] Oral histories gathered from nurses who worked at Baragwanath during that time focused on disturbance and uncertainties. They worked long hours without food, they were unable to contact relatives and commuting was difficult. Above all, nurses feared finding one of their children or relatives among the dead or injured.[37]

A generational schism emerged from interviews. While older nurses continued to condemn protests and strike action, younger nurses supported active ways of voicing their discontent. One older nurse, who began her training in 1955, expressed this point as follows:

I think the change came after '76 to be honest ... this change that we, the older nurses, cannot come to terms with happened after '76 when we realised that the youth were different ... it is a generation of different people.[38]

Matilda Mogale expanded on this by explaining that

the nurses of the age of 20 then, they were different people. There was a difference, these were people who said they would leave their work [to strike], irrespective of what was going on ... There was a dramatic change, people now wanted to be heard, to be seen, to be appreciated.[39]

The power hierarchies were being challenged in a very explicit way. Dr Moira Russell, a white doctor, remembered an event on the morning of 17 June 1976:

> A group of student midwives staged a demonstration in the front of the hospital outside the administration offices [presumably to show support for the youth of Soweto]. They were joined by a small number of 'agitators' from outside the hospital. What happened next was something which was deeply disturbing and totally unexpected. The matrons at Bara had been, up to that point, treated with a marked degree of deference, especially by the most junior ranks of nursing staff or staff in training. When Miss Nola van Eerde, the Chief Matron, came out to speak to the student group someone picked up a stone and threw it at her. This act of defiance and aggression which would have been unthinkable 24 hours previously was no doubt prompted by the group of agitators who were non-staff members, but the fact that it actually happened was indicative of the beginning of the erosion of discipline and a change of attitude towards authority in the hospital which started to permeate throughout the ranks of the nursing staff, spreading over the years to include the ancillary and domestic staff. Things were never quite the same again and I realised later that we had witnessed the beginnings of a culture of unrest which simmered continually beneath the surface, erupting from time to time.[40]

This is the only report I have of this moment, but it was clearly part of a significant change in protest action. Also being challenged was the image of nurses – some younger women sought a more politicised identity.

Against this background a third Nursing Act, No. 50 of 1978, which gave greater power to the Nursing Association, was passed.[41] In the context of the reformist strategies of the time and increasing external pressure on the nursing administration, the Act reversed some of the exclusionary elements of the previous Acts. This made it possible for black nurses to be elected to the SANC.[42] However, the Act contained a number of restrictions that excluded the growing number of nurses who were citizens of the Bantustans. The Act also made strike action by nurses a statutory offence with fines of up to R500 or one year in jail or both.[43] These harsh measures meant that while nurses were increasingly politicised, protests were limited.[44]

This is in no way to suggest that nurses or other hospital employees accepted the conditions in which they were forced to operate. By the early 1980s bed occupancy at the hospital was constantly running at over 100 per cent. The daily average of patients in the medical wards without beds was 293, and this put immense strain on staff, facilities and the hospital's limited resources.[45] Amid growing patient numbers, a severe lack of funding and ever deteriorating conditions, there were indeed some protests. In 1981, 37 Baragwanath radiographers resigned over working conditions and there was a wage strike by non-medical workers at Hillbrow Hospital the following year.[46] The early 1980s also saw a number of food boycotts at hospitals around the country. These boycotts, some of which included nurses, also served to highlight other issues, such as the deteriorating conditions at Baragwanath Hospital. A boycott of the Baragwanath canteen, for example, ostensibly to protest the quality of the food, was also used to call for contracts to protect staff who worked overtime.[47] By the mid-1980s there was increasing dissatisfaction among non-medical hospital staff. Hospital workers had begun to organise around the country, joining unions such as the Black Health and Allied Workers Union; the General and Allied Workers Union; the National Education Health and Allied Workers Union; and, specifically at Baragwanath, the Baragwanath Health Workers' Association.[48]

1985 Strike: Generational divides

In November 1985, 900 student nurses and 800 daily paid workers – including cooks, porters, cleaners, nurses' aides and messengers – began a massive strike at Baragwanath Hospital. Although these groups originally had different grievances, the intolerable working conditions at the hospital affected all of them and they cooperated in an action that had a major impact because of its size.[49] In an interview, Matilda Mogale explained the support for the strike among the student nurses:

> I think it was about broader issues. Nurses were for a very long time barred from joining strikes and joining these political organisations and associating themselves with those who were getting their voices heard. So when they managed it was like when you are putting your hand on a spring mattress and when you move your hand it jumps up![50]

The strike action crippled the hospital. Reports described workers storming the hospital, throwing prepared food on floors and against walls, and turning dustbins upside down.[51] Operating theatres, medical departments and kitchens were closed down. Many doctors left the hospital, which then offered only emergency services.[52] The response of the authorities was harsh: they refused to recognise the trade unions, including those attempting to negotiate on workers' behalf.[53] On the second day of the strike, a large majority of student nurses and daily paid workers were threatened with arrest as they entered the hospital.[54] They were then dismissed and given 24 hours in which to collect their pay.[55] Student nurses were evicted from the hostel.[56]

Three of the dismissed student nurses launched an urgent application in the Rand Supreme Court for an interdict to reinstate the student nurses and auxiliary workers. Mr Justice R. J. Goldstone set aside the dismissal as 'invalid and ineffective' on the grounds that the complaints of the student nurses and auxiliary workers had not been fully heard.[57] The hospital reinstated the dismissed staff. This decision came at a time when the role of the legal system in the struggle against apartheid was changing. During the 1980s a growing public interest law movement achieved a number of minor but important victories. These included legal challenges to the influx control laws, the Group Areas Act and conscription, as well as recognition of trade unions.[58] The court case did not, however, end the incident and nine of the student nurses were made to appear before the all-white SANC disciplinary committee on charges of 'disgraceful conduct' and 'dereliction of duty'.[59] They were cautioned and discharged, but the disciplinary committee demonstrated its control over the student nurses.

This case again highlights the contradictory position of black nurses. They were expected to meet the ideals of the profession and to fulfil their duties to their patients. As Iris Roscher, SANC president, pointed out, 'disciplinary action for patient neglect was the cornerstone of professionalism among nurses worldwide'.[60] Yet the nurses were also part of a divided nursing sisterhood and members of a community suffering discrimination. As a sister tutor at Baragwanath, Mildred Adelaide Makhaya, noted, 'they had no platform to air their frustration and grievances, they had no platform to air their views except at large student nurses meeting where they were single voices crying in the wilderness'.[61] Against this background, many student nurses felt that they had no option but to embark on strike action. Even so, their sense of duty to their patients made any decision to strike a difficult one. A nurse who gave evidence in mitigation of sentence at the disciplinary committee pointed out that 'the strike and in fact any other strike was a traumatic experience for nurses whose job is not only selflessness but a very difficult one'.[62] A nurse whom I interviewed explained that

> things were very tough in that on the one hand one was worried about patients, but you also felt that in your situation no one would ever look at it or listen to what you were saying because they knew you would not go on strike, because of your oath, and because you would think what if that was my mother lying there and there was no one to nurse her?[63]

As Marks points out, nurses were

> caught between their duties to their patients and the demands of the comrades,
> between the pressures of the community and the discipline of the Nursing Council
> ... by the early 1990s nurses could be threatened with death for going on strike and
> threatened with death for not going on strike.[64]

The 1985 strike succeeded in raising the profile of the student nurses' complaints
and allaying some of their short-term grievances. Newspaper coverage appeared
almost daily throughout the latter half of November 1985 and well into 1986, despite
the fact that journalists were restricted from entering the area under the emergency
regulations.[65] This was the first major action since striking was made illegal for nurses
in 1978 and it was followed by similar strikes around the country.[66] However, it is
also significant that student nurses, not registered nurses, took the lead. For Florence
Mudzuli, senior sister at Baragwanath during the 1980s, unionisation was a significant
factor here:

> the old nurses feel that they would not strike, and I think again what caused a lot
> of changes was when the nurses joined the unions ... in the late 80s, DENOSA,
> NEHAWU. You know in all the years we met only at the nursing council and
> nursing association and I think people were more controllable ... when something
> did not satisfy them they would go to the matrons and up to the council or maybe
> to the hospital board and not being radical and going out.[67]

Chris van den Heever, chief superintendent of Baragwanath Hospital in the 1980s, also
identified the shift to unionisation as an important change in nurses' engagement with
the hospital. He explained:

> There were some black nurses that felt the nursing profession benefitted from
> unionisation but they were in the minority, defiantly in the minority. In 1985 with
> that nurses strike these were student nurses that struck and the idea was that it
> was the beginning of unionisation of the nursing profession and the healthcare
> professions ... but from 1985 we saw unionisation coming in and I think a lot of
> hard work and effort went into the mobilisation of the Baragwanath component,
> from the 1980s up to the big strike of 1992.[68]

In June 1987 health care workers joined other, largely public sector workers to launch NEHAWU, the National Education, Health and Allied Workers' Union, affiliated to the Congress of South African Trade Unions (COSATU). Its development was slow; by 1988 NEHAWU had only 6,000 members nationally, drawn mostly from health sector support workers.[69]

1992 strike: Nurses in an untenable position

In 1991 a negotiated amendment to the 1988 Labour Relations Act made provision for limited strike action by employees.[70] This Act still considered strike action a breach of contract, punishable by disciplinary action.[71] Nurses were also still under the firm control of the SANA and in the early 1990s this organisation's view was that 'strike by nurses is a violation of the patient's right to safe and continuous nursing'.[72] But broader militancy by public sector health workers galvanised newly unionised nurses[73] and protests at Baragwanath in June 1992 sparked mass action. Soon twenty to thirty thousand health workers across the country, mostly members of NEHAWU and the Health Workers Union, were on strike over wages and conditions of employment.[74] In the Transvaal alone 29 different institutions were affected and nearly 10,000 employees, mostly general assistants, participated. Of these, about 1,500 were employed at Baragwanath.[75] TPA officials and Baragwanath Hospital management warned the strikers, sent NEHAWU several ultimatums and obtained four Supreme Court interdicts.[76] This did little to quell the escalating violence and destruction of hospital property, and the TPA dismissed 7,400 workers. Hospital management at Baragwanath employed large numbers of replacement workers and in some cases called in army medical staff.[77]

When NEHAWU first balloted for a strike, it claimed the 'capability of having total support for a strike and in a sense [sic] that we would destroy the health services'.[78] As part of this strategy, it called on nurses to join the action.[79] However, nurses themselves had little sustained role in this strike.[80] A senior sister explained that

> the nurses did not fully participate in the strike ... how can you strike if your patient is dying? There was the odd one who will go there and strike and do whatever outside, but the majority stayed in their posts or they did what they call [the] 'skeleton method' where a few would go out and a few would remain in the wards and then they would go out.[81]

Once again nurses were confronted by competing loyalties and identities. Some agreed with the demands of the unions, but during the 1992 strike nurses seemed unsure of whether or not to involve themselves and engaged rather in limited acts of protest, including threats to 'down tools'.[82] It is important to note that in some cases their threats were not in line with the demands of the strikers. In the face of increasing intimidation and with nobody to prepare their pay packets, nurses, and to a lesser extent doctors, threatened to join the strike if they were not paid.[83] Nurses complained that they were having to fetch supplies and carry out non-medical duties.[84]

During this strike a number of nurses and tutors from the Baragwanath Nurses College formed groups that claimed to be representing the nurses' interests. The Bara Professional Health Workers was one such group. They sent a letter to management reinforcing the demands of the striking workers.[85] Other nurses set up a grievance committee and also 'Nurses-for-the-Oppressed-Masses'.[86] Throughout the strike groups of senior nurses wrote letters to management voicing their concerns.[87] In September, registered and enrolled nurses wrote a letter to the state president, F. W. de Klerk, informing him that they could not do their work and that a reinstatement of the fired workers would ease the tensions.[88]

With the exception of the grievance committee, none of these groups interacted with the SANA. This fracturing of nurses' organisations points to two significant issues. Firstly, it weakened the impact of each group's individual campaign. Secondly, it suggests their uneasiness about union discipline and strike action. The number of initiatives clearly suggests that nurses had grievances that they wanted to bring to the fore, but that they were unhappy with the forms of protest action that non-nursing staff were pursuing. More limited protest was indicative of their role and status, but also suggests that they were not totally distancing themselves from the strike.

The few nurses who did actively involve themselves in militant action in 1992 were predominantly student and junior nurses. They called 'upon matrons to join us on this march because they are also BLACK OPPRESSED AND UNDERPAID'.[89] Yet the hierarchical nature of the nursing profession meant that younger nurses were soon brought under the control of SANA and their more conservative seniors, who largely continued work.[90] Regardless of the level of their participation in the strike, nurses were hugely affected by the labour action. Those who remained in the wards had to face massive workloads: 'senior people, the matrons actually rolled up their sleeves and went to work in the kitchens and got food for the patients and came into the wards and helped out and it was very tough, it was so difficult.'[91] Intimidation and violence were directed at nurses. Thinly veiled death treats circulated during the strike. One letter on a NEHAWU letterhead and written in sePedi, stated:

> We also call peacefully on all nursing personnel and all others to strike. The struggle we fight will also be to your advantage. The needs that NEHAWU is demanding are related to the ones received by workers internationally. So we are requesting all government workers to stop working so that government can listen to us. So we are giving a friendly warning to those who are ignoring our pleas to strike. If they don't support us there will be consequences. Tell your brother, sister, mother, friend, partner, neighbour, or anyone who ignores our request that their days are numbered.[92]

During the strike there were three petrol bomb attacks in Soweto, each directed at the home of a hospital employee.[93] In one particularly graphic case, professional nurse Lettie Mmakgang Makgotloe had her house torched by a group of over 50 individuals she considered to be linked to the strike.[94] During the course of the strike a number of nurses were sjamboked and others assaulted as they tried to make their way to work. As a result many nurses hid their uniforms until they were inside the hospital.[95] NEHAWU condemned the violence and claimed that it was not NEHAWU members who were intimidating non-strikers.[96] Rather, it accused 'agent provocateurs or the TPA for carrying out the violence'.[97] In August 1992 NEHAWU marshals were deployed to monitor the situation. After almost ten months of strikes and negotiations an agreement was signed in February 1993. The agreement regulated all aspects of the relationship between the TPA and NEHAWU and served as a guide for dispute resolution, protest action and representation.[98]

At the heart of the 1992 strike was the newly powerful trade union NEHAWU. Its main support base was not professional health workers, but non-medical staff. Neal Thobejane, assistant general secretary of NEHAWU, stated during a meeting with the TPA that 'although the strike is not part of the mass action of the COSATU/ANC alliance, it slots into the program and it cannot be divorced from mass action'.[99] Phillip Dexter, NEHAWU's general secretary, linked the strike more directly to the broader political struggle, maintaining that the strike was part of 'the big political issues such as mass action' and that 'it is part of the total action to ask the Government to go'.[100] Indeed, a number of the pamphlets and posters employed at Baragwanath during the strike made reference to both hospital-related demands and broader political issues. As the strike progressed there was a move away from demands about salaries and working conditions to a broader set of concerns underpinned by a call for a new order.[101] Nurses found themselves in a nearly impossible situation:

> intimidated from all sides from the strikers who see us as scabs, from our bosses who threaten to fire us, from our own disciplinary body, the South African Nursing Council which [now] tells us that we have the right to strike, but which also tells us that if we leave our patients to spend even an hour on the picket-line we will be struck off the roll.[102]

1995 strike: Nurses go it alone

Following South Africa's first democratic election, the latter part of 1994 saw a number of wildcat strikes by hospital employees at all levels, with the exception of doctors. This increase in labour action can be explained in part by the change from a repressive regime intolerant of strikes to a democratic government with a history of mass action.[103]

Yet nurses mobilised around very specific issues. Late in 1994 in the Public Sector Bargaining Chamber health sector unions negotiated a good increase of over 20 per cent for their non-professional members, while nurses and other professionals did not benefit.[104] In August 1995 nurses working for municipal clinics in Gauteng received an increase of 12–15 per cent, while those working in provincial hospitals, such as Baragwanath, received only 5 per cent.[105] This 5 per cent increase was considered appropriate by the SANA and by both NEHAWU and the Health and Other Service Personnel Trade Union of South Africa (HOSPERSA). Nurses considered it degrading and totally unfair, especially in the light of working conditions that had improved little since the 1980s. A nurse with three years of basic training and a year of specialised training in midwifery and community health earned a gross salary of about R3,000 a month. At the same time, a secretary in the public sector with one year of training was earning a minimum of R4,000.[106] Nurses demanded a 33 per cent wage increase, but later revised their demand to 25 per cent.[107] Nursing was no longer the major route of mobility and status for African women, and its rewards were being outstripped by those received for other jobs that nurses perceived as less demanding.

Comparative wage levels prompted wildcat strikes.[108] Nurses demanded equal salaries for all local authority employees and a revised tax system.[109] By mid-August 1995 negotiations between black nurses and government were deadlocked and almost 2,000 Baragwanath nurses embarked on a full-scale strike that lasted almost two months. In contrast to earlier actions by student nurses and the 1992 strike of health workers, it was now registered and qualified nurses who were most militant. The political context was also markedly different. South Africa was now a democratic country and protest action was directed away from the struggle for democracy towards a struggle for social and economic empowerment and labour rights. The new Labour Relations Act No. 66 of 1995 provided workers with the right to take part in a wider range of industrial action and gave them greater protection than ever before.[110] The right to strike was enshrined in both the Act and in the 1996 Constitution. Limitations on civil servants performing essential services were at that stage unclear.[111]

In 1993 the Nursing Act No. 45 of 1944 was amended, abolishing compulsory membership of SANA.[112] This had a profound effect on the ways in which nurses could organise. For the first time since 1944 they were not forced to join a predominantly white-led association that emphasised a certain image and type of behaviour for nurses. Nurses could now more freely join trade unions and some chose to join large multi-sector health worker unions such as NEHAWU and HOSPERSA.[113] Many preferred to form their own national union, the South African Democratic Nurses' Union, which refused to seek affiliation with either of the country's two major union federations, COSATU or the National Council of Trade Unions.[114] However, when tensions between the nurses and government reached boiling point in September 1995, nurses were disillusioned with the union's acceptance of a 5 per cent wage increase.[115] Some nurses used the slogan 'We don't need an organisation; we need money',[116] and Baragwanath nurses embarked on an unofficial strike from which the unions distanced themselves.[117] SANA also totally disassociated itself from the strike and a spokesperson urged the nurses to 'rethink their professional calling to put human lives above all else'.[118] SANA had, however, been forced to loosen its authoritarian control and it no longer had so major a hold on nurses.

During this strike nurses who appealed to their sense of professionalism and ethics to distance themselves from protest action seemed to be in the minority. Instead, many nurses appealed to this image of the qualified professional nurse to endorse their pro-strike position. A spokesperson for the striking nurses said: 'We are qualified women, not just menial labour. We know our skills are needed to save lives. We refuse to subsidise the Government and their fancy cars. Viva RDP. We want some gravy.'[119] Nurses in the newly democratic South Africa, like many other South Africans, expected that their wages and working conditions would improve with the end of apartheid. Many nurses sought to express the fact that nursing is not only a vocation or calling, but also simply a job and a way to earn a living. This attitude was certainly more prevalent among younger nurses. A strike placard displayed during the labour action read 'To hell with Florence Nightingale!'[120]

Nurses were subject to negative media coverage and especially harsh criticism was levelled at their decision not to leave a skeleton staff on duty during the 1995 strike.[121] The ANC-led government instituted dismissal procedures when the striking nurses refused to return to work. Claiming that they could not afford to pay the wage increases, the government appealed to nurses' consciences and repeatedly called on their sense of duty and their moral obligation to their patients.[122] Gauteng Department of Health spokesperson Popo Maja said that 'workers' demands could not be met immediately, but lives had to be saved'.[123] The director general of health further warned nurses that they could face criminal charges if patients died as a result of the strikes.[124] Even President Nelson Mandela spoke out against the strike, urging nurses to leave the profession if they were not prepared to return to work.[125]

Nurses had legitimate grievances on all fronts, yet in the face of government threats of mass dismissal most of the Baragwanath staff had returned to work by the beginning of October.[126] They accepted that nothing would be done until the new budget in March 1996.[127] Nurses also fought back by demanding, and receiving, an apology from Mandela for his statement on the strike and by suggesting that the minister of health, Nkosazana Zuma, should have been at Baragwanath instead of 'staying in comfortable hotels in Beijing' for the UN Women's Conference.[128] The collapse of the 1995 strike did not mark the end of simmering labour tensions at Baragwanath Hospital.[129]

In subsequent years most nurses joined one of the major trade unions. In mid-2007, during the largest public servants' strike since the end of apartheid, Baragwanath Hospital and many others were crippled. The major demands during this strike were for better wages and conditions of employment. However, there were also many underlying issues, including opposition to the government's economic policy and shortcomings in service delivery.[130] Striking nurses again received a large amount of negative media coverage, with headlines such as 'Striking nurses "on thin ice"', which focused on the suffering of patients.[131] This public criticism in turn increased the pressure on government to resolve the strike. Nurses had many reasons to strike in 2007. Their wages and working conditions had improved little during the 13 years of democracy. The mismanagement of the health system under apartheid led to vast understaffing of black hospitals such as Baragwanath and little had changed since 1994. The nursing profession suffered a severe 'brain drain' as highly skilled nurses left for countries such as Dubai and Britain. The status of nursing relative to other opportunities available to black women declined sharply. However, by no means all

Baragwanath nurses participated in this strike. Those affiliated to the Democratic Nursing Organisation of South Africa or HOSPERSA only struck for one or two days and then mostly returned to work. Of the 384 striking health workers dismissed by the Gauteng Health Department, only 20 were nurses and they were later reinstated. This suggests that in Gauteng nurses did not fully back the strike.[132] While more research and a greater sense of historical context are needed regarding these recent events, it seems as if, where nurses are concerned, this strike followed closely the pattern of the 1992 strike.

Conclusion

The strikes discussed in this chapter demonstrate a number of important differences, as well as fundamental continuities. Von Holdt and Maserumule suggest that major strikes at hospitals such as Baragwanath were a product of the transition to democracy rather than of the struggle against apartheid. They suggest that the transition facilitated trade union organisation in the public sector, making strike action a viable and effective method of protest.[133] This is certainly the case with the public sector strikes from 1992, which broadened the range of participants and sectors involved in industrial action. Union organisation in the public sector has been a major feature of the post-apartheid era and by 2007 public sector unions were among the best supported and strongest in COSATU.

The shifts in the nature of nurses' strikes have been more subtle. Change was gradual and highly dependent on a number of circumstances. While the 1949 action was sparked by local, hospital-based grievances, the 1958 and 1985 actions were tied into broader political movements. During all these strikes black nurses fell under the strict control of the white nursing regime. The 1995 strike, however, demonstrated significant new developments. Nurses were more unionised than before, organised themselves and were less constrained by the nursing hierarchy. Broader political changes in the country facilitated more militant action, and comparative wage rates in a rapidly changing context for African women were at the heart of the strike. The evidence suggests that nurses, especially younger nurses coming into the profession during the 1990s, increasingly saw themselves as workers.

Perhaps as important were the continuities to which this chapter has pointed. Throughout the period there is a powerful refrain in black nurses' representations and demands, which highlighted their sense of status and the dignity that they felt was inherent in their profession. Throughout the period nurses' identities as both members of a professional elite and as black women shaped their actions and reactions.

Status and professionalism were important to many nurses, as was their notion that deserting patients was unethical. Thus, many black nurses did not engage in strikes, even where they felt that there were pressing issues in national politics or when they felt their status and position were under acute threat. When they did engage in protest action, these ideas guided their actions. When nurses themselves went out on strike in 1995 it was in part in defence of these ideas about their profession and status.

Some chapters in this collection have tried to look at the detail and diversity of popular protest that was not necessarily part of the liberation movement. It is therefore worth briefly considering whether or not nurses' struggles can be seen as directly part of the anti-apartheid struggle. Are they the 'unsung heroes' of the struggle, as Lubanga suggests?[134] To some extent, nurses' education, training and perception of their role set them apart from the broader struggles, especially in the early years.[135] They were fighting different struggles. However, a number of powerful political women emerged from this nursing elite, who became important leaders in the anti-apartheid struggle.[136] The role of nurses in relation to the anti-apartheid struggle was complex and dynamic. Albertina Sisulu trained as a nurse at the Johannesburg Hospital before the opening of the nurses' college at Baragwanath. Her future husband, prominent ANC and anti-apartheid activist Walter Sisulu, was the brother of a fellow nurse. Adelaide Tambo, wife of Oliver Tambo, worked as a nurse at Baragwanath in the late 1950s. Maggie Resha trained as a nurse at a mission hospital in Pondoland, and in the late 1950s was one of the driving forces behind the nurses' strike at Baragwanath Hospital. Nelson Mandela's first wife, Edith Ntoko, was also a nurse. His second wife, Winnie Madikizela-Mandela, started work at Baragwanath as a social worker after graduating in 1956. She is widely acclaimed as being the first black social worker at the hospital, despite the fact that black graduates from the Jan Hofmeyr School of Social Work had been sent to work at Baragwanath for almost ten years prior to Madikizela-Mandela taking up her post.[137]

On another level, this question can also be seen as being linked to the central contradiction of being a nurse at a black hospital such as Baragwanath and taking part in strike action. When Baragwanath nurses struck it was primarily black patients who suffered. Yet with few channels to voice their grievances, nurses had little alternative. For much of the period under consideration nurses would not turn their backs on the patients. It would be wrong to think that this was only because of the control of the SANA and SANC and that when membership of these bodies was no longer compulsory nurses became uncaring and would engage in strike action. These organisations did, however, disempower black nurses, emphasising the moral and professional costs of protest action. They tended to encourage acceptance of the awful working conditions and poor wages because of nurses' higher 'calling'. The council and association used appeals to professional ethos and the Florence Nightingale image to justify their control over black nurses.

This chapter has explored the complex contradictions faced by black nurses throughout the period under discussion and how they negotiated both identity and power structures when making decisions about protest or labour action. Their identity as nurses and also gender expectations framed their responses. Importantly, this chapter shows that by examining a single group of workers over a long period of time – in this case, black nurses at Baragwanath Hospital – a more nuanced picture of changing patterns of protest and organisation can be developed. The evidence suggests that nurses did become more militant over the period discussed and that they became more organised as workers during and after the transition to democracy. But they still faced multifaceted dilemmas and important constraints when embarking on labour action. The chapter shows that nurses' professional identities interacted with broader political issues in different ways at different times to shape their responses and actions.

11 The 'New Struggle': Resources, networks and the formation of the Treatment Action Campaign (TAC) 1994-1998

Mandisa Mbali

Introduction

Before the African National Congress (ANC) took over the reins of power, the AIDS pandemic barely featured on the agendas of both the white ruling party and the liberation movements. In the early days of ANC rule there were more pressing issues that required urgent attention. Nonetheless, there were scattered pockets of AIDS activism, mostly among gay and lesbian activists, but also within the health professions. By the mid-1990s it seemed that the issue of HIV/AIDS and demands for treatment would be taken up by the new government. However, before long, tensions began to emerge between the state and activists. This chapter addresses the conflict between South African AIDS activists and the ANC-led government in the late 1990s. In particular, it discusses the social and political dynamics behind the emergence of the Treatment Action Campaign (TAC), a radical AIDS-focused social movement formed in December 1998. The central argument in the chapter is that the politics of AIDS activism in post-apartheid South Africa can be understood in relation to *both* the distribution of resources *and* the evolution of networks within the AIDS-related civil society sector. In relation to these two central themes, the discussion puts forward a number of propositions regarding the emergence of TAC in the last years of the twentieth century.

Thereafter, TAC's emergence, in terms of the literature on its links to AIDS-related civil society networks, is fleshed out. Drawing on 'Northern' social movements' scholarship, the chapter critiques some of the existing literature that characterises TAC's emergence as having been in opposition to such networks. Instead, it argues that TAC was born out of the activist component of such civil society networks rather than simply emerging in opposition to them. However, it concurs with the view expressed in the literature on TAC's emergence that the distribution of resources has shaped the politics of AIDS activism. The chapter then goes on to argue that conflict between AIDS activists and the government did not always exist. Indeed, anti-apartheid AIDS activists – including those from the ANC – formed networks and worked together during the transition, a process that culminated in the drafting of the first National AIDS Plan, which was adopted in 1994 by the Mandela administration.

The reorganisation of the state and civil society was critical in shaping the politics of AIDS in the early 'honeymoon period' of the Mandela administration. During this period, civil society networks and the state bureaucracy were reconfigured when activists moved into government. Consequently, activists in civil society initially had good access to activists-turned-bureaucrats in government. However, the bureaucrats faced the immense challenge of transforming the state while simultaneously developing and implementing new policies. Prior to the emergence of AIDS denialism among government leaders, government–non-governmental organisation (NGO) conflicts over issues such as the *Sarafina II* play were also partially related to conflicts over both resource distribution, and access to and influence over policymakers. Sarafina II demonstrated that expensive 'quick fixes' and 'grand gestures' became increasingly attractive to ANC politicians, sometimes pitting them against scientists and activists who had remained rooted in civil society. Nonetheless, for many of these activists, channels to effectively influence policymaking still remained open.

The final section of the chapter argues that the emergence of effective combination antiretroviral therapy in 1996 upped the potential rewards of AIDS activism for activists living with HIV. The fight for treatment became one for life itself, and pressure grew from inside organisations such as the National Association for People Living with AIDS (NAPWA) for the development of a radical AIDS movement, which came about based on social networks among AIDS activists formed through the AIDS Consortium.

Theorising resources and networks in the formation of a new South African social movement

Activists and intellectuals associated with TAC have proposed that a non-governmental network, commonly referred to as the 'AIDS world', pre-dated the movement. They often interpret the politics and characteristics of this network through the lens of how resources are distributed within it. Here, this body of thought will be critiqued using new social movement theory developed in relation to wealthy Northern countries.

The existence of the AIDS world is axiomatic among South African intellectuals associated with TAC. For instance, Mark Heywood, a founding member of TAC, argued that from 1994 many AIDS organisations that had played a key role in shaping AIDS policy in the early 1990s became entangled in the 'eternal circuit of conferences and workshops' at the expense of building a mass-based movement involving people living with and affected by HIV.[1] Similarly, fellow TAC founding member Jack Lewis claimed that AIDS activism prior to the movement's formation was 'all about conferences and per diems'.[2] Although TAC has no official position on AIDS activism prior to its formation, for simplicity of argument I will refer to this critique of earlier AIDS activism as the 'TAC founder critique' of prior AIDS activism.

The idea that there is a civil society AIDS world is widespread in literature on the politics of AIDS in South Africa. For instance, Lesley Lawson's book documenting the story of AIDS in South Africa speaks of the 'AIDS fraternity'.[3] In relation to this fraternity it briefly mentions the growth of 'a large number of non-governmental organisations ... specialising in HIV and AIDS ... represent[ing] a combined workforce of anti-apartheid professionals from the health, education and legal sectors, as well as activists and concerned community members'.[4] However, Lawson primarily attributes TAC's formation to Heywood and Zackie Achmat, a 'great man' approach to writing about the origins of TAC that neglects an analysis of its wider social roots.[5] In particular, TAC's formation can be also attributed to a wider group of activists from AIDS-related NGOs such as the AIDS Law Project and the National Coalition for Gay and Lesbian Equality (NCGLE).

Helen Schneider has similarly argued that there is a post-1994 AIDS world organised around two groupings. The first is an activist grouping including the National AIDS Convention of South Africa (NACOSA), the AIDS Consortium, NAPWA and TAC. Schneider's second grouping is made up of basic and public health scientists based in academic institutions such as the Medical Research Council (MRC) and the Universities of Natal and the Witwatersrand.[6] This chapter primarily discusses the activist part of this AIDS world, which is concerned with lobbying and advocacy-focused civil society organisation. The chapter aims to describe how activists positioned themselves politically within this AIDS world and in relation to the government.

The TAC founder narrative holds that TAC was a completely new social movement that emerged within and partially in reaction to the non-radicalism of many AIDS NGOs in 1998. It suggests that the new movement used novel strategies and was led by people living with HIV, primarily representing members of poor and marginalised communities that were most heavily affected by the epidemic. While this chapter does not set out to substantially refute this narrative, it adds political complexity to the picture of earlier AIDS activism presented in the TAC founder critique. In particular, rather than viewing TAC as emerging in opposition to the AIDS world, the chapter contends that the movement is a product of that world's activist section. It addresses a burgeoning South African social movements literature, which is rich in contemporary ethnographic and political description, but largely weak on discussion of continuities and changes in social movements are over longer periods.[7] The assertion that social movements are built on pre-existing social networks is nothing new in relation to literature on the phenomenon produced in the global North. For instance, John Campbell has argued that social movement mobilising structures are informal and formal networks connecting organisations and individuals. He has defined networks as social structures that

> shape and constrain people's behaviours and opportunities for action. They are conduits through which new models, concepts and practices diffuse and become part of an organisation/movement's repertoire and become available for use in framing and translation by bricoleurs.[8]

Similarly, Sidney Tarrow has argued that while social movements may have a large number of participants, 'they are really much more like an interlocking network of small groups.'[9]

A social network can be easily differentiated from a social movement when the latter is clearly defined. Charles Tilly has offered a particularly useful set of criteria for defining social movements.[10] Firstly, a social movement must involve a campaign. Secondly, it must involve the performance of an established social movement repertoire (a blend of political actions such as boycotts and demonstrations). Lastly, he argues that a social movement must involve displays of moral or political worthiness, unity of members around issues and large numbers of members demonstrating their commitment to 'the cause'.

In dissecting the difference between a social network and a social movement it is also worth noting that it is commonly accepted in Northern social movements literature that all social movements are, in a sense, knowledge based. For instance, Tarrow and Snow have argued that they involve the naming of a particular grievance through 'collective action frames'[11] in terms of which a particular grievance or claim is identified and linked to other grievances. In so doing, a larger frame of meaning is constructed that aims to resonate with the pre-popular culture's predispositions and communicate a uniform message to those in power.[12] Like most social movements, TAC's later social movement activism was knowledge based in that it relied on cognition and effective communication. Having discussed how this chapter draws and builds on these South African and global conceptualisations of the relationship between networks and movements, I will now move on to a brief discussion of late apartheid and transition era AIDS activism.

What had gone before: Late apartheid and transition era AIDS activism

AIDS activism in the early 1990s is widely represented in the literature as having existed in a kind of progressive golden age of AIDS policymaking. For instance, Heywood argues that '[i]n the early 1990s the ANC also worked closely with the first non-governmental organisations ... that emerged to tackle the HIV epidemic'.[13] Similarly, in their article on AIDS policy implementation in post-apartheid South Africa, Stein and Schneider argue:

> The AIDS world just prior to 1994 was characterised by strong networks between non-governmental organisations, researchers and sympathetic health workers, an infrastructure of AIDS counseling and information centres in metropolitan local governments and the anti-apartheid political groupings. The policy space [understood as room for manoeuvre and influence] ... appeared wide.[14]

Transition era AIDS activism was politically focused on assisting the ANC as a government-in-waiting with drawing up an AIDS plan. It was also an era where two large, significant conferences were held dealing with AIDS. The Maputo conference on Health in Southern Africa held in April 1990 marked the beginning of the coordination of national, anti-apartheid activist work around AIDS. The 'Maputo Statement on HIV and AIDS in Southern Africa' asserted that AIDS should be prioritised in a post-apartheid South Africa led by the ANC. The first National AIDS Convention of South Africa was held at the Nasrec convention centre in Johannesburg in 1992. It was a large gathering of several hundred representatives of anti-apartheid political organisations, NGOs, government, business and unions. After the meeting, a small group of people were mandated to draft the first National AIDS Plan, including Mary Crewe, Quarraisha Abdool Karim, Salim Abdool Karim, Edwin Cameron, Manto Tshabalala-Msimang and Nkosasana Zuma (the latter two later both became ministers of health).[15] The UN's Global Programme on AIDS (which would later become the Joint UN Action Plan on HIV/AIDS, or UNAIDS) was also very involved in budgeting and adding time frames to the plan.[16]

So in a sense the transition era was also an era of 'conferences'. These conferences also cost significant amounts of money. For instance the NACOSA conference cost R1.1 million, compared to an overall government AIDS budget of R3.7 million.[17] Despite these comparatively high costs the conferences and meetings were fruitful in that they directly led to the development of the first National AIDS Plan,[18] which was firmly rooted in human rights principles.[19] As Schneider and Stein argue, the plan 'combined the technical with the political and was comprehensive, practical and carefully costed. … It recommended that final authority rest with a co-ordinating structure in the President's office nationally, and the Prime Ministers' offices at provincial level'.[20] The plan had six main components, which were developed by working groups concentrating on education and prevention, counselling, health care, human rights and law reform, and welfare and research.[21] The plan was unique in its emphasis on human rights, the involvement of people living with HIV and in its call for a multi-sectoral response to be implemented through all departments of government.[22]

The stage was thus set for a National AIDS Plan consultatively devised by multiple stakeholders to be implemented by the first legitimate, democratic government. Sadly, for a range of reasons, AIDS policy implementation was postponed. The new government also faced problems of state transformation and delayed delivery. Simultaneously, diverse civil society groupings grappled to formulate appropriate watchdog responses. We now turn to a discussion of the evolution of AIDS activism during the Mandela presidency.

The 'honeymoon period' and the shifting terrain

The immediate post-election period was characterised by warm relations between activists who became bureaucrats and those who remained in civil society. While the latter had excellent access to such activists-turned-bureaucrats in this period, the challenges of transforming the state hindered policy implementation. After the jubilation of the ANC's victory in the 1994 elections, political appointments were made to cabinet and civil servants were appointed. One of these was Quarraisha Abdool Karim, who was head-hunted as the first director of the Department of Health's AIDS unit. Abdool Karim is a microbiologist and epidemiologist by training. She was involved in the anti-apartheid struggle and her husband, Salim Abdool Karim, was involved in the United Democratic Front-aligned National Medical and Dental Association in the 1980s. Both began work at the MRC when they returned to South Africa in the late 1980s. On her appointment, Abdool Karim announced, '[I was] humbled by the request. I knew I wanted to be a scientist in the long run but I wanted to help the government in transformation'.[23]

Nkosasana Zuma, the newly appointed minister of health, and Abdool Karim had done AIDS research together at the MRC and collaborated on the development of the National AIDS Plan that had evolved from the NACOSA process. As co-author of the first post-1994 National AIDS Plan, Abdool Karim had every reason to feel confident that she could make a difference: she enjoyed strong links with the president, the Reconstruction and Development Programme Office, and the Ministry of Health. Soon after her appointment, the AIDS unit was transformed into the Directorate of HIV/ AIDS and Sexually Transmitted Diseases, raising its status. The directorate's budget increased significantly from R3.7 million annually to R21 million, an increase largely based on a massive rise in foreign donor aid, as monies that had previously gone to AIDS NGOs now went to the directorate.[24]

Delivery was complicated by the need to simultaneously transform the state. For instance, one of Abdool Karim's first priorities was to improve the quality of the condoms the government procured for distribution. The first meeting she attended in the department was conducted in Afrikaans and she found it challenging to be a black female who was seven months pregnant in a very white, Afrikaans, male-dominated environment.[25] Initially, the ministry's director general was Kunst Slabber, who had served under the apartheid era minister of health, Rina Venter. He informed Nkosasana Zuma that he would step down once policies and procedures designed for fiduciary responsibility were in place. Abdool Karim also had to familiarise herself and meet with the tender board so that 'much of the first year was spent having to learn about government systems in a department that was in transition'.[26]

In the post-election period, however, AIDS activism was a shifting terrain: while some NACOSA activists moved into government, others remained in civil society, such as Edwin Cameron and Morna Cornell. While these changes were taking place at the national level, NACOSA itself became an umbrella organisation representing civil society on AIDS. The AIDS Law Project (ALP), which had been established in 1992, was based at the Centre for Applied Legal Studies at the University of the Witwatersrand. The ALP had been essential in the formation of the AIDS Consortium, founded in the same year. The AIDS Consortium was made up of several key AIDS activist organisations that pooled their efforts to 'respond quickly and effectively to developments in AIDS policy and the media'.[27] It provided a critical networking space for activists and, hence, a socio-political basis for the emergence of TAC.

By later standards, AIDS activists in the mid-1990s had relatively ready access to senior members of government. For instance, in November 1994 the NACOSA co-chairs, Edwin Cameron and Clarence Mini, met with Deputy Presidents F. W. de Klerk and Thabo Mbeki to urge them to push for Mandela to read a statement in support of the NACOSA plan.[28] As the decade wore on, AIDS activists linked to NACOSA and the AIDS Consortium remained dissatisfied with Mandela not saying enough publicly on AIDS. By early 1996 the co-chairs of NACOSA felt disappointed that 'the President ... [had] not used his high authority and stature to warn South Africans of the dangers of infection, and the dangers of irrational and unfair responses to AIDS'.[29] By contrast, their meetings with Abdool Karim proved more fruitful in shaping the policies of the directorate. Indeed, for Abdool Karim, consultation with NGOs was absolutely central to her role in the Department of Health. Her standpoint was that '[t]he fight against HIV/AIDS can only be won through the joint efforts of all the roleplayers'.[30]

It is clear that goodwill existed on all sides to implement the plan. What soured relations between government and AIDS activists was a scandal over tendering procedures for an AIDS play called *Sarafina II*. This scandal was illustrative of the challenges faced by bureaucrats and those such as Abdool Karim, Zuma and Olive Shisana who were new in government, and is perhaps the first instance where post-apartheid civil society activists played a watchdog role in relation to the actions of their former comrades who were now in government.

AIDS scandals, yet ongoing collaboration

The Mandela administration was the protagonist in the high-profile AIDS scandal over *Sarafina II*. Resource distribution lay at the heart of the debacle. However, AIDS activists began to utilise new political spaces that were created by the interim (1993) and final (1996) constitutions for advocacy. In particular, the public protector and the democratic parliament's Portfolio Committee for Health were used in this manner.

Sarafina II demonstrates the challenges that former activists faced in familiarising themselves with state mechanisms. *Sarafina II*'s genesis can be traced back to the minister deciding to develop an AIDS awareness play as a 'special project'.[31] Mbongeni Ngema had leapt to prominence as a playwright following his highly successful and much-fêted film, *Sarafina*, a political coming-of-age film set during the Soweto uprising starring Whoopi Goldberg (a popular American film star). According to the public protector's report, Ngema was approached by the minister to give his views on producing an AIDS play. At that stage he estimated that the play would cost R800,000.[32] However, when the call was put out for tenders to be submitted, the budget for *Sarafina II* had mushroomed to R14,247,600.[33] This included items such as a 45-seater luxury bus, a 24-ton tractor and a semi-trailer.[34] The only other tender, by Opera Africa, was for a much more modest R600,000.[35] The limited time to respond to the tender made it difficult for other established drama AIDS NGOs to put in counter-bids. Due to the obvious extravagances in the budget, the department's tender committee did not approve the offer. Nevertheless, an official in the department signed a contract with Ngema for the R14.2 million play and immediately wrote a R3 million cheque for the play's development.[36]

Directorate employee Phil Brown, together with consultant Warren Parker, travelled down to Durban to assess and advise on the play's content, as there was no script, and were disappointed with what they saw. In Parker's words, the play was 'a disaster'.[37] Parker met with Ngema and offered a full and detailed critique of what he saw at the rehearsal. Parker left with the impression that Ngema was receptive to the proposed modifications. When the play opened on World AIDS Day, AIDS activists with experience in community-based AIDS awareness work were extremely disappointed by the play. Judy Seidman of Progressive Primary Health Care Network (PPHC) and NAPWA found the play 'depressing'.[38] Morna Cornell, coordinator of the AIDS Consortium, came away from the play upset that it fed into gender stereotypes driving the epidemic: it featured a character, Crocodile, who was lionised for having multiple partners. Female characters wore very short skirts.[39] This critique was not limited to AIDS activists and emerged in a letter to the editor of the *Natal Witness*. A reader, Annesh Ranklown, lashed out at the play as 'totally derogatory to women'.[40]

In early 1996 news of the flouting of tendering procedures hit AIDS activists when they were contacted by the media for comment. Morna Cornell remembers first hearing about the *Sarafina II* and Virodene scandals: 'We would get a call from the press; that's how we would find out.'[41] Both the AIDS Consortium and NACOSA rapidly swung into action around *Sarafina II*. According to Cornell, the AIDS Consortium had an emergency meeting – lasting more than four hours – in which staff sat with the scripts and the notes they had made. The aim was 'to critique the play and be supportive simultaneously'.[42] The comments and suggestions were consolidated into a short document that was sent to the government, but it got no response, 'as usual'.[43] As a result of the media storm, and following calls from NACOSA, parliament's Portfolio Committee on Health held a hearing into the controversy. Mike Ellis, an MP for the Democratic Party, asked the public protector to investigate the tendering procedures around the play. Making a submission to the public protector involved a lot of work for the AIDS Consortium. This included gathering information and fact checking and then there was the submission itself, which took two and a half hours.[44]

The public protector found:

> The awarding of *Sarafina II* contract … was not in accordance with State tender procedures. It was not in accordance even with the agreement with the European Union. It was never budgeted for. I accordingly find that *it was an unauthorised expenditure.*[45]

This outcome precipitated the minister into clutching at straws to minimise the bad press generated by the perceived 'waste' of taxpayers' money. The *Sowetan* reported that Zuma had handed over the play and some of its costs to unnamed private backers.[46] The Health Commission later threatened to prosecute Zuma following its investigation into the debacle.[47]

Without doubt the *Sarafina II* debacle brought serious embarrassment to the government, which 'closed ranks'.[48] The fall-out from the scandal is detailed in the AIDS Consortium's widely publicised statement on the public protector's report, which blamed the minister and director general of health for the debacle and argued that it had 'made the government programme an object of widespread ridicule … put further donor funding of AIDS activities into question … [and] demoralised countless organisations and activists'.[49] The Democratic Party went even further and called for Nkosasana Zuma to be fired.[50] Abdool Karim resigned from the Ministry of Health, ostensibly to resume her career as an epidemiologist; however, some have attributed her move to the scandal.[51]

This narrative adds detail and complexity to the TAC founder critique of the pre-1998 AIDS world. *Sarafina II* showed that the AIDS world attracted politically well-connected, venal opportunists who aimed to benefit from increasing foreign donor funding for AIDS. On the other hand, the two main AIDS activist umbrella bodies operating within this world, NACOSA and the AIDS Consortium, were very outspoken against the inappropriate way the tender was awarded. At this stage they still wanted to keep channels to the government open and were very effectively using the press and new mechanisms such as making submissions before the public protector to influence government AIDS policies. So there was no need at this stage to embark on mass demonstrations or civil disobedience campaigns, as policies could be changed through conventional lobbying coordinated in NGO offices. One ominous development was that the government and civil society began to communicate on matters related to AIDS policy through the media. This is remarkable, given that a mere two years before they had met regularly *as comrades* in NACOSA and affiliated progressive health worker organisations.

The late 1990s was a contradictory period in the AIDS world. While scandals such as *Sarafina II* raged through the press, some channels such as the STD/HIV/ AIDS review (see below) remained open for NGO/community-based organisation activist input into AIDS policymaking. Similarly, a successful activist campaign for the Employment Equity Act to outlaw pre-employment testing of HIV showed that parliament remained a useful space for lobbying for human rights-based legislative responses to AIDS.

While Abdool Karim's exit from the Department of Health was said to be for 'personal reasons', her resignation needs to be seen in the context of the *Sarafina II* scandal. Rose Smart, who was her replacement as the head of the Department of Health's AIDS Directorate, told the media that she was determined to leave the animosity of the *Sarafina* affair behind.[52] Similarly, in a meeting with Clarence Mini and Edwin Cameron, the co-chairs of NACOSA, Zuma was reported to have apologised for commissioning the play.[53] Mandela was also reported to have apologised and argued that the bigger issue was whether the ANC-led government had been prepared to learn from its mistakes.[54] In this spirit of reconciliation and reassessment of policies, the Department of Health commissioned the MRC to do an STD/HIV/AIDS review in July and August 1997.[55] National and provincial site reviews took place over a fortnight in July 1997. On 7 and 8 August a National Consultative Workshop was held where findings and recommendations were discussed.[56] This review was consultative and comprehensive, and its report provides an interesting snapshot of the AIDS world at the time. Schneider argues that '[f]or many AIDS activists, participation in this national review was their first systematic exposure to government'.[57] However, as Schneider and Rose Smart (head of the AIDS Directorate at the time) have suggested, the goodwill and momentum generated nationwide by the provincial reviews were squandered when the minister called for notification – compulsory reporting of AIDS deaths – at a national conference discussing the review's findings.[58]

Despite these scandals, channels certainly remained open for activists to influence government through conventional lobbying to combat AIDS-related discrimination. This was demonstrated in the successful advocacy aimed at having pre-employment HIV testing outlawed. Since their development in the mid-1980s, HIV tests had been used to unjustly discriminate against job candidates and employees with HIV. The ALP launched an advocacy campaign on the issue. Initially, AIDS activists fought for a Code of Good Practice on HIV and Employment and called upon employers and the government to voluntarily subscribe to it.[59] The Southern African Development Community was persuaded to adopt the code and recommended that all member states translate it into domestic legislation. The ALP then used the code to further domestic advocacy.[60]

Around the same time it was decided by the ruling ANC that an employment equity Act ought to be introduced that would force companies to adopt affirmative action and outlaw unfair workplace-based discrimination. AIDS activists saw that the Act presented an opportunity to prohibit unfair pre-employment HIV testing. Activists from the ALP, NACOSA and the NCGLE formed the Employment Equity Alliance in May 1998 to push for the proposed Employment Equity Act to specifically list HIV status as unfair grounds for discrimination.[61] This body made very detailed submissions to the parliamentary Portfolio Committee on Health at the hearings on the Employment Equity Act. At these hearings Zackie Achmat first publicly announced that he was living with HIV.[62] Fatima Hassan, who was an attorney at the ALP, argued that 'parliament wanted to listen' and that the Mandela administration 'saw us as comrades.'[63] Consequently, pre-employment testing of HIV was rendered illegal with the passage of the Employment Equity Act, with the exception of cases where HIV status adversely impacted on an individual's ability to meet a job requirement.[64]

NAPWA and the competing models of AIDS activism

The chapter now turns briefly to the history of NAPWA, to which a significant portion of the TAC founder critique is addressed. NAPWA was formed in 1993 at the first National Conference for People Living with HIV held in Durban.[65] By 1994 it had a national committee with members such as John Pegge, Rick Stephens, Prudence Mabele and Mercy Makhalemele. It was initially a very small organisation, as few people were prepared in those days to be open about living with HIV.[66] AIDS activists who are living with HIV commonly self-identified by the abbreviation People with HIV/AIDS (PWA). NAPWA's mission statement outlined the organisation as aiming to 'be the assertive, legitimate and representative voice of all people living with HIV/AIDS … to ensure that the basic human rights and dignity of all people living with HIV/AIDS are upheld.'[67]

By 1996 the Department of Health, concerned by the lack of visibility of people living with HIV, launched a new 'FACES of AIDS' project. Abdool Karim created 12 posts for people living openly with HIV, many of whom were NAPWA members.[68] It was hard to fill the posts, as many potential applicants were reluctant to be publicly open about living with HIV due to the stigma attached to the disease.[69]

NAPWA was certainly successful in providing the only real nationwide 'space' for PWAs to meet and obtain social and psychological support from one another.

However, from its inception, activists also experienced the organisation as a partially 'problematic' space. For women, disclosure of living with HIV could have serious implications in a society where violence against women was endemic. The murder of AIDS activist Gugu Dlamini in 1998 for revealing her HIV status was a case in point. Dlamini was a young woman who had been diagnosed with HIV at KwaMashu polyclinic in October 1998.[70] Influenced by NAPWA's disclosure campaign, she decided to reveal her HIV status publicly on Radio Zulu in November 1998.[71] She was consequently beaten by four men behind a friend's shack.[72] Following the assault, one of the suspects was heard accusing Dlamini of being a prostitute who had infected people with HIV.[73] She was taken to a clinic and later to a hospital, where she died from her injuries.[74] The investigation was bungled, which meant that successful prosecution was impossible. Eventually, at the ALP's insistence, an inquest was held for Dlamini.

Although Dlamini's death affected all AIDS activists, it did not unify them: while some wanted to continue focusing on social support, others became more radical and political. For instance, Promise Mthembu left NAPWA shortly after Dlamini was murdered. 'I credited Gugu's death to the campaign', said Mthembu, 'because I just felt she was not ready to reveal her HIV status. She had not communicated with her family or her community.'[75] PWA activists who shared her sentiments organised themselves into the Gugu Dlamini Action Committee, which demanded access to AZT to prevent mother-to-child transmission.[76] (See Hodes's chapter in this volume for further details on access to treatment and prevention of mother-to-child transmission.) By March 1999 this committee started collaborating with TAC.

Returning to the TAC founder critique of NAPWA in this period, I would argue that, given these events, it is more accurate to see TAC as partly having emerged out of certain frustrated radical political tendencies or groupings within NAPWA than it is to see it as emerging only in opposition to NAPWA.

Implications of NAPWA's internal politics for the formation of TAC

TAC was born partly out of a coalition of more radical NAPWA activists, but also out of social networks that developed between activists based at AIDS NGOs such as the ALP, the NCGLE and the Positive Women's Network, which were formed through the AIDS Consortium. Moreover, TAC was shaped by scientific developments and the way the epidemic itself was progressing. By the late 1990s AIDS-related mortality was on the rise[77] and the very ranks of AIDS activists were being obliterated by the epidemic. The death of AIDS activist Simon Nkoli came as a big blow to many activists.

At the 1996 Vancouver AIDS Conference, David Ho had announced the startling breakthrough that when three antiretroviral drugs were used in combination there was durable suppression of HIV replication and substantial recovery of the immune system. While their PWA counterparts in the North were living longer due to these new combination antiretroviral therapies, South Africans were dying *en masse* on a daily basis. TAC's increased radicalism compared to earlier AIDS activism may have been related to the greater immediate rewards that treatment offered to people living with HIV. PWA could now fight for their lives as they learned through correspondence, phone conversations and interactions with Northern AIDS activists at international AIDS conferences. As a consequence they began to investigate ways of reducing the cost of the drugs in South Africa.[78]

While some activists left NAPWA outright, others fought for it to match their evolving vision of a radical PWA-led movement for treatment access. Activists who wanted NAPWA to follow the treatment advocacy route tried to convince HIV/AIDS advocate Peter Busse that it should front a big campaign on the issue. Busse was not overtly political in his approach and remained primarily interested in counselling and providing a support network for people living with HIV.[79] Nevertheless, TAC was formed. Prior to its formation, and following AIDS Consortium meetings, there had been months of informal discussions among activists about the need for a treatment access movement.[80] TAC was eventually established at a meeting where, among others, Zackie Achmat (NCGLE), Mark Heywood (ALP), Edwin Cameron, Mazibuko Jara (NCGLE), Prudence Mabele (Positive Women's Network), Mercy Makhalemele (NAPWA), Morna Cornell (AIDS Consortium) and Pumi Mthetwa (NCGLE) were present.[81] This group of founding members helped write TAC's constitution and unofficially managed it for the first two or three months of its existence.

Initially TAC was a NAPWA project. Indeed, early TAC documents such as an April 1999 memo to the minister of health, Nkosasana Zuma, on AZT were issued on behalf of both NAPWA and TAC. In this period, the two organisations were often referred to as NAPWA–TAC.[82] However, the two organisations soon came into conflict. TAC grew rapidly and started using a greater proportion of NAPWA's resources. At a NAPWA board meeting in 2000 Zackie Achmat levelled accusations at Busse of mismanaging the organisation.[83]

This dispute was not resolved.[84] NAPWA left its offices in the South African National NGO Coalition next to the AIDS Consortium and moved to the University of Pretoria.[85] Busse experienced a period of severe AIDS-related illness, but then recovered and reinvented himself as an AIDS consultant, mostly working internationally. A new director, Nkuleleko Nxesi, was appointed to the leadership of NAPWA,[86] which later moved to the East Rand and received large amounts of funding from the Department of Health. In a later period, this government funding to NAPWA was almost certainly used to demobilise PWA and create an artificial political counterweight to TAC.[87]

From 2000 onwards TAC became an organisation in its own right. On the opening day of the 2000 Durban International AIDS Conference a 20,000-strong demonstration of students, unionists, traditional healers, children affected by AIDS, and international AIDS activists from the AIDS Coalition to Unleash Power and the Gay Men's Health Crisis wound its way through the streets of Durban and demonstrated outside Kings Park stadium, where the opening of the conference took place. The infant organisation was well on its way to becoming the first mass-based PWA-led AIDS movement in South Africa. It also began to put the issue of access to treatment by poor people in developing countries firmly on the global agenda.

Conclusion

South African AIDS activism became more radical from the late 1990s onwards. Indeed, TAC was the first radical PWA-driven movement for treatment access in South Africa. However, it also had older socio-political roots. It emerged from a social network consisting of the radical, activist components of the AIDS world, rather than merely in opposition to it. Several reasons can be offered for why AIDS activism preceding TAC's emergence was non-radical in its advocacy approach, other than a lack of radical political ideas and a donor-driven, venal approach to activism.

Firstly, in the transition era, non-governmental AIDS activists worked closely with the ANC to formulate the first National AIDS Plan. Secondly, when the Mandela administration came to power, these activists had every reason to believe that the government would deliver on a plan that it had helped to formulate. Some activists even went into government to assist with implementing the plan. Thirdly, the *Sarafina II* scandal showed the difficulties that these activists-turned-bureaucrats faced in delivering to the people while at the same time trying to transform government from the inside. It also set in motion a harmful pattern of conflict where activists and the government primarily communicated through the media on AIDS.

However, throughout the Mandela administration, effective, office-based lobbying channels remained open to activists. On the one hand, parliamentary committees were effectively used by the Employment Equity Alliance to push for unfair HIV-related discrimination to be outlawed; on the other, warmer engagement with government remained precarious. The STD/HIV/AIDS review process led to a thaw in relations between the government and AIDS activists at the provincial level. Yet this goodwill quickly dissipated when the health minister promoted notification at a national conference to discuss the review's findings.

Much of the TAC founder critique appears to be directed at NAPWA. It is true that there was conflict between TAC and NAPWA soon after TAC's formation, but this was largely over diverging ideas about what AIDS activism should be. Activists grouped around Busse envisioned PWA activism as psycho-social support for people living with HIV. In contrast, activists who rallied around Achmat wanted to form a highly politicised and radical PWA-led movement around treatment access. Networks formed between activists in the AIDS world at the AIDS Consortium provided a vital socio-political basis for TAC's formation.

A far more serious critique of NAPWA's activism is that it was naïve on the gender-based violence that women activists living with HIV faced as a result of disclosure. The murder of Gugu Dlamini most clearly illustrated this and was a lightning rod for incipient radical PWA-led treatment activism, especially in KwaZulu-Natal. The event was a key motive for TAC's formation as an organisation in its own right.

More recently, TAC enjoyed a high degree of consultation with government over the drafting of the 2007 Strategic Plan. TAC has been contemplating its future direction.[88] The ousting of President Thabo Mbeki in September 2008 signalled the end of a long period where AIDS denialism was influential in government policymaking.

At the time of writing, the subsequent administration has proven much more enthusiastic about maximising access to antiretrovirals. But challenges remain in ensuring universal access to HIV treatment and in reducing the number of new infections, not least in addressing the epidemic's disproportionate impact on women. The AIDS world remains politically in flux. In this context, and in light of this volume's focus on continuity and change in popular protest, it is all the more important to contemplate the socio-political origins of TAC, while reflecting on an earlier period where there were rewards for, as well as pitfalls in relations with the government that were, paradoxically, both warm and adversarial.

12 New social movements as civil society: The case of past and present Soweto

Kelly Rosenthal

'*A radical transformation in South Africa will depend more on how the past is remembered than on how the future is plotted.*'[1]

Introduction

Manuel Castells has argued that urban social movements were the front line of ideological revolutions – the sites where new alternatives to dominant hegemony were created.[2] This chapter compares two eras of South African urban social movements, both of which are regarded here as exemplary models of Castells' radical urban movements in that they constitute an attempt to instigate a revolutionary redistribution of power. In an effort to shed light on various dimensions of continuity and change in popular resistance movements in South Africa, the discussion contrasts the Soweto Civic Association (SCA), formed under the apartheid regime in 1976, and the Soweto Electricity Crisis Committee (SECC), formed in 2000 within a democratic political context. The SCA was a prominent part of the civic movement, which witnessed the mobilisation of hundreds of township communities into organised groups that protested effectively against the apartheid state in the 1970s and 1980s. The SECC is a prominent member of the group of community organisations – referred to as the country's 'new social movements' – that have emerged in the last ten years in South Africa. The mobilisation efforts of the SECC's community activists target a wide range of issues, but the key focus of their activism centres on what they call 'the basics', i.e. electricity, water, housing, education, health and employment.

The re-emergence in the last decade of distinct and familiar forms of community organisations in South Africa has understandably prompted comparisons between these new social movements and the anti-apartheid groups that they appear to resemble. Patrick Bond argues that while '[c]ivil society organising in South African cities has a long tradition … the historical memory of activists to the intense apartheid urban repression during the 1960s–70s might be the most important precursor of contemporary civil society.'[3] He argues that the civics movement shared with the new social movements a political vision of being 'for the "globalisation of people", and against "the globalisation of capital"'.[4] The media have offered less nuanced comparisons when reporting the violence that has repeatedly erupted over the last five years in South Africa over the lack of service delivery. An article in the *Guardian* entitled 'Townships in revolt as ANC fails to live up to its promises' carried the subheading: 'Beatings, shootings and petrol bombs see some areas return to violence of apartheid era'. The article began: 'They resemble scenes from another era: angry crowds, clashes with police, shots, teargas and petrol bombs. Twelve years after apartheid ended, some townships are again burning.'[5]

If we are to understand the significance of the new social movements and take seriously their challenges to the African National Congress (ANC) state, these comparisons merit closer investigation. The civics movement and the new social movements both arose under distinct and complex political and economic regimes, which produced different conditions and needs at the grassroots level. The assumption that these two sets of social expressions are ideologically and politically continuous – one that has been explicitly and implicitly expressed in the public and academic domains – belies the key discontinuities between the two. The comparative material presented in this chapter is a starting point in the endeavour to understand popular protest in South Africa across space and time. While an assessment of a wide range of dimensions of comparison would be illuminating, I have limited the discussion in the chapter to one aspect in particular, namely the relationship between the nature of the state and the ideology of resistance. Specifically, the chapter seeks to provide insight into the ways in which different forms of oppression have engendered different forms of resistance.

A note on categories

Comparisons such as this are inherently problematic, as they assume the collective homogeneity of the two groups being compared. In fact,

> the civics movement cannot be spoken of unproblematically as a singular event. The imprints of the particular and the local – with different manifestations in rural areas, urban townships and cosmopolitan inner cities – all mark civic formation, and lend its history a certain unevenness and variety.[6]

Indeed the two most important and prominent civic organisations in the former Transvaal, the SCA and the Alexandra Action Committee (AAC), although they shared many objectives and strategies, had very different ideological positions. The AAC was an explicitly socialist organisation, whereas, as I will argue, the SCA was not. Thus, the civic movement as a whole contained a multitude of political ideologies, and, despite the distinct and recognisable structures of the organisations across the country, they were not homogeneous in all respects.

Similarly, South Africa's new social movements represent a wide array of local concerns and positions. At a gathering of these movements in 2006 under the rubric 'Social Movements Indaba' a list of prominent and 'long-standing' movements was put together. This list revealed the diversity in size, nature and issues that is incorporated by the collective term new social movements. For example, alongside the SECC is listed the Treatment Action Campaign; the Landless People's Movement; the Homeless People's Federation; environmental groups; gay, lesbian, bisexual, transgender and intersex groups; and at least two vigilante organisations: Mapogo-A-Mathamaga and People Against Gangsterism and Drugs. The sheer range of difference in this list threatens to make their collective grouping an absurdity – beyond their opposition to the state in some way, these groups often have very little in common. However, they currently self-identify as being related and conceptualise their various struggles as part of a larger battle against the ANC government's failure to provide adequately for everyone. This grouping of social movements will be referred to in this chapter as the new social movements.

The democratic context: A fertile bed for renewed resistance

For township dwellers in the 1970s and 1980s the apartheid state was omnipresent, coercive and brutal. The ANC state, although sporadically violent when challenged, asserts a different kind of violence; the violence of a retreating state, one failing to take responsibility for the well-being of all its citizens. The apartheid state fostered dynamic and diverse resistance, but the primary common objective of the various organisations that constituted this resistance was to end apartheid. Critiques of capitalism were present and influential, but the exigency of divesting the vast state structure of racial violence and oppression inevitably took precedence. The democratic transition in South Africa occurred shortly after the collapse of the Soviet Union – an internationally legitimated politico-economic alternative to capitalism – and the hegemonic rise of the free market. Any socialist, redistributive or welfarist tendencies within the liberation movement were undermined, co-opted and silenced. A discussion of how the South African liberation movement abandoned its initial attempts at a redistributive and welfarist programme in favour of a neoliberal one will be provided later. The point here is that conditions under democratic transition have fostered an environment where the renewal of grassroots social protest was inevitable:

> [A] particularly sobering aspect of the South African transition to democracy has been the growing recognition that, while South Africa has one of the most progressive constitutions on the planet, the actual realisation of these constitutional rights has not lived up to expectations. Although there have been considerable gains in terms of 'first generation' human rights – political and civil rights, such as freedom from discrimination on the grounds of race, gender, sexual orientation, religion, etc – the same cannot be said concerning the realisation of second generation socio-economic rights.[7]

Democratisation and freedom from racial tyranny has not meant the simultaneous delivery from poverty. South Africa is now ranked as the most unequal country in the world and the poor have reorganised to protest against the violence of neoliberal capitalism and the retreat of the state. In this environment, the new social movements are fighting seemingly old battles: they mobilise around issues of service delivery: water, electricity, housing, employment and education; but this chapter argues that the altered political milieu in which these social movements exist has created the need for a different kind of organisation, one whose primary ideological objective is to demonstrate the systemic injustice of neoliberal capitalism and to offer socialism as a viable alternative.

In many ways the SCA and the SECC appear similar: the former played a central role in the national civic movement and the latter now plays a central role in the new social movements. Much like the SCA, the SECC's campaigns target practical, bread-and-butter issues. Most significantly for the public imagination, the visible protests of the SECC are directly reminiscent of anti-apartheid struggle civics: marches and demonstrations bear witness to *toyi-toyi*-ing (the iconic anti-apartheid dance) and 'struggle songs', which were once directed at Nationalist Party leaders, but which are now sung in modified versions directed at ANC leaders and officials (see Dawson's chapter in this volume on post-apartheid struggle songs). The SECC runs a boycott of service rates, much like the successful and high-profile rent boycott instigated by the SCA. Like the SCA, the SECC is a grassroots organisation, dedicated to building political capacity from the bottom up. Both organisations were or are committed to a broader ideological goal transcending the quotidian nature of their campaigns. It is this last point that this chapter explores in detail, asserting that the ideological goals of the SCA and the SECC are in fact quite different.

Driving the movements: Motlana and Ngwane

This chapter is essentially about the political ideology of two organisations. The argument presented here rests heavily on the oral testimonies of their respective leaders, the late Dr Nthato Motlana, former leader of the SCA, and Trevor Ngwane, a leading figure in the SECC. Motlana was an influential political activist in the 1970s and 1980s who was involved with the ANC from an early age. He qualified as a doctor and opened a practice in Soweto, but remained politically active. In 1976 he was elected chairperson of the Committee of Ten, the institutional forerunner to the SCA, and, shortly afterwards, SCA chairperson. He held this position from 1976 until 1990, while simultaneously developing various business interests. When Nelson Mandela was released from prison, Motlana toured the world as his personal doctor. In 1993 he launched the first black company to be listed on the Johannesburg Stock Exchange: New Africa Investment Limited.

Ngwane enrolled to study sociology at Fort Hare in 1979, where he became involved in radical student politics and was eventually expelled in 1982. During the early 1980s, when Motlana and the SCA were most active, Ngwane registered for a master's degree at the University of the Witwatersrand. It was here that he developed his Marxist ideology and became formally involved with the ANC. In the first democratic municipal elections he was elected as the councillor for Pimville, Soweto, where he was a resident. In 1999 Ngwane wrote an article critiquing the ANC's iGoli 2002 plan, which was published in the South African Municipal Workers' Union newsletter. He was subsequently suspended from the ANC, but was offered his position back on condition that he retract his critique. He refused and became an independent political activist, founding the SECC in 2000.

Admittedly, this focus on the leadership risks conducting a 'big man' or top-down history of resistance. However, due to the limitations of this chapter, it is not possible to engage here with the full complexity of the various levels of organisational ideology or the differences between ideological positions of the leaders and the rank-and-file members. By using the testimonies of these two men, I am not asserting that their ideological positions represent the ideology of all members of their organisations. However, both Motlana and Ngwane represent similar types of leader. Like Motlana in the 1980s, Ngwane today is charismatic and influential, commanding loyalty and respect from a broad spectrum of supporters. Examining their personal political ideologies is a useful way of beginning to understand the nature of the respective organisations. By elucidating the political currents that led to the formation of the SCA and SECC and contrasting the leaders' ideologies with the activities of their organisations, it is possible to understand how two organisations that appear so similar can be understood to represent very different ideological positions.

I first became involved in these issues in 2004, when I spent six weeks living in Soweto and working with the SECC. During this time I conducted interviews and engaged in participant observation with members and non-members of the organisation. I was researching the social implications of cost-recovery practices in water and electricity delivery in Soweto. Much of the insights and some of the material I gathered during that time have been incorporated into this chapter. The relationships I built with residents of Soweto facilitated my return in 2006 to conduct new research. This second period of research, conducted in March and April 2006, again took the form of interviews and participant observation with leaders and members of the SECC. To facilitate a historical comparison with the SCA, I also interviewed some of the surviving members of the SCA leadership. It must be noted that their testimonies rely heavily on memories that are about 30 years old. Certain moments in the history of the SCA may have been more unforgettable to these leaders than others, and their accounts should thus not be interpreted as objective explanations of the entire lifespan of the movement.

The most interesting problem I encountered was a certain degree of inconsistency between the secondary sources on the political ideology of the SCA and the narratives of Nthato Motlana and Tom Manthata. The consensus, whether explicit or implicit in the literature, is that the civics held a socialist ideology.[8] This idea was also articulated by members of the SECC, who remembered or retrospectively constructed the SCA as a socialist organisation. This notion stands in stark contrast with the narratives of Manthata and Motlana, who repeatedly portrayed the SCA as an organisation committed to 'democracy' and driven more by Black Consciousness than socialism. Motlana, who was the leader of the SCA, expressed disillusionment with and distaste for socialism, advocating instead a capitalist, individualistic and entrepreneurial ethos as the panacea for South Africa's socio-economic ills.

This disjuncture was perplexing, and at first I attributed it to the fact that these two men had experienced a shift in political ideology and were both now engaged and invested in capitalist, democratic South Africa, and so it was understandable that they denied a previous adherence to a socialist ideology. However, the explanation that they had created a historical narrative to fit with their current ideologies is unconvincing. Closer examination of the SCA reveals that, although certainly committed to overthrowing the apartheid state and to the principles of participatory democracy, it was by no means a socialist organisation. Motlana's famous 'blueprint for Soweto' listed as its first demand the right to private property and for Sowetans to own the houses that they rented from the state. Further activities, objectives and statements that indicated a strong capitalist discourse within the SCA will be discussed later in this chapter, but the following anecdote recounted by Motlana is a telling example of his early disdain for socialism:

> After 1976, right after we formed the Committee of Ten, they came and arrested all of us. The rioting continued, Soweto was burning, they kept us in for months, and then, around Christmas, they let everyone out, except the Reverend Makatchwa and myself, and the reverend and I spent months in prison together. Now Makatchwa was a Catholic priest and a communist, and all we talked about in prison was communism versus, well I regard myself (and I did then too) as a democrat. Now the interesting thing was that at about that time, the Russians put sputnik[9] around the earth. And I would say to Makatchwa, 'Eh, you bloody communists, what do you know about science?' and he would say 'Hey! We put sputnik in the air!' I lost that argument hands down![10]

The SCA: Structure and ideology

During the 1970s and 1980s academics and political analysts attempting to understand the dynamics of oppression and resistance in apartheid cities began to use urban social movement theory as a theoretical framework.[11] Their efforts facilitated a structuralist approach heavily informed by the work of Manuel Castells, who understood the city as a site of collective consumption with the same potential to be a radical site for revolution as the shop floor – the site of collective production.[12] This approach lends itself to an interpretation of urban social movements as organised attempts at radical social transformation and the redistribution of power and wealth. The civic movement is easily mistaken for a grassroots socialist movement. It was inspired and structured by the principles of 'people's power' and, to a large degree, influenced by the trade union struggles. However, closer scrutiny reveals that the SCA did not wholly fit this description, and its driving ideologies of Black Consciousness, democracy and people's power were indeed compatible with a capitalist ethos.

Political activists in South African townships in the 1980s pioneered a radical new form of resistance and urban governance, precipitating a national movement that became known as the civic movement.[13] This movement 'occupied the vanguard of township rebellions which contributed to apartheid's defeat'.[14] The creation of grassroots, community-based organisations was made possible both by shifts within the resistance movement and by the apartheid government's draconian attempts to crush opposition during the 1980s. A significant enabling factor within the struggle was the move away from the previous separation of community-based organisations (which were predominant in the United Democratic Front, or UDF[15]) and the trade unions. This development in resistance politics can also be partly attributed to the effect of the lifting of influx control in 1986. The demography of hostels began to change dramatically to include large numbers of unemployed, as well as unprecedented numbers of women and children.

The nature of apartheid demanded that structures of protest and resistance were not restricted to a particular arena of life, while the increased prevalence of urban residents (as opposed to hostel dwellers) in factories resulted in 'domestic issues' being raised in forums that had traditionally dealt with shop-floor issues. The first structures that transcended the divide between community and shop floor were the shop stewards councils of the East Rand. These councils met biweekly and essentially co-coordinated the actions of various factories in the area. However, these meetings also provided a forum for workers to express grievances about rent, evictions and other issues that dominated their domestic lives in the townships.[16]

Simultaneously, township youth were appealing to the older generation to join in the struggle against apartheid. Both the Committee of Ten and the AAC were born out of the 1976 crisis.[17] The Committee of Ten, which was the predecessor to the SCA and to various civic structures that developed later across the country,[18] was formed by Sowetans who felt the need to create an organisation whose primary function would be to 'mobilise, lead and to stand by the students'.[19] Thus, this brief period of South African politics witnessed the radicalisation and organisation of the struggle at the grassroots level and the unification of both worker and student demands with community concerns.

In June 1985 P. W. Botha declared the first partial state of emergency, which included Soweto as one of the affected areas. The state of emergency gave the government almost total power to arrest and detain people for long periods without trial, and this had a significant effect on people's ability to mobilise and resist. 'In the first eight months of the 1985 emergency, 8,000 people were detained and 22,000 charged with offences arising from protests.'[20] It was the exigencies of this situation that contributed directly to the creation of the distinctive and highly effective form of mobilisation that characterised the civic movement. The state of emergency forced the SCA to shift its major focus from mass demonstrations to small, underground, grassroots mobilisation. Large-scale rallies and protests became impossible to orchestrate without risking mass arrests. The SCA began to mobilise street committees, i.e. small groups of residents and neighbours who met regularly to discuss both practical and political issues. Community residents would take turns to host the weekly meetings at their homes.

It would be reductionist to assert that the creation of these grassroots institutions was simply a reaction to state repression or material deprivation. The ideological foundations of the civic organisations aimed to build non-hierarchical, participatory forums where everyone was included in decision-making processes. The principles of people's power drove the structure of the civic organisations, and although the movement, which included thousands of local organisations across the country, was in no way homogeneous, the ideals of grassroots organisation were widespread and recognisable structures were established in most townships. The basics of this form of organisation involved the distinctive ordering of township mobilisation into three 'tiers'. Arguably, the most important of these tiers were the street committees, which collectively reported to an area committee, which was, in turn, accountable to the third layer of township authority, namely the local structure of the civic.[21]

The SCA was an organisation whose vision went beyond the coordination of urban resistance to exorbitant rents, evictions, poor services and other conditions that characterised urban life under apartheid. The leaders of the civic were primarily concerned with creating political awareness and presenting a viable alternative to the state. The central objective of people's power was for local organisations to take over the role of the state and to begin to assume key state-like functions.[22] As well as co-coordinating successful rent boycotts, the civic also performed a wide array of other functions in the community:

At the street committee meetings the questions were nearly always about services and problem services. [Around] [t]he one service – the clearing of rubbish – we got together and said, 'The municipality *clearly* cannot keep our townships clean. *We* want to do it ourselves'. And we organised ourselves to say that, in a street like where I lived, we [were] gonna ask Mr Khumalo to buy a truck. Khumalo employed four, five guys, and twice a week, they go from house to house clearing rubbish.

We pay Mr Khumalo R20 a week and if we keep the street clean, Khumalo's men have less to do, we pay them less. The next thing was [that] the market was very far from Soweto, and we said, we are going to organise ourselves to buy in bulk. So we would buy a truck and then once a week, on a Friday, someone from the street committee would go from house to house and say, 'What do you need? ... You are a family of five. How many carrots? How many potatoes?' And we would write it down. Then we would take the truck to Newtown. At that time it was before they built the City Deep huge market, and on Saturday mornings at Regina Mundi, or at a nearby school, people would come to collect their stuff that they had ordered. And of course it was much cheaper for people to do that than to buy from the shops in Soweto.[23]

Arguably one of the most effective means of undermining the authority of the apartheid state was the civics' assumption of a judicial role in the townships:

In some areas of the township, street committees also functioned as people's courts. Pheteni Khumalo explains that in Meadowlands the people's court would 'move from one place to the other, because if it was to be in the same place we would have put the house owner in big trouble ... because the courts were illegal'. In Moroka, on the other hand, a group of elderly residents who belonged to the local civic association established a permanent court at the Inkanyezi Youth centre. The Moroka court dealt mainly with domestic disputes. In other areas courts controlled the hours of the shebeens, searched customers for weapons, and imposed curfews to prevent crime and violence on township streets. Bennet Molokoane believes that the street committees and people's courts had become 'the basic organs of people's power. We were starting to govern ourselves'.[24]

The nature of these activities and the ideological roots of people's power suggest that as well as the condemnation of apartheid, the civics were offering a socialist alternative. However, this assumption is problematic, for while some civics, such as the AAC, were indeed committed to a socialist revolution, the SCA certainly was not. Although the principle of people's power presented a clear mandate in terms of building grassroots organisations, it was not actually prescriptive in terms of economic ideology. Adler and Steinberg assert that the very nature of street committees constitutes a critique of electoral democracy: 'Embodied in the form of the street committee was a distinctive notion of participatory democracy, an assertion that the democracy of the ballot box constituted a truncated and deformed form of citizen power.'[25] But this call for participatory democracy was very different to embracing a wholesale socialist position. Indeed, the leaders of the SCA remembered themselves as being democrats, as opposed to socialists.[26]

Despite the fact that much of the impetus and personnel that constituted the civics movement came from the trade union movement, the assumption that the civics were socialist in nature or particularly concerned with addressing the inherent inequalities of capitalism is inaccurate. While Mayekiso is adamant that the AAC was explicitly socialist in nature, it is apparent that the SCA, despite having paid lip service to certain socialist principles, was actually more concerned with addressing the issues of racial oppression and with the denial of capitalist rights to black citizens.

A far more influential political ideology for the SCA then, was Black Consciousness, an ideology developed and popularised by Steve Biko in the 1970s, which, at its core, asserted the need for black South Africans to reject notions of racial inferiority and embrace their black identity with pride. Tom Manthata, former secretary of the Soweto Committee of Ten, the institutional forerunner to the SCA, describes the ideological roots of the civic movement as arising directly out of the Black Consciousness Movement:

In the Black Consciousness Movement, led by the Black People's Convention, it was felt that closer relations to the people on the ground were required. Our parent organisations, the ANC and PAC [Pan Africanist Congress], it seemed to us, had focused largely on a high political profile which involved only political leaders … so people felt that we needed to organise at civic association levels.[27]

However, like the ideology of people's power, the Black Consciousness Movement was not explicitly prescriptive in nature, and although the principles of Black Consciousness strongly supported the formation of people's power organisations and grassroots political consciousness, it did not necessarily negate capitalist ideology.[28] Black Consciousness augmented the political significance of the civic structures by casting them as critical forums to demonstrate that black communities were capable of governing themselves and demanded an equal quality of life to that of white South Africans. Manthata, secretary and organiser of the SCA, described his political ideology of the time in a narrative that is shaped far more strongly by Black Consciousness than by any other ideological position:

At the time the idea was [that] black people should be responsible for their lives. Black people should assert themselves and their dignity at all times. And black people are in no way inferior. And of course, this was the major issue we faced on the ground; black people believed in their inferiority. They didn't even think that they merited the same quality of life that white people had. … you could not expect the people to get into the struggle against apartheid when they were in that frame of mind. It was not just the conditions we lived in; the job reservation, the pass laws, people having to be put in hostels. All of these things had to be addressed to infuse in the people's minds that to live like that was not human, and to get to the status of a human being it involved *only you*. That is why the Black Consciousness Movement had made it so clear that not everyone could be involved in the struggle against apartheid – not because of their weaknesses, but because they [whites] came from areas where the issues we were facing were not present, and we could not break through to go and live there, side-by-side with them.[29]

Thus, from the viewpoint of its leaders, the success of the 'basic organs of people's power' established by the SCA did not necessarily reflect a pervasive socialist ideology. Nthato Motlana's testimony regarding the development of his own political thought is particularly revealing:

At the time, we, black South Africans, had come under the influence, firstly, of the great Julius Nyerere. Julius Nyerere was a wonderful guy, and … it was a real honour to meet him. And we spoke about African socialism. In the beginning we supported him, but I mean Tanzania became really a failure. One of the greatest mistakes he made, he went after a tribe on the foothills of Kilimanjaro who grew coffee and were very successful, very entrepreneurial, very independent. And his process of 'villagisation', which was good, in that you take a scattered and disparate community and bring them together so that you can build a school for you, a clinic for you and so on, but I mean, he destroyed the entrepreneurial spirit of that tribe. I mean Julius Nyerere's policies, they didn't work. I remember I met him in Zimbabwe, for the United Nations Development Index summit. It's an index which measures infant mortality, health status, education status and so on, and Tanzania, well, Tanzania did not do so well on that index!

While I was active in the beginning, though, I was a socialist, but a little later, I began to believe that entrepreneurship was the way to the future. I became part of the Free Market Foundation, and became chairman of the organisation that we formed, called the Get Ahead Foundation, which in the 1980s basically supplied people with start-up funds for their own businesses. I was always so depressed about black poverty, and my patients couldn't pay. I charged them two rand for a consultation and medicine, but they couldn't pay. And so I really became interested in entrepreneurship, seeing how people can pick themselves up, saying to people I am going to give you a job. As you know I listed the first big black company on the Johannesburg Stock Exchange, NAIL [New Africa Investment Limited]. But in the 1980s under apartheid I tried to encourage my people to do something for themselves, to feed themselves, and I am so sorry that we are not as successful as we should be.

Yes, I started off thinking of socialism, you know in Russia when you have collectivisation of farms, mass production, people work in communes, they work for the state, but then I thought 'no'. You know, the American system, it's flawed but it's very successful in encouraging people to do your own thing, to work for yourself. At one time the richest fellow in the world was a guy called Paul Getty. He died long ago, but he used to say 'If you want to make money, work for yourself, not for another man!' So I abandoned Julius Nyerere's ideas and started the Get Ahead Foundation, and really over many, many years, I've been involved in trying to get my people started in business.[30]

The clear disillusionment with socialism and the embracing of entrepreneurial, individualistic values, described here by its leader, are reflected in some of the actions of the SCA. The SCA at no point demanded free services; rather it protested against poor delivery and exorbitant charges. The rhetoric of the movement suggested that people's right to equality and citizenship was linked to their willingness to pay for their services, in the same way as their white counterparts did. One of the key demands of the SCA, which was eventually successfully achieved in 1996, was for private property rights, i.e. the right for Sowetans to own the houses that they had until then rented from the state. Moreover, instead of demanding that the state should provide services, the SCA frequently mobilised people to do it themselves and to use the provision of services as a business opportunity for local people. Thus, the 'replacement state' that they created was in some ways an interventionist, welfare state in that it was responsible for the provision of services, but in reality it was the community that was mobilised to render these services, and so a kind of entrepreneurial, individualistic ethos was cultivated. These issues were debated internally, and other activists, such as Mzwanele Mayekiso, point to the dangers of this approach. He argues that conceptualising grassroots activism in this way 'risks following the agenda of imperialist development agencies and foreign ministries, namely to shrink the size and scope of third world governments and to force community organisations to take up state responsibilities with inadequate resources'.[31]

The call for 'ungovernability' that swept through South African townships in the mid-1980s was hugely successful in Soweto. The SCA called for a rent boycott in June 1986, which lasted for several years and resulted in the vast majority of Sowetans refusing to pay rent. While this is largely heralded as an extremely successful example of community mobilisation against the oppressive state, the leadership of the SCA was troubled by its implications and the boycott exposed the conflicting political ideologies that existed within the upper echelons of the organisation:

> The rent boycotts became so successful that I became worried. We were talking about services; the services that municipalities need to render, like clearance of rubbish, water, electricity, sewerage and so on. And we said that because the services were not properly provided, and we were being overcharged and so on, we would boycott paying for the services. Unfortunately, the people found it so good not to pay for services, and spent the money on clothes and things, and stopped paying for bonds! With the bank! And then I got really worried, and I said 'Guys, you are going to lose your houses!' So I remember going to Winnie Mandela, going to Reverend Sibidi, who was on the committee, and going to Mrs Sisulu, who was the deputy president of the UDF, and saying to them, 'Please, let's call off the boycott, because I am afraid that if people stop paying their bonds, they will lose their homes'. Winnie agreed, Sibidi agreed, Ma Sisulu said I was talking nonsense! 'How can you say that?' she said. 'We will break this government down!' 'Uh-uh,' I said, 'they are just going to stop building homes.' And they did. Our people incurred huge debt, and when the democratic dispensation came along, so many of our people lost their homes.[32]

Motlana's concerns about the boycott clearly reflect the distinction between applying pressure to the apartheid state and overthrowing a capitalist regime, the latter objective being absent from the SCA's agenda.

The leaders of the SCA moved out of Soweto. Motlana lived on a huge estate in Muldersdrift, just north of Johannesburg. He had his own golf course and a brand new BMW. Tom Manthata now works for the South African Human Rights Commission, an organisation committed to the protection of constitutional democracy. Popo Molefe, another prominent member of the SCA, quit politics in 2004 to 'explore opportunities in the private sector'. Amos Masondo, despite previous alignment to socialist politics in the unions and civics, is now the mayor of Johannesburg, in charge of the downsizing of the public sector and the infamous enemy of the SECC. The common narrative among radical activists is that people like Masondo and Motlana have 'sold out' and betrayed the struggle, but the evidence presented here suggests that, in fact, this is not the case. Rather, it appears that the SCA was never an organisation whose leadership advocated socialist reform, but one that was concerned instead with fighting racial oppression and protecting the human rights of Sowetans. While the rank and file of the SCA may have harboured socialist tendencies, the leadership of the organisation advanced entrepreneurial aspirations and capitalist endeavours.

The re-emergence of adversarial civil society: The roots of the new social movements

The new social movements rose to prominence during the ANC's second term in government under the presidency of Thabo Mbeki. To explain why these groups arose when they did, it is necessary to understand the complex dynamics of the macroeconomic policies that the ANC adopted after coming to power in 1994 and how these policies resulted in a failure to deliver on election promises. The intricacies of the negotiations among the liberation movement, the Nationalist Party and the corporate sector, which began in the late 1980s and led eventually to the end of apartheid, have been the subject of several detailed studies.[33] The common argument presented by these studies is that during the transition to democracy the ANC government, under pressure from global capital and Western political forces, significantly retreated from its redistributive ideals and embraced macroeconomic policies that favoured the domestic and international corporate sector (see Dawson's chapter in this volume).

Terreblanche argues that the ANC as a liberation movement held relatively undefined and confused economic ideologies, and during the struggle against apartheid had never been forced to articulate a particular position:

> Until 1990 the ANC and other liberation organisations paid very little attention to what the economic system and economic policy in a democratized South Africa should be. Two possible reasons can be given for this neglect. Firstly, the ANC was first and foremost a liberation organisation whose main thrust was to overthrow white domination and take over the South African state. It maintained an instrumentalist conception of the state: as soon as political power was in its

257

hands, it would use the state to solve socio-economic problems of unemployment, poverty and inequality. The slogan of Kwame Nkrumah – 'Seek ye first the political kingdom, all else will follow' – resonated in ANC circles. Secondly, the ANC believed that South Africa was an exceptionally rich country, and that the economic deprivation of the black population could easily be rectified after liberation through a state-led process of redistribution and redirection of economic resources and activities.[34]

It was this lack of a firm economic ideology, coupled with a degree of naïveté, that left the ANC 'prone to the counsel of business and mainstream foreign experts that set about schooling ANC leaders in the "realities of the world"'[35] and facilitated a series of compromises and concessions on the part of the democratic movement. The practical result of these negotiations was that the ANC embraced a neoliberal agenda that was a far cry from the redistributive ideals that they had formerly articulated.

A less sympathetic analysis of the ANC's volte-face is articulated by many on the left, who argue that right-wing elements within the ANC overrode the ideological position of those who advocated wariness of global capital, independence from the Bretton Woods institutions, and a welfare-orientated and redistributive state.[36] This shift in ANC ideology is best illustrated by a comparison between the politico-economic plan of its 1994 election campaign, the Reconstruction and Development Programme (RDP) and the Growth, Employment and Redistribution (GEAR) programme that replaced the RDP just two years later. The RDP articulated the ANC's commitment to free basic services for all, whereas GEAR advocated the downsizing of the public sector and called for increased privatisation and cost recovery. Protectionist economic practices were dismantled and thousands of jobs were lost.[37] These characteristics of GEAR have provoked analysts to accuse the ANC of being the only African government to voluntarily impose structural adjustment.[38]

In addition to the shifting terrain of political ideology within the ANC, the transition threw existing civil society, including the civics movement, into considerable confusion. The UDF had operated much like a surrogate for the exiled ANC, and after the democratic transition it was widely felt that the need for adversarial civil society–state relations no longer existed. This was a myth further perpetuated by the coalition among the ruling party, the South African Communist Party (SACP) and the dominant trade union, the Congress of South African Trade Unions (COSATU). Ballard et al. describe how the new government deliberately attempted to institutionalise a collaborative relationship with civil society:

Corporatist institutions, like the National Economic Development and Labour Council (NEDLAC), were established and non-governmental organisations (NGOs) and community-based organisations (CBOs) were provided representation in this forum through the establishment of a development chamber. Legislation was promulgated that enabled the registration of NGOs and CBOs. Public funding agencies, like the National Development Agency (NDA), were established to direct financial resources to the sector, and most importantly, government enabled the subcontracting of development services to a number of civil society actors, thereby entrenching the logic of collegiate state–civil society relations of the immediate post-apartheid phase.[39]

This collaborative arrangement may have worked had the state made good on its election promises. Terreblanche asserts that the ANC's policies represented a systemic continuation of colonial and apartheid segregation and exploitation: 'Neither the political nor the economic part of the new politico-economic system is geared to effectively addressing the predicament of the poorest half of the population, or regard poverty alleviation as a priority.'[40] Thus, the neoliberal economic agenda pursued by the ANC created several social groups whose grievances were not represented by the civil society institutions that had effectively become organs of the state. Buhlungu identifies the three broad groupings of people who, in 2000, formed the Anti-Privatisation Forum, the umbrella organisation of the majority of the new social movements:

First were the left activists within the ANC/SACP/COSATU alliance who felt a sense of frustration, particularly after the adoption of GEAR by the ruling party ... at the same time left activists outside the Alliance, mainly youth, were also searching for relevance, particularly in light of developments in the anti-globalisation movement elsewhere in the world. Many of these were students or youth activists while others worked in various NGOs. Some belonged to remnants of socialist groups like the Marxist Workers Tendency which had faded out of the political scene following the 1994 elections. Some in this group had direct or electronic links with activists in other parts of the world, and were able to exchange views about the state of the burgeoning anti-globalisation movements. The third grouping comprised working class activists drawn from communities that were looking for answers in a context where retrenchments and cost-recovery had combined to destroy their livelihoods and limit their access to basic goods and services.[41]

The new social movements, then, can largely be understood to have emerged as a direct response to the ANC's politico-economic programme, the consequences of which created the need for a new form of civil society that could, on an ideological level, rearticulate a critique of capitalism and, on a quotidian level, protest the socio-economic oppression of the majority of the population. In the void left by a diminished and undermined civil society and in the wake of the retreating and shrinking state, the new social movements emerged to give voice to the myriad concerns and agendas of the increasingly marginalised poor in post-apartheid South Africa.

Importantly, these new movements found echoes of their demands and campaigns within the international anti-globalisation movement, where a particular critique of neoliberal economics and the orthodoxy of the free market was the dominant ideological metanarrative. This affiliation is at least partly responsible for the rhetoric of many new social movements in South Africa, which articulate their critique of the ANC's policies as a critique of the so-called Washington consensus. Thus, the ideological roots of the new social movements in post-apartheid South Africa originate both in the practical consequences of the ANC's policies for the poor and in the coterminous rise in a global movement to resist neoliberalism.

The SECC looks very much like a civic, and it is understandable why this comparison has been made. There are about 22 active branches in Soweto, all of which meet once a week in church halls, classrooms and sometimes under trees. The size of these meetings varies, with some branches drawing hundreds of residents each week, and others only about 20. The meetings are opened with prayer and singing the national anthem, 'Nkosi Sikilel' iAfrika', before the chair opens the floor and invites a discussion about whatever issues the residents might have that week, from power failures and cut-offs to burst water pipes or water meter-related problems. Any messages from the SECC executive are passed onto the residents by the elected leaders of the branches. These leaders all meet once a week in Diepkloof to report on their various communities. The head offices in Diepkloof consist of four small rooms, where the executive operates an advice centre six days a week. This executive body manages the various departments of the SECC: housing, water, electricity, media, pensions, education and organising.

The SECC, like the SCA, mobilises around practical issues, but its ideological position and objective as a socialist political entity that opposes neoliberalism has been clear from the start. The SECC, like many of the new social movements, arose as a reaction to a specific government policy. In this case it was iGoli 2002, the government's initiative to restructure Johannesburg's local government. iGoli 2002 contained a strong commitment to downsizing the public sector and opening up all basic service provision to private tender. Various activist groups, including the Campaign Against Neoliberalism in South Africa (CANSA), the Anti-iGoli 2002 Group, students and academics from the University of the Witwatersrand, and the South African Municipal Workers Union held a series of meetings to discuss the implications of iGoli 2002. In an interview with Peter Alexander, Trevor Ngwane discussed how the SECC was born out of these meetings:

> The meetings that led up to SECC were CANSA meetings. We had a Johannesburg workshop on CANSA, looking at how to spread ideas against neoliberalism. We resolved to set up CANSA in Soweto. ... We met for three months, but we just couldn't find a way forward. ... Then one day we decided, 'Look, let's find an issue.' At that time it was not just Pimvillians, [but] people from Tladi, Zola ... so, we discussed, and electricity was an issue. So, we found money for a workshop, through CANSA, from AIDC [Alterative Information Development Centre] ... and we decided we were going to form an organisation, so we called another workshop, which was addressed by Patrick Bond and Dennis Brutus [well-known activist intellectuals] ... and afterwards we had our own discussion, and we had to find a name, so we decided to call it the Soweto Electricity Crisis Committee.[42]

The SECC demands free basic services for all, claiming that access to water, electricity and housing is a human right and not a commodity, and should not be denied due to the inability to pay. This ideological platform has provided a basis for a repertoire of militant, effective and dramatic forms of resistance. Every day the SECC advice centre is besieged with Sowetans who come and report their problems: electricity cut-offs, forced installation of water meters and evictions. The SECC adopts a strategy of direct action to address each of these issues without delay: it reconnects electricity for several houses a day; digs up water meters and reconnects water supplies; and visits houses from which residents have been evicted, removes the new tenants and reinstates the original inhabitants. Ngwane describes how these forms of activism are important, not only as a vital safety net for the poor, but as vehicles for creating political awareness and for helping to create a grassroots critique of capitalism:

> People do many things to survive under capitalism, they form *stokvels*,[43] burial societies, they rely on their families, they steal. It's all part of survival. Some [are] good; others you can say it's bad. So that's why Operation Khanyisa[44] is popular. It's a practical way of surviving, not just talk. I mean only yesterday, Comrade Boy,

who is now the Operation Khanyisa chief, he was excited because he connected a house that has been cut off since the old days. … It makes it real, not just for the community, but for the comrades also. I mean, Boy … risks going to jail and he gets pushed around, so I could see yesterday it was an important thing, because it's a real connection between him and the working class, so there is a sense of fulfilment. But also it's a political statement. We who are the ideologues, we try and link it to a vision of socialism and a kind of vision for a different government and a society. You know there is a bigger picture, and we say, 'We can't keep on connecting all the time, we need a government which will ensure that there is no need for us [to do so]'. We write pamphlets, and we try to link the electricity issue to the bigger picture. We explain why we demand free basic services for all, and we talk about unemployment and the bigger structural problems. And the issue of calling for free basic services, it is an attack on commodification; we try to attack the capitalist method of making profits from services.[45]

The rhetoric of socialism is strongly supported by the organisation's leadership. Whether or not the rank-and-file members of the SECC advocate a socialist ideology to the same degree as the leadership is debatable, but SECC supporters are very clear in their critique of the ANC government, by whom they feel strongly betrayed. One of the most popular songs sung at almost every meeting and every demonstration is 'That's why I am a socialist' (see Dawson's chapter in this volume for more on the Anti-Privatisation Forum's 'struggle songs'). There is clear support among the SECC's rank and file for the demand for free basic services, despite accusations by the government that these demands encourage a culture of non-payment, an unfortunate hangover from the ungovernability campaigns of the 1980s. Both Motlana and Manthata claimed to know of Sowetans who drove luxury vehicles but refused to pay for services.[46] However, it seems unlikely that these people are the supporters of the SECC. Members of the SECC counter accusations of being unwilling to pay for basic services with the claim that they cannot afford to pay. In light of South Africa's 40 per cent unemployment rate, a rate that is much higher in Soweto, the inability to pay seems a far more likely reason for non-payment of services.

Elderly women make up the bulk of the SECC membership. Collectively known as 'the grannies', these women are predominantly pensioners who are supporting their extended families on their R780 a month state pension. The ANC's insistence that people must pay for services, coupled with rising unemployment, has led to severe disillusionment with the former liberation movement. One of these 'grannies' is a woman called Mrs Masondo. She is the aunt of Amos Masondo, one-time founding member of the SCA and current mayor of Johannesburg. Amos Masondo has been the target of the SECC's most public demonstrations. In 2002 protesters marched to his Kensington home and disconnected his water and electricity in order to protest against the municipality's action taken against poor residents in Soweto who could not afford to pay for their services. The demonstration turned violent when Masondo's bodyguards fired into the crowd. Police arrested 87 protesters, who spent 11 days in prison. The trial dragged on for months, providing welcome publicity for the SECC and the 'Kensington 87', but the charges were eventually dismissed. Mrs Masondo supports five adult children who cannot find work. She lives in a house in Senoane in Soweto where Amos Masondo spent several years of his childhood: 'Amos grew up here', she said.

> He is my brother's son. I sometimes see him when I go to visit his parents' house, but he doesn't come around here anymore. Now he is just another person who has a lot of money but fails to provide for the family … another rich man who has forgotten Soweto.[47]

Mrs Masondo's disenchantment with the ANC is clear:

> I am a member of the ANC. The ANC once helped me to get back into my house when I was being evicted in the 1980s. They sent a lot of comrades to come and help me. Then, I loved the ANC! … Now, Operation Khanyisa has encouraged us not pay for any services. I agree with whoever says that, with whoever says, 'Don't pay', because I cannot pay; because it lessens my burden, my debt. I don't know what to think of the ANC. Age has caught up with me, but I can observe that the youth are unemployed, and I can't fight for them to be employed. … I live off my pension and I have to share with my children. It's hard. I live with my grandchildren and my grandchildren's children, the number is not fixed; they come in and out. My grandchildren bought this wall unit for me. When they were temporary workers, they collected money together and bought it for me, but it has been three years and a couple of months since they have been called to their temporary jobs. As you can see there are no chairs here.[48]

Although Mrs Masondo's narrative of disillusionment with the ANC is worth a special mention because of her family connection to ANC leadership, it is not an uncommon one. A pervasive sense of political exclusion and betrayal in Soweto has created an environment where people are ready to embrace alternatives. The SECC, while not a political party, offers a coherent and compelling ideological alternative to the daily reality of capitalist marginalisation and exclusion.

Concluding remarks: Towards a new understanding of continuities and discontinuities in popular resistance

A key point in this chapter is that, despite apparent similarities, there are significant ideological differences between the popular movements of the 1980s and those of the early twenty-first century. As noted above, a number of sources tend to emphasise the socialist strands in the civic movement and its allies in the trade unions.[49] The analysis presented here suggests that, while there were diverse ideologies in the civics during the 1980s, the leadership of one of the key movements, the SCA, was not essentially socialist. Democratic and Black Consciousness ideologies were a stronger influence, and the principles of people's power did not hinder capitalist aspirations.

By comparing two specific organisations we can see that the apartheid regime and the ANC government have produced two very different kinds of oppositional movements. In part, the new social movements can be understood as almost inevitable revivals of the old resistance movement. The end of apartheid has not meant the end of poverty and inequality. This state of affairs was predicted by socialists within the anti-apartheid struggle who warned against a 'two-phase' approach that sought political power before economic reform:

> We believe that the struggle in South Africa has two aspects (NOT phases or stages). We believe that it is not enough to have 'one person-one vote'. For the majority of South Africans (namely the working people) 'liberation' will be meaningless and empty unless the economy is restructured because that is the only way to guarantee significant and lasting improvements in the quality of life of our working people.[50]

Contemporary South African social movements are now demanding this 'second phase' with a unity of purpose that was, perhaps, not as pronounced in the broad and all-encompassing struggle against apartheid.

It is problematic to reconstruct the history of grassroots resistance in South Africa as a uniformly socialist movement that has been betrayed by the ANC since 1994. The roots of the ANC's current policies are clearly visible in aspects of grassroots mobilisation in the 1970s and 1980s. A historical analysis of the SCA suggests a greater degree of ideological continuity between the 1970s and the 1980s grassroots movement and the current ANC government's policies than between the civics and contemporary social movements in South Africa. As argued in this chapter, the SECC needs to be understood as representing an ideological disjuncture with the SCA. The advent of the new social movements may well be more usefully understood as a significant shift in the ideology of grassroots movements in South Africa than as straightforward 'reincarnations' of older movements.

13 'Phansi Privatisation! Phansi!': The Anti-Privatisation Forum and ideology in social movements[1]

Marcelle C. Dawson

Introduction

At the outset of this volume, attention was drawn to the persistence of inequalities that continue to characterise South African society more than a decade after the transition to democracy. Much of the work presented here concentrates on popular protest and resistance movements during and after apartheid, which have in various ways and to differing degrees shaped the country and continue to influence political debate and policy matters. This chapter is concerned with popular protest in the post-apartheid period and adopts as its vantage point one of South Africa's 'new social movements', namely the Anti-Privatisation Forum (APF). The discussion uses the APF's struggles against the commodification of water services as a lens through which to gain insight into the ideology that drives this movement's grassroots struggles in Johannesburg, South Africa.

The APF is an umbrella organisation that in 2008 comprised 27 community affiliates, three political groupings and a number of individual supporters. The forum defines its main task as mobilising working-class communities against privatisation in the spaces where they live and work.[2] According to the organisation, '[t]he APF links workers' struggles for a living wage and jobs with community struggles for housing, water, electricity and fair rates and taxes'.[3] It sees itself as an open platform where people can collectively discuss the implications of privatisation.

The APF endeavours to bring together communities that may be engaging in isolated struggles, as well as individuals who may have internalised their suffering, to share experiences and strengthen the struggle against privatisation.[4] Key texts on social movements globally characterise such social expressions as single-issue movements. The APF, however, does not have such narrow aims. It frames its mobilisation efforts in terms of broader questions around 'the relationship between new forms of exploitative capitalist reproduction and working class struggle'.[5] Drawing on social movement literature, this discussion offers an explanation for the emergence of movements such as the APF and considers the ideological content and practical forms of the APF's opposition to the commodification of water services. These struggles are considered against the backdrop of popular resistance that characterised the apartheid era and that sparked democratic transition. In taking this approach, the chapter highlights some of the changes and continuities in popular protest in South Africa. It also attempts to assess the extent to which the APF's resistance efforts are able to provide direction in terms of reconceptualising the meaning and content of democracy.

The frame of reference for the following discussion is rooted in a leftist critique of political change in South Africa. Critics on the left regard contemporary popular struggles as symptomatic of ongoing and increasing inequality. For instance, some argue that South Africa has experienced an 'elite transition'[6] that did very little to fundamentally alter the socio-economic realities of the poor. Demonstrators in the post-apartheid period are still overwhelmingly black and poor, but while the eradication of racial oppression was a strong, unifying objective of popular protest during apartheid, race is now a less central, though not absent, fault line. With a Gini-coefficient of 0.679,[7] South Africa now has the highest income inequality in the world. Popular resistance in the contemporary period is rooted in persistent class inequalities, increasing poverty and ongoing social exclusion that continue to plague those who are unemployed or who hover precariously on the edges of the economy in irregular and insecure forms of labour. It is from these densely populated layers of society that the support base of movements like the APF is constituted.

The chapter takes up the issue of grassroots struggles in the post-apartheid period and uses the APF as a vantage point from which to examine continuity and change in popular protest in South Africa, with particular reference to ideology and modes of mobilisation. An important continuity is the furtherance by movements such as the APF of South Africa's long tradition of resistance against social injustice. Some of the methods used to pursue this goal echo the strategies used by freedom fighters during the liberation struggle, while other slogans and tactics employed by APF activists represent a break from anti-apartheid protests, largely because they are underpinned by a distinct socialist ideology, which is openly expressed by the movement's supporters. Another common thread running through past and present grassroots struggles centres on the nature of the demands that emerged during the liberation struggle. Many of the popular protests in the contemporary period continue to revolve around bread-and-butter issues, like access to clean water, for instance. Further examples of continuity with the apartheid period are witnessed in the APF's battles against state machinery and also in the government's response to the movement's actions.

The emergence of new social movements in South Africa: An assessment of the political opportunity structure

To explain how the potential for mobilisation translated into action, renowned social movement theorist Sidney Tarrow proposed the idea of a 'political opportunity structure', which he defined as 'consistent – but not necessarily formal, permanent or national – dimensions of the political environment which either encourage or discourage people from using collective action'.[8] He added that these opportunities must be assessed in relation to 'more stable structural elements, like the strength or weakness of the state, the form of repression employed by it and the nature of the party system'.[9]

The political opportunity structure is not a given within a particular political form and it is open to the influence of a wide range of contextual factors. South Africa has a long history of mass popular organisation that was central in the transition to democracy. In the mid-1990s, following the accession to power by the African National Congress (ANC), there was a brief respite as far as popular movements and black community resistance were concerned. It was a period marked by high levels of hope and expectation. People had faith that the ANC would deliver on its promises contained in the Reconstruction and Development Programme (RDP). Struggle fatigue had perhaps also set in, as political freedom was a hard-won battle for which many paid a very high price. Writing on social movement mobilisation in post-apartheid South Africa, Ballard et al. claimed that 'old avenues of opposition were absorbed into the post-apartheid government, thus leaving opponents of the government without a "voice" with which to express or a mechanism to organise opposition'.[10] These authors suggested further that from the late 1990s onward this void began to be occupied by a number of groups defining themselves as South Africa's 'new' social movements, and they grouped all of these movements together as an oppositional force in relation to the ANC and its alliance partners, namely the South African Communist Party (SACP) and the Congress of South African Trade Unions (COSATU).[11] It is argued here that Ballard and his co-authors have overstated the void or 'vacuum' in popular opposition. In the first instance, the South African National Civic Organisation, although weakened, was still in operation in the mid-1990s and the issue of inadequate service delivery lingered on its agenda. Secondly, the apparent hiatus in grassroots struggle did not last very long at all. Criticism from the left actually began to emerge shortly after the ANC took power, more or less in the mid-1990s, when the government was criticised for putting forward a diluted version of the aims and demands of the liberation struggle in the form of the RDP. In 1996, when the RDP was swept aside in favour of the Growth, Employment and Redistribution (GEAR) programme, condemnation from certain elements within the tripartite alliance was palpable. Thus, in contrast to the view offered by Ballard et al., post-apartheid opposition was not restricted to the 'new' social movements outside of mainstream politics. However, most of the vehement critique of GEAR came later from voices located within these movements, the academy and other positions outside of alliance structures, which opined that GEAR would not improve the lot of the poor.[12]

The waning of local community organisations addressing bread-and-butter issues occurred alongside what some authors refer to as a 'dominant political and economic project that reproduces marginalisation and exclusion'.[13] Part of this exclusion relates to the fact that COSATU represents only 'the core permanent workforce' and thus '[neglects] other workers who do not fit into this paradigm'.[14] Some of the new social movements used this aspect of the political opportunity structure to further the struggles of casual labourers and the unemployed who were not able to look to COSATU to protect their interests. Another criticism of the interpretation of the rise of the 'new' social movements by Ballard et al. claimed that not all the social movements that have emerged since the late 1990s are opposed to the government or its capitalist agenda. For example, the demands of movements like the Treatment Action Campaign (TAC) are not necessarily framed within an alternative political philosophy. In contrast, the APF, since its inception, has espoused a socialist ideology. Indeed, Mark Heywood, founding member of TAC, suggested that the organisation's strategies are based on the following key propositions. Firstly, TAC accepts that '[t]he ANC government is fundamentally a progressive government that is not selling out the poor in this country'. Secondly, TAC does not regard the state as 'inherently antagonistic towards the poor'. Thirdly, TAC believes that '[e]xtensive and lasting reform is possible within the boundaries of capitalism and the current state'. Fourthly, '[t]he Constitution of 1996 can, and has been, used to benefit the poor'.[15]

APF activists disagree very strongly with these propositions. For them 'the chief divide lies in [TAC's] failure to situate its campaign in a critique of government macro-economic policy'.[16] TAC is thus seen by other social movements as a pressure group or lobby organisation that tries to influence government policy within the existing political framework. In an interview with Friedman and Mottiar, activist-intellectual Ashwin Desai commented that '[TAC] seems to work within the corridors of power'.[17]

Heywood's attempt to defend TAC's stance is rather contradictory, however. He argued that '[e]xtensive and lasting reform is possible within the boundaries of capitalism and the current state', but then went on to say that

> capitalism … is an evil system … a system which can't provide jobs for people, can't provide security, can't provide equality for people, but we have to work to try to make sure that some of those vast surpluses which we know are out there are made available to poor people.[18]

Based on their interview with Desai, Friedman and Mottiar suggested that, from the viewpoint of other social movements, TAC appears to be unwilling to cooperate 'because it fears their militancy will jeopardise its attempts to build winning coalitions'.[19] However, long-time APF activist Dale McKinley urged TAC not to see the APF 'as wild troublemakers' and to 'recognise that we could work together'.[20] Acknowledging the correlation between the lack of access to water and increased suffering for those living with HIV/AIDS, the APF attempted to forge links between its own struggles and those of TAC, and it openly demanded that antiretrovirals be provided free of charge.[21] However, the APF's advances were not reciprocated by TAC.

Finally, Ballard et al. claimed that most of the contemporary social movements, in contrast to the oppositional forces that confronted the apartheid government, consider themselves to be 'engaging … with a democratically elected government whose legitimacy they do not question, and within a constitution to which they are loyal'.[22] The ANC government may indeed have been elected legitimately, but much of the social unrest around the country today represents a challenge to its legitimacy. As Greenstein argued, 'the legitimacy of the post-apartheid government must depend on the extent to which it has transcended the practices of its predecessors, and has managed to deal effectively with the legacy of apartheid',[23] and for many APF (and other) activists the ANC government has not succeeded in this regard. Instead, several activists have based their challenge to the state's legitimacy on the assertion that the legacy of apartheid 'is being entrenched and even strengthened by the current government's policies', with the implication that many of 'those who were disadvantaged under apartheid continue to be so under the new dispensation'.[24] Moreover, being legitimately elected through various democratic electoral procedures does not necessarily ensure democracy in practice. Commenting on the ANC's rule, Pretorius suggested that '[t]he party's tendency to discount diversity of interests, to persist with claims to superior understanding of complex issues and to preach hegemony as a virtue might signify government *over* the people rather than government *by* the people'.[25]

In sum, the mid-1990s was not a period of complete absence of opposition to government. Instead, it should be interpreted as a period of significant ideological conflict within the tripartite alliance and attendant criticism of government policy, which provided both a basis and a context for the emergence of the 'new' social movements. By acknowledging this dimension of the political opportunity structure one avoids the pitfall of depicting the new social movements as though they suddenly burst onto the scene out of nowhere. In reality, even though many of the so-called new social movements are new in form, the content of their struggles is rooted in earlier protests against the inequalities that were enforced under apartheid, particularly those related to basic services and housing. Moreover, some of the activists in the new social movements are former members of the tripartite alliance and others had been involved in the United Democratic Front (UDF) and other 'political traditions and ideological tendencies with a long history of struggle'.[26]

While these new social movements symbolise in many respects 'a return to the civic form', they differ from their protest predecessors in that their struggles occur in the absence of 'political party leadership'.[27] This can partly be explained by the fact that in the early years of many of the 'new' social movements there was a strong current of more autonomist and anti-party politics, which was possibly underscored by a conscious decision of some activists to avoid the ideological domination that they had witnessed in the transition, when the ANC became increasingly hegemonic.[28] But there is also the structural reality of the absence of political parties to the left of the ANC and its allies. A related discontinuity between the anti- and post-apartheid protests is that at the height of the struggle in the 1980s 'there were community, youth, student and worker formations *already in existence nationally*'.[29] In contrast, part of the task of the early post-apartheid struggles was to actively seek out and bring together the isolated critical voices into a more coherent formation that was able to challenge the democratic government. This was not an easy undertaking, since some of the ANC dissidents within the alliance who openly criticised GEAR eventually backed down and fell into line, while some decided to fight their battles with the ANC, SACP and COSATU from their vantage point within alliance structures. Others refused to yield and were stripped of, or resigned from, their posts. Still others were expelled. Some of those who were marginalised carved out spaces for themselves in the new social movements.

Critics on the left have suggested that, as a consequence of nodding in a neoliberal direction, the government is increasingly unable to deliver on its promise of a 'better life for all'[30] and that new social movements have emerged in response to the failures of a democratic state 'in the very spaces opened up as a result of the failure of the tactical approaches and strategic visions of the traditional formations to offer any meaningful response to the changing conditions affecting their equally traditional constituencies'.[31] The early post-apartheid years were thus characterised by an opening up of democratic spaces that were conducive to the emergence of the kinds of social movements that crystallised on South Africa's political landscape after apartheid.

Ideological underpinnings of the APF

The APF, although officially launched in September 2000, actually came into being earlier that year amid two important anti-privatisation struggles, namely the opposition to iGoli 2002, a plan for municipal restructuring that entailed increasing involvement by private companies in the provision of basic services, and Wits 2001, which was a two-pronged restructuring plan aimed at downsizing the University of the Witwatersrand by streamlining the service departments (which involved reducing the number of auxiliary staff) and trimming the number of faculties from eight to five (which entailed amalgamating some of the smaller academic departments and creating interdisciplinary schools).

The iGoli 2002 policy, prepared in 1997, represented a blueprint for a new model of local government that was applied to the whole of South Africa. Among other things, iGoli 2002 allowed municipalities to enter into contracts with private companies to outsource the management and distribution of basic services. City councillors and ANC officials believed that iGoli 2002 'offered greater autonomy and flexibility to the management of the service to introduce commercial management practices to the delivery system'.[32] Cost recovery and financial sustainability were key driving forces behind the plan. Councillors firmly believed that the commercialisation of service delivery would allow for improved service delivery and acknowledged that users would have to pay for services. An opposing view came from others, notably trade unions, but also from members of the SACP, who argued that iGoli 2002 was a strategy that would cause further divisions in an already divided Johannesburg.[33] In 1999 the South African Municipal Workers' Union (SAMWU) lodged a formal complaint against the Greater Johannesburg Metropolitan Council, labelling the process that gave birth to iGoli 2002 as undemocratic and accusing the city councillors of being arrogant because of their lack of consultation in the matter.[34] As both municipal workers and 'medium or low income consumers' of basic services, SAMWU members were at risk of experiencing a 'double vulnerability' to corporatised services, which explains why the union was sympathetic to the APF.[35] The anti-iGoli 2002 caucus, some of whom were absorbed into the APF, regarded the policy itself as a neoliberal, anti-labour, anti-poor and business-orientated document that would result in job losses (particularly those held by municipal workers), a decline in labour standards, and increased costs for poor and working-class consumers.[36]

APF activists have accused the ANC of having double standards, which, they argue, are an outcome of its contradictory ideology. For APF supporter Eddie Cottle,

> the biggest onslaught against socialist ideology in South Africa is to be found in the backward orientation of the … ANC and its alliance partners who subscribe to a thesis of a two-stage revolution, precisely because it still holds the aspirations of large sections of ordinary people.[37]

In this vein, Bricks Mokolo, former chairperson of the APF, offered the following view:

> COSATU, SACP they claim that they are socialist … and then it's easy for people to start recruiting or mobilising people under the name of socialism. Socialism for some people is just a stepladder to capitalism. It is the same like in previous years whereby people were addressing people with Black Consciousness politics or philosophy in the black communities. … They are for capitalism. When you chant socialist politics, or socialist slogans, people think, 'Oh! He is a socialist' and then they vote for him. … How many socialists and communists are in parliament? The minister of safety and security[38] is the chairperson of the SACP, but what is he doing now? When the workers are marching in the street, he sends in the police. Now I'm afraid of the comrades from COSATU and SACP telling the people they are socialists, because they are not.[39]

The government's perceived duplicity was further highlighted by Thabo Modisane, an activist in one of the APF's largest affiliates. He accused COSATU leaders of being 'class-collaborators.' He justified his claim in the following way:

> They defend the bosses. They just close our eyes, and say, 'We are socialists', but when we disperse, they negotiate with the capitalists and the bosses and tomorrow they come and say they are socialists, but at the same time they are

on the capitalists' side. While we march [together], COSATU is socialist, SACP is socialist, but on our [own] march, why don't they support our march to show us we are all socialists? Why is the leadership of [the] Communist Party dominating in parliament? … All the socialists [during the liberation struggle] are the leaders now. They are there in the parliament. So if the SACP says, 'We are socialist', they must bring back all the leaders down here on the ground and come back and fight. That is why we say they are class collaborators, because they talk with us like this, then after we [have] left, they talk like that. They've got two languages.[40]

Silumko Radebe, the APF's former national organiser, also spoke of the state's hypocrisy: '[I]t was quite interesting to see them [the government] … coming on board to say, "We are for the people of Palestine; we are for the people of Lebanon", but also not wanting to spoil their relations with Israel, so they always get themselves caught in a 50/50 situation.'[41] Mokolo moreover raised the concern that 'the ANC does not tell them [the people] that, "We, the ANC and the National Party, we are one today"'. He was referring here to the former ruling party, which, in 1994 became known as the New National Party and which was disbanded following the 2004 national elections. Under the leadership of Marthinus van Schalkwyk, many New National Party representatives subsequently joined forces with the ANC.[42] Mokolo continued:

The National Party and the ANC are the capitalists. That is why it was easy for them to come together, to click. It's easy; they are not even fighting. The ANC can fight [the] SACP, it can fight COSATU, it can fight [the] PAC [Pan Africanist Congress], but it cannot fight the National Party. All the nationalists who joined the ANC [albeit a small number], they are settled. They are enjoying their positions. They feel that they are still in the same party. Now this is what the people are not aware of. From the communists, SACP, COSATU leaders, they also try to open spaces for themselves to get into the capitalist group so they can enjoy the benefits. There is no more solidarity because everyone cares for himself now.[43]

The move towards more individualistic modes of operation are, according to Dale McKinley, partly the result of governments – which had initially endorsed a 'commons' approach to the provision of resources like water – caving in in the face of a situation 'where now those things are no longer ideologically popular … because neoliberalism has come'.[44] ANC Councillor Themba Hlatshwayo, who represents Ward 25 in Soweto (which covers Klipruit, Pimville Zones 1, 2, 6, and Power Park) elaborated on the reasons behind the government's conscious ideological shift:

> I think if you put forward the ticket of socialism, you are lost. Before 1994, I was a member of the Communist Party. I was pushing seriously that ticket, but after 1994 I'm no longer pushing that ticket. Everything is changing so speedily. Socialism is not going to make it in this country. You can't push that ticket. You'll die even if you win. In fact the whole world is going in the direction of the capitalists, mixed economy and so on, so why don't we follow?[45]

Reflecting on what he considered an ideological turnaround within the ANC-led alliance, Mokolo lamented:

> I didn't like the way [the] ANC shifted from politics that people were expecting. ... People thought the ANC was a socialist party, but then after 1994, very few people realised that the ANC is not a socialist party and that the ANC has shifted. ... It's like a business, so it's easy for them to be co-opted into the system.[46]

He added:

> Some of the councillors were activists ... [but they] forgot where they come from ... our struggle against apartheid was going along with solidarity. Some people were boycotting rent [payments] to show solidarity with those who don't have money and now today the leaders who are in the government they forgot about solidarity, now they started speaking the same language as the ... apartheid leaders. They forgot about everything and then they start blaming the poor.[47]

Ideological tensions between the APF and the ANC are largely rooted in the government's adoption and implementation of GEAR, which the APF and other critics on the left regard as a neoliberal macroeconomic policy. Commenting on the ANC's abandonment of the already watered-down, but ostensibly pro-poor, policies that were embodied in the RDP, Radebe notes:

> It [the ANC] has clearly shown itself since 1996 ... that it is for neoliberal policies; it's for the capitalists; it's for business. It has made those commitments to business

at the expense of the people. ... [H]aving hopes that the ANC will change is more like waiting for Jesus to return.[48]

However, prior to 1994 the ANC lacked a specific, coherent economic programme and had never fully committed itself to a socialist revolution. Thus, the leap to present-day public–private partnerships in service delivery is not indicative of a sharp ideological about-turn. Reflecting on Rosenthal's work, Beinart's introductory chapter draws attention to the career path of people like Amos Masondo, for example, moving from leadership roles in the civics to positions of power, either at the level of the local state or in the private sector. Some analysts put forward a betrayal thesis, which very likely stemmed from the disjuncture between what the ANC said and what it did. But the APF realised early on that there was a growing political gap as far as championing the interests of the working class was concerned and it positioned itself and framed its demands accordingly.

As far as service delivery is concerned, the City of Johannesburg, of which Amos Masondo is the mayor, has not followed a full-scale privatisation route in the sense of a wholesale selling off of state assets. Instead, the city has opted for a corporate model that has allowed for state-owned – but privately managed – utilities to take over some of the functions of the municipality. For many municipalities faced with added responsibilities and financial pressures following the process of local government restructuring after 1994, transferring service responsibilities to state-owned utilities or entering into long-term contracts with service-providing companies seemed an attractive option. Water services in Johannesburg are under the control of Johannesburg Water (sometimes referred to as the Johannesburg Water Company or JOWCO), which operates as a corporatised municipal utility. The management of its water and sanitation services was outsourced to Johannesburg Water Management, a 'specialised water and sanitation management consortium' that, at the time of conducting this research, was jointly owned by Ondeo (a subsidiary of the French water multinational Suez Lyonnaise des Eaux) and two of its subsidiaries, namely Northumbrian Water (based in Britain) and Water and Sanitation Services South Africa (the local subsidiary).[49] The City of Johannesburg envisaged Johannesburg Water as a utility that 'would operate without significant financial transfers from the City of Johannesburg, and indeed might be so efficient that it could operate at a slight profit'.[50]

The approach to the management and distribution of water services depends largely on the way in which water is conceived. Some – notably local government councillors and representatives from Johannesburg Water, but also township residents who are employed – argue that water, despite being a public good, goes through a number of processes (collection, storage, treatment and piping) before it is 'delivered' to the end user. These processes cost money, hence their argument that water is a commodity. Proponents of this view also stress that the only way to teach people to use water responsibly is to make them pay for it. For example, ANC Councillor Mandla Mtshali, who was responsible for Ward 19 in Soweto, suggested:

> People do not respect water. They don't know how they are blessed with water … one opens the tap, and puts the washing under the tap, and then goes to watch *The Bold and the Beautiful*. Do you mean that particular person does not have the money to pay? He is overspending the water that is being provided for free.[51]

If one were to accept this view, privatisation and cost-recovery strategies would be the logical operating principle. Indeed, as part of the government's cost-recovery plan and in accordance with the terms of iGoli 2002, Johannesburg Water launched 'Operation *Gcin'amanzi*' (which means 'conserving water'), in terms of which pre-paid water meters were installed in homes across Soweto.[52] However, an alternative viewpoint centres on the argument that even if the processing of water costs money, as a public good and a basic need it should remain decommodified and the associated costs should not be borne by the end users, particularly not at the household level. The negative consequences of pre-paid meters for end users are well documented, but it is beyond the scope of this chapter to expand on this discussion here.[53] The APF notes that '[t]here is politics behind the pre-paid meters for the private sector to make money. The motive is profit.'[54] The shift from public to private sector provision of basic resources is aligned with

> somebody's particular class agenda, so of course, if you're sitting on that side of the class fence, then yes, it's going to make absolute sense for you to want to charge for water and to privatise it and to squeeze poor people. And the other side doesn't.[55]

Since the APF accepts the premise that water is a public good and a basic necessity, not a commodity, the organisation considers it unacceptable for water to be 'mediated by the market'.[56] Pre-paid meters would thus be

> out of the question, precisely because water is … something that is an absolute human necessity. It's necessary as a public good; as a public right – if you want

to talk about it in terms of rights, human, constitutional or otherwise – so the question of the recovery of costs to deliver that does not come into the equation.[57]

In a similar vein, Radebe argued,

we have to look at it [water] as a universal issue whereby everybody has [the] right to access it, whether you might be well off or poor … I think it's a fundamental human right that a person has to have access to water, and the way that the government and the private sector has taken up the issue of water as a commodity – that in itself sparks an anger from the community that we have to look at water as a commodity; something that we must buy.[58]

Radebe went on to compare water with other basic services, like electricity, for example, pointing out that while there may be alternatives to electricity, such as gas or paraffin, nothing can replace water.[59] Along these lines, Mokolo insisted that '[people] have got the right to drink water. People can live without Coca-Cola, without beer. They can distance themselves from that, but they cannot distance themselves from water'.[60]

Linking the commodification of basic services to pre-paid meters and oppression, Modisane argued:

Pre-paid is … the way they want to recover that debt, but people cannot afford to pay, because the people are not working. The pre-paid [meters] cause problems [among] the poor, because if you haven't got money, you haven't got water. … You must pay before you use, and that is oppressing the poor. The poor haven't got the right to free basic services. They must buy their own basic services. But they [the government] keep on promising, but at the same time, they attack them with the pre-paid.[61]

While opportunities in the post-apartheid era facilitated the emergence of a miniscule black elite and a burgeoning black middle class, persistent race and class inequalities continue to be experienced most acutely by poor black Africans, many of whom are unemployed or rely on limited grants or casual, insecure forms of employment that provide them with irregular and meagre incomes. Under such circumstances it is difficult – and, in some cases, impossible – to pay for basic services. Modisane explained:

The owners of these [Soweto] homes are old now and they get [a] pension [of R780] and of that ... they want R200 for electricity, R200 for water and then they've got [an] extended family; maybe there are ten [people in the household] and then the balance for those people is R400, which must serve the whole family for the whole month. [Do] you think R400 or R300 ... is enough? It's not enough.[62]

Highlighting dimensions of change and continuity in past and present periods of popular protest, Lehlohonolo, a Pimville (Soweto) resident who is sympathetic to the views of the APF, pointed out that

in the liberation movement we were looking at state intervention more than anything. Water, health care – those are basics, so we didn't foresee a situation where we will be buying those basic services which make people to survive, so for me there is something wrong at the political level.

He added that the country

seem[s] to be adopting what some people call neoliberalism, and that's the kind of policy that is saying we must buy water. It is saying we must privatise more and more. For us it's really a step backwards in terms of what the people have been fighting for in the past.[63]

From these views it is evident that championing the cause of public ownership and the provision of water services is not a novel issue that emerged simultaneously with the rise of the social movements in the late 1990s. Indeed, Rosenthal's chapter in this volume shows that there were socialist strands within the resistance movements under apartheid, but that these tendencies were less dominant than those that promoted democracy and entrepreneurship. Thus, while the ideological roots of some of the new social movements can be traced back to community resistance movements under the apartheid regime, the key difference is that socialism is being vehemently and openly espoused by the leaders of some contemporary social movements.

Ideology in action: Continuity and change in street politics

The APF has threaded its anti-capitalist ideology through its mobilisation efforts as a way of bringing about coherence between what the organisation says and what it does. As part of its campaign against the commodification of water, the APF has engaged in protest action including, among other repertoires, marches and street rallies that have drawn crowds of different sizes, ranging from a few hundred to tens of thousands. Banners on these demonstrations typically read, 'Our Water Is not for Sale!', '*Amanzi Ngawethu*' (The water is ours) or '*Phansi* Privatisation! *Phansi!*' (Down with privatisation) and are sometimes emblazoned with pictures of padlocked taps to symbolise that access to water is denied to some as a result of the increased costs attached to the provision of the service. During these demonstrations, protesters are generally jubilant. '*Amandla!*' (the power) is often shouted out at rallies, on marches and at meetings before a speaker addresses the crowd, and the people assembled respond, '*ngawethu*' or '*awethu!*' (is ours). This rallying cry is commonly associated with the ANC during the liberation struggle, but is still used today by the ruling party and by social movements like the APF. Demonstrators also *toyi-toyi*,[64] chant slogans and sing many of the same 'struggle songs' that were sung at anti-apartheid demonstrations, fund-raising concerts and mass rallies in South Africa and abroad, as well as in prisons across South Africa and at the training camps where soldiers were being prepared for the armed struggle.

At its annual general meeting in 2007 the APF launched a CD of 'working-class songs', which was produced in the 'backyard shack studio' of one of the activists. The APF regards the songs as 'a source of energy' that provides communities and APF supporters with a 'sense of solidarity and determination in the struggles'.[65] Moreover, the organisation claims that

> the CD [reflects] how the APF has been handed over a baton of struggle and resistance by the movement that struggled and defeated apartheid in a formal sense. The cultural heritage that comes from the anti-apartheid struggle and the mass struggles of the 1980s continue to inspire members of the APF and working class communities. The older generation of APF members were part of the liberation movement and songs [o]n the CD reflect this.[66]

One of the songs, '*We nyamazane yiyo ehlala ehlathini*' (which, roughly translated, means, 'The prey lives in the bush'), deals with 'freedom fighters' who lived in exile:

> It has also been adapted to suit new conditions. One of the lines in the song shows the link between the liberation fighters of that time and the APF today. It also calls upon the working class and the poor to join the APF and become self-liberators under the new conditions of capitalist neoliberalism.[67]

These sentiments are clear in the song 'Amanzi ngawethu', meaning 'The water is ours':

[This song] is sung during struggles against water privatisation, water cut-offs, and the installation of water pre-paid meters in the townships. The song tells the ANC government, local authorities and private water companies that access to water is a basic human right and therefore should not be privatised.[68]

The song, 'That's why I am a socialist', which is sung regularly on marches and at meetings, 'is an attempt at defining a vision of, and for, the APF. Socialism here means an egalitarian society governed and controlled by producers of wealth. It is about a society free from wars, occupation, xenophobia, oppression of women and imperialism.[69] Some of the songs are sung in Zulu, some in English, and others in a combination of languages. The APF songs reflect a combination of past and present activism. Some of them pre-date the existence of the APF, but the lyrics of widely known struggle songs have been adapted to suit the context of post-national liberation resistance and new lyrics have been set to well-known beats and melodies. However, some of the songs are distinctive APF creations that have been newly penned and composed. Most of the songs express a desire for an end to social and economic exploitation.

Other forms of street politics – reminiscent of the struggle against apartheid – include threats to local government representatives. In 2001 supporters of the SECC stormed the home of Councillor Ndhlovu of Ward 22 (Pimville, Soweto) and destroyed his electricity meter. In 2002 SECC and APF supporters marched to Amos Masondo's home to confront him on the issue of unaffordable, corporatised services. Mobilisation efforts have also included sit-ins at the offices of Eskom and various forms of direct action aimed at reclaiming people's power. 'Operation Khanyisa', which means 'Operation Light Up', refers to the SECC's scheme to reconnect to the electricity grid residents whose electricity supply was cut by Eskom. Eskom responded by launching an advertising campaign that depicted self-reconnection as a criminal activity and urged people to report illegal connections.

When trenches were dug in 2003 to lay water pipes in Phiri as part of Operation Gcin'amanzi,[70] residents filled them up to halt the progress of the installation of pre-paid water meters. Johannesburg Water then obtained a court interdict preventing community residents and supporters of the APF and the SECC from coming within 50 metres of sites where Operation Gcin'amanzi was being carried out.[71]

'Operation *Vulamanzi*' (literally meaning to open the water, but translated as 'Water for All') represents another direct action strategy informed by the APF's socialist ideology to reclaim public ownership and control of water. Inspired and assisted by the APF, thousands of residents of poor communities in Johannesburg have enabled the water to flow by removing and destroying pre-paid meters and reconnecting residents to the water supply without the interference of these meters. This tactic of 'bypassing' the meter is now widespread and is being carried out by groups and individuals beyond the APF. In 2004 and again in 2006 protesters marched on the Johannesburg Water offices, meters in hand, in an act of defiance against the installation of pre-paid meters.[72] Those performing the reconnections are variously referred to as 'struggle plumbers and electricians' or 'guerrilla technicians'. These direct action strategies are an integral part of the offensive against pre-paid water meters launched by the APF and its affiliates. For example, a strategy used frequently by the Orange Farm Water Crisis Committee (OWCC) involved blockading the main highway into Soweto and Orange Farm.[73] As Bricks Mokolo, a key figure in the OWCC, explained: 'Highways are the arteries and veins of the capitalist body.'[74] As such, they connect townships to the city and wealthier suburbs and serve as a link between workers and their workplaces.[75]

Together with its street struggles and direct action repertoires, the APF also participated in a legal battle against Johannesburg Water, the Department of Water Affairs and Forestry, and the City of Johannesburg.[76] Considering its efforts on the streets and in the courts, it could be argued that the APF has followed a 'legal-activist route' in its water struggles, which, according to Greenstein, aims to 'change policy but also to put in place an expanded definition of rights that may have implications beyond each specific case … [and thus] potentially poses a fundamental challenge to the organisation and the reach of state power'.[77]

The final aspect of continuity and change in street protests that will be addressed here deals with the post-apartheid state's efforts to clamp down on protest by social movements, which have reminded many APF activists of South Africa's apartheid past. Some of those directly involved in the APF argue that, despite significant changes between the former and current political regimes in South Africa, 'the mindsets and practices that structured apartheid responses to dissent and conflict have crept into our new democracy'.[78] Silumko Radebe went as far as to say that '[w]hat we have witnessed in the past six years of the APF has been state repression at its highest, highest, highest force'.[79] Other APF activists, however, adopted a more measured view. For example John Appolis, who was Deputy Chair of the APF at the time of the interview, suggested that while the state's response to protests by social movements has indeed exhibited highly repressive behaviour, the ANC government has not shifted completely into 'a phase of repression'.[80] In response to what some APF activists have perceived as increased levels of repression, the organisation has stepped up its struggle. As McKinley explained:

> The state's response of repression and delegitimisation, of attacking ... as well as describing people as ultra-left, as anarchists ... creates ... an environment where ... the social movements themselves and the community organisations that make them up begin to respond to that. It creates a much more confrontational situation.[81]

Dissidents have been harshly dealt with in the state's effort to 'manufacture consent'. In the arena of basic services, however, APF activists have stood their ground. As is often the case, efforts to clamp down on civil liberties tend to be met with increased commitment to one's principles and goals and, in line with this trend, the APF has not shown any signs of backing down and falling into line with the kind of ideology that underpins the government's economic policies and its approach to service delivery. Commenting on the activities of the OWCC, McKinley and Veriava noted:

> Rather than quieten the OWCC, such attacks spurred the organisation to intensify and broaden its community activism and strengthen its view that the politics of the ANC, its local representative and the policies flowing from the state institutions it controls had become the main 'enemy' of the community.[82]

Thus, instead of repression leading to movements being squashed, it encourages the movements to enter into new and broader terrains of struggle. Histories of resistance – in South Africa and elsewhere – are replete with examples of this trend. Even in cases where a movement is disbanded, its ideology does not necessarily evaporate, thus allowing for ideological continuity over time.

The themes of continuity and change are evident in the work of Charles Tilly and Sidney Tarrow. In his work *The Contentious French*, Tilly introduced the concept of 'repertoires of contention', which he used to refer to 'the whole set of means [a group] has for making claims of different kinds on different individuals or groups'.[83] In a later publication on popular protest in Britain between 1758 and 1834, Tilly refined the definition to read, 'the ways that people act together in pursuit of shared interests'.[84] Customary social movement repertoires include, for example, peaceful demonstrations, sit-ins, the effective use of the media, the destruction of property and other, more violent forms of protest. On the one hand, Tilly emphasises the importance of continuity in collective action and, commenting on this aspect of Tilly's work, Tarrow suggests that repertoires should 'involv[e] not only what people do when they are engaged in conflict with others but what they *know how to do* and what others *expect* them to do'.[85] On the other hand, however, Tilly also acknowledges that repertoires need to be sensitive and responsive to context.[86] Similarly, Tarrow suggests that these modes of mobilisation depend heavily on 'major fluctuations in interests, opportunity and organization',[87] which implies that repertoires can and should change over historical periods, since certain modes of protest, no matter how well versed activists are in the repertoires, may lose their effectiveness or may become obsolete, while others become much more striking and convincing.

Conclusion

Assessing the global picture of popular protest, Dwyer and Seddon point out:

> Towards the end of the 1980s and certainly in the early 1990s ... popular protest was already ... becoming increasingly 'political', both in the sense of [being] self conscious, organised and orchestrated, and in the ideological sense of having longer term aims and objectives than 'protest'.[88]

Some of South Africa's new social movements tend to fit in with this global picture. For example, the APF's approach to grassroots mobilisation has sought to point out how daily struggles around poverty, inequality, lack of access to services, housing evictions, exclusion and unemployment are inextricably linked to the ANC's adoption and implementation of a neoliberal economic policy, and also to imperialism at a regional, international and global level. Thus, the APF is not only fighting against national capital and the black elite in South Africa. Popular politics in the post-apartheid context is defined by the APF as a struggle against neoliberalism and global capitalism. As such, the struggles of the APF, although nominally issue based, are inherently ideological and thus wide ranging.

A closer look at the ideological currents within the tripartite alliance reveals that, within certain quarters, socialism was never upheld as an objective. Instead, the overarching goal was always to incorporate black people into the capitalist economic system. Under the ANC's rule, however, large sections of the black population remain poor and unemployed. The broadly defined socialist ideology of the APF pits the movement against the ANC-led alliance, whose pro-capitalist politics clearly have not benefitted the majority of the population. There have been no trickle-down effect from the rich to the poor, and the country's wealth is still firmly in the hands of an elite, a small part of which is black. Informed by its socialist ideology, the APF's mobilisation strategies around water, for example, are geared towards gaining equal access to, and public ownership and control of, the resource. Some of the APF's mobilisation efforts have evoked a hostile response from the government. Brutal means of control are employed by the police, reminding many activists of state repression during the 1980s.

Organisations like the APF came to the fore from the late 1990s onwards, not only to resist and oppose the ANC's ideological stance, but also to remind the ruling party of the promises it had made. The APF, for example, has continued to engage in struggles aimed at reprioritising some of the objectives that are spelled out in the Freedom Charter and the original demands that were put forward during the liberation struggle, but it also attempts to go beyond these goals. The AFP's attempts to nurture a socialist consciousness at the grassroots level have thus not been forged in a post-apartheid vacuum. Instead, the organisation argues that its efforts have been directed at reclaiming and reintroducing the socialist alternatives that were proposed by many of the very same people who were involved in the liberation struggle, but who distanced themselves from these alternatives when they began to occupy positions of power within the tripartite alliance. While some of the APF's demands are reminiscent of those put forward during anti-apartheid struggles, these battles are now being fought in a changed political context. A key difference between the apartheid period and the current political context is that there are indeed spaces for movements like the APF to operate without being forced to go underground. A certain measure of democracy has made this possible. However, the APF's struggles – which have been largely informed by dire socio-economic circumstances that affect the majority of the population – encourage a rethinking of democracy in ways that reintroduce collective approaches to the political economy and social organisation. In this way, the APF – ideologically and practically – actively resists top-down definitions of democracy that benefit a wafer-thin layer of society and promotes more inclusive and more meaningful forms of democracy under which the majority of the population can flourish.

Endnotes

Chapter 1

1   The so-called tripartite alliance, comprising the ANC, the South African Communist Party and the Congress of South African Trade Unions.

2   C. Bundy, 'Street sociology and pavement politics: Aspects of youth and student resistance in Cape Town, 1985', *Journal of Southern African Studies*, 13, 3 (1987), pp. 303–30.

3   The first was convened and organised by Genevieve Klein, Thula Simpson and William Beinart, and the second by Marcelle Dawson and William Beinart.

4   Hakan Thorn, 'Anti-apartheid and the emergence of a global civil society', South African Popular Politics and Resistance Movements workshop, St Antony's College, Oxford, 10–11 November 2006; H. Thorn, *Anti-apartheid and the Emergence of a Global Civil Society* (Palgrave Macmillan, Basingstoke, 2006).

5   For recent examples, see Tom Lodge, *Mandela: A Critical Life* (Oxford University Press, Oxford, 2006); Mark Gevisser, *Thabo Mbeki: The Dream Deferred* (Jonathan Ball, Johannesburg, 2007); William Mervin Gumede, *Thabo Mbeki and the Battle for the Soul of the ANC* (Zebra Press, Cape Town, 2007); Anthony Butler, *Cyril Ramaphosa* (Jacana, Cape Town, 2008).

6   D. McKinley, 'Democracy and social movements in South Africa', in V. Padyachee (ed.), *The Development Decade? Economic and Social Change in South Africa, 1994–2004* (HSRC Press, Cape Town, 2006); A. Lemon, 'Perspectives on democratic consolidation in Southern Africa: The five general elections of 2004', *Political Geography*, 26 (2007), pp. 824–50.

7   For some examples, see S. Marks, *Reluctant Rebellion: The 1906–8 Disturbances in Natal* (Clarendon Press, Oxford, 1970); C. van Onselen, *Chibaro: African Mine Labour in Southern Rhodesia, 1900–1933* (Pluto Press, London, 1976); T. Lodge, *Black Politics in South Africa since 1945* (Longman, London, 1983); B. Bozzoli (ed.), *Town and Countryside in the Transvaal* (Ravan Press, Johannesburg, 1983); B. Bozzoli (ed.), *Class, Community and Conflict* (Ravan Press, Johannesburg, 1987); W. Beinart & C. Bundy, *Hidden Struggles in Rural South Africa* (James Currey, London, 1987); W. Beinart, *Twentieth-century South Africa* (Oxford University Press, Oxford, 2001).

8   Beinart & Bundy, 1987; H. Bradford, *A Taste of Freedom: The ICU in Rural South Africa, 1920–1930* (Yale University Press, New Haven, 1987); P. Delius, *A Lion amongst the Cattle: Reconstruction and Resistance in the Northern Transvaal* (Ravan Press, Johannesburg, 1996).

9   H. Marais, *South Africa: Limits to Change: The Political Economy of Transition* (Zed Books & UCT Press, London, New York & Cape Town, 2001); P. Bond, *Elite Transition: Globalisation and the Rise of Economic Fundamentalism in South*

Africa (Pluto Press, London, 2000a); R. Southall, 'Introduction: The ANC state, more dysfunctional than developmental?', in S. Buhlungu et al. (eds), *State of the Nation: South Africa 2007* (HSRC Press, Cape Town, 2007); Gumede, 2007; D. McKinley, *The ANC and the Liberation Struggle: A Critical Political Biography* (Pluto Press, London, 1997); A. Desai, *We Are the Poors: Community Struggles in Post-apartheid South Africa* (Monthly Review Press, New York, 2002a).

10 Beinart, 2001; J. Seekings & N. Nattrass, *Class, Race and Inequality in South Africa* (University of KwaZulu-Natal Press, Durban, 2006).

11 C. Ceruti, 'Biggest strikes in South Africa since the end of apartheid', *Socialist Worker Online*, 9 June 2007, <http://www.socialistworker.co.uk/>.

12 J. Beall, S. Gelb & S. Hassim, 'Fragile stability: State and society in democratic South Africa', *Journal of Southern African Studies*, 31, 4 (2005), pp. 681–700.

13 R. Southall, 'The state of party politics: Struggles within the tripartite alliance and the decline of opposition', in J. Daniel, A. Habib & R. Southall (eds), *State of the Nation: South Africa 2003–2004* (HSRC Press, Cape Town, 2003); D. McKinley, 'South Africa's third local government elections and the institutionalisation of "low-intensity" neo-liberal democracy', in J. Minnie (ed.), *Outside the Ballot Box: Preconditions for Elections in Southern Africa 2005/6* (Media Institute of Southern Africa, Windhoek, 2006a).

14 E. Canel, 'New social movement theory and resource mobilization theory: The need for integration', in M. Kaufman & H. D. Alfonso (eds), *Community Power and Grassroots Democracy: The Transformation of Social Life* (Zed Books, London & New Jersey, 1997); S. M. Buechler, *Social Movements in Advanced Capitalism: The Political Economy and Cultural Construction of Social Activism* (Oxford University Press, New York, 2000).

15 Canel, 1997, p. 214; S. Tarrow, *Power in Movement: Social Movements, Collective Action and Politics* (Cambridge University Press, New York, 1994), emphasis added.

16 A. Melucci, *Nomads of the Present: Social Movements and Individual Needs in Contemporary Society* (Temple University Press, Philadelphia, 1989); A. Touraine, *The Voice and the Eye: An Analysis of Social Movements* (Cambridge University Press, Cambridge, 1981).

17 A. Melucci, *Challenging Codes: Collective Action in the Information Age* (Cambridge University Press, Cambridge, 1996).

18 Thorn, 2006.

19 M. Castells, *The City and the Grassroots: A Cross-cultural Theory of Urban Social Movements* (Edward Arnold, London, 1983).

20 M. Dawson, 'Social movements in contemporary South Africa: The Anti-Privatisation Forum and struggles around access to water in Johannesburg', DPhil thesis, University of Oxford, 2008.

21 Canel, 1997, pp. 199, 203.

22 R. Ballard, A. Habib and I Valodia (eds), 'Introduction: From anti-apartheid to post-apartheid social movements', in R. Ballard et al. (eds), *Voices of Protest: Social*

Movements in Post-apartheid South Africa (University of KwaZulu-Natal Press, Durban, 2006); N. Gibson (ed.), *Challenging Hegemony: Social Movements and the Quest for a New Humanism in Post-apartheid South Africa* (Africa World Press, Trenton & Asmara, 2006).

23 Gumede, 2007, p. 351.

24 Ben Cashdan, *Two Trevors Go to Washington*, film (2000).

25 K. Rosenthal in this volume.

26 The song is recorded on the CD, *Songs of the Working Class*, vol. 1, by Patrick 'Patra' Sindane, organiser of the Coalition Against Water Privatisation.

27 Raymond Suttner, *The ANC Underground* (Jacana, Cape Town, 2008).

28 H. Wolpe, 'Capitalism and cheap labour power in South Africa: From segregation to apartheid', *Economy and Society*, 1 (1972), pp. 424–56; R. Turner, *The Eye of the Needle: Toward Participatory Democracy* (Orbis Books, Maryknoll, 1978); M. Legassick, 'South Africa: Forced labour, industrialization, and racial differentiation', in R. Harris (ed.), *The Political Economy of Africa* (Halsted Press, Boston, 1975); F. A. Johnstone, *Class, Race and Gold: A Study of Class Relations and Racial Discrimination in South Africa* (Routledge & Kegan Paul, London, 1976).

29 Beinart & Bundy, 1987; T. Ranger, *Peasant Consciousness and Guerrilla War in Zimbabwe: A Comparative Study* (James Currey, London, 1985); Delius, 1996. The quote is from A. Isaacman et al., '"Cotton is the mother of poverty": Peasant resistance to forced cotton cultivation in Mozambique, 1938–61', *International Journal of African Historical Studies*, 13, 4 (1980), p. 582.

30 S. Horwitz, '"A phoenix rising": A history of Baragwanath Hospital, Soweto, South Africa, 1942–1990', DPhil thesis, University of Oxford, 2006.

31 Dawson, 1997, p. 284.

32 C. Sato, 'Forced removals, land NGOs and community politics in KwaZulu-Natal, South Africa, 1953–2002', DPhil thesis, University of Oxford, 2006.

33 For overviews of land reform, see Deborah James, *Gaining Ground: 'Rights' and 'Property' in South African Land Reform* (Routledge Cavendish, Abingdon, 2006); Cherryl Walker, *Landmarked: Land Claims and Land Restitution in South Africa* (Jacana, Cape Town, 2008).

34 S. Greenberg, 'The Landless People's Movement and the failure of post apartheid land reform', in R. Ballard et al. (eds), *Voices of Protest: Social Movements in Post-apartheid South Africa* (University of KwaZulu-Natal Press, Durban, 2006).

35 Jeremy Gordin, *Zuma: A Biography* (Jonathan Ball, Johannesburg, 2008), p. 225.

36 Jeremy Seekings, *The UDF: A History of the United Democratic Front in South Africa 1983–1991* (James Currey, Oxford, 2000).

37 Seekings & Nattrass, 2006.

38 Michael Neocosmos, 'Civil society, citizenship and the politics of the (im)possible: Rethinking militancy in Africa today', unpublished paper, 2007.

39 Marks, 1970; Jeff Guy, *The Maphumulo Uprising: War, Law and Ritual in the Zulu Rebellion* (University of KwaZulu-Natal Press, Durban, 2005).

40   The AK-47 assault rifle, the weapon of choice for liberation movements/insurgencies throughout the world.

41   Dawson, 2008, chap. 5.

42   Eskom is the parastatal electricity-generating company.

43   S. Johnston & A. Bernstein, *Voices of Anger: Protest and Conflict in Two Municipalities*, report to the Conflict and Governance Facility (Centre for Development, Johannesburg, 2007).

44   G. Miescher & D. Henrichsen, *African Posters* (Basel Afrikaner Bibliographen, Switzerland, 2004); P. Bonner & L. Segal, *Soweto: A History* (Maskew Miller Longman, Cape Town, 1998).

45   A. E. Coombes, *History after Apartheid: Visual Culture and Public Memory in a Democratic South Africa* (Wits University Press, Johannesburg, 2004).

46   A. Sampson, *Mandela: The Authorised Biography* (London, Harper Collins, 1999); Lodge, 2006; Elleke Boehmer, *Mandela: A Very Short Introduction* (Oxford University Press, Oxford, 2008).

47   R. Nixon, 'Mandela, messianism and the media', *Transition*, 51 (1991), pp. 42–55.

48   Belinda Bozzoli, *Theatres of Struggle and the End of Apartheid* (Edinburgh University Press, Edinburgh, 2004).

49   Ibid.

50   C. Cachalia, *Comrade Moss* (Learn and Teach Publications, Johannesburg, 1989).

51   Gumede, 2007; Gevisser, 2007.

52   E. Unterhalter et al. (eds), *Apartheid Education and Popular Struggles* (Ravan Press, Johannesburg, 1991); Jonathan Hyslop, *The Classroom Struggle: Policy and Resistance in South Africa 1940–1990* (University of Natal Press, Pietermaritzburg, 1999).

53   Tracy Carson, 'Black trade unions and consumer boycotts in the Cape Province, South Africa, 1978–82', DPhil thesis, University of Oxford, 2008.

54   T. Barnett & A. Whiteside, *AIDS in the Twentieth Century: Disease and Globalisation* (Palgrave, London, 2006).

55   J. Myburgh, 'The African National Congress under the presidency of Thabo Mbeki (1997 to 2002)', DPhil thesis, University of Oxford, 2006.

56   S. Robins, '"Long live Zackie! long live": AIDS activism, science and citizenship after apartheid', *Journal of Southern African Studies*, 30, 3 (2004), pp. 651–72.

57   R. L. Abel, *Politics by Other Means: Law in the Struggle against Apartheid, 1980–1994* (Routledge, London, 1995).

58   In March 2009, after an appeal by the City of Johannesburg, Johannesburg Water and the Department of Water Affairs and Forestry, the Supreme Court of Appeal set aside the judgement by the High Court and ruled that Phiri residents should be allocated 42 litres per person per day. Moreover, the order relating to the unlawfulness of pre-paid meters was suspended for a period of two years to allow the City of Johannesburg time to take the necessary steps to legalise the devices. In September 2009, following an appeal by the Phiri applicants, the Constitutional Court – in a reversal of the High

Court judgement – ruled that the city's free basic water policy (which allows for a free allocation of six kilolitres per household per month) is reasonable and that pre-paid water meters are lawful.

59   Elizabeth Gunner, 'Jacob Zuma, the social body and the unruly power of song', *African Affairs*, 108, 430 (2009), pp. 27–48.

Chapter 2

1   This figure was quoted by the minister of labour, Marais Viljoen, Hansard, 24 April 1973.

2   M. Horrell, *South Africa's Workers* (South African Institute of Race Relations, Johannesburg, 1969).

3   For an overview of the Ovambo strikes, see M. Kooy, 'The contract labour system and the Ovambo crisis of 1971 in South-West Africa', *African Studies Review*, 16, 1 (1973), pp. 83–105. For strike action in 1972, see D. Hemson, 'Dock workers, labour circulation, and class struggles and the dockworkers of Durban 1940–1959', *Journal of Southern African Studies*, 4, 1 (1977), pp. 88–124; D. Hemson, 'Class consciousness and the migrant workers: The dockworkers of Durban', PhD thesis, University of Warwick, 1978.

4   D. du Toit, *Capital and Labour in South Africa: Class Struggles in the 1970s* (Kegan Paul, London, 1981); S. Friedman, *Building Tomorrow Today: African Workers in Trade Unions, 1970–1984* (Ravan Press, Johannesburg, 1987); J. Baskin, *Striking Back: A History of COSATU* (Ravan Press, Johannesburg, 1991); J. Seekings, *The UDF: A History of the United Democratic Front in South Africa, 1983–1991* (James Currey, Oxford, 2000).

5   A. Sitas & C. Joakimidis, 'A study of strikes in the 1970s', *Work in Progress*, 6 (1978), pp. 105–14; *Work in Progress*, 7 (1979), pp. 30–53; A. Sitas, 'Thirty years since the Durban strikes: Black working-class leadership and the South African transition', *Current Sociology*, 52, 5 (2004), pp. 830–49; R. Toli, 'The origins of the Durban strikes 1973', MA dissertation, University of Durban-Westville, 1991; S. Khwela, '1973 strikes: Breaking the silence', *South African Labour Bulletin*, 17, 3 (1993), pp. 20–27. See also the interviews reprinted after Khwela's article on pp. 28–53 of this edition of *South African Labour Bulletin*.

6   IIE (Institute for Industrial Education), *The Durban Strikes 1973: 'Human Beings with Souls'* (IIE & Ravan Press, Johannesburg, 1974).

7   J. Maree, 'Seeing strikes in perspective', *South African Labour Bulletin*, 12, 9 & 10 (1976), pp. 91–109.

8   SA Statistics (1980), quoted in R. V. Lambert, 'The changing labour market of the seventies and state strategies of reform', in *Black Trade Unions in South Africa: Core of a New Democratic Opposition Movement?* (Friedrich Ebert Stiftung, Bonn, 1983), p. 53.

9   Including, most notably, the debate between liberal and radical historians over the relationship between apartheid and industrialisation.

10   W. Beinart, *Twentieth-century South Africa* (Oxford University Press, Oxford, 2001), p. 181.

11   Ibid., p. 191.

12   Lambert, 1983, pp. 55–56.

13   D. Lewis, 'Black workers and trade unions', in T. Karis & G. Gerhart (eds), *From Protest to Challenge*, vol. 5, *Nadir and Resurgence, 1964–1979* (UNISA, Pretoria, 1997), p. 196.

14   For a survey of these efforts, see D. Horner, 'African labour representation up to 1975', in J. Maree (ed.), *The Independent Trade Unions, 1974–1984* (Ravan Press, Johannesburg, 1987).

15   *Daily News*, 10 January 1973.

16   *Natal Mercury*, 'Workers go back', 11 January 1973.

17   *Natal Mercury*, 15 January 1973; *Daily News*, 15 January 1973.

18   *Natal Mercury*, 'Workers go back', 11 January 1973.

19   'A view of the 1973 strikes', memorandum ca 1973, FOSATU Collection, University of the Witwatersrand, Historical Papers (hereafter WHP), AH1999/C3.15.2.

20   *Natal Mercury*, '650 in new stoppage', 30 January 1973.

21   *Daily News*, 'Strike worsens: Durban service crisis' and 'Fruit, veg. hit', 6 February 1973, p. 1.

22   *Natal Mercury*, 'Incident "work of agitators"', 11 January 1973, p. 15.

23   *Natal Mercury*, '650 in new stoppage', 30 January 1973, p. 9.

24   Department of Information, 'Persverklaring 9/73 (K)', 1 February 1973, SAIRR Collection, WHP. Translations up to this point are taken from *Daily News*, 'Workers are being "used" says Viljoen', 2 February 1973, p. 3.

25   Ibid., my translation.

26   *Daily News*, 15 March 1973; quoted in 'Causes: Newspapers', Gerry Mare Collection, Natal Room, University of KwaZulu-Natal, Pietermaritzburg.

27   Hansard, 5 February 1973, quoted in SAIRR (South African Institute of Race Relations), *Annual Report* (SAIIR, Johannesburg, 1973), p. 283.

28   *Daily News*, 'Workers are being "used" says Viljoen', 2 February 1973, p. 3.

29   *Daily News*, 'NUSAS linked to pay strikes', 6 February 1973, p. 5.

30   Ibid.

31   Ibid.

32   *Natal Mercury*, 'SASO offices raided', 1 February 1973, p. 13.

33   *Sunday Times*, 4 February 1973.

34   The IIE (1974) refers to several moments in which members of the police stated that they were on the alert for agitators, but also emphasises that none of these agitators was ever found.

35   *Daily News*, 'Minister out of touch', 3 February 1973, p. 12.

36   *Daily News*, 'White-tinted spectacles', 6 February 1973, p. 12.

37   *Daily News*, 'Brick strike – was it all necessary?', 5 February 1973, p. 5.

38   *Daily News*, 'Minister out of touch', 3 February 1973, p. 12.

39   *Daily News*, 'More pay call', 9 January 1973, pp. 1–2.
40   *Natal Mercury*, 'No incidents as workers hold', 10 January 1973, p. 9.
41   L. D. Thorne, 'Some comments on labour unrest', 27 February 1973, p. 3, WHP, FOSATU Collection.
42   F. Wilson, *Migrant Labour in South Africa* (SPROCAS, Durban, 1972); B. Freund, *Insiders and Outsiders: The Indian Working Class of Durban, 1919–1990* (University of Natal Press, Pietermaritzburg, 1995); IIE, 1974.
43   *Natal Mercury*, 'Workers go back', 11 January 1973, p. 15.
44   Freund, 1995.
45   *Daily News*, 'Mob invades golf course', 6 February 1973, p. 1.
46   Durban Chamber of Commerce, 'The current Bantu labour stoppage', 9 February 1973, FOSATU Collection, WHP.
47   Ibid., pp. 1–2.
48   South African Institute of Race Relations, 'Table A: Strikes and work stoppages in 1973', 1973, SAIRR Collection, WHP.
49   Durban Chamber of Commerce, 'The current Bantu labour stoppage', 9 February 1973, p. 1, FOSATU Collection, WHP.
50   Ibid.
51   'African workers interview', Gerry Mare Collection, Natal Room, University of KwaZulu-Natal, Pietermaritzburg.
52   Ibid.
53   Ibid.
54   Hansard, 9 February, quoted in SAIRR (South African Institute of Race Relations), *Annual Review (1973)* (SAIRR, Johannesburg, 1974), p. 283.
55   IIE, 1974.
56   Maree, 1976.
57   A. Gouldner, *Wildcat Strike* (Routledge, London, 1955).
58   Durban Chamber of Commerce, 'The current Bantu labour stoppage', 9 February 1973, FOSATU Collection, WHP.
59   Ibid., p. 5.
60   Gouldner, 1955, pp. 54–55.
61   *Daily News*, 'Durban service strike', 6 February 1973.
62   M. Horrell et al., *A Survey of Race Relations in South Africa 1972* (South African Institute of Race Relations, Johannesburg, 1973), pp. 325–28.
63   Durban Chamber of Commerce, 'The current Bantu labour stoppage', p. 3, 9 February 1973, FOSATU Collection, WHP.
64   Ibid.
65   *Natal Mercury*, '650 in new stoppage', 30 January 1973, p. 9.
66   IIE, 1974, pp. 43–44.
67   *Daily News*, 'The protectors', 2 February 1973, p. 12.
68   *Natal Mercury*, 'It's a "dance-in" work stoppage', 27 January 1973, p. 9.
69   Quoted in IIE, 1974, p. 20.

70 *Daily News*, 'Teargas …', 7 February 1973; IIE, 1974, p. 20; M. P. Gwala (ed.), *Black Review 1973* (Durban, Black Community Programmes, 1974), p. 141.

71 *Daily News*, 'Services cut as 3000 strike', 5 February 1973, p. 1.

72 *Daily News*, 'Latest', 5 February 1973, p. 1.

73 *Daily News*, 'Services cut as 3000 strike', 5 February 1973, p. 1.

74 *Daily News*, 'Mob invades golf course', 6 February 1973, p. 1.

75 IIE, 1974, pp. 30, 42–43; *Daily News*, 'Strike worsens', 6 February 1973, p. 1.

76 Gwala, 1974, p. 141; IIE, 1974, pp. 20–21.

77 Hansard, 24 April 1973, quoted in SAIRR, 1974, p. 284.

78 Friedman, 1987; T. Lodge, *Black Politics in South Africa since 1945* (London: Longman, 1983).

Chapter 3

1   I. Morgan, 'The spaghetti siege', *Management* (1980), p. 42.

2   Ibid., p. 44.

3   Ibid.

4   Interview with V. Engel, FCWU Cape Town branch director, 11 May 2006.

5   Interviews with J. Theron, 12 April 2005, 13 May 2006; J. Theron, 'A chronology of the Fatti's & Moni's dispute', 10 August 1979, FCWU Collection, Fatti's & Moni's boycott, BC721:J, UCT Libraries Manuscript and Archives (hereafter, all references to this collection will give only the collection's name and reference number, unless other details are needed). The union first organised workers at Fatti's & Moni's in Bellville in 1953 and negotiated an agreement to improve wages and conditions of work. However, soon after this victory, organisation at the Fatti's & Moni's factory disintegrated.

6   D. Pillay, 'Trade unions and alliance politics in Cape Town 1979–1985', PhD thesis, University of Essex, 1989, p. 100.

7   *Financial Mail*, 2 May 1980, p. 5.

8   Morgan, 1980, p. 42.

9   Interview with P. Moni, managing director of Fatti's & Moni's, 24 November 2006.

10 'Memo of meeting with Mr. Jan Theron', 25 May 1979, FCWU Collection, BC721:J.

11 Pillay, 1989, p. 102.

12 Interview with A. Crawford, FCWU Cape Town branch organiser, 23 May 2006.

13 Interview with S. Ashton, labour consultant and broker for Fatti's & Moni's, 12 November 2006.

14 Interview with Moni.

15 Interview with F. Mabikwe, former Fatti's & Moni's employee, 4 June 2007.

16 Ibid.

17 Interviews with Theron, 12 April 2005; 13 May 2006.

18 Pillay, 1989, p. 101.

19 Interview with Theron, 12 April 2005.

20 Interview with Crawford.

21 Interview with Mabikwe.

22 The third fell under the Industrial Council Agreement for the Biscuit Industry, authorising the union to write a letter of demand and to negotiate on behalf of workers.

23 'Memo of meeting with Mr. Jan Theron', FCWU Collection, BC721:J.

24 Ibid.

25 Liaison committees allowed for a committee split between employers and workers. Workers often saw these as a poor alternative to workers' committees, which enabled workers to democratically elect their representatives.

26 Interview with Moni.

27 'Memo of meeting with Mr. Jan Theron', FCWU Collection, BC721:J; J. Theron, 'A chronology of the Fatti's & Moni's dispute', FCWU Collection, BC721:J.

28 'Memo of meeting with Mr. Jan Theron', FCWU Collection, BC721:J; A. Levy, *Report on Industrial Relations at Bellville and Isando Plants*, unpublished report, 1980, UCT Library. Of the factory's 296 employees, only 22 coloured and two African workers were under the jurisdiction of the biscuit-manufacturing industry. The remaining 272 employees (112 African, 111 coloured and 49 white) could be organised by other unions in the canning and milling industries.

29 L. McGregor, 'The Fatti's & Moni's dispute', *South African Labour Bulletin*, 5, 6 & 7 (1980), p. 123.

30 C. M. Elias, *Report on the Labour Dispute at Fatti's & Moni's* (South African Institute of Race Relations, Johannesburg, ca September 1979), p. 2.

31 Ibid., p. 4.

32 Interview with Theron, 12 April 2005.

33 Ibid.

34 J. Theron, *Annual Report: 37th Annual Conference of the FCWU*, 24–25 September 1979, FCWU Collection, BC721:A.

35 Fatti's & Moni's Workers' Support Committee, 'Stop eating it right now', ca August 1979, FCWU Collection, BC721:J.

36 Interview with Engel.

37 Interview with Crawford.

38 Ibid.

39 Ibid.

40 Interview with Mabikwe.

41 Fatti's & Moni's Workers' Support Committee, 'Stop eating it right now', ca August 1979, FCWU Collection, BC721:J.

42 Pillay, 1989, p. 108. Morgan, 'The Spaghetti Siege', 44–45.

43 Elias, 1979, p. 3.

44 Ibid.

45 *Cape Argus*, '23 jobs at Fattis – unhappy union man', 3 July 1979.

46 *Cape Argus*, 'Hope to end pasta firm deadlock', 20 July 1979.

47 Even while on strike, contract workers continued living in the company's hostels.

48 Interview with Mabikwe.

49 Morgan, 1980, pp. 44–45.

50　R. Price, *The Apartheid State in Crisis* (Oxford University Press, New York, 1991), p. 165. For more on the workerism and populism debate, see P. van Niekerk, 'The trade union movement in the politics of resistance', in S. Johnson (ed.), *South Africa: No Turning Back* (Bloomington: Indiana University Press, 1989), p. 155; R. Davenport & C. Saunders, *South Africa: A Modern History* (London, Macmillan, 2000), p. 491.

51　R. Schroeder, 'Trade unions, politics, and working class struggle: The Food and Canning Workers Union, 1975–86', BA (Hons) research essay, UCT, 1988, p. 81.

52　Following the Fatti's & Moni's boycott there were various union-led consumer boycotts across the country, including the Western Province General Workers' Union boycott of red meat (Cape Town, 1980); the South African Allied Workers' Union boycott of confectioneries (East London, 1981); and the Chemical Industrial Workers' Union boycott of Colgate-Palmolive (Boksburg, 1981).

53　D. Pillay, interview with J. Issel, 29 February 1988; Pillay, 1989, p. 108.

54　Interview with Theron, 12 April 2005.

55　Interview with S. Hassan, WCTA chairperson, 6 June 2007.

56　Ibid.

57　*Evening Post*, 'New boycott threat over PE sackings', 9 November 1978.

58　Interview with Theron, 12 April 2005. Theron suggests that this stance has created a mythology that the union was not part of the boycott.

59　Interview with Engel.

60　Ibid.

61　M. Dlakavu, 'Trade union pioneer dies', *Cape Argus*, 14 June 2001.

62　Interview with F. Engel, chairperson of the Fatti's & Moni's Community Action Support Committee, 11 May 2006.

63　Ibid.

64　Interview with V. Engel.

65　Community Action Support Committee, 'Support Fatti's & Moni's boycott', ca 1979, FCWU Collection. The boycott included all goods manufactured by United Macaroni Factories Ltd. The company also sold products under the brand name of Record Flour and packed pasta for specific supermarket outlets under the brand names Princess, Pot o' Gold, Checkers, Beares and Roma. The company also owned the Wrenchtown Bakery, Ultra Bakeries and Good Hope Bakery.

66　Pillay, 1989, p. 116.

67　Interview with V. Engel.

68　Interview with Moni.

69　E. Kemp, 'Fattis won't transfer scab labour – manager', *Cape Times*, 28 June 1979, p. 3.

70　Pillay, 1989, p. 116.

71　Interview with Z. Achmat, 11 May 2007.

72　Interview with J. de Villiers, former student activist, 25 May 2007.

73　N. Fransman, '500 students support food factory boycott', *Cape Times*, 12 May 1979.

74　'Fatti's & Moni's strike', ca 1979, FCWU Collection, BC721:J.

75　Morgan, 1980, p. 44.

76   N. Fransman, 'Students back boycott', *Cape* Times, 17 May 1979.
77   *Cape Times*, 25 May 1979.
78   Ibid.
79   Pillay, 1989, p. 118.
80   Morgan, 1980, p. 46.
81   Interview with Moni.
82   Ibid.
83   'UCT Wages Commission', 1979, FCWU Collection, BC721:M.
84   *Rand Daily Mail*, 'Fattis suffers, but not from boycott', 9 October 1979.
85   Friedman, 1987, p. 200.
86   Ibid., p. 194.
87   Interview with Theron, 12 April 2005.
88   Interview with F. Engel.
89   J. Theron, Interview, 12 April 2005.
90   Interview with Crawford.
91   Pillay, 1989, p. 133.
92   Interview with F. Engel.
93   Interview with Theron, 12 April 2005.
94   R. Southall, 'African capitalism in contemporary South Africa', *Journal of Southern African Studies*, 7, 1 (1980), p. 59.
95   Interview with Theron, 12 April 2005.
96   Ad Hoc Committee, 'Fatti's & Moni's: Support the boycott', ca June 1979, FCWU Collection, BC721:J.
97   'Neil Aggett obituary', 27 November 1981, AL2457:M5.39, University of the Witwatersrand Library.
98   Interview with Moni.
99   Interview with F. Engel.
100 Morgan, 1980, p. 47; Ad Hoc Committee, 'Fatti's & Moni's: Support the boycott', ca June 1979, FCWU Collection, BC721:J.
101 P. Moni, Interview, 24 November 2006.
102 Pillay, 1989, p. 138.
103 Ibid., p. 134.
104 Interview with Moni.
105 *Cape Argus*, 'The Fatti's & Moni's dispute', 4 October 1979, p. 131.
106 *Cape Times*, 'Trading better – Fattis', 9 October 1979; *Rand Daily Mail*, 'Fattis suffers, but not from boycott', 9 October 1979.
107 *Financial Mail*, 2 May 1980. [see fn 7]
108 Reuters, 'Monis and Fattis set for growth', 1980.
109 Interview with Moni.
110 Ibid.
111 Friedman, 1987, p. 231.
112 Interview with Moni.

113   Interview with Theron, 12 April 2005.

114   S. Friedman, 'Milling giant signs breakthrough deal', *Rand Daily Mail*, 30 June 1981.

115   T. Lodge & B. Nasson, *All Here and Now: Black Politics in South Africa in the 1980s* (David Philip, Cape Town, 1991), p. 43.

116   Interview with Theron, 12 April 2005.

117   Lodge & Nasson, 1991, p. 36.

118   Friedman, 1987, p. 277.

119   Lodge & Nasson, 1991, p. 36.

Chapter 4

1   J. Matsebula, 'Swaziland: Rising tension between government and ANC', IPS-Inter Press Service, 19 December 1984.

2   T. Lodge, '"*Mayihlome!* – Let us go to war!" From Nkomati to Kabwe: The African National Congress, January 1984–June 1985', in South African Research Service (ed.), *South African Review*, vol. 3 (Ravan Press, Johannesburg, 1986), p. 228.

3   H. Barrell, 'Interview with Ronnie Kasrils', 19 August 1989, Historical Papers, University of the Witwatersrand (hereafter WHP), Karis-Gerhart Collection, folder 14, part I, p. 264.

4   H. Barrell, 'Conscripts to their age: African National Congress operational strategy, 1976–1986', DPhil, University of Oxford, 1993, pp. 352–53; *Globe & Mail* (Canada), 'S. African non-whites urged to resist', 5 September 1984; Joint Management Centres, Captain Fouché, 'The UDF: Transkei course', p. 21, 6 September 1985, WHP, A266F.

5   J. F. Smith, 'Guerrilla leader: Crackdown exposes myth of reform in South Africa', Associated Press, 26 October 1984.

6   BBC (British Broadcasting Corporation), 'ANC leader's anniversary address: Call for a people's war', *Summary of World Broadcasts*, 16 January 1985, based on excerpts from a broadcast of the address by the president of the ANC, Oliver Tambo, on the 73rd anniversary of the ANC's founding, Radio Freedom, Lusaka, 8 January 1985.

7   A. Robinson, 'Why the pressures are different this time: Violence in South Africa', *Financial Times* (London), 15 November 1984; J. Herbst, 'Prospects for revolution in South Africa', *Political Science Quarterly*, 103, 4 (1988–89), p. 676.

8   Lodge, 1986, pp. 228, 231, 244.

9   TRC (Truth and Reconciliation Commission), *Truth and Reconciliation Commission of South Africa Report*, vol. 2, *The State inside South Africa between 1960 and 1990* (Juta, Cape Town, 1998), p. 259.

10   Barrell, 1993, pp. 391–92; D. Beresford, 'The killing of Maki Shosana/background report on violence in South Africa following suspicious deaths of black activists', *Guardian* (London), 26 July 1985; G. Frankel, 'A woman lost to mob justice: South African's uncle: "We feel for the people who did this"', *Washington Post*, 29 July 1985; P. Gobodo-Madikizela, *A Human Being Died that Night: Forgiving Apartheid's Chief Killer* (Portobello, London, 2006), p. 29.

11   Associated Press, 'Black independence movement vows to step up war against white rule', 25 June 1985; M. Holman, 'ANC meeting pledges to step up attacks against South Africa', *Financial Times* (London), 26 June 1985; *New York Times*, 'South African rebels promise more attacks', 26 June 1985.

12   TRC, 1998, vol. 3, chap. 1, 'Appendix: National chronology', p. 23.

13   S. Talbot, 'The A.N.C. is taking charge; African National Congress increasing in strength', *Nation*, 3 May 1986.

14   T. Lodge, 'The African National Congress after the Kabwe conference', in G. Moss & I. Obery (eds), *South African Review*, vol. 4 (Ravan Press, Johannesburg, 1987), pp. 10–14.

15   C. Robinson, 'Human rights: Apartheid foes charge that emergency deepens crisis', IPS-Inter Press Service, 23 July 1985; A. Cowell, 'Scores arrested in night raids in South Africa', *New York Times*, 23 July 1985.

16   Associated Press, 29 September 1985.

17   United Press International, 'Anti-apartheid group urges blacks to fight in white neighbourhoods', 4 September 1985.

18   *New York Times*, 'Apartheid foe says protest in white areas is inevitable', 7 September 1985.

19   *Newsweek*, 'We will expect a blood bath', US edition, 16 September 1985.

20   Stephen M. Davis, *Apartheid's Rebels: Inside South Africa's Hidden War* (Yale University Press, New Haven & London, 1987), pp. 123–24.

21   ANC (African National Congress), 'Take the struggle to the white areas' (ca 1985), accessed 8 June 1010, <http://www.anc.org.za/ancdocs/history/ungovern.html>.

22   Barrell, 1993, pp. 388–91.

23   Ibid., pp. 391, 440.

24   Barrell, 1993, pp. 413–19; Sibusiso 'Sihle' Mbongwa, quoted in Laurence Dworkin (director), 'Not the kings and generals, 1983–1990', *Ulibambe Lingashoni: Hold up the Sun: The ANC and Popular Power in the Making*, episode 5; Testimony of Sibusiso Mbongwa & Vejanand Ramlakan to the TRC amnesty hearing at the Durban Christian Centre, 4 September 2000; H. Barrell, interview with Yacoob Abba Omar, 3 December 2003, WHP, Karis-Gerhart Collection, folder 30, part I, pp. 732–44; Interview with Rayman Lalla, 28 April 2004; H. Barrell, interview with Ivan Pillay, 20 July 1989, WHP, Karis-Gerhart Collection, folder 31, part I, p. 767.

25   H. Barrell, interview with Mac Maharaj, 3 February 1991, WHP, Karis-Gerhart Collection, folder 18, part I, p. 525; Barrell, 1993, pp. 446–47.

26   BBC, 'S. African government presents captured ANC "documents"', *Summary of World Broadcasts*, 15 December 1986, based on a SAPA dispatch datelined Pretoria, 12 December 1986; W. Claiborne, 'S. Africa rounds up opposition; Pretoria claims mass arrests needed to deter revolution', *Washington Post*, 13 December 1986; A. Robinson, 'ANC planned to step up action Botha declares', *Financial Times* (London), 13 December 1986; Lodge, 1987, p. 10.

27   C. Cooper et al., *Race Relations Survey 1988/89* (South African Institute of Race Relations, Johannesburg, 1989), p. 609.

28   L. Schuster, 'Grappling with the future', *Christian Science Monitor* (Boston), 17 October 1988.

29   J. D. Battersby, interview with Chris Hani & Steve Tshwete, Lusaka, 3 June 1988, WHP, Karis-Gerhart Collection, folder 12, part I, pp. 3–4.

30   J. D. Battersby, 'South Africa's curbs harden rebels', *New York Times*, 7 June 1988; M. Hornsby, 'Bomb attacks in white city areas to be stepped up: ANC in radical policy switch, South Africa', *Times* (London), 7 June 1988; M. Hornsby, 'Inkatha "warlords" target of new ANC leader, South Africa', *Times* (London), 8 June 1988; J. D. Battersby, 'South African rebel commander: A portrait in erudition and ruthlessness', *New York Times*, 12 June 1988.

31   R. Dowden, 'ANC rift shows up in South African bomb campaign', *Independent*, 24 September 1988.

32   W. J. Booyse, 'The concept "people's war" in the strategy of the ANC and the PAC: A comparative analysis', DPhil thesis, Potchefstroom University, 1990, p. 104.

33   P. Laurence, 'Ten hurt in Johannesburg lunch-hour blast', *Guardian* (London), 23 June 1988; P. Goodspeed, 'Naked terror', *Toronto Star*, 26 June 1988; D. Crary, 'Increasing attacks on civilian targets stir anger, alarm', Associated Press, 29 June 1988.

34   United Press International, 4 July 1988.

35   P. Laurence, 'SA conflict comes to sporting heartland', *Guardian* (London), 4 July 1988.

36   Testimony of Harold Matshididi on day 1 of the TRC amnesty hearing for the Ellis Park arena bomb blast, Johannesburg, 3 August 1997; Testimony of Lester Dumakude on day 2 of the TRC amnesty hearing for the Ellis Park arena bomb blast, Johannesburg, 4 August 1997.

37   V. Mallet, 'ANC apologises for casualties', *Financial Times* (London), 18 August 1988; J. D. Battersby, 'A.N.C. acts to halt civilian attacks', *New York Times*, 21 August 1988; R. Dowden, 'ANC rift shows up in South African bomb campaign', *Independent*, 24 September 1988; Cooper et al., 1989, p. 610.

38   United Press International, 23 August 1988; Associated Press, 'Hamburger restaurant chain hit by another bomb', 24 August 1988.

39   BBC, 'Johannesburg radio says revolutionaries were the election losers', *Summary of World Broadcasts*, 29 October 1988, based on text of commentary on Johannesburg home service on 28 October 1988; *World Insurance Report*, 'S. Africa: Huge increase in pol. riot claims', 11 November 1988; G. Black, 'Nut 'n But', *Nation*, 21 November 1988.

40   G. Black, 'Nut 'n But', *Nation*, 21 November 1988.

41   D. Niddrie, 'ANC increases attacks on civilian targets', *Globe & Mail* (Canada), 24 September 1988.

42   J. Bierman & C. Erasmus, 'Pretoria's gamble', *Maclean's*, 7 November 1988.

43   Ibid.

44   BBC, 'ANC radio says low turnout in S African elections shows rejection of apartheid',
      Summary of World Broadcasts, 31 October 1988, based on the text of a commentary
      on Radio Freedom, 27 October 1988.

45   L. Schuster, 'In South Africa: A tale of two reformers', *Christian Science Monitor*
      (Boston), 23 November 1988.

46   BBC, 'ANC leaders' annual statement reviews achievements of past decade and calls
      for offensive against political structures of apartheid', *Summary of World Broadcasts*,
      12 January 1989, excerpts from first part of recorded annual statement by ANC leader
      Oliver Tambo broadcast by Radio Freedom, 9 January 1989.

47   IPS-Inter Press Service, 'South Africa: Govt announces "National Forum" for urban
      blacks', 18 January 1989.

48   H. Barrell, interview with Bill Anderson, 8 April 1991, WHP, Karis-Gerhart Collection,
      folder 1, pp. 21–22, 29.

Chapter 5

1   Thorn, H., *Anti-apartheid and the Emergence of a Global Civil Society* (Palgrave
      Macmillan, Basingstoke, 2006).

2   For background on the AAM, see R. Fieldhouse, *Anti-apartheid: A History of the
      Movement in Britain* (Merlin, London, 2005).

3   W. Soyinka, 'Views from a palette of the cultural window', in X. Mangcu (ed.), *The
      Meaning of Mandela: A Literary and Intellectual Celebration* (HSRC Press, Cape
      Town, 2006).

4   R. First, *No Easy Walk to Freedom: Articles, Speeches, and Trial Addresses of
      Nelson Mandela* (Heinemann, London, 1965); IDAF (International Defence and Aid
      Fund), *Nelson Mandela: The Struggle Is My Life* (IDAF, London, 1978); M. Benson,
      Nelson Mandela (Penguin, Harmondsworth, 1986); F. Meer, *Higher than Hope:
      The Authorised Biography of Nelson Mandela* (Penguin, Johannesburg, 1988);
      N. Mandela, *Long Walk to Freedom: The Autobiography of Nelson Mandela*
      (Abacus, London, 1994); M. Meredith, *Nelson Mandela: A Biography* (Hamish
      Hamilton, London, 1997); A. Sampson, *Mandela: The Authorised Biography* (Harper
      Collins, London, 1999); T. Lodge, *Mandela: A Critical Life* (Oxford University Press,
      Oxford, 2006); M. Maharaj & A. Kathrada (eds), *Mandela: The Authorised Portrait*
      (Bloomsbury, London, 2006).

5   'Committee minutes and papers, various minutes, 28 October 1963–2 July 1964', Rhodes
      House, Oxford University, Archive of the AAM1778 (hereafter MSSAAM will indicate
      this archive); 'Newsletters and press releases, including the World Committee', 9 January
      1963 and *Report from Prison*, 22 November 1963, MSSAAM1779; 'Transcribed oral
      collection', 'Hilda Bernstein interview with Abdul Minty', pp. 163–90 and 'Telephone
      interview with Lorna Levy', 5 December 2004, University of the Western Cape,
      Mayibuye Archive.

6   'National Committee (NC) minutes, 1960–81', MSSAAM43; 'Committee minutes and
      papers, various minutes, 14 September 1964–25 March 1970', MSSAAM1778; Mary

Benson, 'Speech to UN' and 'telephone interview with Lorna Levy', Rhodes House, Oxford University, Africa Bureau (MSSAfr)1681, box 188, file 3, item 1; J. Johns & R. Hunt Davis (eds), *Mandela, Tambo, and the African National Congress: The Struggle against Apartheid, 1948–1990* (Oxford University Press, Oxford, 1991), pp. 141–42.

7   Alan Brooks at Mandela Witness workshop, Oxford, 1 May 1999.

8   Sampson, 1999, p. 259.

9   First, 1965; IDAF, 1978.

10 Benson, 1986; Meer, 1988.

11 For Mandela's awards, see <http://www.anc.org.za/ancdocs/history/mandela/awards/>, accessed 7 November 2006.

12 'Correspondence/papers OAU, 1971–93', 'Free Mandela Campaign memories', no author, MSSAAM1362.

13 Ibid.; UN press release, 17 August 1973; *Anti-Apartheid News*, April 1973; D. Foster, D. Davis & D. Sandler, *Detention and Torture in South Africa* (James Currey, London & Claremont, 1989), p. 84. The six men on trial were A. Moumbaris, T. T. Cholo, M. J. Mpanza, P. A. Mtembu, G. S. Sijaka and J. W. Hosey; the conference, in Geneva, was organised by the Workers' Group of the ILO Governing Body with the UN Special Committee.

14 'SATIS minutes, 1974–1980', 8 February 1974, MSSAAM1795; 'General correspondence, 1973–80', 'AAM general letter', 4 October 1973, and *Sechaba*, 'South Africa: The imprisoned society', 1974, MSSAAM1802.

15 Email correspondence with Howard Smith, 25 October 2004.

16 Mike Terry at Mandela Witness workshop.

17 Telephone interview with David Hemson, 11 November 2004.

18 S. Ellis & T. Sechaba, *Comrades against Apartheid: The ANC and South African Communist Party in Exile* (James Currey, London, 1992), pp. 141–43.

19 Sampson, 1999, pp. 317–18.

20 Terry at Mandela Witness workshop.

21 S. F. McDonald, 'The black community', in R. E. Bissell & C. A. Crocker (eds), *South Africa in the 1980s* (Westview Press, Boulder, 1979), p. 34.

22 Sampson, 1999, p. 314.

23 Mandela, 1994, pp. 602–3; A. Sparks, *Tomorrow Is Another Country. The Inside Story of South Africa's Negotiated Revolution* (Struik, Sandton, 1994), pp. 61–87; R. Harvey, *The Fall of Apartheid* (Palgrave Macmillan, Basingstoke, 2001), pp. 111–16; Interviews with: Mac Maharaj, 5 January 2005; Abdul Minty, 10 January 2005; Frene Ginwala, by telephone, 13 January 2005; Ismail Ayob, 28 October 2004.

24 AAM, *AAM Annual Report 1979–80*, MSSAAM13.

25 Interview with Gerald Kraak, 14 January 2004.

26 Interview with Maharaj.

27 P. O'Malley, *Shades of Difference: Mac Maharaj and the Struggle for South Africa* (Viking Penguin, New York, 2007), pp. 216–17.

28   'Correspondence/papers OAU, 1971–93', 'Free Mandela Campaign memories', no author, MSSAAM1362; Terry at Mandela Witness workshop; 'NC minutes, 1960–81', 1 July 1978, MSSAAM43; O'Malley, 2007, p. 214; A. Kathrada, *Memoirs* (Struik/Zebra, Cape Town, 2004), pp. 265–66; Mandela, 1994, pp. 567–72.

29   'Nelson Mandela's 60ᵗʰ birthday', MSSAAM1908.

30   W. Mandela & A. Benjamin (eds), *Part of My Soul* (Penguin, Harmondsworth, 1985); A. du Preez Bezdrob, *Winnie Mandela: A Life* (Struik, Cape Town, 2003); N. Harrison, *Winnie Mandela: Mother of a Nation* (Victor Gollancz, London, 1985).

31   'Nelson Mandela's 60th birthday', MSSAAM1908; AAM, *AAM Annual Report 1979–80*, MSSAAM13.

32   R. Nixon, 'Mandela, messianism and the media', *Transition*, 51 (1991), pp. 42–55.

33   'Executive Committee (EC) minutes, 1978–85', 18 June 1980, MSSAAM68; 'Nelson Mandela's 60th birthday', MSSAAM1908; 'Mandela Campaign, 1980–82', MSSAAM1909; Terry at Mandela Witness workshop.

34   *Sunday Post*, 'South Africa's black spokesmen welcome convention call, but say first "Free Mandela"', 9 March 1980.

35   Ibid.

36   Mandela, 1994, p. 602; Sampson, 1999, p. 319.

37   *Sunday Post*, 16 March 1980.

38   *Sunday Post*, 23 March 1980.

39   *Sunday Post*, 30 March 1980.

40   *Sunday Post*, 6 April 1980; 13 April 1980; 20 April 1980; 11 May 1980.

41   *Sunday Post*, 1 June 1980.

42   J. Allen, *Rabble-rouser for Peace: The Authorised Biography of Desmond Tutu* (Rider, London, 2006), pp. 255–58, 182–83.

43   'Appeals for Mandela's release', Mayibuye Archive, Brian Bunting (MCH07), box 125.2.5.3.1.

44   M. Thatcher, *The Downing Street Years* (Harper Collins, London, 1993).

45   'NC minutes, 1960–81', 8 July 1980, MSSAAM43.

46   'Mandela Campaign, 1980–82', MSSAAM1909.

47   Ibid.; correspondence with Mike Terry; interview with Minty.

48   Mandela, 1994, pp. 607–12; Sampson, 1999, pp. 324–26; Mandela & Benjamin, 1985, p. 113; E. Sisulu, *Walter and Albertina Sisulu: In Our Lifetime* (David Philip, Cape Town, 2002), pp. 283–85; F. Buntman, *Robben Island and Prisoner Resistance to Apartheid* (Cambridge University Press, Cambridge, 2003).

49   H. Masekela & D. Michael Cheers, *Still Grazing: The Musical Journey of Hugh Masekela* (Crown, New York, 2004), p. 330.

50   AAM, *AAM Annual Report 1982–83*, MSSAAM13; 'Mandela Campaign, 1983', MSSAAM1910; 'African Sounds Festival, July 1983', MSSAAM1913; 'Nelson Mandela's 65th birthday', MSSAAM1914; South African Democracy Education Trust (SADET) interview with Ruth Mompati, 15 August 2001.

51   AAM, *AAM Annual Report 1983–84*, MSSAAM13; selection of enquiries in response
      to special AKA single, MSSAAM1916.
52   AAM, *AAM Annual Report 1983–84*, MSSAAM13; Thatcher, 1993, pp. 514–15.
53   'NC minutes, 1982–94', 28 February 1985, MSSAAM44; Mandela, 1994, pp. 620–21;
      Sparks, 1994, pp. 48–51.
54   R. Denniston, *Trevor Huddleston: A Life* (Macmillan, London, 1999), pp. 153–84;
      P. McGrandle, *Trevor Huddleston: Turbulent Priest* (Continuum, London & New York,
      2004), pp. 180–87.
55   AAM, *AAM Annual Report 1984–85*, MSSAAM13; 'PM 1967–88', 19 February 1985,
      'Letter from Thatcher', MSSAAM779.
56   P. Waldmeir, *Anatomy of a Miracle* (Penguin, London & New York, 1997), pp. 90–101;
      Mandela, 1994, pp. 624–29.
57   Waldmeir, 1997, pp. 90–101; Mandela, 1994, pp. 636–39.
58   Commonwealth EPG (Eminent Persons Group), *Mission to South Africa: The
      Commonwealth Report. The Findings of the Commonwealth Eminent Persons
      Group on Southern Africa* (Penguin, Harmondsworth, 1986), p. 73; E. Anyaoku,
      The Inside Story of the Modern Commonwealth (Evans Brothers, London, 2004),
      pp. 89–103; Thatcher, 1993, pp. 516–19; R. Sanders (ed.), *Inseparable Humanity: An
      Anthology of Reflections of Shridath Ramphal* (Hansib, London, 1988), pp. 231–37.
59   'Articles: Free Mandela', SA History Archive, University Witwatersrand (hereafter
      SAHA), A2094/Ab (E. S. Reddy).
60   AAM, *Annual Report 1987–88*, MSSAAM13: AAM; 'Nelson Mandela Freedom at 70
      (NMF) general correspondence 1987–5/1988', MSSAAM1920; 'NMF staff meetings and
      reports', MSSAAM1922; 'NMF press releases', MSSAAM1923; interview with Kraak.
61   J. Carlson, *No Neutral Ground* (Quartet Books, London, 1977).
62   AAM, *AAM Annual Report 1987–88*, MSSAAM13.
63   'NMF general correspondence 1987–5/1988', MSSAAM1920; 'NMF media and
      merchandise', MSSAAM1927; 'NMF birthday tribute concert', MSSAAM1929;
      'EC minutes, 1986–95', 7 May 1988, MSSAAM69.
64   'Gallup poll', MSSAAM1932.
65   'NMF birthday tribute concert: letters', 23 October 1987; 9 November 1987;
      11 November 1987, MSSAAM1929.
66   Tony Hollingsworth at Mandela Witness workshop.
67   AAM, *AAM Annual Report 1987–88*, MSSAAM13.
68   Tony Hollingsworth at Mandela Witness workshop.
69   'NMF birthday tribute concert: Statement released by the Department of Foreign
      Affairs, Pretoria', 8 June 1988, MSSAAM1929.
70   AAM, *AAM Annual Report 1987–88*, MSSAAM13; 'NMF birthday tribute concert',
      MSSAAM1929.
71   Masekela & Cheers, 2004.
72   AAM, *AAM Annual Report 1987–88*, MSSAAM13; 'NMF press releases',
      MSSAAM1923; 'Circular letters', MSSAAM1924.

73   *Uncut*, 'Live Aid', 17 October 2004.

74   'NMF staff meetings and reports', MSSAAM1922; 'Circular letters', MSSAAM1924; 'NMF birthday tribute concert', MSSAAM1929.

75   AAM, *AAM Annual Report 1987–88*, MSSAAM13; 'NC minutes, 1982–94', 23 July 1988, MSSAAM44; 'EC minutes, 1986–95', 21 June 1988, MSSAAM69.

76   These conflicts, as well as the AAM's lack of openness to debate and alternative anti-apartheid views, are discussed in more detail in G. L. Klein, 'The Anti-Apartheid Movement (AAM) in Britain and support for the African National Congress (ANC), 1976–1990', DPhil thesis, University of Oxford, 2007.

77   'NMF birthday tribute concert', MSSAAM1929.

78   K. O'Neill (director), *The Nelson Mandela 70th Birthday Concert*, DVD (London, 1988).

79   'Correspondence with Laister Dickson Ltd', MSSAAM1925; 'NMF birthday tribute concert, press cuttings', MSSAAM1930.

80   AAM, *AAM Annual Report 1987–88*, MSSAAM13.

81   'Mandela Freedom March', MSSAAM1934; Denniston, 1999, pp. 178–81.

82   'Mandela Freedom March: Memo to Mike Terry/Alan Brooks', MSSAAM1934.

83   AAM, *AAM Annual Report 1987–88*, MSSAAM13; 'Mandela Freedom March', MSSAAM1934; 'Mandela Freedom March', MSSAAM1935.

84   'Press release', 6 July 1988, Luthuli House Collection, Johannesburg, ANC/UK/Ireland Mission: AAM, series VII, 'Statements', box 16, folder 1.

85   AAM, *AAM Annual Report 1987–88*, MSSAAM13; 'Hyde Park Rally', MSSAAM1933; 'EC minutes, 1986–95', 7 May 1988, MSSAAM69.

86   'Mandela Freedom March', MSSAAM1934.

87   'Hyde Park Rally', MSSAAM1933.

88   Ibid.

89   AAM, *Annual Report 1987–88*, MSSAAM13; 'Mandela Freedom March', MSSAAM1934; Fieldhouse, 2005, pp. 432–34.

90   'Hyde Park Rally', correspondence with Smith, 18 July 1988, internal letter, 16 May 1988, MSSAAM1933.

91   AAM, *AAM Annual Report 1987–88*, MSSAAM13.

92   Mandela, 1994, pp. 640–47; Waldmeir, 1997, pp. 100–5.

93   'Emergency advertisement', MSSAAM1936; 'Emergency petitions', MSSAAM1937.

94   'Circular letters', MSSAAM1924; 'Preparations for Mandela's release', MSSAAAM1939; Meer, 1988, pp. 318–19.

95   Mandela, 1994, pp. 649–61; Waldmeir, 1997, pp. 104–6.

96   'Nelson Mandela International Reception Committee' (NMIRC), MSSAAM1942; A. Butler, *Cyril Ramaphosa* (Johannesburg, Jacana, 2007).

97   'International support, NMIRC', SAHA, AL2457, T11; 'Nelson Mandela National Reception Committee', MSSAAM1943.

98   Mandela, 1994, pp. 666–78; Waldmeir, 1997, pp. 142–45, 156–60.

99   'Mandela's release, January–March 1990: Copy of call circulated to AAM members', MSSAAM1941.

100   Lodge, 2006, pp. 216–21.

101   S. Ngalwa, 'Mandela boost for ANC', *Pretoria News*, 28 July 2008.

Chapter 6

1   Central Statistical Service, *Population Census, Report No. 02-85-01: Geographical Distribution with a Review for 1960–1985* (Government Printer, Pretoria, 1986).

2   SPP (Surplus Peoples Project)), *Forced Removals*, vol. 4, *Natal* (SPP, Cape Town, 1983).

3   Sosibo's claim to be founder of the WECOP was disputed by two other members of the organisation. They told AFRA that WECOP was founded by a local priest in the area, and Sosibo became a chairperson of WECOP when the priest was transferred to Durban (AFRA field report, Weenen, 22 February 1990, AFRA Weenen files [hereafter AWF], AFRA Resource Centre, Pietermaritzburg).

4   Johannes Sosibo, 'The Weenen farm evictions: Sosibo tells the story', ca 1988, AWF; J. M. Sosibo, 'Mngwenya report, 1982 (S.E. Weenen)', p. 1, AWF.

5   From 1979 he began to be quoted in many local newspapers, e.g. see Tim Muil, 'Resentment of black workers in Weenen', *Natal Mercury*, 12 September 1979; Khaba Mkhize, 'Weenen families kicked out', *Echo*, 25 September 1980.

6   J. M. Sosibo, 'As I see it', p. 1, AWF.

7   Weenen Community Project, proposed constitution, 1983, AWF.

8   Sosibo's handwritten essays are currently filed at the AFRA Resource Centre in Pietermaritzburg.

9   Ravan Press declined to publish one of his essays on the grounds that it only talked about one particular locality, Weenen, and one particular ethnic group, the Zulu ('Ravan Press to Sosibo', 20 July 1982, AWF).

10   'Sosibo to Weenen commissioner', 22 September 1981, KwaZulu-Natal Archives, Pietermaritzburg Archives Repository (hereafter NAB: DDA), Pietermaritzburg, vol. 772 N1/15/4.

11   'Minutes, quarterly meeting', 24 September 1981, NAB: DDA, vol. 772 N1/15/4.

12   'Minutes of TBDA', 11 November 1986, AWF.

13   TBDA, *Report on Eviction of Farm Labourers*, January 1987, AWF.

14   'Peter Brown, AFRA, to Viljoen, TBDA', 19 October 1987, PC16/3/5, Alan Paton Centre (hereafter APC), University of KwaZulu-Natal, Pietermaritzburg.

15   'G. B. D. McIntosh to Sosibo', 15 March 1988, AWF; Viljoen, 'TBDA to the editor, *Natal Mercury*', 20 April 1988, AWF; AFRA, *Annual Report 1988–89*, p. 15, PC126/1/3/1/1. APC.

16   AFRA, *Report on Meeting between NPA and Weenen Farm Dwellers*, 13 June 1988, AWF; AFRA, *Annual Report, 1988–89*, p. 15, PC126/1/3/1/1, APC.

17   *Natal Witness*, 24 November 1988.

18   AFRA, 'Press release: Weenen farm evictions', 5 June 1989, AWF; M. Dyer, 'AFRA to the editor, *Natal Witness*', 21 June 1989; 'Statement taken from M. N. Njoko, Weenen emergency camp, 25 July 1989', AWF; *Daily News*, 26 July 1989; *Sowetan*, 27 July 1989.

19   Sosibo, 'The Weenen farm evictions'.

20   'Minutes, AFRA committee', 25 February 1987, AWF; 'Minutes, AFRA legal sub-committee', 19 February 1988, PC16/3/5, APC; AFRA, *Weenen: Report to Legal Sub-committee*, 7 April 1988, AWF.

21   Sosibo, 'WECOP to chairman, AFRA', 23 September 1989, AWF.

22   Brown, 'AFRA to Zungu, WECOP', 31 October 1989, AWF.

23   AFRA, fieldtrip note, 28 April 1990, AWF.

24   AFRA, fieldtrip notes, 18 July 1990; 24 July 1990; 4 August 1990, AWF.

25   AFRA, fieldtrip note, 9 May 1990, AWF.

26   AFRA, fieldtrip notes, 22 February 1990; 22 May 1990; 24 July 1990; 27 January 1991, AWF.

27   'Sosibo to comrades Lekota and Harry Gwala', n.d. [1990?], AWF; 'Sosibo to "comrades"', September 1990, AWF.

28   'AFRA to Sosibo', 19 October 1990, AWF.

29   'Sosibo to AFRA', 7 March 1991, AWF; 'AFRA to Sosibo', 22 March 1991, AWF; AFRA, fieldtrip notes, 23 March 1991; 1 April 1991, AWF.

30   'Creina Alcock to CAP directors', 5 February 1990, 5 November 1990, APC; 'Creina Alcock to Peter Brown', 30 October 1991, APC; CAP, *Trustees' Report*, 28 February 1992, PC16/1/4/2, APC.

31   'Proposals, Weenen communities', November 1991, AWF.

32   'Minutes, Weenen meeting (NPA)', 12 December 1991, AWF; 'Minutes, Weenen work group (NPA)', 27 February 1992, AWF; 'Minutes, CAP management committee', 22 February 1992, 20 June 1992, PC16/1/4/2, APC; *CAP Newsletter*, January 1993, pp. 1–3, PC16/1/4/3, APC.

33   NPA, *Weenen Development Strategy*, September 1989, Thuthuka-Mngwenya files (old file number KNA/4/4/2; new file number DC23/KZ234/160), Department of Land Affairs Registry (hereafter DLA: TMF), Ladysmith; NPA, *Weenen: Expansion Proposals for Entokozweni*, October 1990, AWF. Both documents proposed the same six scenarios, but used a different alphabetical order. Here I use the one in the 1989 document.

34   'Sosibo to NPA', 20 April 1992; 30 June 1992, AWF.

35   'Graham McIntosh to AFRA', 15 May 1992, AWF.

36   *CAP Newsletter*, January 1993, pp. 4–8, PC16/1/4/3, ACP; 'Minutes, CAP management committee', 23 January 1993, pp. 1–3, PC16/1/4/3, ACP.

37   'NPA to Department of Regional and Land Affairs', 23 September 1993, DLA: TMF.

38   'Minutes, meeting between V. A. Volker and KwaNobamba', 19 May 1993, DLA: TMF; 'Minutes, Special Committee on Displacees', 4 June 1993, DLA: TMF.

39   According to the Act, the community had to bear 20 per cent of the purchase price of the farm, while the government would pay the remaining 80 per cent. Of the

community's 20 per cent share of the purchase price, its members were required to raise at least 5 per cent as an initial deposit at the time of purchase and would pay the remaining 15 per cent to the government over a period of five years ('Minutes, Special Committee on Displacees', 29 July 1993, DLA: TMF).

40   'Minutes, Special Committee on Displacees', 5 August 1993, DLA: TMF.

41   'Minutes, meeting of the community of the green tent town', 24 August 1993, DLA: TMF.

42   Based on the carrying capacity of a total of 484 LSUs (large stock units) and 4–6 LSUs per family, the department estimated that the three farms, in total about 3,000 hectares, could support between 146 and 161 families (D. R. Twiddy & W. Urquhart, *Cedara Reports*, no. N/A/93/40, no. N/A/93/41 and no. N/A/93/42, DLA: TMF).

43   'Graham McIntosh to NPA', 29 August 1993, AWF.

44   'Minutes, meeting regarding purchase of land for evictees', 16 September 1993, DLA: TMF.

45   *Natal Witness*, 13 April 1993; *Daily News*, 15 April 1993; Harry Wells, 'The origin and spread of private wildlife conservancies and neighbour relations in South Africa, in a historical context of wildlife utilisation in southern Africa', paper presented to the conference on African Environments, Past and Present, St Antony's College, Oxford, UK, 5–8 July 1999, pp. 25–26; Anne Vaughn & Peter Sapsford, *A Report on the Proposed Weenen Nature Reserve Land Swop*, mimeo, undated, AWF.

46   Interview with Conrad Rottcher, 19 August 2004, Weenen.

47   NPA, 'Weenen: Physical planning's evaluation of Woodford, Alma, Weltevreden, and North Kolombe, for settlement purposes in terms of the Act 126 of 1993', pp. 1–4, undated [April 1994?], DLA: TMF.

48   Trust deed: Thuthuka Mngwenya Community Trust, signed on 1 June 1994, DLA: TMF.

49   'Minutes, CAP management committee', 21 May 1994, p. 1, PC16/1/4/3, APC.

50   'George Opperman to DLA', 3 February 1995, DLA: TMF.

51   Interviews with Rauri Alcock, 23 August 2004, Weenen; Mphephethe Masondo, 18 August 2004, Weenen; Lindelani Sibisi, 23 August 2004, Weenen.

52   *Natal Witness*, 28 September 1994.

53   CAP, *Report on Land Claims Programme*, August 1995, p. 2, PC16/1/4/3, APC.

54   DLA, 'Notes, meeting with committees of Weenen and Muden', 27 September 1994, AWF.

55   Ibid.

56   *Natal Witness*, 28 September 1994.

57   *Star*, 13 October 1994.

58   Ibid.

59   KZN Provincial Administration, 'Submission to the land reform pilot project coordinating committee: The Estcourt/Weenen/Msinga magisterial districts', October 1994, pp. 4, 21–23, DLA: TMF.

60   'Minutes, CAP management committee', 12 November 1994, pp. 1–2, PC16/1/4/3, APC.

61   CAP, *Report on Land Claims Programme*, August 1995, p. 3, PC16/1/4/3, APC.

62 'Minutes, CAP management committee', 23 January 1995, pp. 2–5, PC16/1/4/3, APC; 'Jotham Myaka to Minister Hanekom', 17 January 1995, DLA: TMF.
63 'Darryl Twiddy to DLA', 11 January 1995, DLA: TMF.
64 'Draft minutes, Weenen meeting with Minister Hanekom', 6 October 1994; 'Draft minutes', Weenen committee, 27 October 1994, AWF.
65 DLA, handwritten memo, 17 November 1994, DLA: TMF; 'Minutes, meeting with Nyawo's sub-committee', 8 December 1994, DLA: TMF.
66 'Minutes, meeting between DLA, a seller and Weenen community', 2 May 1995, DLA: TMF. Eventually the DLA decided to incorporate the Thuthuka Mngwenya purchase into the pilot programme by mid-1995 (Harold Riversage, *Detailed Report on the Mngwenya Farm Purchases*, 14 August 1995, p. 1, DLA: TMF).
67 'Thuthuka Mngwenya Community Trust to DLA', 8 May 1995, DLA: TMF.
68 Harold Riversage, 'Meeting with Nyawo, Nkabinde and Manana', undated [August 1995?], DLA: TMF; Riversage, *Detailed Report*, pp. 3–5, DLA: TMF.
69 Riversage, *Detailed Report*, p. 3, DLA: TMF.
70 DLA memorandum: 'Designation of land for settlement purposes: Act 126 of 1993: Woodford, North Kolombe, Alma, Weltevreden in Weenen, KZN', 5 December 1995, DLA: TMF.
71 Riversage, *Detailed Report*, p. 4; 'Volsum, Chetty and Laz to DLA', 21 June 1995, 2 October 1995, DLA: TMF; 'DLA pilot office to Maree and Pace', 23 October 1995, DLA: TMF.
72 Riversage, *Detailed Report*, pp. 5–6; Riversage, 'Phone call discussion with McIntosh', 26 August 1995, DLA: TMF.
73 Harold Riversage, *Progress Report on the Thuthuka Mngwenya Project*, 4 April 1996; 'Provincial Land Reform Steering Committee to Nyawo', 26 April 1996, DLA: TMF; 'DLA to Nyawo', 7 June 1996, DLA: TMF.
74 Jonathan Clegg, 'Ukubuyisa isidumbu – "bring back the body": An examination into the ideology of vengeance in the Msinga and Mpofana rural locations, 1882–1944', in Philip Bonner (ed.), *Working Papers in South African Studies*, vol. 2 (Ravan Press, Johannesburg, 1981), pp. 186–87; Helen Bradford, *A Taste of Freedom: The ICU in Rural South Africa, 1920–1930* (Yale University Press, New Heaven, 1987), p. 194.
75 Interview with Sihle Mkhize, Pietermaritzburg, 2 May 2002.
76 Interview with Johannes Sosibo, Weenen, 6 November 2002.
77 Interview with Annah Nyawo, KwaNobamba, 16 January 2003.
78 Harold Riversage, 'Briefing on Mngwenya farm purchase', 11 March 1996, p. 7, DLA: TMF; interviews with Lisa del Grande, 26 November 2002, Pietermaritzburg; Rauri Alcock, 23 August 2004, Weenen; Jotham Myaka, 11 July 2002, Greytown.
79 Riversage, 'Briefing on Mngwenya', pp. 4–6.
80 Harold Riversage, 'Proposals, Mngwenya farm purchases', 2 May 1996, pp. 2–3, DLA: TMF.
81 'DLA pilot office to Nyawo', 27 June 1996, DLA: TMF.
82 Harold Riversage, 'Proposals, Magenta', p. 3, DLA: TMF.

83   Interviews with Jotham Myaka, 4 September 1998, Muden; Annah Nyawo, 16 January
      2003, KwaNobamba.

84   'DLA to Thuthuka Mngwenya Trust', 30 October 1998, DLA: TMF.

85   'O. Diack to S. Edwards, deputy master of High Court', 22 September 1999, DLA: TMF.

86   Interview with Johannes Sosibo, 19 August 2004, Weenen; 'Minutes, Thuthuka
      Mngwenya meeting', 30 May 2002, DLA: TMF.

87   I consulted the following files at the Ladysmith district office of the DLA: Ncunjane,
      Nomoya, KwaJeke, Nkaseni farms, and Blaauwkrantz farm-Mpungu CPA. Of these five
      projects, the KwaJeke project suffered the same tragic fate as the Thuthuka Mngwenya
      project when the boundary dispute between the Mthembu and the Mchunu groups
      emerged on the farm Blaauwkrantz after the land was transferred to the KwaJeke Trust
      (DLA, 'Status of KwaJeke project', undated [2000?], DLA: KwaJeke file; DLA, 'Minutes,
      KwaJeke project', 7 May 2000, DLA: KwaJeke file; 'DLA to WPDC', 22 May 2000,
      29 August 2000, 12 December 2000, DLA: KwaJeke file).

88   CAP, untitled document given to author by Rauri Alcock, 2002.

89   Interviews with Rauri Alcock, 23 August 2004, Weenen; Graham Oates, 20 August 2004,
      Estcourt.

90   'Minutes, Nkaseni meeting', 20 December 2000, DLA: Nkaseni farms file.

91   Interviews with Zanzile Dladla, Tugela Estates, 18 August 2004; Lungisile Duma,
      Nomoya, 18 August 2004.

92   Interview with Lindelani Sibisi, WPDC, Weenen, 23 August 2004.

93   Interviews with Joseph le Roux, Weenen, 19 August 2004; Thokozani Mkhize, Estcourt,
      20 August 2004.

94   Interviews with Johannes Sosibo, Weenen, 2 November 2002; Lisa del Grande,
      AFRA, Pietermaritzburg, 26 November 2002; Tom Malinga, Land Commission,
      Pietermaritzburg, 3 December 2002; Promise Makhaya and Mavis Shabalala, DLA,
      Ladysmith, 17 August 2004; Conrad Rottcher, Weenen, 19 August 2004; attendance at
      the Gongolo meeting, Weenen, 22 August 2004.

95   Jonny Steinberg, *Midlands* (Jonathan Ball, Johannesburg, 2002).

Chapter 7

1   P. Delius, *A Lion amongst the Cattle: Reconstruction and Resistance in the Northern
      Transvaal* (James Currey, Oxford, 1996); W. Beinart & C. Bundy, *Hidden Struggles in
      Rural South Africa: Politics and Popular Movements in Transkei and the Eastern
      Cape, 1890–1930* (James Currey, London, 1987).

2   C. J. de Wet, *Moving Together, Drifting Apart: Betterment Planning and
      Villagisation in a South African Homeland* (Wits University Press, Johannesburg,
      1995).

3   S. Marks, *The Ambiguities of Dependence in South Africa: Class, Nationalism and
      the State in 20th Century Natal* (Johns Hopkins University Press, Baltimore, 1986),
      p. 8; C. Murray, *Black Mountain: Land, Class and Power in the Eastern Orange Free
      State, 1880s–1980s* (Edinburgh University Press, Edinburgh, 1992).

4   This literature fits into a wider body of work that considers how national and ethnic
     identities were 'socially constructed' in Africa. See, for instance, L. Vail, *The Creation
     of Tribalism in Southern Africa* (James Currey, London, 1989); J. Lonsdale, 'The moral
     economy of Mau Mau: Wealth, poverty and civic virtue in Kikuyu political thought', in
     J. Lonsdale & B. Berman (eds), *Unhappy Valley: Conflict in Kenya and Africa* (James
     Currey, London, 1992); B. Berman, 'Ethnicity, patronage and the African state: The
     politics of uncivil nationalism', *African Affairs*, 97, 388 (1998), pp. 305–41.

5   Delius, 1996; I. van Kessell & B. Oomen, 'One chief, one vote: The revival of traditional
     authorities in post apartheid South Africa', *African Affairs*, 96 (1994), pp. 561–85;
     L. Ntsebeza, *Democracy Compromised: Chiefs and the Politics of Land in South
     Africa* (HSRC Press, Cape Town, 2006).

6   M. Mamdani, *Citizen and Subject: Contemporary Africa and the Legacy of Late
     Colonialism* (James Currey, London, 1996); T. Ranger, 'The invention of tradition
     revisited', in T. Ranger & O. Vaughn (eds), *Legitimacy and the State in 20th Century
     Africa* (Macmillan Press, Oxford, 1993).

7   For approaches that consider the mutually constitutive relationship between state
     and society, see J. Migdal, A. Kohli & V. Shue (eds), *State Power and Social Forces:
     Domination and Transformation in the Third World* (Cambridge, Cambridge
     University Press, 1994).

8   'Press statement by chief minister', 19 August 1964, Cape Town Archives, Chief
     Magistrate Transkei (CMT, to which reference will be made in subsequent notes),
     box 1841, file 42/17.

9   *Daily Dispatch*, 10 March 1964.

10   *Daily Dispatch*, 15 April 1964; *Debates of the National Assembly, Republic
     of Transkei (TNA)* (The Assembly, Umtata, 1978), p. 212; DAF (Department of
     Agricultural & Forestry), *Transkei Agricultural Development Study* (DAF, Umtata,
     1991), p. 91.

11   F. Hendricks, *The Pillars of Apartheid: Land Tenure, Rural Planning and the
     Chieftaincy* (Wicksell International, Stockholm, 1990), p. 135.

12   'Press statement by chief minister', 19 August 1964, CMT box 1841, file 42/17; *Debates
     of the Transkei Legislative Assembly, Republic of Transkei (TLA)* 1965, p. 187.

13   *TLA* 1965, p. 187; *Daily Dispatch*, 25 October 1983.

14   *TLA* 1972, p. 83.

15   DAF (Department of Agriculture & Forestry), *Annual Report, 1971–72*, p. 10.

16   *TLA* 1970, p. 282.

17   DAF, *Annual Report 1980–81*, p. 81; cf. *TLA* 1969, p. 188; *TLA* 1970, p. 179; *TLA*
     1972, p. 259; *TLA* 1973, p. 371; DAF, *Annual Report 1972–73*, p. 84; DAF, *Annual
     Report 1974–75*, p. 72.

18   *TLA* 1978, p. 165; DAF, 1991, p. 264; *Daily Dispatch*, 29 May 1985.

19   DAF, 1991, p. 209; *Daily Dispatch*, 20 June 1986.

20   Cf. R. Southall, *South Africa's Transkei: The Political Economy of an 'Independent'
     Bantustan* (Heinemann, London, 1982).

21 *TLA* 1984, p. 157.
22 'Letter from Hugh White to Professor G. M. Carter', 26 July 1963, University of Cape Town Archives, Cater-Karis Microfilm Collection, reel 17.
23 *TLA* 1971, p. 80.
24 *Daily Dispatch*, 23 October 1981.
25 *Daily Dispatch*, 27 April 1988.
26 *TLA* 1969, p. 199.
27 *TLA* 1971, p. 221.
28 *TLA* 1973, p. 216.
29 *TLA* 1975, p. 184.
30 T. J. Bembridge, *Problems of Agricultural Development in the Republic of Transkei: A Preliminary Summary*, research report for the Urban–Rural Workshop, Stellenbosch, 2–4 June, 1982, p. 45.
31 Department of Agriculture Ciskei, 'Agricultural extension', memo, Cape Town Archives, Commissioner General Transkei (KGT), box 112, file N1/3/2/6/T. This memo dealing with 'problems experienced by Bantu Extension Officers' was written in 1971.
32 *TLA* 1975, p. 240.
33 *TLA* 1975, p. 189.
34 *TLA* 1973, p. 226.
35 *TLA* 1969, p. 191; *TLA* 1970, p. 197.
36 *TLA* 1973, p. 216.
37 *TNA* 1981, p. 186; *TLA* 1972, p. 265.
38 *TNA* 1982, p. 155.
39 Hendricks, 1990; Mamdani, 1996.
40 *TLA* 1965, p. 198; *TLA* 1968, p. 143; *TLA* 1976, p. 126.
41 Office of the Auditor General, *Report of the Auditor General on the Appropriation and Miscellaneous Accounts and on the Accounts of Lower Authorities in the Area, 1966–67* (Ministry of the Interior, Umtata, 1967); *Report of the Auditor General, 1976–77*.
42 *TNA* 1978, p. 117.
43 *TLA* 1970, p. 181.
44 *TLA* 1975, p. 183.
45 *TLA* 1972, p. 424.
46 *TLA*, 1973, pp. 360–61.
47 'Letter from Bantu Affairs commissioner, Mqanduli, to the chief Bantu affairs commissioner', 8 September 1961, Cape Town Archives, Mqanduli Magistrate (hereafter 1MQL), box 6/1/103, file N11/1/2.
48 'Letter from Bantu affairs commissioner, Mqanduli, to the chief Bantu affairs commissioner', November 1962, Cape Town Archives, 1MQL, box 6/1/100, file N11/1/4; *TLA* 1973, *Report of the Public Accounts Committee*.
49 *TLA*, 1973, p. 360; *TLA* 1976, p. 121. The transcripts of the *Reports of the Public Accounts Committee*, which was a committee of the Transkei Legislature, were

recorded in the *TNA* and *TLA*. Sometimes these pages are numbered, other times they are not.

50   A. Spiegel, 'A trilogy of tyranny and tribulation: Village politics and administrative intervention in Matatiele during the early 1980s', *Journal of Contemporary African Studies*, 11, 2 (1992), pp. 31–54; J. Segar, *The Fruits of Apartheid: Experiencing 'Independence' in a Transkeian Village* (Anthropos, Bellville, 1989).
51   'Conference of Bantu Affairs Commissioners at Umtata on 9 and 10 March 1962', Cape Town Archives, 1MQL, box 6/1/103, file N11/1/2.
52   Hendricks, 1990.
53   Pretoria Archive, Department of Native Administration and Development, BAO 5/515, file 109/1294, *Report: Meeting of the Chiefs in the Thembu Region*, 26 May 1964.
54   *TLA* 1973, pp. 62, 223.
55   *TLA* 1972, p. 273; *TNA* 1982, p. 154.
56   *TLA* 1974, p. 196; DAF, *Annual Report 1974–75*, p. 3.
57   *TLA* 1976, *Report of the Public Accounts Committee*.
58   DAF, *Annual Report 1977–78*, p. 2.
59   *TLA* 1976, p. 52.
60   *TNA* 1978, p. 117.
61   'After 1975/6 … the level of budget support [from Pretoria] … declined in real terms' and Customs Union transfers remained flat too (DAF, 1991, p. 50).
62   *Rand Daily Mail*, 16 October 1979.
63   Ibid.
64   *TNA* 1980, p. 262.
65   *TNA* 1977, p. 67.
66   *Daily Dispatch*, 24 March 1977.
67   Republic of Transkei, *The Development Strategy, 1980–2000* (Republic of Transkei, Umtata, 1979), pp. 27–28.
68   *TNA* 1977, pp. 204, 357.
69   Hawkins Associates, *The Physical and Spatial Basis for Transkei's First Five Year Development Plan* (Hawkins Associates, Salisbury, October 1980), p. 109; *TNA* 1977, p. 69.
70   *Cape Times*, 24 March 1977.
71   DAF, 1991, pp. 9, 55; Bembridge, 1982, p. 19; W. Beinart, 'Agrarian history and reconstruction', in J. Lonsdale (ed.), *South Africa in Question* (James Currey, Oxford, 1988), p. 138.
72   *TNA* 1977, p. 309.
73   *TNA* 1977, p. 69; *TLA* 1970, *Report of the Public Accounts Committee*.
74   *Daily Dispatch*, 9 May 1974; the article referred to an incident that took place in 1973.
75   *TNA* 1977, p. 71.
76   *Daily Dispatch*, 7 August 1986.
77   *TNA* 1977, p. 330.
78   *TNA* 1977, p. 334.

79   *TNA* 1978, p. 117; *TNA* 1979, p. 147.

80   *Daily Dispatch*, 25 October 1989.

81   Cf. the series of annual reports on TRACOR in *Reports of the Auditor General on Transkei Agricultural Corporation*.

82   This is the thrust of the reports of research organisations such as Public Services Accountability Monitor (<http://www.psam.org.za>), as well as the tenacious reporting of newspapers such as the *Daily Dispatch*, <http://www.dispatch.co.za>.

83   On Tsolo College, see *Daily Dispatch* 16 August 1996; on the Magwa tea plantation, see T. Kepe, 'Magwa tea venture in South Africa: Politics, land and economics', *Social Dynamics*, 31, 1 (2005), pp. 261–79; on the Ncora irrigation scheme, see *Daily Dispatch*, 25 March 1995.

84   Cf. J. Peires, 'Traditional leaders in purgatory: Local government in Tsolo, Qumbu and Port Saint Johns, 1990–2000', *African Studies*, 59, 1 (2000), pp. 97–114.

85   R. Southall, *Making Government Work for Poor People in the Eastern Cape: A Report for the Department for International Development, UK*, 2001, Cory Library, pamphlet box 226.

86   *Daily Dispatch*, 20 April 1995.

87   *Daily Dispatch*, 2 July 1996.

88   *Daily Dispatch*, 23 May 1996.

89   Southall, *Making Government Work for Poor People: A Report for the Department for International Development, UK*, 2001, Cory Library, pamphlet box 226.

90   Ministry of Agriculture & Land Affairs, 'Agriculture policy in South Africa: A discussion document' (Pretoria, 1998).

91   Southall, *Making Government Work for Poor People: A Report for the Department for International Development, UK*, 2001, Cory Library, pamphlet box 226.

92   *Daily Dispatch*, 11 July 1996; 7 May 1998; 13 March 1999.

93   *Daily Dispatch*, 5 November 1998.

94   *Daily Dispatch*, 6 November 1996; 25 January 1997; 7 February 1997.

95   *Daily Dispatch*, 7 May 1997; 7 May 1998.

96   *Daily Dispatch*, 28 August 1997.

97   *Daily Dispatch*, 7 May 1997; 17 September 1997.

98   *Daily Dispatch*, 2 July 1996; 15 November 1996.

99   *Daily Dispatch*, 11 January 1997; 8 August 1999.

100 *Daily Dispatch*, 7 February 1997.

101 DALA (Department of Agriculture & Land Affairs), *Annual Report, 2001–2002* (DALA, Grahamstown, 2002), p. 40.

102 Interview with Mcebisi Magadla, East London, 31 October 2008.

103 DALA (Department of Agriculture & Land Affairs), *Annual Report, 2000–2001* (DALA, Grahamstown, 2001), p. 59.

104 Interviews with Kenny Jafta, Dutywa, 10 November 2008; Simphiwe Somdyola, East London, 18 November 2008.

105 Interview with Jafta. The proposed scheme was mentioned in the 'State of the province address' at the start of 2008, but neglected in 2009; cf. <http://www.polity.org.za/article/sa-balindlela-state-of-the-province-address-2008-02-15> and <http://www.polity.org.za/article/e-cape-sogoni-state-of-the-province-address-by-eastern-cape-premier-mbulelo-sogoni-13022009-2009-02-13>.

106 *Engineering News*, 12 October 2007.

107 William Beinart and Tim Gibbs, interviews with Dr Kassim Kasule, Lusikisiki, April 2008 and in Mbotyi village.

108 DALA, 2001, p. 59; *Daily Dispatch*, 20 March 1998.

109 Interview with Zoleka Capa, Flagstaff, 9 November 2008.

110 Interview Magadla. This theoretical point is made by Lonsdale, 1992.

111 *Daily Dispatch*, 4 June 1999.

112 DALA (Department of Agriculture & Land Affairs), *Strategic Plan 2006* (DALA, Grahamstown, 2006), p. 1.

113 Interview with Mashwaba Msizi, Bhisho, 17 November 2008.

114 Interview with Simphiwe Somdyola, East London, 18 November 2008.

115 DALA, 2006, p. 36.

116 Interviews with Mashwaba Msizi, Bhisho, 17 November 2008; John Allwood, King William's Town, 14 November 2008.

117 *Daily Dispatch*, 26 March 1999.

118 Hansard policy speech 2007–08 (Eastern Cape government, Bhisho, 2008), p. 17.

119 Most notably, the closed-down teacher training colleges; cf. South African Press Association, 15 April 2008.

Chapter 8

1 My thanks to Nicoli Nattrass for her many helpful comments on this article.

2 As cited in K. McDonald, *Global Movements: Action and Culture* (Blackwell, Malden, MA & Oxford, 2006), p. 70.

3 The show is known by its combined isiXhosa and English names, but for the sake of convenience, only the English name will be referred to throughout this chapter.

4 The SABC calculates its audience ratings based on Living Standards Measurements (LSMs). Members of LSM 1–3, representing the lowest income groups, are not measured as their purchasing power is regarded as negligible and they are not attractive to advertisers. As *Beat It!* is aimed at LSM 1–3, it is therefore difficult to determine the size of its audience. The most recent survey revealed that *Beat It!*'s audience from LSM 4 upwards exceeded a million viewers. The show's production staff infer from their audience targeting and from the burgeoning access to television in poor communities that the real viewership exceeds three million.

5 J. Lewis et al., 'Community Health Media Trust: The role of HIV/AIDS media and moving us into action', paper presented at the South African AIDS Conference, Durban, 5–8 June 2007, pp. 6–7.

6 Ibid., p. 8.

7   P. Rotha, S. Road & R. Griffin (eds), *Documentary Film: The Use of the Film Medium to Interpret Creatively and in Social Terms the Life of the People as It Exists in Reality* (Faber & Faber, London, 1968), p. 75.

8   A. Ek, 'Perilous silence and discriminatory visibility: On absent and present representations of HIV-positive individuals in the South African press, 1998–2003', in M. Foller & H. Thorn (eds), *No Name Fever: AIDS in the Age of Globalization* (Studentlitteratur, Lund, 2005), p. 284.

9   W. Benn, as cited in T. Burns, 'The organization of public opinion', in J. Curran, M. Gurevitch & J. Woollacott (eds), *Mass Communication and Society*, 2nd ed. (Arnold, London, 1984), p. 69.

10   D. McQuail, 'The influence and effects of mass media', in J. Curran, M. Gurevitch & J. Woollacott (eds), *Mass Communication and Society*, 2nd ed. (Arnold, London, 1984), pp. 90–91; S. Hall, 'Culture, the media and the 'ideological effect', in ibid., pp. 341–42.

11   A. Melucci, *Challenging Codes: Collective Action in the Information Age* (Cambridge University Press, Cambridge, 1996), p. 8.

12   Take, for example, the slogan of the women's movement: 'Equality now', further underscored by the acronym for their leading body, NOW (National Association of Women), or the ACT UP slogan 'SILENCE = DEATH', which confronted its members with the stark choice to either join the movement and take action, or to perish.

13   McDonald, 2006, p. 74.

14   Melucci, 1996, pp. 2, 67.

15   The Community Health Media Trust was renamed the Community Media Trust in 2009.

16   Membership of the support group was fluid; however, there were certain long-standing members, particularly in the later series, including Vuyani Jacobs, Busisiwe Maqungo and Lihle Dlamini.

17   D. Gould, '"Rock the boat, don't rock the boat, baby": Ambivalence and the emergence of militant AIDS activism', in J. Goodwin, J. Jasper & F. Polletta (eds), *Passionate Politics: Emotions and Social Movements* (University of Chicago Press, Chicago, 2001), p. 143.

18   Ibid., p. 135.

19   S. Epstein, 'AIDS activism and state policies in the United States', in M. Foller & H. Thorn, *No Name Fever: AIDS in the Age of Globalization* (Studentlitteratur, Lund, 2005), p. 176.

20   B. R. Rich, as cited in B. Horrigan, 'Notes on AIDS and its combatants: An appreciation', in M. Renov (ed.), *Theorizing Documentary* (Routledge, New York, 1993), p. 168; B. Shepard & R. Hayduk, 'Media and the new social movements', in B. H. Shephard & R. Hayduk (eds), *From ACT UP to the WTO: Urban Protest and Community Building in the Era of Globalization* (Verso, London & New York, 2002), pp. 261–63.

21   Interview with Jack Lewis, Cape Town, 23 May 2007.

22   J. Iliffe, *The African AIDS Epidemic: A History* (Double Storey, Cape Town, 2006), pp. 144–45. This working group is known as the Treatment Action Group, and an

important exchange has built up between the two organisations. Treatment Action Group members also made guest appearances on *Beat It!*

23 M. Heywood, 'Preventing mother-to-child-HIV transmission in South Africa: Background, strategies and outcomes of the Treatment Action Campaign case against the minister of health', *South African Journal on Human Rights*, 19 (2003), p. 278.

24 Idol Productions & J. Lewis (producer), *Beat It!* series 2000, episode 3.

25 *Beat It!* series 2000, episode 7.

26 Ibid.

27 Ibid.

28 Ibid.

29 Ibid.

30 Ibid.

31 M. Feldman, cited in R. Shilts, *And the Band Played On: People, Politics and AIDS Epidemic* (St Martin's Press, New York, 1987), p. 286.

32 Epstein, 2005, p. 177.

33 *Beat It!* series 2005, episode 15.

34 Cited in E. Cameron, *Witness to AIDS* (Tafelberg, Cape Town, 2005), p. 137.

35 This was confirmed in numerous interviews with the production staff of *Beat It!* The commissioning editor at the SABC instructed Community Health Media Trust production staff to either change content that was deemed too critical of government or face the channel's refusal to air episodes.

36 *Beat It!* series 2005, episode 12.

37 Ibid. See N. Nattrass, *Mortal Combat: AIDS Denialism and the Struggle for Antiretrovirals in South Africa* (University of KwaZulu-Natal Press, Scottsville, 2007), for an example of Mseleku's obfuscation regarding HIV. In kowtowing to pressure from the Department of Health, in 2003 Mseleku misrepresented South Africa's growing mortality rates by attributing them to a TB epidemic rather than an AIDS epidemic (ibid., p. 140). Mseleku also publicly supported traditional remedies for HIV that had not been subjected to the rigorous drug testing procedures of the South African medical authorities (ibid., p. 183).

38 R. Spottiswoode (director), *And the Band Played On: Politics, People and the AIDS Epidemic* (USA, 1993).

39 An AIDS-defining opportunistic infection.

40 R. Lyon, as cited in Shilts, 1987, p. 360.

41 Epstein, 2005, p. 177.

42 H. Schneider, 'On the fault-lines: The politics of AIDS policy in contemporary South Africa', in *African Studies*, 61, 1 (2002), p. 155. The term 'health citizen' derives from Robins' article on the emergence of new subjectivities in the South African treatment access movement: S. Robins, '"Long live Zackie, long live": AIDS activism, science and citizenship after apartheid', *Journal of Southern African Studies*, 30, 3 (2004), pp. 651–72.

43 P. A. Treichler, *How to Have Theory in an Epidemic: Cultural Chronicles of AIDS* (Duke University Press, Durham, 1999), p. 129.
44 V.-K. Nguyen, 'Antiretroviral globalism, biopolitics, and therapeutic citizenship', in A. Ong & S. Collier (eds), *Global Assemblages: Technology, Politics and Ethics as Anthropological Problems* (Blackwell, Malden, MA, 2005), pp. 125–26.
45 A triazole antifungal drug patented by Pfizer, and the first-line treatment for oral thrush (one of the most common opportunistic infections in HIV-positive people).
46 *Beat It!* series 2003, episode 8.
47 Shilts, 1987, p. 564.
48 *Beat It!* series 2005, episode 13.
49 A. de Waal, *AIDS and Power: Why There Is No Political Crisis – Yet* (David Philip, Cape Town, 2006), p. 36.
50 Interview with Michael Rautenbach, Cape Town, 24 April 2007.
51 Interview with Vuyani Jacobs, Cape Town, 22 March 2007.
52 *Beat It!* series 2004, episode 4.
53 *Beat It!* series 2004, episode 8.
54 *Beat It!* series 2002, episode 12.
55 Z. Achmat as cited in De Waal, 2006, p. 37.
56 E. Sawyer, 'An ACT UP founder "acts up" for Africa's access to AIDS', in B. Shepard & R Hayduk, *From ACT UP to the WTO: Urban Protest and Community Building in the Era of Globalization* (Verso, London & New York, 2002), p. 92; Epstein, 2005, p. 178.
57 *Beat It!* series 2000, episode 13.
58 *Beat It!* series 2000, episode 2.
59 Robins, 2004, p. 651.
60 Cameron, 2005, p. 164.
61 A. Sitas, 'The making of the "comrades" movement in Natal, 1985–1991', *Journal of Southern African Studies*, 18, 3 (1992), pp. 629–41; P. Delius & C. Glaser, 'Sexual socialisation in South Africa: A historical perspective', *African Studies*, 61, 1 (2002), p. 18. See M. Gevisser, 'A different fight for freedom: A history of South African lesbian and gay organisation from the 1950s to 1990s', in M. Gevisser & E. Cameron, *Defiant Desire: Gay and Lesbian Lives in South Africa* (Routledge, New York, 1995), for a discussion on the masculinist dimensions of the comrades movement and the ways in which this related to homophobia within the anti-apartheid movement.
62 *Beat It!* series 2005, episode 12.
63 N. Masilela, 'The New African Movement and the beginnings of film culture in South Africa', in I. Balseiro & N. Masilela (eds), *To Change Reels: Film and Film Culture in South Africa* (Detroit, Wayne State University Press, 2003), p. 19.
64 Interview with Prudence Mabele, Johannesburg, 18 March 2007.
65 Interview with Jacobs.
66 Interview with Busisiwe Maqungo, Cape Town, 24 April 2007.

Endnotes

Chapter 9

1   R. Florida, *The Rise of the Creative Class: And How It's Transforming Work, Leisure, Community and Everyday Life* (Basic Books, New York, 2002); S. Zukin, *The Cultures of Cities* (Blackwell, Oxford, 1995).

2   G. Evans, 'Hard branding the cultural city: From Prado to Prada', *International Journal of Urban and Regional Research*, 27, 2 (2003), pp. 417–40.

3   G. A. Myers, 'Naming and placing the other: Power and the urban landscape in Zanzibar', *Tijdschrift voor Economische en Sociale Geografie*, 87 (1996), pp. 237–46; C. Nash, 'Placenames: Postcolonial locations', *Transactions of the Institute of British Geographers*, 24, 4 (1999), pp. 457–80.

4   I use the concept of 'Global Africanisation' to depict the new political culture that constitutes the new discourse for building a new South Africa. It is a site of power for the government of South Africa in which the contemporary consolidation of globalisation is taking place and a turning point around which the South African public defines its new African cultural outlook under the influence of its new political class.

5   V. D. Dora, 'The rhetoric of nostalgia: Postcolonial Alexandria between uncanny memories and global geographies', *Cultural Geographies*, 13, 2 (2006), pp. 207–38.

6   L. Davie, 'Community backs Mandela Yard', 2 June 2005, <http://joburgnews. co.za/2005/june/jun2_mandela.stm>.

7   Alexandra Renewal Project, 'Heritage overview', 26 May 2006, <http://www.alexandra. co.za/08_social/heritage_0.htm>.

8   N. Dlamini, 'Mandela Yard tells Alex's history', 1 February 2005, accessed 30 September 2006, <http://www.joburg.org.za/2005/feb/feb1_museum.stm>.

9   D. Hill, *Body of Truth: Leveraging What Consumers Can't or Won't Say* (Wiley, Hoboken, 2003).

10   J. H. Gilmore, 'Frontiers of the experience economy', *Batten Briefings: From the Darden Graduate School of Business Administration* (Barden Institute, Charlottesville, 2003).

11   N. Mandela, *Long Walk to Freedom: The Autobiography of Nelson Mandela* (Little, Brown, London, 2001).

12   R. Nixon, 'Mandela, messianism, and the media', *Transition*, 51 (1991), p. 49.

13   Dlamini, 2005.

14   Ibid.

15   Ibid.

16   The Heritage Resource Agency is part of the South African Heritage Council, which seeks to provide for the identification, conservation, protection and promotion of the country's heritage for present and future generations. Mafisa offers a range of services in conservation, development, tourism and land reform. The company's mission is to facilitate economic growth, skills development and job creation through responsible forms of tourism and related land uses.

17   These are significant sites where significant incidents/events in the anti-apartheid struggle took place.

18   See Corporate Tours to Soweto, <http://www.soweto.co.za/html/gallery.htm>.

19   Gauteng Tourism Authority website, accessed 26 September 2006, <http://www. gauteng.net/home/home.asp>.

20   B. Bramwell & L. Rawding, 'Tourism marketing images of industrial cities', *Annals of Tourism Research*, 23 (1996), pp. 201–21.

21   C. M. Rogerson, 'Urban tourism and small tourism enterprise development in Johannesburg: The case of township tourism', *GeoJournal*, 60, 3 (2004), pp. 249–57.

22   N. Morgan, A. Pritchard & R. Pride, *Destination Branding: Creating the Unique Destination Proposition* (Butterworth-Heinemann, Oxford, 2002), p. 5.

23   T. Eetgerink, 'Feel the heartbeat of South Africa', *Mail & Guardian*, 26 June 2006.

24   L. Masha, 'Mandela Centre for Alexandra', 21 October 2004, accessed 29 September 2006, <http://www.southafrica.info/mandela/mandelacentre-alexandra.htm>.

25   K. Meethan, *Tourism in a Global Society: Place, Culture, Consumption* (Palgrave, Hampshire, 2001).

26   Interview with Siphesihle, Alex resident, 7th Avenue, 24 January 2006.

27   Interview with Lucky, Alex resident from 8th Avenue who used to stay in 1st Avenue, 25 January 2006.

28   Interview with Virginia, who came to Alex in 1985, but is now living in a transit camp, 27 January 2006.

29   Interview with angry anonymous resident, 7th Avenue, 25 January 2006.

30   Interview with Vusumuzi, Alex resident, 7th Avenue, 25 January 2006.

31   Interview with George, Alex resident, 7th Avenue, 24 January 2006.

32   Abram Louis Fischer, commonly known as Bram Fischer (1908–75), was a South African lawyer of Afrikaner descent notable for anti-apartheid activism and for the legal defence of anti-apartheid figures, including Nelson Mandela at the Rivonia trial. Bram Fischer settlement is located west of Johannesburg, 60 km from Alex.

33   Interview with Virginia, 27 January 2006.

34   Interview with Agnes, originally from Newcastle, now a camp resident, 27 January 2006.

35   Interview with Jacob, project manager for safety and security in Region 7, 1 February 2006.

36   Interviews with Mama Zandile, *maskhandi* musician and Alex Organising Committee member against removals, a mother of one; Mama Mandlovu, mother of one and small tuck shop operator from 6th Avenue, 27 January 2006.

37   Interview with Virginia, 27 January 2006.

38   Interview with Agnes, a mother of two, who is not staying with her children in the camp, 27 January 2006

39   Interview with anonymous Alex resident, 7th Avenue, 25 January 2006.

40   Interview with David, Alex resident, 7th Avenue, 25 January 2006.

41   Interview with Alex resident, 7th Avenue, 25 January 2006.

42   London Road is the main road going through Alex from Sandton to the airport and is soon to be renamed after a youth activist, Vincent Tshabalala. Born in 1964, Tshabalala was one of the martyrs of the struggle. He left the country in 1983 and joined the ranks

of Umkhonto we Sizwe, the armed wing of the ANC, later returning on military and underground missions in the country. He was killed in a street battle with the police at the corner of London Road and 12th Avenue in 1985.

43   N. Dlamini, 'Alex streets to be renamed', Johannesburg News Agency, 26 September 2007, <http://www.joburg.org.za/2007/sep/sep26_azikhwelwa.stm>.

44   Interview with an anonymous Alex resident, now resident at the camp, 27 February 2006.

45   Zionist Christian Church.

46   Interview with Jacob, 1 February 2006.

47   Interview with Virginia, 27 January 2006.

48   Jolly is originally from Durban and now a camp resident (interview, 27 February 2006).

49   Interview with an anonymous Alex resident now resident at the camp, 27 February 2006.

50   Interview with an anonymous Alex resident now based at the camp, 27 February 2006.

51   Interview with an anonymous Alex resident now based at the camp, 27 February 2006.

52   Interview with Maina, pregnant, a mother of one and a camp resident, 27 January 2006.

53   Interview with Tholakele, an Alex resident since 1962 and a grandmother, now a camp resident, 27 January 2006.

54   Dlamini, 2005.

55   K. Marx, Capital, vol. 1 (Penguin, Harmondsworth, 1976).

56   S. Best, 'The commodification of reality and the reality of commodification: Baudrillard, Debord, and postmodern theory', in D. Kellner (ed.), Baudrillard: A Critical Reader (Blackwell, Oxford, 1994), p. 44.

57   Interview with two Xuma family members in the company of some neighbours, 25 January 2006.

58   Mandela, 2001, p. 89.

59   E. Cassirer, The Myth of the State (Yale University Press, New Haven, 1964).

60   D. Lowenthal, 'Past time, present place: Landscape and memory', Geographical Review, LXV, 1 (1974), p. 27.

61   M. Crang, 'Envisioning urban histories: Bristol as palimpsest, postcards, and snapshots', Environment and Planning, 28 (1996), p. 441.

62   P. Bonner & N. Nieftagodien, Alexandra: A History (Wits University Press, Johannesburg, 2008), pp. 408–10.

63   L. Sinwell, 'The Alexandra Development Forum (ADF): The tyranny of invited participatory spaces?', Transformation, forthcoming.

Chapter 10

1   For a detailed discussion of this, as well as the reasons why nursing was a more popular choice, see S. Horwitz, '"Black nurses in white": Exploring young women's entry into the nursing profession at Baragwanath Hospital, Soweto, 1948–1980', Social History of Medicine, 20, 1 (2007), pp. 131–46.

2   S. Marks, *Divided Sisterhood: Race, Class and Gender in the South African Nursing Profession* (Wits University Press, Johannesburg, 1994), p. 2.

3   Exceptions include H. Sweet, "'Wanted: 16 nurses of the better educated type": Provision of nurses to South Africa in the late nineteenth and early twentieth centuries', *Nursing Inquiry*, 11 (2004), pp. 176–84; H. Sweet & A. Digby, 'Race, identity and the nursing profession in South Africa, c. 1850–1958', in B. Mortimer & S. McCann (eds), *New Directions in the History of Nursing in International Perspective* (Routledge, London, 2005), which is the only one of these to talk briefly about nursing strikes; A. Digby & H. Sweet, 'Nurses as cultural brokers in twentieth-century South Africa', in W. Ernst (ed.), *Plural Medicine, Tradition and Modernity, 1800–2000* (Routledge, London, 2002).

4   Marks, 1994, pp. 2–3.

5   Sweet & Digby, 2005, p. 109.

6   On unrest in educational institutions, see J. Hyslop, *The Classroom Struggle: Policy and Resistance in South Africa 1940–1990* (University of Natal Press, Pietermaritzburg, 1999), pp. 22–43; B. Hirson, *Year of Ash, Year of Fire: The Soweto Revolt: Roots of a Revolution?* (Zed Books, London, 1979), pp. 30–36. On unrest in medical institutions, see Marks, 1994, p. 107; Sweet & Digby, 2005, pp. 113–20; A. K. Mager, *Gender and the Making of a South African Bantustan: A Social History of the Ciskei, 1945–1959* (James Currey, Oxford, 1999), p. 204 on a strike at the Lovedale Mission Hospital in 1949.

7   K. F. Mills, superintendent, Johannesburg Hospital, to the chairman and members of the Special Purposes Committee, 'Baragwanath Hospital: Disturbance among nursing staff', 18 July 1949, South African National Archives Depository (SAB), JHM 121, 625/48(5).

8   Ibid.

9   See also, Marks, 1994, pp. 127, 138; C. Searle, *The History of the Development of Nursing* (Struik, Cape Town, 1965), pp. 278–79; *Nursing RSA*, 'Obituary: Jane McLarty (1893–1989)', *Nursing RSA*, 4, 3 (1989), p. 8.

10 T. Mashaba, *Rising to the Challenge of Change: A History of Black Nursing in South Africa* (Juta, Kenwyn, 1995), p. 40.

11 N. Lubanga, 'Nursing in South Africa: Black women workers organize', in M. Turshen (ed.), *Women and Health in Africa* (Africa World Press, Trenton, 1991), p. 61.

12 Marks, 1994, pp. 123–25.

13 Interviews used in this chapter were conducted between 2003 and 2004 as part of a larger study. For more information, see Horwitz, 2007.

14 T. O. Kentron, 'Anti-apartheid nursing body to confer: Protest against act growing', *Contact: The SA News Review*, 14 June 1958, p. 8.

15 *Nursing RSA*, 1989; *Rand Daily Mail*, 'In the House of Assembly: Nursing Amendment Bill criticised by Mrs. Ballinger', 1 April 1950; Marks, 1994, p. 138.

16 S. Horwitz, "'A phoenix rising": A history of Baragwanath Hospital, Soweto, South Africa, 1942–1990', DPhil thesis, University of Oxford, 2006, p. 174.

17 See Marks, 1994, pp. 12, 106–12, 142.

18 H. Joseph, *Side by Side: The Autobiography of Helen Joseph* (Zed Books, London, 1986), p. 64. See also M. Resha, *Mangoana o Tsoara Thipa ka Bohaleng: My Life in the Struggle* (Congress of South African Writers, Johannesburg, 1991), p. 118.

19 '1957 Bill', undated, University of the Witwatersrand, Historical Papers (hereafter WHP), AD1137, FEDSAW, C.C.4.7; 'Conference of women', 23 June 1957, WHP, AD1137, FEDSAW, C.C.4.7; Lubanga, 1991, p. 64.

20 Kentron, 1958, p. 8; L. Baldwin-Ragaven, J. de Gruchy & L. London, *An Ambulance of the Wrong Colour: Health Professionals, Human Rights and Ethics in South Africa* (UCT Press, Cape Town, 1999), p. 168; Joseph, 1986, p. 64; Marks, 1994, p. 161.

21 *Sunday Times*, 'Non-white nurses protest against passes', 23 March 1958; Resha, 1991, p. 120.

22 M. Jarrett-Kerr, *African Pulse: Scenes from an African Hospital Window* (Faith Press, London, 1960), p. 70.

23 Joseph, 1986, p. 64; Resha, 1991, p. 120.

24 Jarrett-Kerr, 1960, p. 71. It is probable that the word 'mother' is used here not to mean the actual mothers of nurses – although that might have been the case for some women – but more generally to indicate older African women.

25 Resha, 1991, p. 120.

26 Joseph, 1986, p. 64.

27 M. Cooper, 'New pattern of protest', *Contact: The SA News Review*, 1, 5 (1958), p. 4; *Sunday Times*, 'Non-white nurses protest against passes', 23 March 1958.

28 Joseph, 1986, p. 64; see also Cooper, 1958, p. 4.

29 'To the matron of Baragwanath Hospital and the principal of the Training College for Non-European Nurses', undated, pp. 1–2, WHP, AD1137, FEDSAW, C.C.4.5; Resha, 1991, p. 120; Joseph, 1986, p. 64.

30 'To the matron of Baragwanath Hospital and the principal of the Training College for Non-European Nurses', undated, p. 2, WHP, AD1137, FEDSAW, C.C.4.5.

31 Searle, 1965, p. 237.

32 Jarrett-Kerr, 1960, p. 71; Marks, 1994, pp. 166–72.

33 Interviews with Annah Montso, 13 October 2004 and [name changed for anonymity] Florence Mudzuli, 14 September 2004. See also A. P. Cheater, 'A marginal elite? African registered nurses in Durban, South Africa', *African Studies*, 33 (1974), p. 146 and Resha, 1991, p. 139, who suggests that nurses did not feel that they were represented adequately by the SANA.

34 Interview with Margaret Mohlala, 27 September 2004.

35 Interview with Virginia Ramogale, 1 September 2004.

36 See, for example, E. Brink & G. Malungane, *Soweto 16 June 1976: It All Started with a Dog* (Kwela Books, Cape Town; 2001); S. M. Ndlovu, *The Soweto Uprisings: Counter-memories of June 1976* (Ravan Press, Johannesburg, 1998).

37 Interviews with Zodwa Mfete, 9 January 2003; Annah Montso, 13 October 2004; Harriet Gwebu, 16 August 2003.

38 Inteview with Margaret Mohlala, 27 September 2004.

39 Interview with Matilda Mogale, 14 September 2004.

40 Moira Russell, letter to Simonne Horwitz, 6 April 2004; Interview with Chris van den Heever, 6 October 2004. See also J. A. Hunt, *White Witch Doctor: A Surgeon's Life in Apartheid South Africa* (Durban House, Dallas, 2002), p. 254.

41 L. Uys, 'Racism and the South African nurse', *Nursing RSA*, 2, 11/12 (1987), p. 55.

42 Marks, 1994, pp. 167–68.

43 *Nursing News* (1983), p. 1; Lubanga, 1991, p. 71.

44 Anon., 'Health workers' struggles', *Critical Health*, 15 (1986a), pp. 16–19; Anon., 'An historical overview of nursing struggles in South Africa', *Critical Health*, 24 (1998), p. 55.

45 *Saturday Star*, 'Defiant doc puts career on the line for sake of free speech', 6 August 1988.

46 Anon., 'Other strikes at other hospitals', *Critical Health*, 15 (1986b), p. 12.

47 Anon., 1998, p. 57. Similar boycotts occurred at Coronation and Hillbrow hospitals during the same period.

48 Lubanga, 1991, p. 71.

49 Anon., 'Baragwanath Hospital strike 1985: Divided interests and joint action', *Critical Health*, 15 (1986c), p. 4.

50 Interview with Matilda Mogale, 14 September 2004.

51 *Sowetan*, 'Bara reports false – official', 22 November 1985; W. Utting, 'Hospital chaos as hundreds of strikers arrested', *Weekly Mail*, 15 November 1985.

52 W. Utting, 'Hospital chaos as hundreds of strikers arrested', *Weekly Mail*, 15 November 1985.

53 Lubanga, 1991, p. 73.

54 Ibid.; M. Moseki, '700 held at Bara', *Sowetan*, 15 November 1985.

55 *Business Day*, '900 striking Bara nurses given notice', 19 November 1985.

56 Ibid.; *Sowetan*, 'BARA: Court move', 19 November 1985; *Star*, 'Bara dismissal notice "invalid and ineffective"', 25 November 1985.

57 *Sowetan*, 'BARA: Court move', 19 November 1985; *The Star*, 'Bara dismissal notice "invalid and ineffective"', 25 November 1985. The application was brought by Mardulate Tshabalala, Themba Nbobo and Macbeth Nxumalo.

58 On the changing role of the courts, see R. Abel, *Politics by Other Means: Law in the Struggle Against Apartheid, 1980–1994* (Routledge, New York, 1995).

59 *Sowetan*, 'Comment', 28 May 1986; *Sowetan*, 'Pardon Bara 9', 28 May 1986. The nine nurses were K. Mophosho, F. Morafe, M. T. Papo, M. Mpshe, J. Nbobo, P. M. Morodi, W. H. Shibambo and A. Shilote.

60 Cited in *Citizen*, 'Nurses join forces to condemn "radical Bara activities"', 23 May 1986.

61 Cited in *Sowetan*, 'Pardon Bara 9', 28 May 1986.

62 *Sowetan*, 'Comment', 28 May 1986.

63 Interview with Harriet Gwebu, 16 August 2003.

64   S. Marks, 'The legacy of the history of nursing for post-apartheid South Africa', in
     A. M. Rafferty, J. Robinson & R. Elkan (eds), *Nursing History and the Politics of*
     Welfare (Routledge, New York, 1997), p. 34.
65   W. Utting, 'Hospital chaos as hundreds of strikers arrested', *Weekly Mail*, 15 November
     1985.
66   Marks, 1994, p. 203.
67   Interview with Florence Mudzuli, 14 September 2004.
68   Interview with Chris and Hester van den Heever, Chris Hani Baragwanath Hospital,
     6 October 2004.
69   K. von Holdt & B. Maserumule, 'After apartheid: Decay or reconstruction? Transition
     in a public hospital', in E. Webster & K. von Holdt, *Beyond the Apartheid Workplace:*
     Studies in Transition (University of KwaZulu-Natal Press, Scotsville, 2005), p. 6.
70   Labour Relations Amendment Act No. 9 of 1991.
71   C. Heunis & A. J. Pelser, 'Down the needle! Should public sector nurses in South Africa
     have the right to strike?' *Curationis*, 20, 3 (1997), p. 43.
72   *Nursing News*, 'Editorial', 1992, p. 2.
73   'B. Adair for Cheadle, Thompson and Haysom, Attorneys, Notaries and Conveyances to
     Dr. G. Marais, MP, the minister for administration and tourism', 11 June 1992, personal
     papers of Dr Chris van den Heever (hereafter CVDH), file 1; 'NEHAWU's proposals on
     Friday 12 June 1992'; J. Roos, 'Actions of NEHAWU members', 19 May 1992, CVDH, file
     1, p. 21.
74   'NEHAWU's proposals on Friday 12 June 1992'.
75   J. de Lange, 'TPA kry hofbevel teen stakers by Bara', *Beeld*, 6 June 1992.
76   'Cheadle, Thompson and Haysom, Attorneys, Notaries and Conveyances to Dr. G.
     Marais, MP, the minister for administration and tourism', 11 June 1992, CVDH, file 2;
     'Summary of the current position regarding the strike action as well as other forms of
     protest action of NEHAWU and its members', CVDH, file 1, p. 41.
77   Von Holdt & Maserumule, 1995, p. 14.
78   'NEHAWU's proposals on Friday 12 June 1992'.
79   NEHAWU, 'State sector workers unite and fight the apartheid regime', undated handout.
80   Von Holdt & Maserumule, 1995.
81   Interview with Florence Mudzuli, 14 September 2004.
82   Baragwanath Hospital, 'Minutes of the emergency meeting held 18 June 1992', CVDH,
     file 1; 'Staff meeting', 17 June 1992, CVDH, file 1; 'Staking by TPA instellings', p. 11,
     CVDH, file 1.
83   'Meeting with Mrs Langley', 17 June 1992, CVDH, file 2.
84   'Meeting Dr. Bruwer–SANA president with Bara nurses', 25 June 1992, CVDH files.
85   'Bara Professional Health Workers', ca 20 June 1992, CVDH, file 1.
86   'Staff meeting', 16 June 1992, CVDH, file 1; 'Doctors, nurses, students', undated, p. 297,
     CVDH, file 3.
87   'Meeting of trained personnel held in nurses dining hall on 20 August 1992', CVDH,
     file 3.

88 'Letter from Mrs Adele Tjale, on behalf of the Baragwanath registered and enrolled nurses, RE Baragwanath registered and enrolled nurses', 10 September 1992, CVDH, file 3.

89 'March for workers rights, issued by strike crisis committee', undated, CVDH, file 3.

90 'Meeting of chief nursing service manager with self selected "leaders" for feedback on the 2 memoranda handed over by the students on 17th and 18th July 1992', CVDH, file 3; 'Notes on events at the hospital', 20 June 1992, CVDH, file 1.

91 Interview with Harriet Gwebu, 16 August 2003.

92 'National Education Health and Allied Workers Union', undated, CVDH, file 3.

93 Joe Mdhlela & Sonti Maseko, '7 hurt in attack', *Sowetan*, 9 July 1992; *Sowetan*, 'Fired workers and job-seekers in clash', 10 July 1992.

94 'RE: Burnet House, statement by L. M. Makgotloe', 16 August 1991, CVDH, file 3.

95 'Meeting notes', 18 June 1992, CVDH files; 'Meeting of trained personnel', nurses dining hall, 20 August 1992, CVDH, file 3.

96 'Kunene, notes of meeting between NEHAWU and TPA', 9 June 1992, CVDH, file 2; Joe Mdhlela & Sonti Maseko, '7 hurt in attack', *Sowetan*, 9 July 1992.

97 'Intimidation and violence, Bara Health Workers Crisis Committee', CVDH, file 3.

98 'Recognition and procedural agreement between the Transvaal Provincial Administration (TPA) and National Education, Health and Allied Workers Union (NEHAWU)', 1 February 1993, p. 4, CVDH, file 2.

99 'NEHAWU's proposals on Friday 12 June 1992'.

100 B. Templeton, 'Conflicting views of the hospital dispute', *Saturday Star*, 20 June 1992.

101 'White supers to be fired from Hillbrow Hospital', CVDH, file 3.

102 Marks, 1997, p. 35.

103 R. Kale, 'Impressions of health in the new South Africa: A period of convalescence', *British Medical Journal*, 310 (1995), pp. 1119–22.

104 T. Bernhardt, 'The nurses' strike: A well organised plea for recognition', *Industrial Democracy Review*, 4, 5 (1996), p. 11; P. Sidley, 'Nurses strikes in South Africa', *British Medical Journal*, 311 (1995), p. 707.

105 Bernhardt, 1996, p. 11.

106 G. Mantashe, 'The nurses' strike: Organising nurses', *South African Communist Party*, 142 (1995), <http://www.sacp.org.za/main.php?include=pubs/acommunist/1995/issue142.html#Nurses>.

107 Heunis & Pelser, 1997, pp. 44.

108 Sidley, 1995; Von Holdt & Maserumule, 1995, p. 14.

109 Bernhardt, 1996, p. 14.

110 Heunis & Pelser, 1997, p. 42.

111 Ibid, pp. 42–43.

112 V. J. Ehlers, 'Nursing and politics: A South African perspective', *International Nursing Review*, 47 (2000), p. 77.

113 Ibid.

114 H. Adam, 'Corporatism as minority veto under ANC hegemony in South Africa', in H. Giliomee & C. Simkins (eds), *The Awkward Embrace: One-party Domination and Democracy* (Routledge, London, 1999), p. 272.

115 Von Holdt & Maserumule, 1995, p. 14; Bernhardt, 1996, p. 12.

116 Heunis & Pelser, 1997, p. 46; Mantashe, 1995.

117 Sidley, 1995.

118 Bernhardt, 1996, p. 13.

119 Ibid., p. 16.

120 Heunis & Pelser, 1997, p. 46.

121 *Sunday Tribune*, 'The strike killed our babies', 10 September 1995; Ehlers, 2000, p. 78.

122 S. Adams, 'What's left? The South African Communist Party after apartheid', *Review of African Political Economy*, 72 (1997), p. 243.

123 Bernhardt, 1996, p. 13.

124 Adam, 1999, p. 272.

125 Sidley, 1995.

126 Adams, 1997, p. 243.

127 Bernhardt, 1996, pp. 11–20.

128 Ibid., p. 16; Adam, 1999, p. 272.

129 For a fuller discussion of this, see Von Holdt & Maserumule, 1997, but more work remains to be done on the multitude of labour actions during this period.

130 P. Sidley, 'Striker cripples health services in South Africa', *British Medical Journal*, 334 (2007), pp. 1240–41.

131 SAPA, 'Striking nurses "on thin ice"', 9 June 2007; E. Momberg & J. Gordin, 'Nurses fired as shutdown looms', *Sunday Independent*, 10 June 2007.

132 C. Benjamin, 'Cleaners in firing line amid health strike chaos', *Business Day*, 26 June 2007.

133 Von Holdt & Maserumule, 1997, pp. 6–20.

134 Lubanga, 1991, p. 51.

135 Horwitz, 2007.

136 Ibid.

137 Unrecorded discussion with Albertina Sisulu, 7 July 2004; Resha, 1991, pp. 118–20; A. du Preez Bezdrob, *Winnie Mandela: A Life* (Struik, Cape Town, 2003), p. 51.

Chapter 11

1 M. Heywood, 'The price of denial', *Development Update*, 5, 3 (2004), p. 97.

2 Interview with Jack Lewis, Idol Pictures offices, Muizenburg, Cape Town, 22 January 2007.

3 L. Lawson, *Side Effects: The Story of AIDS in South Africa* (Double Storey, Cape Town, 2008), p. 175.

4 Ibid., p. 68.

5 Ibid.

6   H. Schneider, 'The AIDS impasse in South Africa as a struggle for symbolic
      power', paper presented at the AIDS in Context conference at the University of the
      Witwatersrand, Johannesburg, 2001, p. 6.

7   Here I am referring to S. Friedman & S. Mottiar, 'Seeking the high ground: The
      Treatment Action Campaign and the politics of morality', in R. Ballard, A. Habib &
      I. Valodia (eds), *Voices of Protest: Social Movements in Post-apartheid South Africa*
      (University of KwaZulu-Natal Press, Durban, 2006); A. Desai, *We Are the Poors:*
      Community Struggles in Post-apartheid South Africa (Monthly Review Press, New
      York, 2002a); and Patrick Bond's earlier work on social movements. This is a critique
      I made in M. Mbali, 'TAC in the history of patient-driven AIDS activism: The case for
      historicising South Africa's new social movements', in N. Gibson (ed.), *Challenging*
      Hegemony: Social Movements and the Quest for a New Humanism in Post-
      apartheid South Africa (Africa World Press, Trenton & Asmara, 2006).

8   J. Campbell, 'Where do we stand? Common mechanisms in organisational and social
      movement research', in G. F. Davis et al. (eds), *Social Movements and Organization*
      Theory (Cambridge University Press, Cambridge, 2005), p. 61.

9   S. Tarrow, *Power in Movement: Social Movements and Contentious politics*, 2nd ed.
      (Cambridge University Press, Cambridge, 1998).

10   C. Tilly, *Social Movements, 1768–2004* (Paradigm, Boulder, 2004), p. 23.

11   Tarrow, 1998, p. 110. David Snow was the first to argue this: D. A. Snow, 'Framing
      processes, ideology and discursive fields', in D. A. Snow, S. A. Soule & H. Kriesi (eds),
      The Blackwell Companion to Social Movements (Blackwell, Oxford, Malden, MA &
      Victoria, 2004).

12   Ibid., p. 110.

13   Heywood, 2004, p. 96.

14   H. Schneider & J. Stein, 'Implementing AIDS policy in post-apartheid South Africa',
      Social Science and Medicine, 52, 2 (2001), p. 723.

15   'Letter to Helen Schneider from Ralph Mgijima dated 13 October 1993', Centre for
      Health Policy (hereafter CHP), University of the Witswatersrand, Historical Papers,
      box B1–B5, Centre for Health Policy, Department of Health, p. 1.

16   Mary Crewe is quite critical of UNAIDS's involvement in the process as too time
      consuming and the targets as too unrealistic, creating a plan that was too unwieldy
      (interview with Mary Crewe, University of Pretoria, 2006).

17   According to Dr Itzak Fourie, NACOSA's funding sources broke down as follows:
      the Department of Health and Population Development provided R600,000, the
      Commission for European Communities R450,000 contributed via Kagiso Trust, and
      the Chamber of Mines provided R50,000 (*Draft Report: First Meeting of the National*
      AIDS Council, Parktonian Hotel, Braamfontein, 27 January 1994, under 'Item B6:
      Funding and priorities', p. 21, CHP, box B6–C8, Centre for Health Policy, Department
      of Health, NACOSA file B6, 'Misc. minutes and reports 1995–7'). Olive Shisana told
      the author that the total government budget was seven million rand when she entered
      public office, while Quarraisha Abdool Karim put the amount at three or four million

rand. Either way, it is clear that the NACOSA conference consumed a large proportion of the 1992/93 AIDS budget (interviews with Olive Shisana, 27 March 2007 and Quarraisha Abdool Karim, Nelson R. Mandela Medical School, University of KwaZulu-Natal, 18 October 2006).

18   J. Frohlich & P. Moodley, 'The National Aids Convention of South Africa: NACOSA', in Department of Health, *The South Africa STD/HIV/AIDS Review Situational Analysis* (Department of Health, Pretoria, 1997), p. 24.

19   CHP Resource Room, 'Highlights of the law reform and human rights strategy', *AIDS Bulletin*, 3, 2 (1994), p. 9.

20   Schneider & Stein, 2001; pp. 725.

21   Janet Frohlich, *National STD/HIV/AIDS Review: Comprehensive Report*, vols. 1–4 (Department of Health, Pretoria, 1997), p. 43.

22   Ibid.

23   Interview with Abdool Karim.

24   Ibid.

25   Ibid.

26   Ibid.

27   CHP Resource Room, '*The AIDS Consortium Project: Bulletin*, issue 1, August 1992, Centre for Applied Legal Studies, University of the Witwatersrand', p. 1.

28   'Facsimile transmission to the Honourable Deputy President F W de Klerk dated 21 November 1994', p. 1, CHP, file C8, Centre for Health Policy, NACOSA, miscellaneous documents.

29   'Statement by NACOSA co-chairs, dated Thursday 1 February 1996', CHP, box B1–B5, Centre for Health Policy, Department of Health, file C8, Centre for Health Policy, NACOSA, miscellaneous documents, p. 1.

30   *HIV/AIDS/STD Directorate Progress Reports 1995–6*, 'Department of Health: HIV/AIDS and STD Program: Strategy, business and structure plans 1995–1996', CHP, box B1–B5, Centre for Health Policy, Department of Health, file B2, p. 2

31   Interview with Abdool Karim.

32   Ibid.; *Report in terms of Section 8(2) of the Public Protector Act (No. 23 of 1994). Report No. 1 (Special Report) Investigation of the Play Sarafina II*, p. 3, CHP, box D–E, CHP special topics and correspondence, file D1 CHP Sarafina 2.

33   Ibid., p. 4.

34   Ibid.

35   Ibid.

36   Ibid.

37   Interview with Warren Parker, Johannesburg, 31 January 2007.

38   Interview with Judy Seidman, Johannesburg, 4 December 2006.

39   Interview with Morna Cornell, School of Public Health, University of Cape Town Medical School, 28 March 2007.

40   A. Ramklown, 'Musical fails', *Natal Witness*, 9 January 1996, p. 6.

41   Interview with Cornell.

42   Ibid.

43   Ibid.

44   Ibid.

45   *Report in terms of Section 8(2) of the Public Protector Act (No. 23 of 1994). Report No. 1 (Special Report) Investigation of the Play Sarafina II*, p. 46, CHP, box D–E, CHP special topics and correspondence, file D1 CHP Sarafina 2.

46   *Sowetan*, 'Comment', 21 February 1996, p. 6.

47   *Citizen*, 'Heath unit rejects Omar's Zuma claim', 24 November 1998, p. 5.

48   Interview with Abdool Karim.

49   'Media statement by NACOSA co-chairs on *Sarafina 2* and the public protector's report, status: Immediate', fax, 8 June 1996, pp. 1–2, CHP, box D–E, Special Topics and Correspondence, file D1, *Sarafina 2*.

50   J. Malala, '"Sarafina" saga: Zuma in the firing line', *Star*, 3 June 1996, p. 1.

51   In an interview with the author, Abdool Karim implied that she left the department to advance her career as a scientist; however, Lesley Lawson (2008) has attributed her departure to the scandal.

52   Lawson, 2008, p. 4.

53   A. Salie, 'Zuma apologises for Sarafina 2', *Cape Times*, 28 February 1996, p. 1.

54   A. Salie, 'Top health official out to undo Sarafina 2 damage', *Cape Times*, 13 January 1997, p. 5.

55   Frohlich, 1997, p. 9.

56   Ibid., p. 10.

57   Schneider, 2001, p. 5.

58   Ibid., p. 5; telephonic interview with Rose Smart, 8 May 2007.

59   Interview with Smart.

60   Ibid.

61   Ibid.

62   Ibid.

63   Interview with Fatima Hassan, ALP offices, Cape Town, 16 March 2008.

64   Ashraf Grimwood & Kevin Osborne, *National AIDS Convention of South Africa Western Cape: Advocating for Change in HIV/AIDS Policies and Strategies 1997/8 Annual Report*, p. 9, Gay and Lesbian Archives (hereafter GALA), Triangle Project Collection, AM2974, box C.2.5.2–C.2.2.8, file C.2.2.5.5, Lesbian conference.

65   NAPWA, 'NAPWA SA statement (dated 3 October 1995)', p. 1, GALA, Triangle Project Collection, AM2974, box C.2.5.2–C.2.2.8, file C.2.2.5.2.

66   NAPWA, 'Letter dated 18 May 1994 from Shaun Mellors', p. 1, GALA, Triangle Project Collection, box C2.5.2–C2.2.8, file C.2.2.5.2.

67   Ibid., p. 2.

68   Interview with Abdool Karim.

69   Ibid.

70   Inquest no. KwaMashu CAS 375:12:98, p. 63.

71   Ibid.; interview with Promise Mthembu, Gender AIDS Forum offices, Durban, 19 August 2003.

72   Inquest no. KwaMashu CAS 375:12:98, p. 51.

73   Ibid., p. 18.

74   Ibid., p. 52.

75   Interview with Mthembu.

76   Ibid.; interview with Thabo Cele, TAC KwaZulu-Natal provincial office, Durban, 25 April 2007.

77   A 2001 MRC study showed that 'about 40% of the adult deaths aged 15–49 that occurred in the year 2000 were due to HIV/AIDS'. From the few hundred AIDS deaths in the late 1980s, AIDS had become South Africa's leading cause of death by the early 2000s. See R. Dorrington et al. *The Impact of HIV/AIDS on Adult Mortality in South Africa: Technical Report* (Burden of Disease Research Unit, MRC, Cape Town, 2001), <http://www.africa.upenn.edu/Urgent_Action/apic-101501.html>.

78   Interview with Seidman.

79   Interviews with Cornell and Crewe.

80   Interview with Mazibuko Jara, Olympia Cafe, Kalk Bay, Cape Town, 26 March 2007.

81   Ibid.; interview with Cornell.

82   Treatment Action Campaign, 'Memorandum to minister of health: Dr Nkosasana Zuma, dated Friday 30 April 1999', p. 7, CHP Resource Room, *TAC HIV & AIDS Treatment Action Campaign. A Reading Package for Treatment Action Campaign Volunteers HIV/AIDS: An Activists Guide to Treatment Rights and Literacy. Building a Movement to Secure the Rights to Dignity and Access to Treatment for People with HIV and AIDS.*

83   Interview with Crewe.

84   Ibid.; interview with Cornell.

85   Interview with Crewe.

86   Ibid.

87   TAC, 'TAC statement on auditor-general's qualified audit opinion of the Department of Health', 18 October 2004, <http://www.tac.org.za/newsletter/TACStatementonAuditor. htm>; L. Mazibuko, 'Scandalous shenanigans', repr. from *Sowetan*, 12 October 2004, <http://www.tac.org.za/newsletter/TACStatementonAuditor.htm>.

88   As of early 2007 it was undergoing a process of strategic planning and evaluation (interview with Mazibuko Jara, 26 March 2007).

Chapter 12

1   J. Depelchin, cited in S. Terreblanche, *A History of Inequality in South Africa: 1652–2002* (University of KwaZulu-Natal Press, Pietermaritzburg, 2002).

2   M. Castells, *The Urban Question* (Edward Arnold, London, 1977).

3   P. Bond, *South Africa's Resurgent Urban Social Movements: The Case of Johannesburg, 1984, 1994, 2004*, Centre for Civil Society, research report, no. 22, 2004, p. 15, <http://www.ukzn.ac.za/CCS/files/Bond-sm.pdf>.

4   Ibid., p. 3.

5   R. Carroll, 'Townships in revolt as ANC fails to live up to its promises', *Guardian*, 22 February 2006, p. 5.

6   G. Adler & J. Steinberg (eds), *From Comrades to Citizens: The South African Civics Movement and the Transition to Democracy* (Macmillan, London, 2000), p. 4.

7   S. L. Robins, 'Introduction', *Limits to Liberation after Apartheid* (James Currey, Oxford, 2005), p. 3.

8   Adler & Steinberg, 2000; T. Lodge & B. Nasson *All, Here, and Now: Black Politics in South Africa in the 1980s* (David Philip, Cape Town, 1991); M. Mayekiso, *Township Politics: Civic Struggles for a New South Africa* (Monthly Review Press, New York, 1996).

9   The original sputnik was, of course, launched in 1957, but it is likely that Motlana is using the term as a generic to refer to the Russian space technology of the time.

10   Interview with Nthato Motlana, 18 March 2006.

11   J. Seekings, 'South Africa's townships 1980–1991: An annotated bibliography', University of Stellenbosch, Research Unit for Sociology of Development, occasional paper, no. 16, 1992.

12   Castells, 1977.

13   Lodge & Nasson, 1991; Adler & Steinberg, 2000.

14   Adler & Steinberg, 2000, p. 1.

15   In 1983 the UDF was constituted by 565 organisations, 83 of which were listed as 'civics', 313 as 'youth' and 32 as 'women' (Lodge & Nasson, 1991, p. 51).

16   For a fuller account, see M. Mamdani, *Citizen and Subject: Contemporary Africa and the Legacy of Late Colonialism* (James Currey, London, 1996).

17   Interview with Motlana; Mayekiso, 1996.

18   Interview with Tom Manthata, 23 March 2006.

19   Interview with Motlana.

20   W. Beinart, *Twentieth-century South Africa* (Oxford University Press, Oxford, 1994), p. 247.

21   Adler & Steinberg, 2000.

22   Lodge & Nasson, 1991.

23   Interview with Motlana.

24   P. Bonner & L. Segal, *Soweto: A History* (Maskew Miller Longman, Cape Town, 1998), p. 124.

25   Adler & Steinberg, 2000, p. 8.

26   Interviews with Motlana and Manthata.

27   Interview with Manthata.

28   Lodge and Nasson (1991) describe the Black Consciousness Movement as 'ideologically eclectic', containing some activists who were more inclined to class analysis and some who asserted the central tenet to be the exclusion of white activists from the struggle.

29   Interview with Manthata.

30   Interview with Motlana.

31   Mayekiso, 1996, p. 12.

32   Interview with Motlana.

33   Terreblanche, 2002; P. Bond, *Against Global Apartheid: South Africa Meets the World Bank, IMF and International Finance* (UCT Press, Cape Town, 2001); H. Marais, *South Africa: Limits to Change: The Political Economy of Transition,* 2nd ed. (Zed Books, London, New York & Cape Town, 2001).

34   Terreblanche, 2002, p. 85.

35   Marais, 2001, p. 123.

36   Bond, 2001; N. Gibson (ed.), *Challenging Hegemony: Social Movements and the Quest for a New Humanism in Post-apartheid South Africa* (Africa World Press, Trenton & Asmara, 2006).

37   Terreblanche, 2002; Bond, 2001.

38   Bond, 2001; Pithouse, 2005.

39   R. Ballard et al., 'Globalisation, marginalization and contemporary social movements in South Africa', *African Affairs*, 104 (2005), p. 616.

40   Terreblanche, 2002, p. 422.

41   S. Buhlungu, *The Anti-Privatisation Forum: A Profile of a Post-apartheid Social Movement*, Centre for Civil Society, research report, p. 4, <http://www.nu.ac.za/ccs/>.

42   P. Alexander, 'Anti-globalisation movements, identity and leadership: Trevor Ngwane and the Soweto Electricity Crisis Committee', Centre for Civil Society, n.d., <http://www.nu.ac.za/ccs/>.

43   Groups or clubs that act as rotating credit unions or informal savings associations.

44   Operation Khanyisa refers to the strategy used by SECC members to reconnect people's electricity when it is cut off for non-payment. Many of these men are skilled electricians or have learnt how to perform these complex electrical operations from their comrades. Some are even ex-Eskom employees (Eskom is the South African parastatal electricity-generating company). They do this work on a voluntary basis.

45   Interview with Ngwane.

46   Interviews with Motlana and Manthata.

47   Interview with Mrs Masondo, 19 July 2004.

48   Ibid.

49   Mayekiso, 1996; Lodge & Nasson, 1991; Bond, 2004; Gibson, 2006.

50   Pamphlet distributed in the Vaal area, 1984, cited in Lodge & Nasson, 1991, p. 132.

Chapter 13

1   I am grateful to Dale McKinley for commenting on this chapter.

2   APF (Anti-Privatisation Forum), 'About the Anti-Privatisation Forum', 2001, <http://www.apf.org.za>.

3   Ibid.

4   Ibid.

5   D. McKinley & P. Naidoo, 'New social movements in South Africa: A story in creation', *Development Update*, 5, 2 (2004), p. 15.

6   P. Bond, *Elite Transition: Globalisation and the Rise of Economic Fundamentalism in South Africa* (Pluto Press, London, 2000).

7   The Gini-coefficient is a statistical measure of wealth or income inequality. It can range from 0 to 1, where 0 is indicative of an equal distribution of wealth, while a higher Gini-coefficient indicates a higher level of inequality.

8   S. Tarrow, *Power in Movement: Social Movements, Collective Action and Politics* (Cambridge University Press, New York, 1994), p. 18.

9   Ibid., pp. 81–82.

10   R. Ballard et al., 'Introduction: From anti-apartheid to post-apartheid social movements', in R. Ballard et al. (eds), *Voices of Protest: Social Movements in Post-apartheid South Africa* (University of KwaZulu-Natal Press, Durban, 2006), p. 15.

11   Ibid.

12   Bond, 2000; H. Marais, *South Africa: Limits to Change: The Political Economy of Transition* (Zed Books & UCT Press, London, New York & Cape Town, 2001); P. Dwyer, 'South Africa under the ANC: Still bound to the chains of exploitation', in L. Zeilig (ed.), *Class Struggle and Resistance in Africa* (New Clarion Press, Cheltenham, 2002); D. McKinley, 'The political economy of the rise of social movements in South Africa', seminar paper presented at the Centre for Policy Studies, Johannesburg, 2003a; D. McKinley, 'Democracy and social movements in South Africa', in V. Padayachee (ed.), *The Development Decade? Economic and Social Change in South Africa, 1994–2004* (HSRC Press, Cape Town, 2006b); D. McKinley, 'South Africa's third local government elections and the institutionalisation of "low-intensity" neo-liberal democracy', in J. Minnie (ed.), *Outside the Ballot Box: Preconditions for Elections in Southern Africa 2005/6* (Media Institute of Southern Africa, Windhoek, 2006a).

13   S. Greenberg & N. Ndlovu, 'Civil society relationships', *Development Update*, 5, 2 (2004), p. 45.

14   Ibid., p. 39.

15   M. Heywood, 'Social movements: Challenging the state', paper prepared for the Harold Wolpe Memorial Seminar and presented at The Edge Institute, 4 May 2005, pp. 3–4, <http://www.the-edge.org.za/seminars.htm>.

16   S. Friedman & S. Mottiar, 'Seeking the high ground: The Treatment Action Campaign and the politics of morality', in R. Ballard et al. (eds), *Voices of Protest: Social Movements in Post-apartheid South Africa* (University of KwaZulu-Natal Press Durban, 2006), p. 38.

17   Ibid.

18   Heywood, 2005, p. 5.

19   Friedman & Mottiar, 2006, p. 34.

20   McKinley, cited in Friedman and Mottiar, 2006, p. 38.

21   APF (Anti-Privatisation Forum), 'Anti-Privatisation Forum local government platform', press release, 6 February 2006.

22   R. Ballard et al., 'Globalization, marginalization, and contemporary social movements in South Africa' (Centre for Civil Society, 2003), p. 13, <http://www.nu.ac.za/ccs/>.

Endnotes

23   R. Greenstein, *State, Civil Society and the Reconfiguration of Power in Post-apartheid South Africa*, Centre for Civil Society, research report, no. 8 (CCS, Durban, 2003), p. 42.
24   Ibid.
25   L. Pretorius, 'Government *by* or *over* the people? The African National Congress's conception of democracy', *Social Identities*, 12, 6 (2006), p. 745, emphasis in original.
26   McKinley & Naidoo, 2004, p. 13.
27   Greenberg & Ndlovu, 2004, p. 41.
28   Ibid., pp. 41–42.
29   N. Benjamin, 'Organisation building and mass mobilisation', *Development Update*, 5, 2 (2004), p. 90, emphasis added.
30   A. Desai, *Neo-liberalism and Its Discontents: The Rise of Community Movements in Post-apartheid South Africa*, Centre for Civil Society, research report (2002), p. 14, <http://www.nu.ac.za/ccs/>; McKinley & Naidoo, 2004, p. 11; D. McKinley & A. Veriava, *Arresting Dissent: State Repression and Post-apartheid Social Movements* (Centre for Violence and Reconciliation, Braamfontein, 2005), p. 25.
31   McKinley & Naidoo, 2004, pp. 9, 14–15.
32   City of Johannesburg, *City of Johannesburg: An African City in Change* (Zebra Press, Johannesburg, 2001), p. 32.
33   J. Beall, O. Crankshaw & S. Parnell, *Uniting a Divided City: Governance and Social Exclusion in Johannesburg* (Earthscan, London, 2002), p. 99.
34   Ibid., pp. 99–100.
35   Afrol, 'SA unions see hope for economic recovery', *Afrol*, 19 August 2003; F. Barchiesi, 'Classes, multitudes and the politics of community movements in post-apartheid South Africa', in N. Gibson (ed.), *Challenging Hegemony: Social Movements and the Quest for a New Humanism in Post-apartheid South Africa* (Africa World Press, Trenton & Asmara, 2006), p. 233.
36   J. Pape & D. A. McDonald, 'Introduction', in D. A. McDonald & J. Pape (eds), *Cost Recovery and the Crisis of Service Delivery in South Africa* (HSRC Press & Zed Books, Cape Town, London & New York, 2002), pp. 6–7; see also Beall, Crankshaw & Parnell, 2002, pp. 101–2 for a useful tabulated summary of the iGoli 2002 debate.
37   E. Cottle, 'Ideology and social movements', *Development Update*, 5, 2 (2004), p. 99.
38   Mokolo was referring here to Charles Nqakula, who held the position of minister of safety and security at the time of the interview.
39   Interview with Bricks Mokolo, 24 August 2006.
40   Interview with Thabo Modisane, 4 April 2006.
41   Interview with Silumko Radebe, 1 September 2006.
42   Interview with Mokolo.
43   Ibid.
44   Interview with Dale McKinley, 10 August 2006.
45   Interview with Themba Hlatshwayo, 15 March 2007.
46   Interview with Mokolo.

47 Ibid.

48 Interview with Radebe.

49 Public Citizen, APF (Anti-Privatisation Forum) & CAWP (Coalition Against Water Privatisation), *Nothing for Mahala: The Forced Installation of Prepaid Water Meters in Stretford, Extension 4, Orange Farm, Johannesburg, South Africa*, report (2004), p. 8, <http://www.wateractivist.org>; City of Johannesburg, *Reflecting on a Solid Foundation: Building Developmental Local Government* (2006), p. 31, <http://www.joburg.org.za/>.

50 City of Johannesburg, 2006, p. 113.

51 Interview with Mtshali.

52 For information on how the pre-paid meter should work in practice, see Johannesburg Water, 'Prepayment water meter' (Johannesburg Water, n.d.a), p. 1; Johannesburg Water, 'Operation *Gcin'amanzi*: Free payment user guide' (Johannesburg Water, n.d.b), pp. 4, 8–9.

53 See, for example, Public Citizen, APF & CAWP, 2004; CAWP (Coalition Against Water Privatisation), 'The struggle against silent disconnections: Prepaid meters and the struggle for life in Phiri, Soweto' (CAWP, Johannesburg, 2004); E. Harvey, 'Managing the poor by remote control: Johannesburg's experiments with prepaid water meters', in D. A. McDonald & G. Ruiters (eds), *The Age of Commodity: Water Privatisation in Southern Africa* (Earthscan, London, 2005), pp. 120–27; E. Harvey, 'The commodification of water in Soweto and its implications for social justice', PhD thesis, University of the Witwatersrand, 2007; M. Dawson, 'Social movements in contemporary South Africa: The Anti-Privatisation Forum and struggles around access to water in Johannesburg', DPhil thesis, University of Oxford, 2008, pp. 195–236.

54 Interview with Mokolo.

55 Interview with McKinley.

56 Ibid.

57 Ibid.

58 Interview with Radebe.

59 Ibid.

60 Interview with Mokolo.

61 Interview with Modisane.

62 Ibid.

63 Interview with Lehlohonolo (surname not known), Pimville, 7 July 2006.

64 A militant dance associated with anti-apartheid protest action, but still performed today during demonstrations.

65 APF (Anti-Privatisation Forum), 'APF launches CD of songs', press release, 5 May 2007.

66 Ibid.

67 Ibid.

68 Ibid.

69 Ibid.

Endnotes

70 As part of the government's cost-recovery plan, and in accordance with the terms of iGoli 2002, Johannesburg Water started introducing pre-paid water meters into the homes of township residents. This project is called 'Operation *Gcin'amanzi'*, which means 'conserving water'.

71 D. McKinley, 'Water is life: The Anti-Privatisation Forum and the struggle against water privatisation' (2003), <http://www.sarpn.org.za/>.

72 Ibid.; C. Smith, 'Guerrilla technicians challenge the privatization of South Africa's public resources', *In These Times*, 30 August 2002, <http://www.inthesetimes.com/>; J. Beall, 'Decentralizing government and decentring gender: Lessons from local government reform in South Africa', *Politics and Society*, 33, 2 (2005), p. 263; A. Earle, J. Goldin & P. Kgomotso, 'Domestic water provision in the democratic South Africa: Changes and challenges', paper produced for the Nordic Africa Institute's Conflicting Forms of Citizenship Programme (2005), p. 22; M. M. Kavanagh, 'South Africa's Freedom Charter at 50', *ZMag* (2005), <http://zmagsite.zmag.org/>.

73 A township situated approximately 45 kilometres south of Johannesburg.

74 AFP (Anti-Privatisation Forum), 'Orange Farm residents continue protest actions to demand basic services', press release, 13 September 2006, <http://www.polarisinstitute. org>.

75 For more on the water struggles of the OWCC, see OWCC (Orange Farm Water Crisis Committee), AFP (Anti-Privatisation Forum) & CAWP (Coalition Against Water Privatisation), 'Destroy the meter/enjoy free water' (OWCC, APF & CAWP, Johannesburg, 2004), <http://apf.org.za/IMG/pdf/orange_farm_prepaid_booklet.pdf>.

76 It is beyond the scope of this chapter to elaborate on the court case. More information can be found in Dawson, 2008, pp. 294–304; J. Dugard, 'Rights, regulation and resistance: The Phiri water rights campaign', *South African Journal of Human Rights*, 24, 3 (2009), pp. 593–611; J. Dugard, 'Legal mobilisation in the struggle for water in Phiri, Soweto', in A. Nilsen & S. Motta (eds), *Social Movements and the Development of Resistance in the Global South* (Palgrave, London, 2010).

77 Greenstein, 2003, p. 37.

78 Ibid., p. 44.

79 Interview with Radebe.

80 Interview with John Appolis, 30 March 2007.

81 Interview with McKinley.

82 McKinley & Veriava, 2005, pp. 41–42.

83 C. Tilly, *The Contentious French* (Harvard University Press, Cambridge, MA, 1986), p. 2.

84 C. Tilly, *Popular Contention in Great Britain, 1758–1834* (Harvard University Press, Cambridge, MA, 1995), p. 41.

85 S. Tarrow, *Power in Movement: Social Movements and Contentious Politics*, 2nd ed. (Cambridge University Press, Cambridge, 1998), p. 30, emphasis in original.

86 Tilly, 1986.

87   Tarrow, 1998, p. 31.

88   P. Dwyer & D. Seddon, 'The new wave? A global perspective on popular protest', in
      C. Barker & M. Tyldesley (eds), *8th International Conference on Alternative Futures
      and Popular Protest Conference Proceedings* (Manchester Metropolitan University,
      Manchester, 2002).

Bibliography

Abel, R. L., *Politics by Other Means: Law in the Struggle against Apartheid, 1980–1994* (Routledge, London, 1995).

Adam, H., 'Corporatism as minority veto under ANC hegemony in South Africa', in H. Giliomee & C. Simkins (eds), *The Awkward Embrace: One-party Domination and Democracy* (Routledge, London, 1999).

Adams, S., 'What's left? The South African Communist Party after apartheid', *Review of African Political Economy*, 72 (1997), pp. 237–48.

Adler, G. & Steinberg, J. (eds), *From Comrades to Citizens: The South African Civics Movement and the Transition to Democracy* (Macmillan, London, 2000).

Alexander, P., 'Anti-globalisation movements, identity and leadership: Ngwane, T. and the Soweto Electricity Crisis Committee', Centre for Civil Society, n.d., <http://www.nu.ac.za/ccs/>.

Alexandra Renewal Project, 'Heritage overview', 26 May 2006, <http://www.alexandra.co.za/08_social/heritage_0.htm>.

Allen, J., *Rabble-rouser for Peace: The Authorised Biography of Desmond Tutu* (Rider, London, 2006).

ANC (African National Congress), 'Take the struggle to the white areas' (ca 1985), accessed 27 November 2007, <http://www.anc.org.za/ancdocs/history/ungovern.html>.

Anon., 'Health workers' struggles', *Critical Health*, 15 (1986a), pp. 16–19.

——, 'Other strikes at other hospitals', *Critical Health*, 15 (1986b), pp. 12–14.

——, 'Baragwanath Hospital strike 1985: Divided interests and joint action', *Critical Health*, 15 (1986c), pp. 4–10.

——, 'An historical overview of nursing struggles in South Africa', *Critical Health*, 24 (1998), pp. 53–62.

Anyaoku, E., *The Inside Story of the Modern Commonwealth* (Evans Brothers, London, 2004).

Baldwin-Ragaven, L., De Gruchy, J. & London, L., *An Ambulance of the Wrong Colour: Health Professionals, Human Rights and Ethics in South Africa* (UCT Press, Cape Town, 1999).

Ballard, R. et al., 'Globalization, marginalization, and contemporary social movements in South Africa' (Centre for Civil Society, 2003), <http://www.nu.ac.za/ccs/>.

Ballard, R. et al., 'Globalisation, marginalization and contemporary social movements in South Africa', *African Affairs*, 104 (2005), pp. 615–34.

——, 'Introduction: From anti-apartheid to post-apartheid social movements', in R. Ballard et al. (eds), *Voices of Protest: Social Movements in Post-apartheid South Africa* (University of KwaZulu-Natal Press, Durban, 2006).

Balseiro, I. & Masilela, N. (eds), *To Change Reels: Film and Film Culture in South Africa* (Wayne State University Press, Detroit, 2003).

Barchiesi, F., 'Classes, multitudes and the politics of community movements in post-apartheid South Africa', in N. Gibson (ed.), *Challenging Hegemony: Social Movements and the Quest for a New Humanism in Post-apartheid South Africa* (Africa World Press, Trenton & Asmara, 2006).

Barker, C. & Tyldesley, M. (eds), *8th International Conference on Alternative Futures and Popular Protest Conference Proceedings* (Manchester Metropolitan University, Manchester, 2002).

Barnett, T. & Whiteside, A., *AIDS in the Twentieth Century: Disease and Globalisation* (Palgrave, London, 2006).

Barrell, H., 'Conscripts to their age: African National Congress operational strategy, 1976–1986' (unpublished DPhil, University of Oxford, 1993).

Baskin, J., *Striking Back: A History of COSATU* (Ravan Press, Johannesburg, 1991).

Beall, J., 'Decentralizing government and decentring gender: Lessons from local government reform in South Africa', *Politics and Society*, 33, 2 (2005), pp. 253–76.

Beall, J., Crankshaw, O. & Parnell, S., *Uniting a Divided City: Governance and Social Exclusion in Johannesburg* (Earthscan, London, 2002).

Beall, J., Gelb, S. & Hassim, S., 'Fragile stability: State and society in democratic South Africa', *Journal of Southern African Studies*, 31, 4 (2005), pp. 681–700.

Beinart, W., 'Agrarian history and agrarian reconstruction', in J. Lonsdale (ed.), *South Africa in Question* (James Currey, Oxford, 1988).

——, *Twentieth-century South Africa* (Oxford University Press, Oxford, 1994).

——, *Twentieth-century South Africa* (Oxford University Press, Oxford, 2001).

Beinart, W. & Bundy, C., *Hidden Struggles in Rural South Africa: Politics and Popular Movements in Transkei and the Eastern Cape, 1890–1930* (James Currey, London, 1987).

Bembridge, T. J., *Problems of Agricultural Development in the Republic of Transkei: A Preliminary Summary*, research report for the Urban–Rural Workshop, Stellenbosch, 2–4 June, 1982.

Benjamin, N., 'Organisation building and mass mobilisation', *Development Update*, 5, 2 (2004), pp. 73–93.

Benson, M., *Nelson Mandela* (Penguin, Harmondsworth, 1986).

Berman, B., 'Ethnicity, patronage and the African state: The politics of uncivil nationalism', *African Affairs*, 97, 388 (1998), pp. 305–41.

Bernhardt, T., 'The nurses' strike: A well organised plea for recognition', *Industrial Democracy Review*, 4, 5 (1996), pp. 11–20.

Best, S., 'The commodification of reality and the reality of commodification: Baudrillard, Debord, and postmodern theory', in D. Kellner (ed.), *Baudrillard: A Critical Reader* (Blackwell, Oxford, 1994).

Bierman, J. & Erasmus, C., 'Pretoria's gamble', *Maclean's* (7 November 1988).

Bissell, R. E. & Crocker, C. A. (eds), *South Africa in the 1980s* (Westview Press, Boulder, 1979).

Boehmer, E., *Mandela: A Very Short Introduction* (Oxford University Press, Oxford, 2008).

Bond, P., *Elite Transition: Globalisation and the Rise of Economic Fundamentalism in South Africa* (Pluto Press, London, 2000a).

——, *Cities of Gold, Townships of Coal: Essays on South Africa's New Urban Crisis* (Africa World Press, Trenton & Asmara, 2000b).

——, *Against Global Apartheid: South Africa Meets the World Bank, IMF and International Finance* (UCT Press, Cape Town, 2001).

——, *South Africa's Resurgent Urban Social Movements: The Case of Johannesburg, 1984, 1994, 2004*, Centre for Civil Society, research report, no. 22, 2004, <http://www.ukzn. ac.za/CCS/files/ Bond-sm.pdf>.

Bonner, P. (ed.), *Working Papers in South African Studies*, vol. 2 (Ravan Press, Johannesburg, 1981).

Bonner, P. & Nieftagodien, N., *Alexandra: A History* (Wits University Press, Johannesburg, 2008).

Bonner, P. & Segal, L., *Soweto: A History* (Maskew Miller Longman, Cape Town, 1998).

Booyse, W. J., 'The concept "people's war" in the strategy of the ANC and the PAC: A comparative analysis', DPhil thesis, Potchefstroom University, 1990.

Bozzoli, B. (ed.), *Town and Countryside in the Transvaal* (Ravan Press, Johannesburg, 1983).

——, (ed.), *Class, Community and Conflict* (Ravan Press, Johannesburg, 1987).

——, *Theatres of Struggle and the End of Apartheid* (Edinburgh University Press, Edinburgh, 2004).

Bradford, H., *A Taste of Freedom: The ICU in Rural South Africa, 1920–1930* (Yale University Press, New Haven, 1987).

Bramwell, B. & Rawding, L., 'Tourism marketing images of industrial cities', *Annals of Tourism Research*, 23 (1996), pp. 201–21.

Brink, E. & Malungane, G., *Soweto 16 June 1976: It All Started with a Dog* (Kwela Books, Cape Town, 2001).

Buechler, S. M., *Social Movements in Advanced Capitalism: The Political Economy and Cultural Construction of Social Activism* (Oxford University Press, New York, 2000).

Buhlungu, S., *The Anti-Privatisation Forum: A Profile of a Post-apartheid Social Movement*, Centre for Civil Society, research report, <http://www.nu.ac.za/ccs/>.

Bundy, C., 'Street sociology and pavement politics: Aspects of youth and student resistance in Cape Town, 1985', *Journal of Southern African Studies*, 13, 3 (1987), pp. 303–30.

Buntman, F., *Robben Island and Prisoner Resistance to Apartheid* (Cambridge University Press, Cambridge, 2003).

Burns, T., 'The organization of public opinion', in J. Curran, M. Gurevitch & J. Woollacott (eds), *Mass Communication and Society*, 2nd ed. (Arnold, London, 1984).

Butler, A., *Cyril Ramaphosa* (Jacana, Johannesburg, 2007).

——. *Cyril Ramaphosa* (Jacana, Cape Town, 2008).

Cachalia, C., *Comrade Moss* (Learn & Teach Publications, Johannesburg, 1989).

Cameron, E., *Witness to AIDS* (Tafelberg, Cape Town, 2005).

Campbell, J., 'Where do we stand? Common mechanisms in organisational and social movement research', in G. Davis et al. (eds), *Social Movements and Organization Theory* (Cambridge University Press, Cambridge, 2005).

Canel, E., 'New social movement theory and resource mobilization theory: The need for integration', in M. Kaufman & H. D. Alfonso (eds), *Community Power and Grassroots Democracy: The Transformation of Social Life* (Zed Books, London & New Jersey, 1997).

Carlson, J., *No Neutral Ground* (Quartet Books, London, 1977).

Carson, T., 'Black trade unions and consumer boycotts in the Cape Province, South Africa, 1978–82', DPhil thesis, University of Oxford, 2008.

Cashdan, B. (director), *Two Trevors Go to Washington* (2000).

Cassirer, E., *The Myth of the State* (Yale University Press, New Haven, 1964).

Castells, M., *The Urban Question* (Edward Arnold, London, 1977).

——, *The City and the Grassroots: A Cross-cultural Theory of Urban Social Movements* (Edward Arnold, London, 1983).

CAWP (Coalition Against Water Privatisation), 'The struggle against silent disconnections: Prepaid meters and the struggle for life in Phiri, Soweto' (CAWP, Johannesburg, 2004).

Central Statistical Service, *Population Census, Report No. 02-85-01: Geographical Distribution with a Review for 1960–1985* (Government Printer, Pretoria, 1986).

Centre for Health Policy Resource Room, 'Highlights of the law reform and human rights strategy', *AIDS Bulletin*, 3,2 (1994).

Cheater, A. P., 'A marginal elite? African registered nurses in Durban, South Africa', *African Studies*, 33 (1974), pp. 143–58.

City of Johannesburg, *City of Johannesburg: An African City in Change* (Zebra Press, Johannesburg, 2001).

——, *Reflecting on a Solid Foundation: Building Developmental Local Government* (2006), <http://www.joburg.org.za>.

Clegg, J., '*Ukubuyisa isidumbu* – "bring back the body": An examination into the ideology of vengeance in the Msinga and Mpofana rural locations, 1882–1944', in P. Bonner (ed.), *Working Papers in South African Studies*, vol. 2 (Ravan Press, Johannesburg, 1981).

Collier, S. & Ong, A. (eds), *Global Assemblages, Technology, Politics and Ethics as Anthropological Problems* (Blackwell, Malden, MA, 2005).

Commonwealth EPG (Eminent Persons Group), *Mission to South Africa: The Commonwealth Report. The Findings of the Commonwealth Eminent Persons Group on Southern Africa* (Penguin, Harmondsworth, 1986).

Coombes, A. E., *History after Apartheid: Visual Culture and Public Memory in a Democratic South Africa* (Wits University Press, Johannesburg, 2004).

Cooper, M., 'New pattern of protest', *Contact: The SA News Review*, 1, 5 (1958).

Cooper, C. et al., *Race Relations Survey 1988/89* (South African Institute of Race Relations, Johannesburg, 1989).

Cottle, E., 'Ideology and social movements', *Development Update*, 5, 2 (2004), pp. 95–128.

Crang, M., 'Envisioning urban histories: Bristol as palimpsest, postcards, and snapshots', *Environment and Planning*, 28 (1996), pp. 429–52.

Curran, J., Gurevitch, M. & Woollacott, J. (eds), *Mass Communication and Society*, 2nd ed. (Arnold, London, 1984).

DAF (Department of Agricultural & Forestry), *Transkei Agricultural Development Study* (DAF, Umtata, 1991).

DALA (Department of Agriculture & Land Affairs), *Annual Report 2000–2001* (DALA, Grahamstown, 2001).

——, *Annual Report, 2001–2002* (DALA, Grahamstown, 2002).

——, *Strategic Plan 2006* (DALA, Grahamstown, 2006).

Daniel, J., Habib, A. & Southall, R. (eds), *State of the Nation: South Africa 2003–2004* (HSRC Press, Cape Town, 2003).

Davenport, R. & Saunders, C., *South Africa: A Modern History* (Macmillan, London, 2000).

Davis, Stephen M., *Apartheid's Rebels: Inside South Africa's Hidden War* (Yale University Press, New Haven & London, 1987).

Davis, G. F. et al.(eds), *Social Movements and Organization Theory* (Cambridge University Press, Cambridge, 2005).

Dawson, M.C., 'Social movements in contemporary South Africa: The Anti-Privatisation Forum and struggles around access to water in Johannesburg', DPhil thesis, University of Oxford, 2008.

Delius, P., *A Lion amongst the Cattle: Reconstruction and Resistance in the Northern Transvaal* (James Currey, Oxford, 1996).

Delius, P. & Glaser C., 'Sexual socialisation in South Africa: A historical perspective', *African Studies*, 61, 1 (2002), pp. 27–54.

Denniston, R., *Trevor Huddleston: A Life* (Macmillan, London, 1999).

Desai, A., *Neo-liberalism and Its Discontents: The Rise of Community Movements in Post-apartheid South Africa*, research report, Centre for Civil Society, 2002a, <http://www.nu.ac.za/ccs/>.

——, *We Are the Poors: Community Struggles in Post-apartheid South Africa* (Monthly Review Press, New York, 2002b).

De Waal, A., *AIDS and Power: Why There Is No Political Crisis – Yet* (David Philip, Cape Town, 2006).

De Wet, C. J., *Moving Together, Drifting Apart: Betterment Planning and Villagisation in a South African Homeland* (Witwatersrand University Press, Johannesburg, 1995).

Digby, A. & Sweet, H., 'Nurses as cultural brokers in twentieth-century South Africa', in W. Ernst (ed.), *Plural Medicine, Tradition and Modernity, 1800–2000* (Routledge, London, 2002).

Dora, V. D., 'The rhetoric of nostalgia: Postcolonial Alexandria between uncanny memories and global geographies', *Cultural Geographies*, 13, 2 (2006), pp. 207–38.

Dorrington, R. et al., *The Impact of HIV/AIDS on Adult Mortality in South Africa: Technical Report* (Burden of Disease Research Unit, Medical Research Council, Cape Town, 2001), <http://www.africa.upenn.edu/Urgent_Action/apic-101501.html>.

Dugard, J., 'Rights, regulation and resistance: The Phiri water rights campaign', *South African Journal of Human Rights*, 24, 3 (2009), pp. 593–611.

——, 'Legal mobilisation in the struggle for water in Phiri, Soweto', in A. Nilsen, & S. Motta (eds), *Social Movements and the Development of Resistance in the Global South* (Palgrave, London, 2010).

Du Preez Bezdrob, A., *Winnie Mandela: A Life* (Struik, Cape Town, 2003).

Du Toit, D., *Capital and Labour in South Africa: Class Struggles in the 1970s* (Kegan Paul, London, 1981).

Dwyer, P., 'South Africa under the ANC: Still bound to the chains of exploitation', in L. Zeilig (ed.), *Class Struggle and Resistance in Africa* (New Clarion Press, Cheltenham, 2002).

Dwyer, P. & Seddon, D., 'The new wave? A global perspective on popular protest', in C. Barker & M. Tyldesley (eds), *8th International Conference on Alternative Futures and Popular Protest Conference Proceedings* (Manchester Metropolitan University, Manchester, 2002).

Earle, A., Goldin, J. & Kgomotso, P., 'Domestic water provision in the democratic South Africa: Changes and challenges', paper produced for the Nordic Africa Institute's Conflicting Forms of Citizenship Programme (2005).

Ehlers, V. J., 'Nursing and politics: A South African perspective', *International Nursing Review*, 47 (2000), pp. 74–82.

Ek, A., 'Perilous silence and discriminatory visibility: On absent and present representations of HIV-positive individuals in the South African press, 1998–2003', in M. Foller & H. Thorn (eds), *No Name Fever: AIDS in the Age of Globalization* (Studentlitteratur, Lund, 2005).

Elias, C. M., *Report on the Labour Dispute at Fatti's & Moni's* (South African Institute of Race Relations, Johannesburg, ca September 1979).

Ellis, S. & Sechaba, T., *Comrades against Apartheid: The ANC and South African Communist Party in Exile* (James Currey, London, 1992).

Epstein, S., 'AIDS activism and state policies in the United States', in M. Foller & H. Thorn (eds), *No Name Fever: AIDS in the Age of Globalization* (Studentlitteratur, Lund, 2005).

Ernst, W. (ed.), *Plural Medicine, Tradition and Modernity, 1800–2000* (Routledge, London, 2002).

Evans, G., 'Hard branding the cultural city: From Prado to Prada', *International Journal of Urban and Regional Research*, 27, 2 (2003), pp. 417–40.

Fieldhouse, R., *Anti-apartheid: A History of the Movement in Britain* (Merlin, London, 2005).

First, R., *No Easy Walk to Freedom: Articles, Speeches, and Trial Addresses of Nelson Mandela* (Heinemann, London, 1965).

Florida, R., *The Rise of the Creative Class: And How It's Transforming Work, Leisure, Community and Everyday Life* (Basic Books, New York, 2002).

Foller, M. & Thorn, H. (eds), *No Name Fever: AIDS in the Age of Globalization* (Studentlitteratur, Lund, 2005).

Foster, D., Davis, D. & Sandler, D., *Detention and Torture in South Africa* (James Currey, London & Claremont, 1989).

Freund, B., *Insiders and Outsiders: The Indian Working Class of Durban, 1919–1990* (University of Natal Press, Pietermaritzburg, 1995).

Friedman, S., *Building Tomorrow Today: African Workers in Trade Unions, 1970–1984* (Ravan Press, Johannesburg, 1987).

Friedman, S. & Mottiar, S., 'Seeking the high ground: The Treatment Action Campaign and the politics of morality', in R. Ballard, A. Habib & I. Valodia (eds), *Voices of Protest: Social Movements in Post-apartheid South Africa* (University of KwaZulu-Natal Press Durban, 2006).

Frohlich, J., *National STD/HIV/AIDS Review: Comprehensive Report*, vols. 1–4 (Department of Health, Pretoria, 1997).

Frohlich, J. & Moodley, P., 'The National Aids Convention of South Africa: NACOSA', in Department of Health, *The South Africa STD/HIV/AIDS Review Situational Analysis* (Department of Health, Pretoria, 1997).

Gevisser, M., 'A different fight for freedom: A history of South African lesbian and gay organisation from the 1950s to 1990s', in M. Gevisser & E. Cameron (eds), *Defiant Desire: Gay and Lesbian Lives in South Africa* (Routledge, New York, 1995).

——, *Thabo Mbeki: The Dream Deferred* (Jonathan Ball, Johannesburg, 2007).

Gevisser, M. & Cameron, E. (eds), *Defiant Desire: Gay and Lesbian Lives in South Africa* (Routledge, New York, 1995).

Gibson, N. (ed.), *Challenging Hegemony: Social Movements and the Quest for a New Humanism in Post-apartheid South Africa* (Africa World Press, Trenton & Asmara, 2006).

Giliomee, H. & Simkins, C., *The Awkward Embrace: One-party Domination and Democracy* (Routledge, London, 1999).

Gilmore, J. H., 'Frontiers of the experience economy', *Batten Briefings: From the Darden Graduate School of Business Administration* (Batten Institute, Charlottesville, 2003).

Gobodo-Madikizela, P., *A Human Being Died that Night: Forgiving Apartheid's Chief Killer* (Portobello, London, 2006).

Goodwin, J., Jasper, J. & Polletta, F. (eds), *Passionate Politics: Emotions and Social Movements* (University of Chicago Press, Chicago, 2001).

Gordin, J., *Zuma: A Biography* (Jonathan Ball, Johannesburg, 2008).

Goudie, S. C., Khan, F. & Killian, D., 'Transforming tourism: Black empowerment, heritage and identity beyond apartheid', *South African Geographical Journal*, 81, 1 (1999), pp. 22–31.

Gould, D., "'Rock the boat, don't rock the boat, baby'": Ambivalence and the emergence of militant AIDS activism', in J. Goodwin, J. Jasper & F. Polletta (eds), *Passionate Politics: Emotions and Social Movements* (University of Chicago Press, Chicago, 2001).

Gouldner, A., *Wildcat Strike* (Routledge, London, 1955).

Greenberg, S., 'The Landless People's Movement and the failure of post-apartheid land reform', in R. Ballard et al. (eds), *Voices of Protest: Social Movements in Post-apartheid South Africa* (University of KwaZulu-Natal Press, Durban, 2006).

Greenberg, S. & Ndlovu, N., 'Civil society relationships', *Development Update*, 5, 2 (2004), pp. 23–48.

Greenstein, R., *State, Civil Society and the Reconfiguration of Power in Post-apartheid South Africa*, Centre for Civil Society, research report, no. 8 (CCS, Durban, 2003).

Gumede, W. M., *Thabo Mbeki and the Battle for the Soul of the ANC* (Zebra Press, Cape Town, 2007).

Gunner, E., 'Jacob Zuma, the social body and the unruly power of song', *African Affairs*, 108, 430 (2009), pp. 27–48.

Guy, J., *The Maphumulo Uprising: War, Law and Ritual in the Zulu Rebellion* (University of KwaZulu-Natal Press, Durban, 2005).

Gwala, M. P. (ed.), *Black Review 1973* (Durban, Black Community Programmes, 1974).

Hall, S., 'Culture, the media and the "ideological effect"', in J. Curran, M. Gurevitch & J. Woollacott (eds), *Mass Communication and Society*, 2nd ed. (Arnold, London, 1984).

Harrison, N., *Winnie Mandela: Mother of a Nation* (Victor Gollancz, London, 1985).

Harvey, E., 'Managing the poor by remote control: Johannesburg's experiments with prepaid water meters', in D. A. McDonald & G. Ruiters (eds), *The Age of Commodity: Water Privatisation in Southern Africa* (Earthscan, London, 2005).

——, 'The commodification of water in Soweto and its implications for social justice', PhD thesis, University of the Witwatersrand, 2007.

Harvey, R., *The Fall of Apartheid* (Palgrave Macmillan, Basingstoke, 2001).

Hawkins Associates, *The Physical and Spatial Basis for Transkei's First Five Year Development Plan* (Hawkins Associates, Salisbury, October 1980).

Hemson, D., 'Dock workers, labour circulation, and class struggles in Durban, 1940–1959', *Journal of Southern African Studies*, 4, 1 (1977), pp. 88–124.

——, 'Class consciousness and the migrant workers: The dockworkers of Durban', PhD thesis, University of Warwick, 1978.

Hendricks, F., *The Pillars of Apartheid: Land Tenure, Rural Planning and the Chieftaincy* (Wicksell International, Stockholm, 1990).

Heunis, C. & Pelser, A. J., 'Down the needle! Should public sector nurses in South Africa have the right to strike?' *Curationis*, 20, 3 (1997), pp. 41–46.

Heywood, M., 'Preventing mother-to-child-HIV transmission in South Africa: Background, strategies and outcomes of the Treatment Action Campaign case against the minister of health', *South African Journal on Human Rights*, 19 (2003), pp. 278–315.

——, 'The price of denial', *Development Update*, 5, 3 (2004), pp. 93–102.

—, 'Social movements: Challenging the state', paper prepared for the Harold Wolpe Memorial Seminar, presented at The Edge Institute, 4 May 2005, <http://www.the-edge.org.za/seminars.htm>.

Herbst, J., 'Prospects for revolution in South Africa', *Political Science Quarterly*, 103, 4 (1988–89), pp. 665–85.

Hill, D., *Body of Truth: Leveraging What Consumers Can't or Won't Say* (Wiley, Hoboken, 2003).

Hirson, B., *Year of Ash, Year of Fire: The Soweto Revolt: Roots of a Revolution?* (Zed Books, London, 1979).

Horner, D., 'African labour representation up to 1975', in J. Maree (ed.), *The Independent Trade Unions, 1974–1984* (Ravan Press, Johannesburg, 1987).

Horrell, M., *South Africa's Workers* (South African Institute of Race Relations, Johannesburg, 1969).

Horrell, M. et al., *A Survey of Race Relations in South Africa 1972* (South African Institute of Race Relations, Johannesburg, 1973).

Horrigan, B., 'Notes on AIDS and its combatants: An appreciation', in M. Renov (ed.), *Theorizing Documentary* (Routledge, New York, 1993).

Horwitz, S., '"A phoenix rising": A history of Baragwanath Hospital, Soweto, South Africa, 1942–1990', DPhil thesis, University of Oxford, 2006.

—, '"Black nurses in white": Exploring young women's entry into the nursing profession at Baragwanath Hospital, Soweto, 1948–1980', *Social History of Medicine*, 20, 1 (2007), pp. 131–46.

Hughes, H. & Vaughan, A., 'The incorporation of historically disadvantaged communities into tourism initiatives in the new South Africa: Case studies from KwaZulu-Natal', in M. Robinson et al. (eds), *Management, Marketing and the Political Economy of Travel and Tourism* (Centre for Travel and Tourism and Business Education, Sunderland, 2000).

Hunt, J. A., *White Witch Doctor: A Surgeon's Life in Apartheid South Africa* (Durban House, Dallas, 2002).

Hyman, R., *Strikes* (Fontana, London, 1972).

Hyslop, J., *The Classroom Struggle: Policy and Resistance in South Africa 1940–1990* (University of Natal Press, Pietermaritzburg, 1999).

IDAF (International Defence and Aid Fund for Southern Africa), 'South Africa: The imprisoned society', *Sechaba*, 8, 4 (1974).

—, *Nelson Mandela: The Struggle Is My Life* (IDAF, London, 1978).

IIE (Institute for Industrial Education), *The Durban Strikes 1973: 'Human Beings with Souls'* (IIE & Ravan Press, Johannesburg, 1974).

Iliffe, J., *The African AIDS Epidemic: A History* (Double Storey, Cape Town, 2006).

Isaacman, A. et al., '"Cotton is the mother of poverty": Peasant resistance to forced cotton cultivation in Mozambique, 1938–61', *International Journal of African Historical Studies*, 13, 4 (1980), pp. 581–615.

James, D., *Gaining Ground: 'Rights' and 'Property' in South African Land Reform* (Routledge Cavendish, Abingdon, 2006).

Jarrett-Kerr, M., *African Pulse: Scenes from an African Hospital Window* (Faith Press, London, 1960).

Johannesburg Water, 'Prepayment water meter' (Johannesburg Water, n.d.a).

——, 'Operation *Gcin'amanzi*: Free payment user guide' (Johannesburg Water, n.d.b).

Johns, J. & Hunt Davis, R. (eds), *Mandela, Tambo, and the African National Congress: The Struggle against Apartheid, 1948–1990* (Oxford University Press, Oxford, 1991).

Johnston, S. & Bernstein, A., *Voices of Anger: Protest and Conflict in Two Municipalities: Report to the Conflict and Governance Facility* (Centre for Development, Johannesburg, 2007).

Johnstone, F. A., *Class, Race and Gold: A Study of Class Relations and Racial Discrimination in South Africa* (Routledge & Kegan Paul, London, 1976).

Joseph, H., *Side by Side: The Autobiography of Helen Joseph* (Zed Books, London, 1986).

Kale, R., 'Impressions of health in the new South Africa: A period of convalescence', *British Medical Journal*, 310 (1995), pp. 1119–22.

Kane-Berman, J., *Political Violence in South Africa* (South African Institute of Race Relations, Johannesburg, 1993).

Kaplan, L., 'Skills development for tourism in Alexandra Township, Johannesburg', *Urban Forum*, 15, 4 (2004), pp. 380–98.

Karis, T. & Gerhart, G. (eds), *From Protest to Challenge*, vol. 5, *Nadir and Resurgence, 1964–1979* (Indiana University Press, Bloomington, 1997).

Kathrada, A., *Memoirs* (Struik/Zebra, Cape Town, 2004).

Kaufman, M. & Alfonso, H. D. (eds), *Community Power and Grassroots Democracy: The Transformation of Social Life* (Zed Books, London & New Jersey, 1997).

Kavanagh, M., 'South Africa's Freedom Charter at 50', *ZMag* (2005), <http://zmagsite.zmag.org/>.

Kellner, D. (ed.), *Baudrillard: A Critical Reader* (Blackwell, Oxford, 1994).

Kentron, T. O., 'Anti-apartheid nursing body to confer: Protest against act growing', *Contact: The SA News Review* (14 June 1958).

Kepe, T., 'Magwa tea venture in South Africa: Politics, land and economics', *Social Dynamics*, 31, 1 (2005), pp. 261–79.

Khwela, S., '1973 strikes: Breaking the silence', *South African Labour Bulletin*, 17, 3 (1993), pp. 20–27.

Klein, G. L., 'The Anti-Apartheid Movement (AAM) in Britain and support for the African National Congress (ANC), 1976–1990', DPhil thesis, University of Oxford, 2007.

Kooy, M., 'The contract labour system and the Ovambo crisis of 1971 in South-West Africa', *African Studies Review*, 16, 1 (1973), pp. 83–105.

Lambert, R. V., 'The changing labour market of the seventies and state strategies of reform', in *Black Trade Unions in South Africa: Core of a New Democratic Opposition Movement?* (Friedrich Ebert Stiftung, Bonn, 1983).

Lawson, L., *Side Effects: The Story of AIDS in South Africa* (Double Storey, Cape Town, 2008).

Legassick, M., 'South Africa: Forced labour, industrialization, and racial differentiation', in R. Harris (ed.), *The Political Economy of Africa* (Halsted Press, Boston, 1975).

Lemon, A., 'Perspectives on democratic consolidation in Southern Africa: The five general elections of 2004', *Political Geography*, 26 (2007), pp. 824–50.

Levy, A., 'Report on Industrial Relations at Belville and Isando Plants', unpublished report, 1980, UCT Library.

Lewis, D., 'Black workers and trade unions', in T. Karis & G. Gerhart (eds), *From Protest to Challenge*, vol. 5, *Nadir and Resurgence, 1964–1979* (UNISA, Pretoria, 1997).

Lewis, J. et al., 'Community Health Media Trust: The role of HIV/AIDS media and moving us into action', paper presented at the South African AIDS Conference, Durban, 5–8 June, 2007.

Lodge, T., *Black Politics in South Africa since 1945* (Longman, London, 1983).

—, *The ANC after Nkomati* (South African Institute of Race Relations, Johannesburg, 1985).

—, "'Mayihlome! – Let us go to war!" From Nkomati to Kabwe: The African National Congress, January 1984–June 1985', in South African Research Service (ed.), *South African Review*, vol. 3 (Ravan Press, Johannesburg, 1986).

—, 'The African National Congress after the Kabwe conference', in G. Moss & I. Obery (eds), *South African Review*, vol. 4 (Ravan Press, Johannesburg, 1987).

—. *Mandela: A Critical Life* (Oxford University Press, Oxford, 2006).

Lodge, T. & Nasson, B., *All, Here and Now: Black Politics in South Africa in the 1980s* (David Philip, Cape Town, 1991).

Lonsdale, J., 'The moral economy of Mau Mau: Wealth, poverty and civic virtue in Kikuyu political thought', in J. Lonsdale & B. Berman (eds), *Unhappy Valley: Conflict in Kenya and Africa* (James Currey, London, 1992).

Lonsdale, J. & Berman, B. (eds), *Unhappy Valley: Conflict in Kenya and Africa* (James Currey, London, 1992).

Lowenthal, D., 'Past time, present place: Landscape and memory', *Geographical Review*, LXV, 1 (1974), pp. 1–36.

Lubanga, N., 'Nursing in South Africa: Black women workers organize', in M. Turshen (ed.), *Women and Health in Africa* (Africa World Press, Trenton, 1991).

Mager, A. K., *Gender and the Making of a South African Bantustan: A Social History of the Ciskei, 1945–1959* (James Currey, Oxford, 1999).

Maharaj, A. & Kathrada, A. (eds), *Mandela: The Authorised Portrait* (Bloomsbury, London, 2006).

Mamdani, M., *Citizen and Subject: Contemporary Africa and the Legacy of Late Colonialism* (James Currey, London, 1996).

Mandela, N., *Long Walk to Freedom: The Autobiography of Nelson Mandela* (Abacus, London, 1994).

——, *Long Walk to Freedom: The Autobiography of Nelson Mandela* (Little, Brown, London, 2001).

Mandela, W., *A Life* (Zebra Press, Cape Town, 2003).

Mandela, W. & Benjamin, A. (eds), *Part of My Soul* (Penguin, Harmondsworth, 1985).

Mangcu, X. (ed.), *The Meaning of Mandela: A Literary and Intellectual Celebration* (HSRC Press, Cape Town, 2006).

Mantashe, G., 'The nurses' strike: Organising nurses', *South African Communist Party*, 142 (1995), <http://www.sacp.org.za/main.php?include=pubs/acommunist/1995/issue142.html#Nurses>.

Marais, H., *South Africa: Limits to Change: The Political Economy of Transition* (Zed Books & UCT Press, London, New York & Cape Town, 2001).

Maree, J., 'Seeing strikes in perspective', *South African Labour Bulletin*, 2, 9 & 10 (1976), pp. 91–109.

Marks, S., *Reluctant Rebellion: The 1906–8 Disturbances in Natal* (Clarendon Press, Oxford, 1970).

——, *The Ambiguities of Dependence in South Africa: Class, Nationalism and the State in 20th Century Natal* (Johns Hopkins University Press, Baltimore, 1986).

——, *Divided Sisterhood: Race, Class and Gender in the South African Nursing Profession* (Wits University Press, Johannesburg, 1994).

——, 'The legacy of the history of nursing for post-apartheid South Africa', in A. M. Rafferty, J. Robinson & R. Elkan (eds), *Nursing History and the Politics of Welfare* (Routledge, New York, 1997).

Marx, K., *Capital*, vol. 1 (Penguin, Harmondsworth, 1976).

Masekela, H. & Michael Cheers, D., *Still Grazing: The Musical Journey of Hugh Masekela* (Crown, New York, 2004).

Mashaba, T., *Rising to the Challenge of Change: A History of Black Nursing in South Africa* (Juta, Kenwyn, 1995).

Masilela, N., 'The New African Movement and the beginnings of film culture in South Africa', in I. Balseiro & N. Masilela (eds), *To Change Reels: Film and Film Culture in South Africa* (Wayne State University Press, Detroit, 2003).

Mayekiso, M., *Township Politics: Civic Struggles for a New South Africa* (Monthly Review Press, New York, 1996).

Mbali, M., 'TAC in the history of patient-driven AIDS activism: The case for historicising South Africa's new social movements', in N. Gibson (ed.), *Challenging Hegemony: Social Movements and the Quest for a New Humanism in Post-apartheid South Africa* (Africa World Press, Trenton & Asmara, 2006).

McDonald, K., *Global Movements: Action and Culture* (Blackwell, Malden, MA & Oxford, 2006).

McDonald, S. F., 'The black community', in R. E. Bissell & C. A. Crocker (eds), *South Africa in the 1980s* (Westview Press, Boulder, 1979).

McDonald, D. A. & Ruiters, G. (eds), *The Age of Commodity: Water Privatisation in Southern Africa* (Earthscan, London, 2005).

McGrandle, P., *Trevor Huddleston: Turbulent Priest* (Continuum, London & New York, 2004).

McGregor, L., 'The Fatti's & Moni's dispute', *South African Labour Bulletin*, 5, 6 & 7 (1980), pp. 118–22.

McKinley, D., *The ANC and the Liberation Struggle: A Critical Political Biography* (Pluto Press, London, 1997).

——, 'The political economy of the rise of social movements in South Africa', seminar paper presented at the Centre for Policy Studies, Johannesburg, 2003a.

——, 'Water is life: The Anti-Privatisation Forum and the struggle against water privatisation', Anti Privatisation Forum, 2003b, <http://www.sarpn.org.za/>.

——, 'Democracy and social movements in South Africa', in V. Padayachee (ed.), *The Development Decade? Economic and Social Change in South Africa, 1994–2004* (HSRC Press, Cape Town, 2006a).

——, 'South Africa's third local government elections and the institutionalisation of "low-intensity" neo-liberal democracy', in J. Minnie (ed.), *Outside the Ballot Box: Preconditions for Elections in Southern Africa 2005/6* (Media Institute of Southern Africa, Windhoek, 2006b).

McKinley, D. & Naidoo, P., 'New social movements in South Africa: A story in creation', *Development Update*, 5, 2 (2004), pp. 9–22.

McKinley, D. & Veriava, A., *Arresting Dissent: State Repression and Post-apartheid Social Movements* (Centre for Violence and Reconciliation, Braamfontein, 2005).

McQuail, D., 'The influence and effects of mass media', in J. Curran, M. Gurevitch & J. Woollacott (eds), *Mass Communication and Society*, 2nd ed. (Arnold, London, 1984).

Meer, F., *Higher than Hope: The Authorised Biography of Nelson Mandela* (Penguin, Johannesburg, 1988).

Meethan, K., *Tourism in a Global Society: Place, Culture, Consumption* (Palgrave, Hampshire, 2001).

Melucci, A., *Nomads of the Present: Social Movements and Individual Needs in Contemporary Society* (Temple University Press, Philadelphia, 1989).

——, *Challenging Codes: Collective Action in the Information Age* (Cambridge University Press, Cambridge, 1996).

Meredith, M., *Nelson Mandela: A Biography* (Hamish Hamilton, London, 1997).

Miescher, G. & Henrichsen, D., *African Posters* (Basel, Afrikaner, Bibliographen, Switzerland, 2004).

Migdal, J., Kohli, A. & Shue, V. (eds), *State Power and Social Forces: Domination and Transformation in the Third World* (Cambridge, Cambridge University Press, 1994).

Ministry for Agriculture and Land Affairs, 'Agriculture policy in South Africa: A discussion document' (Ministry for Agriculture and Land Affairs, Pretoria, 1998).

Minnie, J. (ed.), *Outside the Ballot Box: Preconditions for Elections in Southern Africa 2005/6* (Media Institute of Southern Africa, Windhoek, 2006).

Morgan, I., 'The spaghetti siege', *Management* (1980), pp. 42–48.

Morgan, N., Pritchard, A. & Pride, R., *Destination Branding: Creating the Unique Destination Proposition* (Butterworth-Heinemann, Oxford, 2002).

Mortimer, B. & McCann, S. (eds), *New Directions in the History of Nursing in International Perspective* (Routledge, London, 2005).

Murray, C., *Black Mountain: Land, Class and Power in the Eastern Orange Free State, 1880s–1980s* (Edinburgh University Press, Edinburgh, 1992).

Myburgh, J., 'The African National Congress under the presidency of Thabo Mbeki (1997 to 2002)', DPhil thesis, University of Oxford, 2006.

Myers, G. A., 'Naming and placing the other: Power and the urban landscape in Zanzibar', *Tijdschrift voor Economische en Sociale Geografie*, 87 (1996), pp. 237–46.

Naidoo, K., 'The politics of youth resistance in the 1980s: The dilemmas of a differentiated Durban', *Journal of Southern African Studies*, 18, 1 (1992), pp. 143–65.

Nash, C., 'Placenames: Postcolonial locations', *Transactions of the Institute of British Geographers*, 24, 4 (1999), pp. 457–80.

Nattrass, N., *Mortal Combat: AIDS Denialism and the Struggle for Antiretrovirals in South Africa* (University of KwaZulu-Natal Press, Scottsville, 2007).

Ndlovu, S. M., *The Soweto Uprisings: Counter-memories of June 1976* (Ravan Press, Johannesburg, 1998).

Neocosmos, M., 'Civil society, citizenship and the politics of the (im)possible: Rethinking militancy in Africa today', unpublished paper, 2007.

Nguyen, V.K., 'Antiretroviral globalism, biopolitics, and therapeutic citizenship', in S. Collier & A. Ong (eds), *Global Assemblages, Technology, Politics and Ethics as Anthropological Problems* (Blackwell, Malden, MA, 2005).

Nilsen, A. & Motta, S. (eds), *Social Movements and the Development of Resistance in the Global South* (Palgrave, London, 2010).

Nixon, R., 'Mandela, messianism and the media', *Transition*, 51 (1991), pp. 42–55.

Ntsebeza, L., *Democracy Compromised: Chiefs and the Politics of Land in South Africa* (HSRC Press, Cape Town, 2006).

Nursing RSA, 'Obituary: Jane McLarty (1893–1989)', *Nursing RSA*, 4, 3 (1989), p. 8.

Office of the Auditor General, *Report of the Auditor General on the Appropriation and Miscellaneous Accounts and on the Accounts of Lower Authorities in the Area, 1966–67* (Ministry of the Interior, Umtata, 1967).

O'Malley, P., *Shades of Difference: Mac Maharaj and the Struggle for South Africa* (Viking Books, New York, 2007).

OWCC (Orange Farm Water Crisis Committee), AFP (Anti-Privatisation Forum) & CAWP (Coalition Against Water Privatisation), 'Destroy the meter/enjoy free water' (OWCC, APF & CAWP, Johannesburg, 2004), <http://apf.org.za/IMG/pdf/orange_farm_prepaid_booklet.pdf>.

Padyachee, V. (ed.), *The Development Decade? Economic and Social Change in South Africa, 1994–2004* (HSRC Press, Cape Town, 2006).

Paley, D., 'Only the poor have pre-paid water meters', *Alternatives* (17 November 2003), <http://www.alternatives.ca/>.

Pape, J. & McDonald, D. A., 'Introduction', in D. A. McDonald & J. Pape (eds), *Cost Recovery and the Crisis of Service Delivery in South Africa* (HSRC Press & Zed Books, Cape Town, London & New York, 2002).

Peires, J., 'Traditional leaders in purgatory: Local government in Tsolo, Qumbu and Port Saint Johns, 1990–2000', *African Studies*, 59, 1 (2000), pp. 97–114.

Pillay, D., 'Trade unions and alliance politics in Cape Town 1979–1985', PhD thesis, University of Essex, 1989.

Pretorius, L., 'Government *by* or *over* the people? The African National Congress's conception of democracy', *Social Identities*, 12, 6 (2006), pp. 745–69.

Price, R., *The Apartheid State in Crisis* (Oxford University Press, New York, 1991).

Public Citizen, AFP (Anti-Privatisation Forum) & CAWP (Coalition Against Water Privatisation), *Nothing for Mahala: The Forced Installation of Pre-paid Water Meters in Stretford, Extension 4, Orange Farm, Johannesburg, South Africa* (2004), <http://www.wateractivist.org>.

Public Citizen & OWCC (Orange Farm Water Crisis Committee), *South Africa: The Forced Implementation of Prepaid Meters* (Public Citizen, OWCC, 2004), <http://www.wateractivist.org>.

Rafferty, A. M., Robinson, J. & Elkan, R. (eds), *Nursing History and the Politics of Welfare* (New York, 1997).

Ranger, T., *Peasant Consciousness and Guerrilla War in Zimbabwe: A Comparative Study* (James Currey, London, 1985).

——, 'The invention of tradition revisited', in T. Ranger & O. Vaughn (eds), *Legitimacy and the State in 20th Century Africa* (Macmillan Press, Oxford, 1993).

Renov, M., *Theorizing Documentary* (Routledge, New York, 1993).

Republic of Transkei, *The Development Strategy, 1980–2000* (Republic of Transkei, Umtata, 1979).

Resha, M., *Mangoana o Tsoara Thipa ka Bohaleng: My Life in the Struggle* (Congress of South African Writers, Johannesburg, 1991).

Robins, S., '"Long live Zackie! long live": AIDS activism, science and citizenship after apartheid', *Journal of Southern African Studies*, 30, 3 (2004), pp. 651–72.

——, *Limits to Liberation after Apartheid* (James Currey, Oxford, 2005).

Robinson, M. (ed.), *Management, Marketing and the Political Economy of Travel and Tourism* (Centre for Travel and Tourism and Business Education, Sunderland, 2000).

Rogerson, C. M., 'Urban tourism and small tourism enterprise development in Johannesburg: The case of township tourism', *GeoJournal*, 60, 3 (2004), pp. 249–57.

Rosenthal, K., 'New social movements as civil society: The case of past and present Soweto', MSc dissertation, University of Oxford, 2006.

Rotha, P., Road, S. & Griffin, R. (eds), *Documentary Film: The Use of the Film Medium to*

Interpret Creatively and in Social Terms the Life of the People as It Exists in Reality (Faber & Faber, London, 1968).

SAIRR (South African Institute of Race Relations), *Annual Report* (SAIRR, Johannesburg, 1973).

——, SAIRR (South African Institute of Race Relations), *Annual Review (1973)* (SAIRR, Johannesburg, 1974).

Sampson, A., *Mandela: The Authorised Biography* (Harper Collins, London, 1999).

Sanders, R. (ed.), *Inseparable Humanity: An Anthology of Reflections of Shridath Ramphal* (Hansib, London, 1988).

Sapire, H., 'Politics and protest in shack settlements of the Pretoria-Witwatersrand-Vereeniging region, South Africa, 1980–1990', *Journal of Southern African Studies*, 18, 3 (1992), pp. 670–97.

Sato, C., 'Forced removals, land NGOs and community politics in KwaZulu-Natal, South Africa, 1953–2002', DPhil thesis, University of Oxford, 2006.

Sawyer, E., 'An ACT UP founder "acts up" for Africa's access to AIDS', in B. H. Shepard & R. Hayduk (eds), *From ACT UP to the WTO: Urban Protest and Community Building in the Era of Globalization* (Verso, London & New York, 2002).

Schneider, H., 'The AIDS impasse in South Africa as a struggle for symbolic power', paper presented at the AIDS in Context conference at the University of the Witwatersrand, Johannesburg, 2001.

——, 'On the fault-lines: The politics of AIDS policy in contemporary South Africa', *African Studies*, 61, 1 (2002), pp. 145–67.

Schneider, H. & Stein, J., 'Implementing AIDS policy in post-apartheid South Africa', *Social Science and Medicine*, 52, 2 (2001), pp. 723–31.

Schroeder, R., 'Trade unions, politics, and working class struggle: The Food and Canning Workers Union, 1975–86', BA (Hons) research essay, University of Cape Town, 1988.

Searle, C., *The History of the Development of Nursing* (Struik, Cape Town, 1965).

Seekings, J., 'South Africa's townships 1980–1991: An annotated bibliography', University of Stellenbosch, Research Unit for Sociology of Development, occasional paper, no. 16, 1992.

——, *The UDF: A History of the United Democratic Front in South Africa 1983–1991* (James Currey, Oxford, 2000).

Seekings, J. & Nattrass, N., *Class, Race and Inequality in South Africa* (University of KwaZulu-Natal Press, Durban, 2006).

Segar, J., *The Fruits of Apartheid: Experiencing 'Independence' in a Transkeian Village* (Anthropos, Bellville, 1989).

Shepard, B. & Hayduk, R., 'Media and the new social movements', in B. H. Shepard & R. Hayduk (eds), *From ACT UP to the WTO: Urban Protest and Community Building in the Era of Globalization* (Verso, London & New York, 2002).

Shilts, R., *And the Band Played On: People, Politics and AIDS Epidemic* (St Martin's Press, New York, 1987).

Sidley, P., 'Nurses strikes in South Africa', *British Medical Journal*, 311 (1995), p. 707.

—, 'Strikes cripples health services in South Africa', *British Medical Journal*, 334 (2007), pp. 1240–41.

Sinwell, L., 'The Alexandra Development Forum (ADF): The tyranny of invited participatory spaces?', *Transformation*, forthcoming.

Sisulu, E., *Walter and Albertina Sisulu: In Our Lifetime* (David Philip, Cape Town, 2002).

Sitas, A., 'The making of the "comrades" movement in Natal, 1985–1991', *Journal of Southern African* Studies, 18, 3 (1992), pp. 629–41.

—, 'Thirty years since the Durban strikes: Black working-class leadership and the South African transition', *Current Sociology*, 52, 5 (2004), pp. 830–49.

Sitas, A. & Joakimidis, C., 'A study of strikes in the 1970s', *Work in Progress*, 6 (1978), pp. 105–14; *Work in Progress*, 7 (1979), pp. 30–53.

Snow, D. A., 'Framing processes, ideology and discursive fields', in D. A. Snow, S. A. Soule & H. Kriesi (eds), *The Blackwell Companion to Social Movements* (Blackwell, Oxford, Malden, MA & Victoria, 2004).

Southall, R., 'African capitalism in contemporary South Africa', *Journal of Southern African Studies*, 7, 1 (1980), pp. 38–70.

—, *South Africa's Transkei: The Political Economy of an 'Independent' Bantustan* (Heinemann, London, 1982).

—, 'The state of party politics: Struggles within the tripartite alliance and the decline of opposition', in J. Daniel, A. Habib & R. Southall (eds), *State of the Nation: South Africa 2003–2004* (HSRC Press, Cape Town, 2003).

—, 'Introduction: The ANC state, more dysfunctional than developmental?' in S. Buhlungu et al. (eds), *State of the Nation: South Africa 2007* (HSRC Press, Cape Town, 2007).

Soyinka, W., 'Views from a palette of the cultural window', in X. Mangcu (ed.), *The Meaning of Mandela: A Literary and Intellectual Celebration* (HSRC Press, Cape Town, 2006).

Sparks, A., *Tomorrow Is Another Country: The Inside Story of South Africa's Negotiated Revolution* (Struik, Sandton, 1994).

Spiegel, A., 'A trilogy of tyranny and tribulation: Village politics and administrative intervention in Matatiele during the early 1980s', *Journal of Contemporary African Studies*, 11, 2 (1992), pp. 31–54.

Spottiswoode, R. (director), *And the Band Played On: Politics, People and the AIDS Epidemic* (USA, 1993).

SPP (Surplus Peoples Project), *Forced Removals*, vol. 4, *Natal* (SPP, Cape Town, 1983).

Steinberg, J., *Midlands* (Jonathan Ball, Johannesburg, 2002).

Suttner, R., 'Democratic transition and consolidation in South Africa: The advice of "the experts"', *Current Sociology*, 52, 5 (2004), pp. 755–73.

—, *The ANC Underground* (Jacana, Cape Town, 2008).

Sweet, H., '"Wanted: 16 nurses of the better educated type": Provision of nurses to South Africa in the late nineteenth and early twentieth centuries', *Nursing Inquiry*, 11 (2004), pp. 176–84.

Sweet, H. & Digby, A., 'Race, identity and the nursing profession in South Africa, c. 1850–1958', in B. Mortimer & S. McCann (eds), *New Directions in the History of Nursing in International Perspective* (Routledge, London, 2005).

Tarrow, S., *Power in Movement: Social Movements, Collective Action and Politics* (Cambridge University Press, New York, 1994).

——, *Power in Movement: Social Movements and Contentious Politics*, 2nd ed. (Cambridge University Press, Cambridge, 1998).

Terreblanche, S., *A History of Inequality in South Africa: 1652–2002* (University of KwaZulu-Natal Press, Pietermaritzburg, 2002).

Thatcher, M., *The Downing Street Years* (Harper Collins, London, 1993).

Thorn, H., *Anti-apartheid and the Emergence of a Global Civil Society* (Palgrave Macmillan, Basingstoke, 2006).

Tilly, C., *The Contentious French* (Harvard University Press, Cambridge, MA, 1986).

——, *Popular Contention in Great Britain, 1758–1834* (Harvard University Press, Cambridge, MA, 1995).

——, *Social Movements, 1768–2004* (Paradigm, Boulder, 2004).

Toli, R., 'The origins of the Durban strikes 1973', MA dissertation, University of Durban-Westville, 1991.

Touraine, A., *The Voice and the Eye: An Analysis of Social Movements* (Cambridge University Press, Cambridge, 1981).

TRC (Truth and Reconciliation Commission), *Truth and Reconciliation Commission of South Africa Report* (Juta, Cape Town, 1998).

Treichler, P. A., *How to Have Theory in an Epidemic: Cultural Chronicles of AIDS* (Duke University Press, Durham, 1999).

Turner, R., *The Eye of the Needle: Toward Participatory Democracy* (Orbis Books, Maryknoll, 1978).

Turshen, M. (ed.), *Women and Health in Africa* (Africa World Press, Trenton, 1991).

Unterhalter, E., Wolpe, H., Botha, T. Badat, S., Dlamini, T., and Khotseng, B. (eds), *Apartheid Education and Popular Struggles* (Ravan Press, Johannesburg, 1991).

Uys, L., 'Racism and the South African nurse', *Nursing RSA*, 2, 11/12 (1987), pp. 55–56.

Vail, L., *The Creation of Tribalism in Southern Africa* (James Currey, London, 1989).

Van Kessell, I. & Oomen, B., 'One chief, one vote: The revival of traditional authorities in post apartheid South Africa', *African Affairs*, 96 (1994), pp. 561–85.

Van Niekerk, P., 'The trade union movement in the politics of resistance', in S. Johnson (ed.), *South Africa: No Turning Back* (Bloomington, Indiana University Press, 1989).

Van Onselen, C., *Chibaro: African Mine Labour in Southern Rhodesia, 1900–1933* (Pluto Press, London, 1976).

Von Holdt, K. & Maserumule, B., 'After apartheid: Decay or reconstruction? Transition in a public hospital', in E. Webster & K. von Holdt (eds), *Beyond the Apartheid Workplace: Studies in Transition* (University of KwaZulu-Natal Press, Scotsville, 2005).

Waldmeir, P., *Anatomy of a Miracle* (Penguin, London & New York, 1997).

Walker, C., *Landmarked: Land Claims and Land Restitution in South Africa* (Jacana, Cape Town, 2008).

Wells, H., 'The origin and spread of private wildlife conservancies and neighbour relations in South Africa, in a historical context of wildlife utilisation in southern Africa', paper presented to the conference on African Environments, Past and Present, St Antony's College, Oxford, 5–8 July 1999.

Wilson, F., *Migrant Labour in South Africa* (SPROCAS, Durban, 1972).

Wolpe, H., 'Capitalism and cheap labour power in South Africa: From segregation to apartheid', *Economy and Society*, 1 (1972), pp. 424–56.

Zeilig, L. (ed.), *Class Struggle and Resistance in Africa* (New Clarion Press, Cheltenham, 2002).

Zukin, S., *The Cultures of Cities* (Blackwell, Oxford, 1995).

Index